THE CAMBRIDGE COMPANION TO

LEO STRAUSS

Leo Strauss was a central figure in the twentieth-century renaissance of political philosophy. The essays of *The Cambridge Companion to Leo Strauss* provide a comprehensive and nonpartisan survey of the major themes and problems that animated Strauss's work. These include his revival of the great "quarrel between the ancients and the moderns," his examination of the tension between Jerusalem and Athens, and, most controversially, his recovery of the tradition of esoteric writing. The volume also examines Strauss's complex relation to a range of contemporary political movements and thinkers, including Edmund Husserl, Martin Heidegger, Max Weber, Carl Schmitt, and Gershom Scholem, as well as the creation of a distinctive school of "Straussian" political philosophy.

Steven B. Smith, the Alfred Cowles Professor of Political Science at Yale University, is the author of *Reading Leo Strauss*, *Spinoza's Book of Life*, and *Spinoza, Liberalism, and Jewish Identity*. His publications have appeared most recently in *Hebraic Political Studies*, *Review of Politics*, and *Political Theory*, and he has lectured throughout the United States, Europe, and Israel. Professor Smith has held the position of Master of Branford College at Yale since 1996.

To Jan –
For your continuing
education
Best wishes
Steven
5.27.09

CAMBRIDGE COMPANIONS TO PHILOSOPHY

OTHER VOLUMES IN THE SERIES OF CAMBRIDGE COMPANIONS:

Continued after the Index

The Cambridge Companion to

LEO STRAUSS

Edited by Steven B. Smith
Yale University

CAMBRIDGE
UNIVERSITY PRESS

CAMBRIDGE UNIVERSITY PRESS
Cambridge, New York, Melbourne, Madrid, Cape Town, Singapore,
São Paulo, Delhi

Cambridge University Press
32 Avenue of the Americas, New York, NY 10013-2473, USA

www.cambridge.org
Information on this title: www.cambridge.org/9780521703994

First published 2009

Printed in the United States of America

A catalog record for this publication is available from the British Library.

Library of Congress Cataloging in Publication data

The Cambridge companion to Leo Strauss / edited by Steven B. Smith.
    p.   cm. – (Cambridge companions to philosophy)
Includes bibliographical references and index.
ISBN 978-0-521-87902-6 (hardback : alk. paper)
1. Strauss, Leo – Criticism and interpretation.   2. Political science –
Philosophy.   I. Smith, Steven B., 1951–   II. Title.   III. Series.
JC251.S8C36   2009
181′.06–dc22   2009007870

ISBN 978-0-521-87902-6 hardback
ISBN 978-0-521-70399-4 paperback

"The highest subject of political philosophy is the philosophic life: philosophy – not as a teaching or as body of knowledge, but as a way of life – offers, as it were, the solution to the problem that keeps political life in motion."

– Leo Strauss

CONTENTS

ix

x   Contents

CONTRIBUTORS

LEORA BATNITZKY is Professor of Religion at Princeton University and director of the new Tikvah Project on Jewish Thought at Princeton. She is the author of *Idolatry and Representation: The Philosophy of Franz Rosenzweig Reconsidered* (Princeton University Press, 2000) and *Leo Strauss and Emmanuel Levinas: Philosophy and the Politics of Revelation* (Cambridge University Press, 2006).

NASSER BEHNEGAR is an Associate Professor in the Department of Political Science at Boston College. His writings include *Leo Strauss, Max Weber, and the Scientific Study of Politics* (University of Chicago Press, 2003). He is currently working on a book-length study of early liberalism and in particular of the thought of Locke, Spinoza, and Hume.

TIMOTHY FULLER is the Lloyd E. Worner Distinguished Service Professor and Professor of Political Science at Colorado College. He is the author and editor of several works, including Michael Oakeshott's *The Voice of Liberal Learning* (Yale University Press, 1989) and most recently, with Corey Abel, *The Intellectual Legacy of Michael Oakeshott*.

WILLIAM A. GALSTON holds the Ezra Zilkha Chair in Governance Studies at the Brookings Institution and is also College Park Professor at the University of Maryland. The author most recently of *Liberal Pluralism* (Cambridge University Press, 2002), *The Practice of Liberal Pluralism* (Cambridge University Press, 2005), and *Public Matters* (Rowman & Littlefield, 2006), Galston was elected to the American Academy of Arts and Sciences in 2004.

JOEL L. KRAEMER, John Henry Barrows Professor Emeritus in the Divinity School and member of the Committee on Social Thought at the University of Chicago, is the author of the recent *Maimonides: The Life and World of One of Civilization's Greatest Minds* (Doubleday, 2008) and *Humanism in the Renaissance of Islam* (E. J. Brill, 1993) and editor

xi

of *Perspectives on Maimonides: Philosophical and Historical Studies* (Oxford University Press, 1991).

LAURENCE LAMPERT is Emeritus Professor of Philosophy at Indiana University Indianapolis. He is the author of *Leo Strauss and Nietzsche* (University of Chicago Press, 1966) and of three other books on Nietzsche, one of which develops Strauss's history of philosophy: *Nietzsche and Modern Times: A Study of Bacon, Descartes, and Nietzsche* (Yale University Press, 1992).

STANLEY ROSEN is the Borden Parker Bowne Professor Emeritus and University Professor of Philosophy at Boston University. He has lectured widely in America and Europe and holds an honorary doctorate from The New University of Lisbon. Among his many books are *Hermeneutics as Politics* (Oxford University Press, 1987), *The Elusiveness of the Ordinary* (Yale University Press, 2002), and *Plato's 'Republic': A Study* (Yale University Press, 2005).

SUSAN MELD SHELL is Professor and Chair of the Political Science Department at Boston College. She is the author of *The Embodiment of Reason: Kant on Spirit, Generation, and Community* (University of Chicago Press, 1996) and *Kant and the Limits of Autonomy* (Harvard University Press, 2009).

STEVEN B. SMITH is the Alfred Cowles Professor of Political Science and Master of Branford College at Yale University. His recent work includes *Spinoza, Liberalism and the Question of Jewish Identity* (Yale University Press, 1997), *Spinoza's Book of Life: Freedom and Redemption in the 'Ethics'* (Yale University Press, 2003), and *Reading Leo Strauss: Philosophy, Politics, Judaism* (University of Chicago Press, 2006).

CATHERINE H. ZUCKERT is Nancy Reeves Dreux Professor of Political Science at the University of Notre Dame and editor-in-chief of *The Review of Politics*. Her books include *Natural Right and the American Imagination* (Rowman & Littlefield, 1990), *Postmodern Platos* (University of Chicago Press, 1996), and (with Michael Zuckert) *The Truth About Leo Strauss* (University of Chicago Press, 2006).

MICHAEL ZUCKERT is the Nancy Reeves Dreux Professor and Chair of the Political Science Department at University of Notre Dame. He is the author of *Natural Rights and the New Republicanism* (Princeton University Press, 1994), *Launching Liberalism: On Lockean Political Philosophy* (University of Kansas Press, 2002) and (with Catherine Zuckert) *The Truth About Leo Strauss*.

ABBREVIATIONS

AAPL *The Argument and Action of Plato's Laws* (Chicago: University of Chicago Press, 1975)

CCM *Correspondence Concerning Modernity*, trans. George Elliott Tucker *Independent Journal of Philosophy*, 4 (1983): 105–119 and 5/6 (1988): 177–192

CM *The City and Man* (Chicago: University of Chicago Press, 1964)

EW *The Early Writings (1921–32)*, ed. and trans. Michael Zank (Albany, NY: State University of New York Press, 2002)

FPP *Faith and Political Philosophy: The Correspondence Between Leo Strauss and Eric Voegelin, 1934–1964*, ed. and trans. Peter Emberley and Barry Cooper (University Park, PA: Pennsylvania University Press, 1993)

GN "Geman Nihilism," *Interpretation* 26 (1999): 352–378

GS, 1–3 *Gesammlte Schriften, vols. 1–3*, ed. Heinrich and Wiebke Meier (Stuttgart: J. B. Metzler, 1996–2001)

JPCM *Jewish Philosophy and the Crisis of Modernity*, ed. Kenneth Hart Green (Albany, NY: State University of New York Press, 1997)

LAM *Liberalism Ancient and Modern* (New York: Basic Books, 1968)

NRH *Natural Right and History* (Chicago: University of Chicago Press, 1953)

OT *On Tyranny: Including the Strauss-Kojève Correspondence*, ed. Victor Gourevitch and Michael S. Roth (Chicago: University of Chicago Press, 2000)

PAW *Persecution and the Art of Writing* (Chicago: University of Chicago Press, 1952)

PL *Philosophy and Law: Contributions to the Understanding of Maimonides and His Predecessors*, trans. Eve Adler (Albany, NY: State University of New York Press, 1995)

PPH *The Political Philosophy of Hobbes: Its Basis and Its Genesis*, trans. Elsa M. Sinclair (Oxford: Clarendon Press, 1936)

RCPR *The Rebirth of Classical Political Rationalism*, ed. Thomas Pangle (Chicago: University of Chicago Press, 1989)

SCR *Spinoza's Critique of Religion*, trans. Elsa M. Sinclair (New York: Schocken, 1965)

SPPP *Studies in Platonic Political Philosophy*, ed. Thomas Pangle (Chicago: University of Chicago Press, 1983)

TM *Thoughts on Machiavelli* (Chicago: University of Chicago Press, 1958)
TWM "Three Waves of Modernity," *An Introduction to Political Philos-ophy: Ten Essays by Leo Strauss,* ed. Hilail Gildin (Detroit, MI: Wayne State University Press, 1975), 81–98
WPP *What is Political Philosophy and Other Studies* (Glencoe, IL: The Free Press, 1959)

1 Introduction

Leo Strauss Today

Leo Strauss (1899–1973) was a central figure in the revival of the study of political philosophy. He was highly controversial during his lifetime, and the debates over his ideas and his legacy have only deepened in the years after his death. His writings attracted passionate defenders and equally passionate critics. His name itself has become an "ism": *Straussianism*.[1]

There is considerable disagreement over the nature of Strauss's achievement even among those most intimately acquainted with his work. His attempt to revive the famous "quarrel between the ancients and the moderns" led many to wonder whether his loyalties were more with the world of ancient philosophy and politics than with modernity. His writings on the theme of what he metaphorically called "Jerusalem and Athens" led some to question whether his commitments were to the theistic tradition of revealed law or to secular forms of rationality. His recovery of the tradition of esoteric writing has led many to speculate whether his own writings conveyed a secret teaching intended for those initiated into the art of "careful reading." And his concern with the problems created by the philosophies of historicism, relativism, and

---

[1] Among the recent works on Strauss, see the following: Steven B. Smith, *Reading Leo Strauss: Politics, Philosophy, Judaism* (Chicago: University of Chicago Press, 2006); Catherine and Michael Zuckert, *The Truth About Leo Strauss: Political Philosophy and American Democracy* (Chicago: University of Chicago Press, 2006); Heinrich Meier, *Leo Strauss and the Theologico-Political Problem*, trans. Marcus Brainard (Cambridge, UK: Cambridge University Press, 2006); Thomas L. Pangle, *Leo Strauss: An Introduction to His Thought and Intellectual Legacy* (Baltimore, MD: John Hopkins Press, 2006); Eugene R. Sheppard, *Leo Strauss and the Politics of Exile: The Making of a Political Philosopher* (Waltham, MA: Brandeis University Press, 2006); Daniel Tanguay, *Leo Strauss: An Intellectual Biography*, trans. Christopher Nadon (New Haven, CT: Yale University Press, 2007); David Janssens, *Between Jerusalem and Athens: Philosophy, Prophecy, and Politics in Leo Strauss's Early Thought* (Albany, NY: SUNY Press, 2008).

nihilism has led many to wonder about Strauss's politics. Was he a Platonist attempting to educate a new generation of philosopher-kings, or a closet nihilist who affected conventional opinions ultimately to subvert them? Who was Leo Strauss and what did he stand for?

Strauss was a member of a remarkable generation of émigré-scholars who helped to revive a decaying field called "the history of political thought," which was widely considered moribund if not dead. He did this by introducing into the English-speaking world an interest in what has come to be called "the modernity problem." In particular, Strauss called into question the concept of progress upon which the great hopes of the Enlightenment had been pinned. Along with other refugees from Hitler's Germany, he questioned at its most fundamental level the Enlightenment idea of progress and human perfectibility that had been a central part of the modern project since the seventeenth century. The great catastrophes of the twentieth century – two world wars and the Holocaust – convinced Strauss that the steady triumph of scientific and technological rationality had not been a blessing in every respect. The very idea of progress – the use of scientific and technological power for the "relief of man's estate" – had come to appear to thoughtful observers as increasingly problematic.

Strauss's response to the problem of modernity was to reopen the issue with which the modern era began, namely the quarrel between the ancients and the moderns. Initially a literary and aesthetic debate, Strauss inquired into the grounds for rejecting the ancients, beginning with Machiavelli and extending through a number of "waves" of modernity from Hobbes and Locke to Rousseau and Kant, and culminating in the radical modernity – today we might say "postmodernity" – of Nietzsche and Heidegger. Rather than exhibiting a steady, cumulative progress of knowledge over error and superstition, Strauss showed how modernity exhibited a dangerous tendency toward "historicism" or what became known as "nihilism," that is, the view that all standards of justice and morality are historically relative, limited to the perspective of the age in which they are expressed. This type of historical relativism, given powerful expression by Oswald Spengler and other interwar German thinkers, had made its way into the Anglo-American world where, Strauss believed, it was beginning to erode the core structure of liberal beliefs about justice and natural rights.

Strauss was not originally a student of political theory or political philosophy. He came to an appreciation of the importance of politics through his early investigation into the philosophy of Spinoza, Maimonides, and other medieval Jewish and Arabic philosophers. These thinkers had adopted a manner of writing that was deliberately intended to conceal their deepest and most important teachings from public scrutiny. This was done in part because they lived in communities that held powerful injunctions against philosophical questioning of the religious law, but also out of a sense of respect for or loyalty to those communities of which they were a part. The doctrine of esotericism or the "double truth" had long been noted by Strauss's scholarly predecessors but he gave it a new meaning. In particular, he came to believe that all philosophers insofar as they desire to communicate to others must take account of the political situation of philosophy, that is, what can be said and what must be kept under wraps. From this, Strauss inferred the primacy of political philosophy.

This insight into the primacy of political philosophy gave Strauss a platform from which to reinterpret the standard works of the tradition from Plato onward. It provided him with a way of interpreting works written under what might be called "regimes of persecution." Rather than simply assuming that works like Plato's *Republic*, Spinoza's *Theologico-Political Treatise*, or Locke's *Second Treatise* mean precisely what they say on the surface, one must be attuned to contradictions, repetitions, and ambiguities down to the smallest points of detail as containing possible clues to what the author secretly intended. Strauss brought the skills of a literary detective to the study of philosophical texts. This discovery of what he called "a forgotten kind of writing" led him to pose such questions as: "What are the limits of free expression?" "To what degree is the freedom to philosophize consistent with the underlying premises of social order?" "What is the social responsibility of philosophers?" and in its broadest and most comprehensive form, simply "Why philosophy?"

Strauss knew that his discovery – actually, he always referred to it as a "recovery" – of esotericism would set off a bombshell. He was correct. Almost immediately, critics took aim. Perhaps the most disturbing suggestion was that the great thinkers wrote in a way that would deliberately deceive the majority of their readers. Strauss admitted that such a charge was bound to be shocking to "every decent modern reader."[2] There were further questions raised by the recovery of esotericism. How could the interpretation of an esoteric meaning be verified if the very meaning of the text was hidden? When was an author's contradiction simply a contradiction and not a clue to some deeper problem? Further, was esoteric interpretation a historical phenomenon, limited to texts written in preliberal or nonliberal societies, or was it an imperative for all philosophical writers, even those living in free societies that valued, or at least claimed to value, the expression of heterodox points of view? Was Strauss himself such a writer?[3]

---

[2] Strauss, "Persecution and the Art of Writing," in *PAW*, 35.

[3] For the idea that Strauss was an esoteric writer, see Laurence Lampert, *Leo Strauss and Nietzsche* (Chicago: University of Chicago Press, 1996); Shadia

At the same time that Strauss questioned some of the basic tenets of the Enlightenment's faith in progress and science, he reawakened an interest in the importance and vitality of religion. This grew out of his experience as a German Jew who had been raised in an orthodox family and for whom what was called "the Jewish Question" was a lifelong concern. The Enlightenment had attempted to solve the traditional problem of church-state relations by cordoning religion off into its own private sphere within civil society. Influenced by writers like Franz Rosenzweig within the Jewish tradition and Karl Barth within Christianity, Strauss viewed this type of liberal theology as inadequate to deal with the full scope of the "theologico-political predicament." Strauss began to raise questions about whether the Enlightenment had succeeded in disproving the possibility of revealed religion or whether the citadel of orthodoxy had managed to survive the "Napoleonic" assault of the modern critique of religion. The question of Jerusalem or Athens, of whether revealed law or human reason was the ultimate guide of life, was still an issue that remained to be decided.

The theologico-political theme, considered until only recently a somewhat peripheral aspect of Strauss's interests, has in recent years come to take center stage. The Jewish Question was not just a parochial aspect of Strauss's biography but became for him the very symbol of the human predicament. The Jewish Question meant more for him than the failure of even democratic governments to end the problem of "discrimination." "The Jewish problem," he would write, "is the most manifest symbol of the human problem."[4] In addressing this issue, Strauss sometimes took upon himself the language of the prophet or sage.

The importance of the theologico-political problem was recognized just over a decade ago by the literary critic George Steiner writing in the pages of the *Times Literary Supplement*:

If, in the traditional pairing which Strauss adopts, the life-long labors turn around Jerusalem and Athens, it is the former which, at the last, radiates at the center. It is in the light or dark of Jewish identity and history, made dramatically intense

Drury, *The Political Ideas of Leo Strauss* (New York: Saint Martin's, 1988); Steven Lenzner, *Leo Strauss and the Problem of Freedom of Thought* (Ph.D. Dissertation, Harvard University, Department of Government, 2003); for an excellent account of Strauss's esotericism and its relation to contemporary literary theory, see Paul A. Cantor, "Leo Strauss and Contemporary Hermeneutics," *Leo Strauss's Thought: Toward a Critical Engagement*, ed. Alan Udoff (Boulder, CO: Lynne Reinner, 1991), 267–314; see also Gérald Sfez, "Leo Strauss: Un Criticisme de la Preuve," *Revue Philosophique* 130 (2005): 3–19; Arthur Melzer, "Esotericism and the Critique of Historicism," *American Political Science Review* 2 (2006): 279–295.
4 Strauss, "Preface to *Spinoza's Critique of Religion*," in *LAM*, 230.

by the twentieth century, that Leo Strauss, Hermann Cohen's dissenting successor in the development and tragedy of German Judaism, reads, that he "lives"
the interaction between classical Greek, Islamic, Renaissance, and Judaic views
of the meaning of man. Even where the declared topic is outwardly remote from
Judaica, in the somewhat strange book on Aristophanes and Socrates, for example, we need, as Strauss himself would have it, to read between the lines. The
Hebrew characters are never far off.[5]

As Steiner maintains here, if it was Jerusalem that "radiates at the
center" of Strauss's thought, it is important – even imperative – to note
that he addressed the problem of revelation not essentially as a man of
faith but in the spirit of a Socratic philosopher raising or asking questions. Of course, this is already to stake a claim in a contested field –
one that is addressed in several of the essays in this book. Strauss
accepted the view, widely shared by a number of his contemporaries,
that philosophy had not yet refuted the claims of revelation. This alone
puts him in a long skeptical tradition from Montaigne and Pascal to
Kierkegaard and even Wittgenstein. But this did not lead to a call for
a revival of orthodoxy but a return to classical political philosophy, a
return compelled by Strauss's awareness of the self-destruction of modern philosophy and its descent into nihilism.

Strauss's call for a "return" to classical political philosophy – a return
always described by him as "tentative or experimental" – was not some
reactionary effort to revive an ancient metaphysical system or some
antiquated cosmology. Still less was it a call to revive the ancient polis
and its forms of social hierarchy. Long before philosophy became the
name of an academic discipline, it was associated by its practitioners
with a way of life. To practice philosophy meant not to adhere to a
specific set of doctrines, a method, or much less anything like a system
of ideas but to live in a certain way. The way of life of the philosophers
was intended as an answer to the question, "How ought I to live?" or
"What is the best way of life?"

Strauss's resurrection of the Socratic model of the philosophical life
has naturally led readers to wonder whether Strauss had a political philosophy of his own, perhaps even communicated secretly "between the
lines." This is an issue on which he remained tantalizingly and, I suspect, deliberately oblique, even though it has not prevented all manners of readers from attributing all manners of doctrinal positions to
him from neo-conservatism to a nihilistic antimodernity. But Strauss
declared himself to be a skeptic in the original Greek sense of the term,
that is to say, wary of all political solutions that claim certainty for

[5] George Steiner, "Inscrutable and Tragic: Leo Strauss's Vision of the Jewish
Destiny," *Times Literary Supplement* (November 11, 1997), 4.

themselves and certainly wary of political movements and causes. He claimed to be a "friend" of liberal or constitutional democracy but on skeptical grounds as the least harmful of the different alternatives.[6] Given these ambiguities and the importance that Strauss has come to assume, it remains more urgent than ever to come to an assessment of his complex legacy for the study of philosophy and politics.

The essays contained in this volume attempt to canvass the wide range of Strauss's interests. Although Strauss's writings typically took the form of the commentary – a form to which he gave very high philosophical expression – I have preferred to avoid reprising his often dense and detailed interpretations of specific figures within the tradition (Plato, Maimonides, Hobbes, Nietzsche) and to focus instead on the general themes or problems that these writings are intended to illustrate. I believe this approach follows Strauss's own method that always regarded his case studies in the history of ideas as the best means of stimulating awareness of the "fundamental" or "permanent" problems of philosophy. This approach should give readers a sense of the scope and breadth of the problems that Strauss felt it important to address.

The essays in the first half of this volume deal broadly with Strauss's various contributions to the history of philosophy (ancient, medieval, modern), the theologico-political predicament, the recovery of esotericism, and the modernity problem, to name just the most prominent. Those in the second half of the book survey his views on politics and twentieth-century thought, in particular. These include his views on his German contemporaries, on modern political ideologies (Liberalism, Communism, National Socialism), his judgment on America as a regime, his critique of the social sciences, and his views on the role of education and the university in a free society. The volume concludes with a consideration of Strauss's legacy.

This volume opens with a biographical essay by the editor that puts Strauss's writing in the context of an extraordinary life that moved from a small town in Germany to Berlin, Paris, and England, and from there to New York, Jerusalem, and Chicago. Strauss's life intersected with some of the giants of twentieth-century European thought including not only Husserl, Heidegger, and Cassirer but Gershom Scholem, Alexandre Kojève, and Hans-Georg Gadamer. Special attention is given to the decade Strauss spent at the New School for Social Research, where he first began to develop his distinctive approach to philosophy.

[6] Strauss, "Liberal Education and Responsibility," in *LAM*, 24.

Leora Batnitzky then takes up Strauss's understanding of the theologico-political predicament. She argues that although Strauss initially examined this problem within the context of German Jewry, he came to regard it as expressing the enduring challenge posed by revelation to the claims of reason and philosophy. As such, the term "theologico-political predicament" links Strauss's early development to his later themes, including his revival of the great "quarrel between the ancients and the moderns," the relation between Jerusalem and Athens, and his diverse studies in the history of political philosophy. Her essay concludes that the challenge posed by revelation remains of enduring significance not just for believers but especially for nonbelievers.

Laurence Lampert addresses the controversial theme of Strauss's "recovery" of esotericism. Drawing heavily upon Strauss's recently published correspondence and especially the letters to his friend Jacob Klein from 1938 to 1939, these letters record Strauss's excitement at the discovery of esoteric writing first in Maimonides and later in Plato and other classical Greek writers. Strauss's recovery of the esoteric tradition is then illustrated by a close reading of his essay on Judah Halevi's *Kuzari*, composed originally in 1943. Lampert argues that following his great medieval and classical masters, Strauss decided to practice his own form of esoteric writing, having deemed that the reasons for the practice were still valid in an age that regarded itself as open to the expression of all views, however heterodox.

Catherine Zuckert considers Strauss's repeated and widely discussed proposals for a "return" to premodern thought. Focusing on his lecture "Progress or Return," she argues that Strauss's call for a return was based on a new understanding of both of the "roots" of the Western tradition, namely biblical morality and Greek rationalism. Strauss presents the history of the West as a series of attempts to harmonize or synthesize these conflicting tendencies, but because ancient philosophy is fundamentally incompatible with the biblical conception of the Creator God, these attempts have failed. It is the tension between rather than any synthesis of these roots that is the secret of the vitality of the West and the best promise for its future.

Stanley Rosen reprises Strauss's analysis of the problem of modernity by drawing attention to the two modern thinkers who arguably exercised the greatest influence on Strauss: Nietzsche and Heidegger. Modernity, they agreed, was marked by the steady triumph of scientific and technological progress, while being simultaneously incapable of understanding the very works that constitute that progress. This inability is represented by the terms "relativism" and "historicism," which claim there is no stable basis for ranking values in accordance with excellence; the resulting denial can only lead to nihilism. Rosen concludes that Strauss's analysis of the modernity problem is itself a characteristically modern trope and that he fails to prove the superiority of the Socratic-Platonic alternative.

Joel Kraemer considers one of Strauss's most enduring intellectual legacies, his recovery of the "medieval Enlightenment" in Jewish and Arabic thought. Turning to Strauss's 1935 book *Philosophy and Law*, Kraemer argues that Strauss's understanding of Maimonides's *Guide of the Perplexed* ("the classic of rationalism") was decisively shaped by his reading of Alfarabi and the Arabic *Falasifa* (philosophers). Like his brother-in-law Paul Kraus, Strauss helped to direct attention to the Arabic contribution to philosophy and in so doing come to a richer understanding of philosophy. Because Islam and Judaism both have the character of a comprehensive body of Law (Sharia, Torah) and not a faith or creedal religion like Christianity, each helps vividly to illustrate the enduring tensions between philosophy and revelation. Strauss's approach to the medievals was not that of a conventional historian of ideas but rather of a philologically gifted philosopher challenging the attack on classical rationalism by the modern Enlightenment.

The second half of this volume begins with two essays on Strauss's politics and his relation to both his country of birth and his adopted homeland. Susan Shell discusses Strauss's views on the German philosophy of the early twentieth century that helped give rise to Hitler and National Socialism. She focuses on Strauss's 1941 lecture on "German Nihilism," in particular his use of the Virgilian motto, "to crush the proud and spare the vanquished." She argues this essay marks the turn in Strauss's thought where he distanced himself from his earlier harsh criticism of liberal democracy and the doctrine of the "rights of man," as expressed in his now widely cited letter to Karl Löwith of 1933, to his unhesitating support of liberal democracy as a vehicle for civilized statecraft.

William Galston disagrees with those critics who regard Strauss as a dangerous enemy of liberal democracy. Galston maintains that Strauss valued the U.S. Constitution as a bulwark against the tyrannies of both the Left and the Right, but he did so for positive reasons as well. Strauss endorsed the public-private distinction so valuable to liberalism, as the best way of reducing – even if not completely eliminating – the various forms of discrimination and social injustice. This separation also helps ensure the survival of certain distinctive forms of liberal virtue necessary for the survival of self-government. Strauss emphasized that liberal democracy is the modern regime that is the closest approximation of the ancient idea of *politeia* or mixed government, and to this extent it remained open to the claims of human excellence. Galston concludes that Strauss provided a "qualified embrace" of liberal democracy, qualified only by his fears about modern democracy's tendency toward complacency, philistinism, and mass conformity.

Nasser Behnegar explores Strauss's interest in the modern social sciences, examining his critique of behavioral and Weberian social science, respectively. Both are understood in the light of Strauss's attempt to restore classical political science, especially in its Aristotelian visage. Strauss's critique centered on the modern social scientific endorsement of the fact/value distinction and the claim that only the "Is" can be an object of knowledge, whereas the "Ought" belongs to the irrational sphere of private values. He once colorfully compared this situation to "beings who are sane and sober when engaged in trivial business and who gamble like madmen when confronted with serious issues – retail sanity and wholesale madness."[7] Behnegar also explains the close kinship between Strauss and Edmund Husserl and the reasons for Strauss's preference for classical political science over phenomenology.

In his essay, Timothy Fuller places Strauss among the distinguished scholars who restored political philosophy to a central place in the university study of politics in the years after World War II, advocating also the complementary restoration of the classical tradition of liberal learning. Strauss was not only a teacher; he reflected carefully on teaching as a vocation and on the aims of liberal education in the context of a liberal democracy. What he offered as a scholar was complemented by what he wrote on teaching and learning. He insisted on clearly distinguishing the study of politics from the life of action while recognizing that these distinct teachings are dialectically related.

One of the most controversial aspects of Strauss's legacy is that group known as "Straussians." Michael Zuckert attempts to dispel both the notion that there exists a single-minded clique of followers of Strauss and the mystery surrounding the existence of several groups or factions of Straussians. Although the number of those influenced by Strauss is now quite large and their interests diverse, Zuckert attempts to get to the heart of the matter by identifying two issues upon which they disagree, namely morality and religion. He attempts to show that these disagreements derive at least in part from certain unresolved puzzles in Strauss's own thinking. The different factions of Straussians – the East Coast and West Coast as well as different Straussian grouplets – derive not only from issues in Strauss's thought but center on some of the most significant and abiding human questions.

---

[7] Strauss, *NRH*, 4.

These issues and others have intrigued and perplexed Strauss's readers from the time of his earliest publications. Strauss was the author of more than a dozen books and around a hundred articles and reviews, among which the best known are *On Tyranny* (1948), *Persecution and the Art of Writing* (1952), *Natural Right and History* (1953), *Thoughts on Machiavelli* (1958), *What Is Political Philosophy* (1959), and *Liberalism Ancient and Modern* (1968). These works and many others have been reissued several times over the years and are now widely translated into a number of European and Asian languages. New editions and collections of Strauss's works are being made available, and conferences have been devoted to his ideas in countries throughout the world. What is clear is that Strauss's writings and teachings – rivaling that of other giants of twentieth-century political thought such as Isaiah Berlin, Hannah Arendt, and John Rawls – have had a major impact on the revival of political philosophy in our time.

Strauss's own achievements cannot be entirely divorced from the phenomenon known as "Straussianism." To be sure, this has been exacerbated recently by certain high-profile discussions of Strauss and his alleged influence from beyond the grave on American policymakers in the Bush administration.[8] Of course, what Strauss would have thought of this is impossible to know. What is clear is that these discussions have often ended up reifying Straussianism by turning it into some sort of monolith. There are many different types of Straussians with quite different interests; there are liberal Straussians and conservative Straussians, Democratic Straussians and Republican Straussians, secular Straussians and religious Straussians. With some plausibility, all can claim to find their ideas and positions ratified by Strauss's own writings.

Strauss was a teacher and, like all great teachers, he attracted students. Many of these students have gravitated to the university and can be found in departments of political science, philosophy, classics, and

[8] Among those claiming to find some type of political agenda in Strauss's writings, see Robert Devigne, *Recasting Conservatism: Oakeshott, Strauss, and the Response to Postmodernism* (New Haven, CT: Yale University Press, 1994); Shadia Drury, *Leo Strauss and the American Right* (New York: Saint Martin's 1997); Anne Norton, *Leo Strauss and the Politics of American Empire* (New Haven, CT: Yale University Press, 2004); Alain Frachon and Daniel Vernet, *L'Amérique Messianique: Les guerres des néo conservateurs* (Paris: Editions du Seuil, 2004); Myles Burnyeat, "Sphinx Without a Secret," *New York Review of Books* (May 30, 1985), 30–36; Stephen Holmes, "Truths for Philosophers Alone," *Times Literary Supplement* (December 1–7, 1989), 1319–1323; James Atlas, "Leo-Cons: A Classicist's Legacy," *New York Times* (May 4, 2003), sec. 4.

even literature; others can be found in the world of journalism, think tanks, and public administration. This diversity is represented by the various contributors to this volume, all of whom have been inspired in one way or another by the work of Strauss. This does not mean that they understand Strauss in the same way or even that they agree about the overall purpose of his work. Any attempt to impose some type of unity of perspective would be false to the subject. Some of the contributors were students of Strauss, others students of his students, and still others simply found their way to Strauss's writings on their own. There is no individual known to me who can claim mastery of all of the subjects about which Strauss wrote. Therefore, each contributor has been chosen for their command of one or the other of the wide range of problems and themes that constituted Strauss's life's work.

Strauss did not see himself as offering a road map to utopia. There are no books by Strauss with titles like *A Theory of Justice* or *Anarchy, State, and Utopia*. He eschewed the temptation to engage in ambitious, reconstructive efforts to remake society in accordance with a theory or a program. At certain times, he even denied that he was a philosopher at all, preferring to regard himself as a "scholar" or, even better, as a teacher and reserving the term philosopher only for the greatest thinkers.[9] Strauss did not write analytical treatises on politics nor did he, except indirectly, attempt to give practical guidance to statesmen and fellow citizens. His writings remain firmly nested within the genre of the commentary, leading some critics to wonder whether he should even be considered a philosopher at all. Nevertheless, Strauss often spoke of the commentary as a unique form of philosophical communication – a form brought to perfection by the great medieval Arabic Platonist Alfarabi – and which he sought to renew in our age.

Strauss did not offer a philosophy of politics in the conventional sense of the term. He was concerned instead with the prior and almost unasked question, "What is political philosophy?" a term that he did more than anyone else to revive. The question to which he devoted his life and that shaped his work was the classic theme of the relation between philosophy and the city. What is philosophy and how does it differ from other forms of knowledge and ways of life? What benefits, if any, does philosophy confer on the city? Strauss presented philosophy and the philosophical way of life as an alternative to two powerful but deeply felt delusions to which human beings are perpetually attracted. I think it is best to conclude by letting Strauss speak in his own voice:

Men are constantly attracted and deluded by two opposite charms: the charm of competence which is engendered by mathematics and everything akin to

9 Strauss, "An Introduction to Heideggerian Existentialism," in *RCPR*, 29–30.

mathematics, and the charm of humble awe, which is engendered by meditation on the human soul and its experiences. Philosophy is characterized by the gentle, if firm, refusal to succumb to either charm. It is the highest form of the mating of courage and moderation. In spite of its highness or nobility, it could appear as Sisyphean or ugly, when one contrasts its achievement with its goal. Yet it is necessarily accompanied, sustained, and elevated by eros. It is graced by nature's grace.[10]

[10] Strauss, "What Is Political Philosophy," in *WPP*, 40.

2   Leo Strauss
The Outlines of a Life

"[Strauss's] primary interests were two questions: one, the question of God; and two, the question of politics."[1]
– Jacob Klein

THE YOUNG STRAUSS AND THE THEOLOGICO-POLITICAL PROBLEM

Leo Strauss was born in the small German town of Kirchhain in Hesse on September 20, 1899. According to a later autobiographical statement, he was brought up in "a conservative, even orthodox Jewish home" where the "ceremonial laws were rather strictly observed."[2] This did not prohibit his parents from sending him to study at the prestigious Gymnasium Philippinum in nearby Marburg, where among his classmates was the future Harvard political scientist Carl J. Friedrich. It was here that Strauss was first introduced both to the classics of Greek philosophy and the tradition of German humanism.

Strauss's upbringing was conventional for the era. He said that the Jews of his area "lived in a profound peace" with their non-Jewish neighbors. This was due to a government – the *Kaiserreich* – "not in every respect admirable" but that managed to maintain "an admirable order everywhere."[3] This sense of certainty was shaken, when he was a child, by the experience of observing a group of refugees from a Russian pogrom

[1] Strauss, "A Giving of Accounts," in *JPCM*, 458.
[2] The rough outline of Strauss's early life is given in his "A Giving of Accounts," in JPCM, 459–460. The so-called European or Weimar Strauss has recently attracted considerable attention; for some of the contributors to this interest see, David Biale, "The Philosopher as Weimar Jew," *Leo Strauss's Thought: Toward a Critical Engagement* (Boulder, CO: Lynne Rienner, 1991), 31–40; Daniel Tanguay, *Leo Strauss: An Intellectual Biography*, trans. Christopher Nadon (New Haven, CT: Yale University Press, 2007), 10–49; for a detailed biographical account, see Eugene R. Sheppard, *Leo Strauss and the Politics of Exile: The Making of a Political Philosopher* (Waltham, MA: Brandeis University Press, 2006).
[3] Strauss, "Why We Remain Jews," in *JCPM*, 312–313.

13

on their way to Australia. This made a profound impression on the young Strauss ("It was an unforgettable moment."), leading him to wonder if such things might yet happen in Germany. It was perhaps this experience that led Strauss to embrace Zionism – "simple straightforward political Zionism" – at the age of seventeen.[4]

After a year of military service that he spent as a translator in Belgium, Strauss attended the University of Marburg not far from his home. Marburg was then the center of the great neo-Kantian movement that dominated German philosophy from the late nineteenth to the early twentieth centuries. The person at the center of this neo-Kantian tendency was Hermann Cohen (1842–1918), whom Strauss later described as "a passionate philosopher and a Jew passionately devoted to Judaism."[5] Although it is extremely doubtful that the two ever met, Cohen's philosophy exerted a powerful influence on the young Strauss, leading him to pursue a doctorate in philosophy at the University of Hamburg under the supervision of Cohen's student, Ernst Cassirer (1874–1945). Strauss later described his dissertation on *Das Erkenntnisproblem in der philosophischen Lehre Fr. H Jacobi* (1921) (*The Problem of Knowledge in the Philosophical Doctrine of F. H. Jacobi*) as a "disgraceful performance." It nevertheless allowed him to pursue a postdoctoral year at Freiburg, where he went to study with the phenomenological philosopher Edmund Husserl.[6]

Among Strauss's friends at Marburg was the future philosopher of mathematics Jacob Klein (1899–1978).[7] A Russian Jew from Libau, Klein early impressed Strauss as "wholly non-provincial in a wholly provincial environment."[8] He expressed disappointment only that he had failed to

[4] Strauss, "A Giving of Accounts," in *JPCM*, 460; for Strauss's early Zionist sympathies, see Michael Zank, "Introduction," in *EW*, 3–11.
[5] Strauss, "A Giving of Accounts," in *JPCM*, 460. For Strauss's other writings on Cohen, see in particular "Jerusalem and Athens: Some Preliminary Observations," in *SPPP*, 167–173; "Preface to 'Spinoza's Critique of Religion,'" in *LAM*, 243–254; "Introduction to Hermann Cohen, *Religion of Reason Out of the Sources of Judaism*," in *SPP*, 233–247.
[6] Strauss, "Das Erkenntnisproblem in der philosophischen Lehre Fr. J. Jacobis (1921)," in *GS*, 2: 237–292. For the importance of Jacobi on Strauss's thought, see Steven B. Smith, "Strauss's Spinoza," *Reading Leo Strauss: Politics, Philosophy, Judaism* (Chicago: University of Chicago Press, 2006), 65–83; see also, David Janssens, "The Problem of the Enlightenment: Strauss, Jacobi, and the Pantheism Controversy," *Review of Metaphysics* 56 (2003): 605–632.
[7] Among Klein's best known works are *Greek Mathematical Thought and the Origins of Algebra*, trans. Eva Brann (Cambridge, MA: MIT Press, 1968); *A Commentary on Plato's Meno* (Chapel Hill, NC: University of North Carolina Press, 1965); *Plato's Trilogy: Theaetetus, the Sophist, and the Statesman* (Chicago: University of Chicago Press, 1977).
[8] Strauss, "A Giving of Accounts," in *JPCM*, 460.

win Klein over to the cause of Zionism. The two were to develop a life-long friendship. Strauss recalled how they would frequently meet in a café with other young scholars after spending the day working in the Prussian State Library in Berlin. According to Strauss, Klein had a fear of appearing to be a part of a group of young bohemians out on the town, and insisted on seeming to be utterly conventional businessmen or office workers. Occasionally, Strauss would interrupt their conversation by shouting "Nietzsche," much to the discomfort of Klein.[9] This shows the playful and somewhat mischievous side of Strauss's personality.

Strauss's year at Freiburg seems to have marked a turning point in his early development. He had gone there initially to study natural theology but was immediately attracted to Husserl's assistant, a young scholar named Martin Heidegger. Strauss would describe Heidegger as "one of the unknown young men in Husserl's entourage," who at that time was lecturing on Aristotle's *Metaphysics*.[10] Strauss also made the acquaintance of a group of young students – Hans-Georg Gadamer, Karl Löwith, and later Hannah Arendt – who were part of the Heidegger circle. Years later, he could still recount the profound affect that Heidegger exercised on him and so many of his generation:

I remember the impression he made on me when I heard him first as a young Ph.D. in 1922. Up to that time I had been particularly impressed, as many of my contemporaries in Germany were, with Max Weber: by his intransigent devotion to intellectual honesty, by his passionate devotion to the idea of science – a devotion that was combined with a profound uneasiness regarding the meaning of science. On my way north from Freiburg, where Heidegger then taught, I saw, in Frankfurt-am-Main, Franz Rosenzweig...and I told him of Heidegger. I said to him that, in comparison with Heidegger, Weber appeared to me as an "orphan child" in regard to precision and probing and competence. I had never seen before such seriousness, profundity, and concentration in the interpretation of philosophic texts.[11]

Upon completing his postdoctoral year, Strauss became affiliated with Franz Rosenzweig's *Freies Jüdisches Lehrhaus* (Free Jewish House of Study) in Frankfurt, where he turned his attention to Jewish themes. In an as-yet unpublished letter to Nahum Glatzer written in Hebrew in 1925, Strauss noted that he had been teaching Hebrew in Kassel – Rosenzweig's hometown – and was reading Rashi and Abravanel.[12] It was during this period that Strauss also met the future biblical scholar

---

[9] Strauss, "An Unspoken Prologue to a Public Lecture at Saint John's College in Honor of Jacob Klein," in *JPCM*, 449–450.

[10] Strauss, "A Giving of Accounts," in *JPCM*, 461.

[11] Strauss, "An Introduction to Heideggerian Existentialism," in *RCPR*, 27–28.

[12] An unpublished letter from Strauss to Nahum Glatzer, dated Purim Eve, 1925; this was made available to me by Glatzer's daughter, Professor Judith Wechsler of the Department of Art History at Tufts University.

Nechama Leibowitz (1905–1997), who agreed to tutor him in the Hebrew text of Saadya Gaon's *The Book of Beliefs and Opinions* in exchange for teaching her the Greek text of Plato's *Gorgias*.[13]

His earliest publications date from this period and appeared in Jewish periodicals like the *Jüdische Rundschau* and Martin Buber's *Der Jude*. A lengthy article criticizing Hermann Cohen's critique of Spinoza caught the attention of Julius Guttmann (1880–1950), who was then head of the Academy for the Science of Judaism in Berlin.[14] As its name implied, the Academy was dedicated to the pursuit of a scientific or scholarly study of Judaism based on careful attention to historical sources and influences. Strauss was appointed to the position of a research assistant in charge of editing the Academy's jubilee edition of the works of Moses Mendelssohn – to which he, along with Alexander Altmann (1906–1987), contributed several introductory essays.[15] It was here also that Strauss began work on a book on Spinoza's philosophy of religion. Not published until 1930 due to disagreements with Guttmann, *Die Religionskritik Spinozas* was dedicated to the memory of Franz Rosenzweig, who had died the previous year.[16]

Strauss's book on Spinoza appeared at just the moment that the reputation of Spinoza was undergoing a serious reassessment. Throughout Europe, conferences were being planned to commemorate the 300th anniversary of Spinoza's birth. For many who were participating in these celebrations, it represented an unprecedented opportunity to correct what was seen as a deep historical injustice, namely, the excommunication of Spinoza from the Sephardic community of Amsterdam and from the Jewish world in general. Of course, the rehabilitation of Spinoza had been under way for more than a century. Beginning in the last quarter of the eighteenth century, Spinoza was canonized by the German

[13] Alan Udoff, "Leo Strauss: An Introductory Account," *Leo Strauss's Thought*, 26–27.

[14] Strauss, "Cohens Analyse der Bibel-Wissenschaft Spinozas (1924)," in *GS*, 1: 363–386; trans. Michael Zank, "Cohen's Analysis of Spinoza's Bible Science," in *EW*, 140–172. Strauss's essay was a review of Hermann Cohen, "Spinoza über Staat und Religion, Judentum und Christentum (1915)," *Jüdische Schriften*, ed. B. Strauss (Berlin: C. A. Schwetschke, 1924), 3: 290–372.

[15] The longest of Strauss's prefaces is the introduction to "Morgenstunden" and "An die Freunde Lessings," in *GS*, 2: 528–605; for an important analysis, see Janssens, "The Problem of the Enlightenment," 605–632.

[16] For Strauss's disagreement with Guttmann, see Meier, *GS*, 1: xvii–xix; for Strauss's farewell to Rosenzweig, see "Franz Rosenzweig und die Akakemie für die Wissenschaft des Judentums (1929), in *GS*, 2: 363–364; trans, Michael Zank, "Franz Rosenzweig and the Academy for the Science of Judaism," in *EW*, 212–213.

romantics as the "God-intoxicated man," and by the first third of the nineteenth century he was being treated by the German Jewish community as a secular saint promising redemption through a religion of reason. Spinoza may have been seen as a heretic but he was still a Jewish heretic, and his heresies were vital steps toward the age of emancipation. Everyone – whether they admitted it or not – had been a beneficiary of his sacrifice. This era of good feeling came to an abrupt end exactly one year after the Spinoza tercentennial, when Adolf Hitler came to power.[17]

Strauss's book made no mention of the Spinoza retrospective then underway, although one can see a theme emerging that would become central to his life's work, namely, the "theologico-political problem" that he would later call "*the* theme of my investigations."[18] As the term suggests, the theologico-political problem was intimately connected to the so-called Jewish Question or Jewish Problem, that is, the Jewish condition in modern liberal society. To what extent can a liberal democracy – a regime that professes official neutrality toward religion – provide an answer to the age-old problem of persecution? This question had been debated throughout Europe at least since the French Revolution, but nowhere more widely than in Germany.

German Jews in particular looked to the philosophy of Spinoza to provide an answer to the Jewish Question. Spinoza envisaged modern democracy as constituted by a bond of universal and rational morality rather than by religion. Religion would henceforth be consigned to the sphere of individual conscience or private belief, thus elevating the state to a position of neutrality toward the various competing religious denominations. Nevertheless, it was recognized that this purely "formal" separation of the public and private spheres could not entirely eliminate persecution or anti-Jewish prejudice; it could only shift it from the public to the private side of the ledger. At the same time, Spinoza's philosophy also intimated that there could be no solution to the Jewish Question without a Jewish state. Liberal democracy points toward or makes possible political Zionism.[19]

For particular historical reasons, the liberal solution to the theologico-political problem was weaker in Germany than in other European nations. The Weimar Republic was regarded by many intellectuals of Strauss's generation as a foreign import without roots in the German tradition. Furthermore, it was a symbol of Anglo-French domination that could be traced back to the French Revolution. The very

---

[17] Strauss, "Preface to *SCR*," in *LAM*, 227: "The German-Jewish problem was never solved. It was annihilated by the annihilation of the German Jews."
[18] Strauss, "Preface to 'Hobbes Politische Wissenschaft,'" in *JPCM*, 453.
[19] Strauss, "Preface to *SCR*," in *LAM*, 227–230.

weakness of Weimar was made manifest in its failure to provide safety and protection to its Jewish citizens. "The Weimar Republic," Strauss later remarked, "was succeeded by the only German regime – the only regime ever anywhere – which had no other clear principle except murderous hatred of the Jews."[20] It was the very weakness and fragility of liberal democracy, its susceptibility to demagoguery of both the Left and the Right, that would become a central problem of Strauss's life's work.

YEARS IN EXILE

Under the auspices of a grant from the Rockefeller Foundation, Strauss left Germany for Paris where he lived from October 1932 to December 1933. One of the minor ironies of twentieth-century history is that his fellowship was made possible in part because of letters of recommendation written by Carl Schmitt, who would later become the infamous legal philosopher of National Socialism. Strauss had come to the attention of Schmitt because of a lengthy review he had written of Schmitt's *Der Begriff der Politischen (The Concept of the Political)*.[21] Schmitt would later admit that Strauss's review "saw through me and X-rayed me as nobody else had."[22] Strauss himself would later claim that his review of Schmitt coincided with "a change of orientation" that would lead him to focus on the priority of political philosophy. This change of orientation that would emerge over a period of several years consisted of the growing awareness of the role of esoteric writing, and therefore a new approach to premodern philosophy.[23]

Little is known of Strauss's year in Paris. He married Marie (Miriam) Bernsohn in 1933. In a letter to Schmitt, he mentions "the Arabist Massignon" as having left a strong impression on him.[24] Louis Massignon (1883–1962) held the chair of Arabic at the Collège de France and was the benefactor and friend of Strauss's brother-in-law, the Czech Arabist Paul Kraus (1904–1944). Kraus was married to Strauss's sister Bettina, whom he had met in Berlin. While in Paris, Kraus lectured on Islamic philosophy at the École Pratique des Hautes Études but was unable to find

[20] Strauss, "Preface to *SCR*," in *LAM*, 226.
[21] Leo Strauss, "Anmerkungen zu Carl Schmitt, *Der Begriff des Politischen* (1932)" *GS*, 3: 217–238; trans. E. M. Sinclair in Carl Schmitt, *The Concept of the Political* (New Brunswick, NJ: Rutgers University Press, 1976), 81–105; reprinted in Heinrich Meier, *Carl Schmitt and Leo Strauss; The Hidden Dialogue*, trans. Harvey Lomax (Chicago: University of Chicago Press, 1995), 91–119.
[22] Cited in Meier, *The Hidden Dialogue*, xvii.
[23] Strauss, "Preface to *SCR*," in *LAM*, 257.
[24] Letter to Schmitt, July 10, 1933, cited in Meier, *The Hidden Dialogue*, 127.

permanent employment due to French restrictions on foreign nationals. Massignon, a French aristocrat, regarded Kraus as a prodigy and helped arrange a position for him at the Egyptian University in Cairo. It was in Cairo that Bettina died shortly after childbirth, and Kraus himself died under mysterious circumstances in 1944. Their daughter, Jenny, was sent to live on a kibbutz near Jerusalem and was later adopted by the Strausses, who were then living in the United States.[25]

Strauss viewed the Nazi takeover of power from the outside. He seems to have been unaware of Schmitt's involvement with the Nazi movement when he wrote the previous letter to Schmitt. It was from this same period that he wrote an unnerving letter to his fellow refugee Löwith regarding the triumph of National Socialism and what Strauss regarded as the proper response to it: "Just because the right-wing Germany does not tolerate us [the Jews] says nothing against the principles of the right. To the contrary, only on the basis of the principles of the right – fascist, authoritarian, *imperial* – is it possible, with decency and without the ridiculous and pitiable appeal to the 'unwritten rights of man,' to protest against this shabby nuisance [i.e., Hitler]."[26]

Strauss's disparaging references here to Western liberalism and the rights of man are consistent with his analysis of the failure of Weimar to protect its Jewish citizens. Given the weakness of liberalism in Germany, where was one to turn? If liberalism could not protect the Jews, perhaps the only alternative was some type of neo-Roman imperial ideology conceived along Augustan lines. In the same letter, Strauss remarks that he had been reading Caesar's *Commentaries* and notes a new-found appreciation for Virgil's judgment that under the Roman empire, "the subjected are spared and the proud are subdued (*Tu regere imperio parcere subjectis et debellare superbos*)."[27] *Pax et princeps* had been the watchword of the Augustan age. Perhaps a "spark" of Romanism could yet be found in the modern world, but where this might come from Strauss could not say.[28]

This letter has been widely discussed (and often gleefully cited) as evidence of a strong authoritarian streak in Strauss's thought. This

[25] The story of Kraus's life and his relation to Strauss is beautifully told by Joel Kraemer, "The Death of an Orientalist: Paul Kraus from Prague to Cairo," *The Jewish Discovery of Islam: Studies in Honor of Bernard Lewis*, ed. Martin Kramer (Tel Aviv: The Moshe Dayan Center, 1999), 181–223.

[26] Letter to Löwith, May 19, 1933, in *GS*, 3; 625.

[27] *GS*, 3: 625; the Latin phrase comes from Virgil, *Aeneid*, 6: 853; see also the passage from Livy cited at the end of *OT*, 212.

[28] This letter has recently received considerable attention; for one of the more thoughtful treatments, see Sheppard, *The Politics of Exile*, 60–63.

judgment may not be altogether false. Strauss clearly flirted with dangerous ideas during this period. We have already seen that he rejected the neo-Kantianism of his mentors Cohen and Cassirer for the "new thinking" advocated by Heidegger and Rosenzweig. At the core of the new thinking was the philosophy of Nietzsche. In another letter to Löwith, Strauss wrote: "Nietzsche so dominated and charmed me between my 22nd and 30th years that I literally believed everything I understood of him."[29] Unfortunately, Strauss does not elaborate on what he claimed to understand of Nietzsche, but as the dating suggests the allure of German nihilism that did so much to inform the philosophy of National Socialism came to an end for him around 1930.

Simultaneous with the events discussed previously, Strauss began working on a projected study of Maimonides that would eventually see fruition under the title *Philosophie und Gesetz* (*Philosophy and Law*).[30] The purpose of this book was to some degree strategic: to gain an academic position at the Hebrew University where his friend Gershom Scholem (1897–1982) had already become established as a specialist in the field of Jewish mysticism. Strauss had originally met Scholem in Berlin in 1927 and the two formed a lifelong friendship, although one not without rivalry and occasional touches of malice.[31] A professorship in medieval Jewish philosophy at the Hebrew University had been awarded to Julius Guttmann, Strauss's former boss at the Academy, and Scholem encouraged Strauss to apply for another position that was to be filled. This did not come to pass.[32]

While encouraging Strauss to apply for the position, Scholem also advised him to try to publish something in the area of Jewish studies. The result was a broadside against Guttmann's reading of Maimonides. The central problem of medieval philosophy was not, as Guttmann thought, the reconciliation of reason and revelation; it was the primacy

[29] Letter to Löwith, June 23, 1935, in *CCM*, 183; this letter has figured prominently in Laurence Lampert, *Leo Strauss and Nietzsche* (Chicago: University of Chicago Press, 1996).

[30] Strauss, *Philosophie und Gesetz: Beiträge zum Verständnis Maimunis und seiner Vorläufer* (1935), *GS*, 2: 3–123; trans. Eve Adler, *Philosophy and Law: Essays Toward the Understanding of Maimonides and his Predecessors* (Albany, NY: SUNY, 1995).

[31] Smith, "Gershom Scholem and Leo Strauss: Notes Toward a German-Jewish Dialogue," *Reading Leo Strauss*, 43–64.

[32] Letter to Strauss, January 27, 1934, in *GS*, 3: 710. A sense of Strauss's desperation is conveyed in an undated letter to Alexandre Kojève in Strauss, *OT*, 224: "I am deep in work and worries – in other words in a situation similar to yours. Nothing will come of Palestine: Guttmann is going there. So far the prospects are the same as in France. But one must not lose courage."

of law and the authority of the lawgiver. It is the primacy of law under-stood in the broadest sense as the domain of the prophet that supplies the ultimate grounding of philosophy. It was this insight actually first discovered by Strauss in his reading of Avicenna's *On the Divisions of the Rational Sciences* that would provide the key to all his later attempts to recover the premodern tradition of philosophical rationalism.[33]

Strauss's focus on the political justification of prophecy led in turn to an enhanced awareness of the Platonic influence on medieval thought. The problem of revelation was no longer to be seen as a problem for the philosophy of religion but for political philosophy. Just exactly what this meant gave rise to great perplexity among Strauss's friends and associates. In a letter to Walter Benjamin of March 29, 1935, Scholem wrote bluntly about how this would affect Strauss's candidacy for a position in Jerusalem:

Any day now, Schocken will bring out a book by Leo Strauss [*Philosophie und Gesetz*] (I have devoted great energy to obtaining an appointment for Strauss in Jerusalem), marking the occasion of the Maimonides anniversary. The book begins with an unfeigned and copiously argued (if completely ludicrous) affir-mation of atheism as the most important Jewish watchword. Such admirable boldness for a book that will be read by everybody as having been written by a candidate for Jerusalem . . . I admire this ethical stance and regret the – obviously conscious and deliberately provoked – suicide of such a capable mind. As is to be expected here, only three people at the very most will make use of the freedom to vote for the appointment of an atheist to a teaching position that serves to endorse the philosophy of religion.[34]

On May 20, 1935, Benjamin replied: "I am also very interested in Leo Strauss's book. What you tell me about him fits in with the pleasant image of him I have always made for myself."[35] Almost a year later, Benjamin wrote to Scholem inquiring about Strauss's whereabouts. "Is Leo Strauss in Palestine?" he asked. "I would not be adverse to address-ing his works in the journal *Orient und Okzident* . . . Perhaps you'll soon be seeing the author; if so, you can prevail upon him to send me

---

[33] Strauss, "A Giving of Accounts," in *JPCM*, 463. The importance of Strauss's reading of Avicenna has been stressed by Heinrich Meier, "How Strauss Became Strauss," *Enlightening Revolutions: Essays in Honor of Ralph Lerner*, ed. Svetozar Minkov (Boulder, CO: Rowman & Littlefield, 2006), 367; see also Tanguay, *Leo Strauss: An Intellectual Biography*, 57; the importance of this theme is discussed by Joel Kraemer, "The Medieval Arabic Enlightenment," this volume.

[34] Letter from Scholem to Benjamin, March 29, 1935, in *The Correspondence of Walter Benjamin and Gershom Scholem, 1932–1940*, ed. Gershom Scholem, trans. Gary Smith and Andre Lefevre (New York: Schocken, 1989), 156–157.

[35] Letter from Benjamin to Scholem, May 20, 1935, *The Correspondence*, 160.

the books."[36] Scholem had to inform Benjamin that by this time Strauss was already living in England.

STRAUSS IN ENGLAND

Strauss arrived in England in early 1934 with Miriam, her son Thomas, and little more than his foundation grant and an academic letter of reference from the French historian Henri Sée.[37] Even though the Strausses lived in a boarding house on Russell Square and were desperately short of money, his letters from this period express a strong liking for England and the English way of life. "The English people is [much] politer than the Frenchmen," he wrote in broken English in an undated letter to Alexandre Kojève (1902–1968), whom he knew from Paris.[38] "I cannot realize a greater difference than that between the Préfecture de Police and the Aliens Registration Office. We feel much better here than in Paris."[39] He enthused about the delicious English breakfasts that he also preferred to French food. "The hams taste too good as to consist of pork and therefore they are allowed by the Mosaic law according to atheistic interpretation," he joked.[40] In another letter he wrote: "I like this country about which one might say what Diderot said of Hobbes: dry (the pubs close at 10 P.M. sharp here and the stuff is expensive!)." By contrast to the Bibliothèque Nationale, "the British Museum is a place to which one *enjoys* going."[41]

Strauss developed a strong Anglophilia that was to remain a part of his makeup. In an early letter, he remarked on the "strong impression" left on him from a visit to Downing Street, "the seat of the greatest power in the world – much much smaller than the Wilhelmstrasse."[42] England cultivated a strong tradition of the gentleman that was not to be found

---

[36] Letter from Benjamin to Scholem, May 3, 1936, *The Correspondence*, 179.

[37] S. J. D. Green, "The Tawney-Strauss Connection: On Historicism and Values in the History of Political Ideas," *The Journal of Modern History* 67 (1995): 256.

[38] Kojève, a Russian émigré and a distinguished Hegel scholar, formed a strange bond of friendship with Strauss; the Strauss-Kojève relation is explored in Smith, "Tyranny Ancient and Modern," *Reading Leo Strauss*, 131–155; see also Victor Gourevitch, "Philosophy and Politics, I–II," *Review of Metaphysics*, 22 (1968): 58–84, 281–328; Michael Roth, "Natural Right and the End of History: Leo Strauss and Alexandre Kojève," *Revue de Métaphysique et de Morale* 3 (1991): 407–422; Robert Pippin, "Being, Time, and Politics: The Strauss-Kojève Debate," *History and Theory* 2 (1993): 138–161.

[39] Letter to Kojève, undated, in *OT*, 222.

[40] Letter to Kojève, undated, in *OT*, 222.

[41] Letter to Kojève, April 9, 1934, in *OT*, 225.

[42] Letter to Kojève, January 16, 1934, in *OT*, 224.

in continental Europe. Strauss later came to identify this English idea of the gentleman with the Aristotelian notion of the *megalopsychos*, or "great-souled" man. This was a quality that he found exemplified in the statecraft of Winston Churchill, who would become a hero of his. In a letter to Löwith penned shortly after World War II, Strauss wrote: "A man like Churchill proves that the possibility of *megalopsychia* exists today *exactly* as it did in the fifth century B.C."[43] He also contracted an appreciation for English prose. He was a reader of Shakespeare, Macaulay, Thackeray, Disraeli, and P. G. Wodehouse. He remarked that the quiet understatement of Jane Austen was a better entree to the classics than the romantic self-disclosure of Dostoyevsky.[44]

Strauss applied to and was accepted at Sidney Sussex College at Cambridge University as a research student beginning in January 1935 to conduct continuing research on Hobbes.[45] In a letter to Kojève, he boasted that he had become "a real Hobbes philologist: Mss, etc."[46] When his Hobbes book was eventually published in 1936, it attracted several admirers. Ernest Barker was a reader of the manuscript for Clarendon Press and contributed a Foreword – later removed from the American edition. He praised the "great merit" of the book as its application of the same "genetic method" to Hobbes that Werner Jaeger had earlier applied to Aristotle.[47] Michael Oakeshott, who would contribute important Hobbes scholarship of his own, reviewed it favorably three times. Oakeshott praised the work, not without some qualifications, as of "the first importance" and "the most original book on Hobbes which has appeared for many years."[48] And R. H. Tawney, then professor of economic history at the London School of Economics, described Strauss as knowing "more [about Hobbes] than any Englishman" and "the greatest living authority on Hobbes."[49]

The Hobbes book has always been the book of Strauss's most admired by non-Straussians. It was in many ways a conventional history of ideas studying Hobbes's development. Nevertheless, the book pioneered

[43] Letter to Löwith, August 20, 1946, in *CCM*, 111.
[44] Strauss, *OT*, 185; on Jane Austen, see Stanley Rosen, "Leo Strauss and the Problem of the Modern," this volume.
[45] Leo Strauss File, Sidney Sussex College Archive, Cambridge University; I owe this information to Teresa Bejan.
[46] Letter to Kojève, April 9, 1934, in *OT*, 225.
[47] Ernest Barker, "Foreword" to Strauss, *PPH*, vii.
[48] Michael Oakeshott, "Dr. Strauss on Hobbes," *Politica*, 2 (1936–37): 364–379; reprinted in *Hobbes and Civil Association* (Indianapolis, IN: Liberty Fund, 2000), 141–158; Oakeshott's other, much shorter, reviews appeared in *The Cambridge Review* 57 (1936–37): 150 and in *Philosophy*, 12 (1937): 239–241.
[49] Cited in Green, "The Tawney-Strauss Connection," 261.

certain themes that would be crucial to Strauss's later thought. Strauss treated Hobbes as the crucial break between the ancients and the moderns. Hobbes transformed the ancient and medieval doctrine of natural law into a theory of modern natural rights. He introduced a new dimension of subjectivity or freedom into philosophy. Furthermore, Hobbes's revolution was not the result of a new scientific outlook, as many readers had attributed to him, but was constructed out of "humanistic" sources, especially Thucydides's history and Aristotle's *Rhetoric*. On the basis of his critique of the Aristotelian theory of pride – honor, vanity, glory – Hobbes constructed a "new morality" of "bourgeois" civilization. Strauss's Hobbes was the true founder of liberal modernity.

Despite the respectful treatment of Strauss's Hobbes book, there seemed little or no chance that an academic position in England would be forthcoming. Tawney, who acted as a benefactor to the young German émigré, did his best to convince his friend, the economist John U. Nef, to hire Strauss at the University of Chicago. Tawney was unsuccessful in securing a position for Strauss, although his good opinion may have helped to lay the basis for his later tenure there. Strauss eventually made his way to America in 1937 at the invitation of Salo Baron as a lecturer in the history department at Columbia University. The following year, he accepted a temporary and then a permanent position at the New School for Social Research.

THE NEW YORK YEARS

The New School had been established originally in 1918 by John Dewey and a group of "progressive" intellectuals to foster adult education and independent research outside the official university system. By the early 1930s, the New School had opened its doors to European scholars fleeing fascism and National Socialism. The University-in-Exile became the place where European scholarship found a place of refuge on American soil. Under the leadership of economist Alvin Johnson (1874–1971), the New School attracted a remarkable body of luminaries including psychologists Max Wertheimer and Alfred Schutz, sociologists Hans Speier and Max Ascoli, political theorists Arnold Brecht and Erich Hula, and economists Adolph Lowe and Frieda Wunderlich. Into this extraordinary constellation of scholars at the age of almost forty, Strauss found his first academic home.[50]

[50] For a useful overview of the New School, see Peter Rutkoff and William B. Scott, *New School: A History of the New School for Social Research* (New York: Free Press, 1986); Strauss is discussed on pages 143–149; see also Claus-Dieter Krohn, *Intellectuals in Exile: Refugee Scholars and the New School for Social Research*, trans. Rita and Robert Kimber (Amherst, MA: University of Massachusetts Press, 1993), 74–76.

Strauss's letters from this period reveal both the great relief and the great anxiety of settling into life in the New World. In a letter to Klein dated January 20, 1938, he wrote that "things aren't nearly as bad as I had reason to expect." In the same letter, he noted that a position with "powerful backing" has opened up at Harvard, but "it is unlikely that anything should come of it for me because, as you know, I am a Jew."[51] Shortly later he warned Klein: "You must not expect it to be easier here than in England: have no illusions." "The Jewish-protective tendencies of the Americans change from month to month. But they could also change for you."[52]

Life was continually beset by worries about family and friends back in Germany as well as Miriam, who had remained for a time back in England. In addition, there was a constant shortfall of cash. In an especially poignant letter, Strauss wrote to Klein: "I ask you to *please* loan me forty dollars between 12/1 and 12/15. I know no one in the USA, and consequently no one on this planet, and no one in this universe whom I could go to, and on 12/1 my pockets will be completely empty."[53] At the same time, Strauss's financial worries were offset by the experience of teaching his first classes: "This evening I had my first seminar: Aristotle's *Politics*," he wrote. "It really happened! But I am a charlatan. I asserted a thousand things that didn't add up or that I didn't know anything about."[54] Most importantly, it was during this period that Strauss was making his first discoveries of the esoteric tradition. Sometimes these discoveries were mixed with everyday concerns: "I am now reading Herodotus who – I would swear as a Catholic Christian – is an esoteric writer (*esoterischer Schriftsteller*) and one to perfection. In short life goes on. If only money-calamities weren't lurking in the future."[55]

The decade that Strauss spent at the New School was one of the most remarkable of his career. It was during this time that he discovered his distinctive voice and his own idiomatic forms of expression. Strauss was an active contributor to the intellectual life of the New School through his participation in the graduate faculty's General Seminar, contributing papers on Germany and contemporary politics. This seminar met on Wednesday evenings and, in the words of a former student, seemed like "a convocation on Mount Olympus."[56] In 1941, Strauss delivered

[51] Letter to Klein, January 20, 1938, in *GS*, 3; 544.
[52] Letter to Klein, February 11, 1938, in *GS*, 3: 548,
[53] Letter to Klein, November 27, 1938, in *GS*, 3: 558.
[54] Letter to Klein, February 7, 1938, in *GS*, 3: 546.
[55] Letter to Klein, October 15, 1938, in *GS*, 3: 556; for Strauss's discovery of esotericism, see Laurence Lampert, "Strauss's Recovery of Esotericism," this volume.
[56] This description was provided in a telephone interview with Harry V. Jaffa.

a paper on "German Nihilism" where he traced Hitler's rise to power back to a group of conservative intellectuals before and shortly after World War I who had rejected the principles of liberalism and European civilization.[57] As his analysis demonstrated, he was not entirely unsympathetic to the motivations of this group, but the gist of the paper was to show how even justified moral intentions can lead to horror. In the summer of 1942, he presented a paper titled "What Can We Learn from Political Theory?" and in November of 1943 he addressed the annual meeting of the Conference on Jewish Relations at the New School on the topic, "The Re-education of Axis Countries Concerning the Jews."[58]

This last paper was a sober and often somber reflection upon the possibility of liberalism taking root in postwar Germany. Strauss was deeply skeptical as to whether democracy could be imposed on Germany from the outside, and argued that there was no group with sufficient authority to do so from within. He speculated the best that one could expect from a defeated Germany would be a form of bureaucratic collectivism based on a resuscitated interpretation of Christianity. Fortunately, he proved to be wrong about this.

During this same period, Strauss began to publish in the New School's flagship journal *Social Research*, then under the editorial direction of Hans Speier (1905–1993).[59] Here he ventured into his first forays into classical political philosophy that would occupy so much of his later work. An article, "The Spirit of Sparta or the Taste of Xenophon," appeared in 1939, "On Classical Political Philosophy" in 1945, and "On a New Interpretation of Plato's Political Philosophy" in 1946.[60] At the

---

[57] Strauss, "German Nihilism," *Interpretation* 26 (1999): 353–378; this theme is discussed by Susan Shell, "'To Spare the Vanquished and Crush the Arrogant': Leo Strauss's Lecture on 'German Nihilism,'" this volume.

[58] Strauss, "What Can We Learn from Political Theory?" and "The Re-education of Axis Countries Concerning the Jews," *Review of Politics* 69 (2007): 515–529, 530–538; see Nathan Tarcov, "Will the Real Leo Strauss Please Stand Up?" *The American Interest* (September/October, 2006): 120–128.

[59] Speier and Strauss had met in 1929; their wives had been school friends from Erfurt; see Hans Speier, *Truth in Hell and Other Essays on Politics and Culture, 1935–1987* (New York: Oxford University Press, 1989), 9; Speier later contributed an essay ("Grimmelshaussen's Laughter") to a *festschrift* for Strauss *Ancients and Moderns: Essays on the Tradition of Political Philosophy in Honor of Leo Strauss*, ed. Joseph Cropsey (New York: Basic Books, 1964), 177–212.

[60] Strauss, "The Spirit of Sparta or the Taste of Xenophon," *Social Research*, 6 (1939): 502–536; "On Classical Political Philosophy," *Social Research*, 12 (1945): 98–117; reprinted in *WPP*, 78–94; "On a New Interpretation of Plato's Political Philosophy," *Social Research*, 13 (1946): 326–367.

same time, Strauss had not lost touch with his interests in medieval Jewish and Islamic thought, writing important essays on Abravanel, Alfarabi, Maimonides, and Judah Halevi.[61]

It is not a stretch to say that it was during this period at the New School that Strauss became a "Straussian." In a remarkable series of letters to Klein, Strauss marveled at his discovery of esoteric writing in the works of various ancient and modern philosophical figures. These thoughts came together in an unpublished essay from 1939 called simply "Exoteric Teaching," and two years later in his famous essay, "Persecution and the Art of Writing," which later served as the lead essay of a book of the same title.[62] This short essay may have received more attention than anything Strauss ever wrote. Here he drew upon the discovery that certain writers of the past expressed themselves in a language of caution and discretion both to avoid the real danger of persecution but also as an exercise in "social responsibility," not wishing to rock the ship of state. This insight – that some thinkers do not always say what they seem to say – would not have been particularly upsetting if it had not been combined with a further claim, namely, that liberal regimes that endorse maximum freedom of thought and opinion often find themselves prone to distinctive forms of intellectual complacency and conformity. Much to everyone's embarrassment, liberalism may be as prone to thoughtlessness as authoritarianism. With this insight, Strauss had discovered what would later become known as "the dialectic of the Enlightenment."

Strauss's work during the New York years culminated in his first book actually written in English called *On Tyranny: An Interpretation of Xenophon's "Hiero."* Published originally in 1948, this short book anticipated the wave of studies seeking to understand the causes of fascism, the appearance of the "authoritarian personality," and the advent of a new phenomenon called "totalitarianism." Strauss approached this problem through a circuitous route, namely, through a densely detailed reading of an ancient and largely forgotten dialogue by Xenophon. The

---

[61] Strauss, "On Abravanel's Philosophical Tendency and Political Teaching," *Isaac Abravanel,* ed. J. B. Trend and H. Loewe (Cambridge, UK: Cambridge University Press, 1937), 93–129; "The Literary Character of the 'Guide of the Perplexed,'" *Essays on Maimonides,* ed. Salo Baron (New York: Columbia University Press, 1941); reprinted in *PAW,* 38–94; "The Law of Reason in the *Kuzari,*" *Proceedings of the American Academy of Jewish Research* 13 (1943): 47–96; reprinted in *PAW,* 95–141; "Farabi's Plato," *Louis Ginzberg Jubilee Volume* (New York: American Academy for Jewish Research, 1945), 357–393.

[62] Strauss, "Exoteric Teaching," in *RCPR,* 63–71; "Persecution and the Art of Writing," *Social Research* 8 (1941): 488–504; reprinted in *PAW,* 33–37.

original edition of *On Tyranny* ran to just over 100 pages and included an introduction ("On Xenophon and Dr. Strauss") by Alvin Johnson, the president of the New School.[63] In the introduction – which has been unfortunately dropped from the later editions – Johnson wrote: "I often marvel at Dr. Strauss. He is a scholar of scholars. Yet his approach to a classical author is as direct as that of Erasmus or Montaigne." Johnson concluded his introduction with the hope that Strauss's little book "may mark a new direction in classical scholarship, a systematic effort to excavate the classical authors from the successive strata of ashen scholarship and win back for us the original freshness and splendor of a great literature."[64]

On Tyranny brought to the surface four themes that would form the backbone of all of Strauss's later work. Although each of these had been present or at least intimated in his earlier work, here for the first time they appear as part of a unified package. First, the work demonstrated the art of "careful reading," which was closely tied to Strauss's discovery of the problem of esotericism. Strauss paid particular attention to the literary form or the "action" of the dialogue, the give-and-take between the two protagonists, the poet Simonides and the tyrant Hiero. By focusing on the rhetoric of the work, Strauss was able to uncover what he believed to be the central, animating theme of philosophical writing, namely, the "disproportion between the intransigent quest for truth and the requirements of society."[65]

Second, Strauss used the work to highlight the fundamental conflict between the ancients and the moderns. Modern tyranny – and here Strauss is thinking of the tyrannies of Hitler's Germany and Stalin's Russia – "surpassed the boldest imagination of the most powerful thinkers of the past." But modern tyranny is based on modern political science, and modern political science has its basis in Machiavelli. In contrast to the ancients, modern tyranny is armed with the twin weapons of mass ideology ("propaganda") and technology. Yet Strauss affirms that to understand modern tyranny in its specific sense, it remains necessary to grasp "the elementary and in a sense natural form of tyranny which

---

[63] For Johnson's role in establishing the University-in-Exile, see Rutkoff and Scott, *New School*, 84–106; Krohn, *Intellectuals in Exile*, 22–23, 58–59. For a valuable character sketch of Johnson and his role in the encouragement of emigré intellectuals, see Arnold Brecht, *The Political Education of Arnold Brecht: An Autobiography, 1884–1970* (Princeton, NJ: Princeton University Press, 1970), 471–472.

[64] Alvin Johnson, "On Xenophon and Dr. Strauss," foreword to Leo Strauss, *On Tyranny: An Interpretation of Xenophon's "Hiero"* (New York: Political Science Classics, 1948), ix.

[65] Strauss, *OT*, 27.

is pre-modern tyranny."[66] The ancients still remain the best guide to understanding the moderns.

Third, Strauss attacked the dominant "historicist" manner of reading texts that consisted in seeing them as relative to their times. But by trying to understand the thought of the past as the product of its time, the historicist scholar is led to distort that thought by forcing it to conform to the principles of modern relativism. To understand the thought of the past "as it really has been" means considering it in a nonhistoricist manner. This means distrusting all scholarly conventions that stand between the reader and the text, or as Strauss put it, "I never believed that my mind was moving in a larger 'circle of ideas' than Xenophon's mind."[67]

Finally, Strauss made a central theme of his reading the question of the best way of life. The exchange between the two protagonists in the dialogue is ultimately a contest over whether the political life or the philosophical life – the way of the statesman or the way of the philosopher – is best. This problem, along with the related problem of Jerusalem and Athens, is one that would inform virtually all of Strauss's later thinking.

Among his many friends and colleagues at the New School, Strauss formed a special bond with Kurt Riezler (1882–1955).[68] Several years Strauss's senior, Riezler had been a German diplomat during World War I and was deeply affected by Heidegger after the war. Forced to leave Germany due to his anti-Nazi activities, Rielzer joined the New School the same year as Strauss. In a moving tribute to Riezler on the occasion of his death, Strauss stressed those aspects of Riezler's thought that were most sympathetic to his own, notably, his defense of the tradition of European nationalism against the emerging tendency toward cosmopolitanism.[69] Riezler contended cosmopolitanism was supported by modern economic and technological developments that could ultimately increase our power over nature but would also led to a coarsening or deadening of the spirit. Such cosmopolitanism forced individuals into ever more specialized tasks and functions while "exciting all kinds of curiosities and stimulating all kinds of interests," thus making "ever more difficult concentration on the few things on which man's wholeness entirely depends."[70] In particular, the cosmopolitan ideal made

[66] Strauss, *OT*, 23.

[67] Strauss, *OT*, 26.

[68] For a useful biography, see Wayne C. Thompson, *In the Eye of the Storm: Kurt Riezler and the Crisis of Modern Germany* (Iowa City, IA: University of Iowa Press, 1980).

[69] For Strauss's later thoughts on the role of Europe, see "Preface," in *LAM*, v–vii.

[70] Strauss, "Kurt Riezler (1882–1955)," in *WPP*, 236.

difficult the possibility of reverence that at all times takes the form of loyalty to one's particular heritage and tradition. Unlike Riezler, Strauss was not a German nationalist but Riezler's emphasis on the particular as opposed to the universal may have reinforced Strauss's belief about the importance of the regime as the fundamental concept of political life.

From an early time, Strauss began to attract students. Among the "first generation" of his students was Howard B. White (1912–1974), Strauss's successor at the New School, who was married to Riezler's daughter and who wrote on Francis Bacon and Shakespeare;[71] Harry V. Jaffa (b. 1918), who completed a dissertation on *Thomism and Aristotelianism* before going on to contribute works on Lincoln and American political thought;[72] and Henry Magid (1917–1979), who worked on John Stuart Mill and English political thought.[73] To this list must also be added the name of Joseph Cropsey (b. 1918), who was to write on Adam Smith and Plato.[74] Strictly speaking, Cropsey was not a student of Strauss's at the New School, having completed his Ph.D. in economics at Columbia, but he began auditing courses from Strauss shortly after returning from military service at the prompting of his friend Jaffa. He would join Strauss about a decade later as a colleague and collaborator at the University of Chicago.[75]

---

[71] Howard B. White, *Peace Among the Willows: The Political Philosophy of Francis Bacon* (The Hague: Martinus Nijhoff, 1960); "Bastards and Usurpers: Shakespeare's 'King John,'" *Ancients and Moderns*, 148–176; *Copp'd Hills Towards Heaven: Shakespeare and the Classical Polity* (The Hague: Martinus Nijhoff, 1970).

[72] Harry V. Jaffa, *Thomism and Aristotelianism: A Study of the Commentary by Thomas Aquinas on the "Nicomachean Ethics"* (Chicago: University of Chicago Press, 1952); *Crisis of the House Divided: An Interpretation of the Issues in the Lincoln-Douglas Debates* (New York: Doubleday, 1958); *How to Think About the American Revoution* (Durham, NC: Carolina Academic Press, 1978); *A New Birth of Freedom: Abraham Lincoln and the Coming of the Civil War* (Lanham, MD: Rowman & Littlefield, 2000).

[73] Henry Magid, *English Political Pluralism: The Problem of Freedom and Organization* (New York: Columbia University Press, 1941); "Political Philosophy as the Search for Truth," *Ancients and Moderns*, 304–315.

[74] Joseph Cropsey, *Polity and Economy: An Interpretation of the Principles of Adam Smith* (The Hague: Martinus Nijhoff, 1957); Ed. with Leo Strauss, *History of Political Philosophy* (Chicago: Rand McNally, 1972); *Political Philosophy and the Issues of Politics* (Chicago: University of Chicago Press, 1977); *Plato's World: Man's Place in the Cosmos* (Chicago: University of Chicago Press, 1995).

[75] Telephone interview with Joseph Cropsey.

THE UNIVERSITY OF CHICAGO

Strauss joined the faculty of the University of Chicago in the fall of 1949. The terms of his appointment are worth retelling. According to sociologist Edward Shils in his biography of Robert Maynard Hutchins – the President of the university and the founder of the famous "Hutchins College" – a vacancy in the field of political philosophy had come up after the retirement of Charles Merriam. The appointment committee consisted of economist Theodore Schultz, international relations specialist Hans Morgenthau, and Shils himself. According to Shils, there were three candidates under consideration for the position: Alexandre Passerin d'Entrèves, the distinguished medievalist from Oxford; Alfred Cobban, a scholar of the French Revolution from London; and Strauss. The committee was divided. Schultz claimed to be unable to pass judgment on an area not his own. Morgenthau favored Strauss but was reluctant to push for him suspecting that the chair of his department, Leonard White, might not be so inclined. Shils also favored Strauss but knew that John Nef, the influential chair of the Committee on Social Thought, favored d'Entrèves. Shils tells what happened next:

I proceeded without consulting Nef; I wrote a long cautious memorandum to Hutchins, reviewing the merits of all three candidates but making it clear that Strauss was my preference. I did not want to ride roughshod over Nef's desire but I did not wish to be subservient to it either. The memorandum went to Hutchins and I called on him shortly afterward in order to speak more freely than I had written. Hutchins had obviously read my long-winded memorandum very closely and he saw my preference. He said simply something like, "Who is the best of them?" I replied that Strauss was very much the best. He then replied, "All right, let's have Strauss." The matter was settled.[76]

And so it was.

The move to Chicago seemed to have been a pleasure in contrast to the uncertainties of his arrival in New York a decade previous. In a letter to Klein written shortly after arriving, he described the apartment as "majestic" and went on to enumerate the number of rooms. He added that lying on his desk was a book given to him as a farewell gift titled "How to Live Within Your Income." The university neighborhood, Hyde Park, was described as "the Chicago Washington Heights," full of German-Jewish refugees. "The man who works at our delicatessen went to school with me in Marburg and the owner of the animal hospital in

[76] Edward Shils, "Robert Maynard Hutchins, 1899–1977," *Remembering the University of Chicago: Teachers, Scientists, Scholars* (Chicago: University of Chicago Press, 1991), 192.

which Schwulch stayed while we were living in a hotel is an in-law of mine from Biebrich."[77]

Strauss introduced himself to the faculty and students of the University of Chicago with a series of six lectures given in the autumn of 1949 under the title "Natural Right and History." These were subsequently expanded and turned into a book published in 1953. This book – along with *Persecution and the Art of Writing* published the year before – turned Strauss from an unknown into a major voice in American political philosophy. *Natural Right and History* remains even today Strauss's most widely read book. It canvassed the entire range of the Western tradition of political philosophy from the Greeks to the Germans. But Strauss's book was more than a neutral or disinterested piece of historical scholarship. It was a work that put the analysis of the modernity problem front and center.

From the outset, *Natural Right and History* set an ominous tone. The tradition of natural right or natural rights conceived as all but self-evident to an earlier generation of Americans was in danger of being eclipsed by German historicism. "[This] would not be the first time," Strauss warned, "that a nation defeated on the battlefield . . . has deprived its conquerors of the most sublime fruit of victory by imposing on them the yoke of its own thought."[78] The German "historical sense" today has threatened to become a complete relativism or even nihilism, the belief that all standards of truth, justice, and morality are relative to their historical time and place. Strauss argued further that this form of historicism has crept into the modern academy by way of the sociology of Max Weber with his insistence on the rigorous separation of "facts" and "values," and the related belief that social science must restrict itself only to the "is" and not the "ought." The result of Weber's particular form of ethical neutrality is that social scientists who enjoy the benefits of intellectual freedom, tolerance, and the exchange of ideas are denied the ability to provide that liberalism with a rational foundation. The deepest and most pressing moral principles have become no more than a matter of individual choice or arbitrary decision. Lurking just behind this analysis of modernity was the Schmittian ethic of *Decionismus* that Strauss believed had played such an important role in the implosion of the Weimar Republic.[79]

Space does not permit a more detailed account of *Natural Right and History*. The book offers a breathtaking (and sometimes breathless)

---

[77] Letter to Klein, February 6, 1949, in *GS*, 3: 596.
[78] Strauss, *NRH*, 2.
[79] Strauss, *NRH*, 40–42, 45–47, 65–67; the importance of Weber is discussed by Nasser Behnegar, "Strauss and Social Science," this volume.

account of not only the contrast between the ancients and the moderns but the gradual "lowering of the sights" of modernity by its focus on the historicization of the principles of natural right. Just as he had in *On Tyranny*, Strauss showed how the claims of historicism are self-contradictory. If all claims to truth are historically relative, this must hold true for historicism itself, but historicism claims – inconsistently – to represent a truth that stands above history.[80]

Strauss's return to nature as a standard of political judgment is sometimes believed to give his thought a dogmatic or absolutist character. This is false. Invoking Aristotle against the traditions of both Thomism and Kantianism, he constantly maintained the flexibility of standards of natural right within the context of normal politics. "There is a universally valid hierarchy of ends," he maintained, "but there are no universally valid rules of action."[81] However, Strauss's insistence on the need for flexibility should not be confused with Machiavellianism. Machiavelli, Hobbes, and Locke's "first wave" of modernity gave way to a more radical second wave inaugurated by Rousseau and the tradition of German idealism, only to be supplanted by a third wave of "radical historicism" brought about by Nietzsche and later Heidegger. These philosophical transformations were themselves related to profound political and historical changes culminating in the monstrous tyrannies of the twentieth century. Strauss's book was intended as a wake-up call to the complacent progressivism and pragmatism that had characterized the recent American philosophical past.

Almost immediately, Strauss began to attract students. Among the next generation of Strauss's students were the brilliant and eccentric classicist Seth Benardete (1930–2001),[82] the philosopher Stanley Rosen (b. 1929),[83] and political theorist Allan Bloom (1930–1992).[84] It was from

---

[80] Strauss, *NRH*, 25.

[81] Strauss, *NRH*, 162.

[82] Seth Benardete, *Herodotean Inquiries* (The Hague: Maratinus Nijhoff, 1969); *The Being of the Beautiful: Theaetetus, Sophist, and Statesman* (Chicago: University of Chicago Press, 1984); *Socrates's Second Sailing: On Plato's "Republic,"* (Chicago: University of Chicago Press, 1989); *Plato's "Laws": The Discovery of Being* (Chicago: University of Chicago Press, 2000).

[83] Stanley Rosen, *Nihilism: A Philosophical Essay* (New Haven, CT: Yale University Press, 1969); *Hermeneutics as Politics* (New York: Oxford University Press, 1987); *Ancients and Moderns: Rethinking Modernity* (New Haven, CT: Yale University Press, 1989); *The Elusiveness of the Ordinary: Studies on the Possibility of Philosophy* (New Haven, CT: Yale University Press, 2002); *Plato's Republic: A Study* (New Haven, CT: Yale University Press, 2005); this last work is dedicated to "the genuine Leo Strauss."

[84] Allan Bloom, *Shakespeare's Politics* (New York: Basic Books, 1964); *The Closing of the American Mind* (New York: Simon & Schuster, 1987): *Giants and*

this period – Benardete dates it from around 1955 – that a self-conscious school of "Straussians" began to take shape.[85]

What was it that attracted students to Strauss? Did he exercise some strange and cultlike control over their minds, as some of Strauss's most hostile critics have alleged?[86] According to Victor Gourevitch, who studied with him during this period, it was Strauss's "total absorption in the materials" and the fact that "he spoke directly about the things that concerned us in a non-technical way" that students found enticing. But there was more: Strauss showed how it was possible "that one can be a serious and dignified Jew in an academy that was still highly suspicious of Judaism."[87] This was confirmed by another student, Werner Dannhauser, who also reflected on this theme: "He astounded us with the care with which he studied books by Jews like Maimonides thus showing us that one could not afford to treat the whole tradition of Jewish learning as relics in one's mind."[88]

AN INTERLUDE IN ISRAEL

Strauss spent the academic year of 1954 to 1955 as a visiting professor at the Hebrew University. The background to his visit is of some interest. As early as 1950, Scholem had been approaching Strauss about a move. In a letter from Scholem, he asked Strauss "whether you are ready to be the successor to [Buber's] chair." "I assume," he wrote, "that it would be potentially more satisfying for you to accept a position in Jerusalem in their non-Jewish area of study, if one could study theoretical sociology, or however it is currently called, than to accept the professorship in Jewish philosophy that will also possibly be free in two years."[89]

Strauss apparently seriously considered this possibility but in the end decided to decline. "The decision was very difficult for me as no one could know better than you," he wrote. "I feel myself too old and exhausted, incapable of doing anything more than to learn the little I am granted, *si fortunae placet* [if fate allows] with the greatest possible

---

Dwarfs: Essays 1960–1990 (New York: Simon & Schuster, 1990); *Love and Friendship* (New York: Simon & Schuster, 1993).

[85] Seth Benardete, *Encounters and Reflections: Conversations with Seth Benardete*, ed. Ronna Burger (Chicago: University of Chicago Press, 2002), 46.

[86] See Myles Burnyeat, "Sphinx Without a Secret," *New York Review of Books* 32 (May 30, 1985): 30–36.

[87] Interview with Victor Gourevitch, July 12, 2007.

[88] Werner Dannhauser, "Leo Strauss as Citizen and Jew," *Interpretation* 17 (1990): 446.

[89] Letter from Scholem, January 20, 1950, in *GS*, 3: 718,

degree of clarity and, as one says, to nail it down."[90] He then went on to add a revealing clarification: "Thus I need *all* the scant strength I have. Because of the incidents since 1933 and especially the difficulties I have had since 1936, I have fragmented myself too much – only now am I beginning to concentrate on the real problem (*eigentliche Problem*): I should not interrupt this process."[91]

Scholem was clearly hurt by Strauss's refusal. He declared himself "discouraged and distressed" that Strauss was backing out. "You don't know how much, even in your own field (if you had a taken a professorship for example) you could have affected *without* inflicting harm on your desire for productive work," he wrote. "We could have accomplished *much* here together and that would have been good for all concerned."[92]

About a month later, Scholem wrote again this time to report on the death of Guttmann ("it was a long and hard death"). Adding guilt to his earlier expression of hurt, Scholem added: "He [Guttmann] was conscious almost to the end and spoke repeatedly of you especially when he found out about your turning down the invitation to come here which struck him as a tremendous pity. He wanted so badly to see you here." Whether the dying Guttmann, who had clashed twenty years earlier with the young Strauss, would have felt remorse about this is anyone's guess. But Scholem concluded, "Well, what's impossible is impossible" (*Nun, was nicht geht, geht nicht*).[93]

In the meantime, Strauss urged the appointment of Shlomo Pines (1908–1990) for the position of Guttmann's successor. A Franco-Russian Jew born in Paris but raised in Archangel, Pines, who knew both Strauss and Kraus from his Berlin days, was principally a student of Hellenistic and Islamic philosophy. The appointment did eventually go through, and later Pines and Strauss collaborated on Pines's magisterial English translation of Maimonides's *Guide of the Perplexed*.[94]

It was in Jerusalem that Strauss delivered his famous lecture series "What is Political Philosophy?" published in English in 1959. He began these lectures with a beautiful tribute to his hosts: "In this city, and in this land, the theme of political philosophy – 'the city of righteousness, the faithful city' – has been taken more seriously than anywhere else

---

[90] Letter from Strauss, April 4, 1950, in *GS*, 3: 720.

[91] *GS*, 3: 720.

[92] Letter from Scholem, April 27, 1950, in *GS*. 3: 720–721.

[93] Letter from Scholem, May 20, 1950, in *GS*, 3: 722.

[94] Maimonides, *The Guide of the Perplexed*, trans. Shlomo Pines; intro. Leo Strauss (Chicago: University of Chicago Press, 1963); see Joel Kraemer and Josef Stern, "Shlomo Pines on the Translation of Maimonides' 'Guide of the Perplexed,'" *The Journal of Jewish Thought and Philosophy* 9 (1998): 13–24.

on earth. Nowhere else has the longing for justice and the just city filled the purest hearts and the loftiest souls with such zeal as on this sacred soil."[95] Strauss was deeply tempted by the offer of a position in Jerusalem but, according to his daughter Jenny, "he felt he was too old to learn to teach in Hebrew and he felt that for the Israelis, the study of political philosophy was at that point not the highest priority."[96]

THE FINAL YEARS

The period after Strauss's return from Israel was one marked by intense and sustained productivity. In certain respects, the works written from this period onward mark a new and distinctive phase of his thought. This phase has been described by Allan Bloom as "characterized by a complete abandonment of the form as well as the content of modern scholarship" because "Strauss no longer felt bound to make any compromises or to see the texts through the screen of scholarly method and categories." Strauss had finally "liberated himself [from historicism] and could understand writers as they understood themselves."[97] This may be true enough but, more to the point, Strauss's writings were characterized by a more intense focus on the theologico-political problem. What earlier had appeared to be a distinctively German-Jewish problem was now seen in terms of a much broader problem that he began to think of in terms of the bipolarities of Jerusalem and Athens.[98]

As Strauss understood these terms, Jerusalem and Athens do not represent two cities or two cultures but rather two profoundly different ways of life: the city of faith – the holy city – and the city of reason. He believed the permanence of these alternatives constituted the decisive refutation of historicism. The objects to which these names refer constitute two fundamentally different human alternatives – the life of faith and piety or the life of rational self-sufficiency, the moral life or the philosophical life. Which of these is right and, just as important, how are we to choose between them? Even more than the themes of ancients and moderns or esoteric and exoteric writing did the problem of Jerusalem and Athens come to preoccupy Strauss's thought in the last years of his

---

[95] Strauss, "What is Political Philosophy," in *WPP*, 9.

[96] From an e-mail exchange with Jenny Strauss Clay.

[97] Allan Bloom, "Leo Strauss (September 20, 1899–October 18, 1973), *Political Theory* 2 (1974): 384–385.

[98] For Strauss's writings on this subject, see "Jerusalem and Athens: Some Preliminary Reflections, in *SPP*, 147–173; "On the Interpretation of Genesis," in *JPCM*, 359–376; "Progress or Return?" in *RCPR*, 227–270; for an overview of the issues, see Smith, "How Jewish Was Leo Strauss?" *Reading Leo Strauss*, 23–42.

life. In some respects, Strauss's writings moved beyond questions of politics to a confrontation with these two visions of eternity. "The question *quid sit deus*," he wrote at the conclusion of an essay on Thucydides, "is the all-important question which is coeval with philosophy although the philosophers do not frequently pronounce it."[99]

Ironically, the full impact of this problem was developed in his book, *Thoughts on Machiavelli*. What exactly did Machiavelli, the most politic of writers, have to teach about the themes of philosophy and theology? Strauss's answer: everything. More than any other of his works, *Thoughts on Machiavelli* was greeted with disbelief often bordering on scorn. This derision often comes from those who seem not to have gone beyond the famous opening sentence in which Strauss expressed himself "inclined to the old-fashioned and simple opinion according to which Machiavelli was a teacher of evil."[100] The idea that Machiavelli, or any political writer, could be described as evil struck many readers as moralistic, unhistorical, and naïve.[101] It was this last claim, that he was naïve, that to some degree confirmed Strauss in the truth of his view. Rather than looking outside the text for the historical, economic, or intellectual context in which it was written, it is better to look at the text itself and whatever context or information the author chooses to supply. It is a mistake to too quickly ignore the surface for the depth. This was simply following Strauss's own hermeneutic principle: "The problem inherent in the surface of things, and only in the surface of things, is the heart of things."[102]

The title of Strauss's *Thoughts on Machiavelli* is clearly modeled on Machiavelli's *Discourses on Livy*. Scholars who rebuke Strauss for misreading Machiavelli clearly miss the point. His book is less a scholarly commentary on Machiavelli than a prolonged meditation on the problem of political theology. As early as *On Tyranny*, Strauss had identified Machiavelli as the true founder of modernity. Knowingly or unknowingly, all later political philosophy has been an outgrowth of Machiavellianism. Strauss read Machiavelli's work as one of those great theologico-political discourses of early modernity opposed to revealed religion in any of its traditional forms. It was Machiavelli who introduced an "anti-theological ire" that became the originating moment of the Enlightenment. He transformed the ancient Epicurean critique of

---

[99] Strauss, *CM*, 241.

[100] Strauss, *TM*, 9.

[101] For the range of responses to Strauss's Machiavelli, see Kim A. Sorensen, *Discourses on Strauss: Revelation and Reason in Leo Strauss and His Critical Study of Machiavelli* (Notre Dame, IN: University of Notre Dame Press, 2006).

[102] Strauss, *TM*, 13.

religion into a new spirit of activism and revolt. His goal was to replace the God of Scripture with *Fortuna*, a more pliant deity that can be made amenable to human ingenuity. Not humble awe or obedience but cunning and audacity become the new Machiavellian virtues. He wished to do to Christianity what Christianity had done to the older Roman civil religions. He hoped to bury them. This is where Strauss emphasizes the closest point of contact between Machiavelli and Jesus: both were "unarmed prophets" who succeeded despite their lack of military hardware. Strauss called this the power of "propaganda." Machiavelli became the bringer of a new Decalogue, a new tablet of laws, which would replace both philosophy and religion. This new Law could be called the progressive theory of history.

Strauss's most eloquent expression of the problem of Jerusalem and Athens is contained in the 1965 Preface to the English translation of *Spinoza's Critique of Religion*. Here he reprised the issues of his youth but from a deepened perspective. What had appeared thirty years before as a German-Jewish problem now appeared as a much deeper, even intractable, problem, as one of those "infinite, absolute problems that cannot be solved."[103] The idea that there could be a human or political solution to the Jewish question could not but be regarded as "blasphemous." "From every point of view," he wrote, "it looks as if the Jewish people were the chosen people at least in the sense that the Jewish problem is the most manifest symbol of the human problem insofar as it is a social or political problem."[104]

Strauss now expressed doubt that philosophy could ever refute or overcome the possibility of revelation. Reason and revelation would always remain two equally vital, but equally antagonistic, possibilities. But even here Strauss's thought expressed a new direction. While earlier he had treated Judaism as a purely political or sociological phenomenon, he now regarded it as the carrier of a profound truth. Revelation is given in Judaism its most profound and unconditional expression. In the penultimate paragraph of the Preface, he refers to Deuteronomy 4:6: "Keep them and do them; for that will be your wisdom and your understanding in the sight of the peoples, who, when they hear all these statutes, will say, 'Surely this great nation is a wise and understanding people.'" This passage confirmed Strauss in the belief that Judaism could not be reduced to the claims of civil theology or a Platonic noble lie, but that "Jewish orthodoxy based its claim to superiority to other religions from the beginning on its superior rationality."[105]

---

[103] Strauss, "Preface to *SCR*," in *LAM*, 230.
[104] Strauss, "Preface to *SCR*," in *LAM*, 230.
[105] Strauss, "Preface to *SCR*," in *LAM*, 256.

The publication of the Preface to *Spinoza's Critique of Religion* was the closest thing to a philosophical autobiography that Strauss ever wrote. Scholem, to whom Strauss had sent a copy of the manuscript, declared the work "more remarkable" than anything Strauss had produced previously. In a letter of November 28, 1962, Scholem wrote: "I regard it as an intellectual autobiography of yourself where one adventure of the spirit (and its mishaps) follows upon another." He claimed to find fault in Strauss's omission of several important stages of his life's story, but then goes on to add: "The readers, who know less about you than I, especially the poor Americans, who have heard little of horn-blowing will probably be very much astonished (in English "baffled") by your reading." Scholem expressed some surprise that such a work would actually be published and concluded: "I will keep the copy of the manuscript pristine, for who knows if you won't at the last minute declare the manuscript 'apocryphal,' thereupon hiding it in a loft or cellar as was usual from time immemorial for such easily shocking literature."[106]

This last remark seems to have taken Strauss by surprise. Just over a week later, he wrote back professing to be "intrigued" by Scholem's words of caution and asked: "Should I understand it as an extremely polite and reserved counsel not to print my Preface?"[107] Responding to Scholem's inquiry as to why he was now undertaking to publish such a testimony, Strauss's reply was extremely revealing:

When studying Hobbes, I observed that what he said and did not say was a function of the heresy laws obtaining at the time of publication of his various works. But then I saw that in one of his works published at a time of considerable restriction he was more outspoken than ever before. I was baffled until I noted that this book was published when he was already very old, with one foot in the grave and I learned that this condition is conducive to courage. As for me I have had my first two heart attacks, Ergo.[108]

A week later, Scholem responded to Strauss hoping to dispel "the anxieties that seem to have lain so gloomily over your heart." "I, too, am agreeable to the printing of your autobiographical forward to that old heretic Spinoza," Scholem wrote. He then added: "You have my blessing, have no doubt, and most likely I (along with perhaps five or six other readers who might barely constitute a Hessian minyan) shall form the only legitimate nucleus of readers for this opuscule. For you will hardly be able to have any great illusions that these pages might

---

[106] Letter from Scholem, November 28, 1962, in *GS*, 3: 747.
[107] Letter to Scholem, December 6, 1962, in *GS*, 3: 748.
[108] Letter to Scholem, December 6, 1962, in *GS*, 3: 748.

be as good as impenetrable to American readers."[109] No doubt he was right.

Strauss was named Robert Maynard Hutchins Distinguished Service Professor in 1960. In 1964, he accepted an invitation to teach philosophy at the University of Hamburg, from where he had received his doctorate over forty years before, but the visit had to be cancelled at the last minute for reasons of health.[110] Strauss retired in 1967. The following year, he taught at Claremont Men's College in California and in 1969, at the invitation of Klein, he became the Scott Buchanan Distinguished Scholar-in-Residence at St. John's College in Annapolis, Maryland. His last book, *The Argument and Action of Plato's "Laws,"* was published posthumously in 1975. Here he returned to the insight gleaned from Avicenna years before in the Prussian State Library: "The treatment of prophecy and the divine law is contained in [Plato's] *Laws.*"[111]

Strauss continued to teach and write despite declining health. In a letter to Scholem of September 30, 1973, he wrote: "I believe, I told you more than once that 1972–73 were hitherto my worst years: my fingers tremble, and I am not sure whether you can decipher this note. Nevertheless I finished an essay on *Jenseits von Gut und Böse*, on the gods in Thucydides, and on Xenophon's *Anabasis*. Rather apiquorsic stuff but I have a feeling that the BOSS will not condemn me."[112] Strauss died less than a month later on October 18, 1973. He had traveled a long way from the man who had once stated that he desired nothing more from life than to read Plato and breed rabbits while supporting himself as a rural postmaster in a small German town.[113]

---

[109] Letter from Scholem, December 13, 1962, in *GS*, 3: 749.

[110] Letter to Löwith, June 3, 1964, in *GS*, 3, 690–691; see also letter to Kojève, June 3, 1965, in *OT*, 313; Heinrich Meier, *Leo Strauss and the Theologico-Political Problem*, trans. Marcus Brainard (Cambridge, UK: Cambridge University Press, 2006), 4.

[111] Strauss, *AAPL*, 1.

[112] Letter to Scholem, September 30, 1973, in *GS*, 3: 771; the word "apiquorsic" is derivative of the Hebrew "apikoros," which refers to a form of learned heresy, e.g., Epicureanism; for Strauss' thoughts on Epicureanism, see "Notes on Lucretius" in *LAM*, 76–139; *SCR*, 37–52; *NRH*, 188–189.

[113] Strauss, "A Giving of Accounts," in *JPCM*, 460.

3 Leo Strauss and the "Theologico-Political Predicament"

In the 1965 preface to the English translation of his first book, *Spinoza's Critique of Religion*, Leo Strauss describes the beginnings of his intellectual journey by stating that "This study of Spinoza's *Theologico-Political Treatise* was written during the years 1925–28 in Germany. The author was a young Jew born and raised in Germany who found himself in the grip of the theologico-political predicament."[1] Also in 1965, Strauss's *The Political Philosophy of Hobbes* was published for the first time in German. There Strauss refers to the "theologico-political problem," deeming it "*the* theme of my investigations."[2] With the term "theologico-political predicament,"[3] Strauss links his early intellectual development to his later intellectual themes, including what he calls the quarrel between the ancients and the moderns, the relation between Jerusalem and Athens, and to his diverse studies in the history of political philosophy, of Plato, Hobbes, Maimonides, Alfarabi, and Spinoza, among many others.

This essay considers what Strauss meant by "theologico-political predicament," suggesting that there are at least two senses in which he employs the term, the first diagnostic, the second reconstructive. In its diagnostic sense, "theologico-political predicament" refers to the ultimate results of the early modern attempt to separate theology from politics. However, Strauss in no way favors a return to theocracy or, like his contemporary Carl Schmitt, a turn toward political theology. Strauss attempts to recover classical political philosophy, not to return to the political structures of the past, but to reconsider ways in which

---

[1] Strauss, "Preface to *SCR*," in *LAM*, 224.

[2] Strauss, "Preface to 'Hobbes Politische Wissenschaft,'" in *JPCM*, 453; emphasis in the original.

[3] Strauss uses "predicament" in the "Preface to *SCR*" and "problem" in the "Preface to *PPH*." For the sake of simplicity, throughout this essay we use the terms interchangeably, although the different senses of "predicament" and "problem" may also refer to the diagnostic and reconstructive senses in which Strauss uses the term, with predicament corresponding to the diagnostic sense and problem to the reconstructive sense.

premodern thinkers thought it necessary to grapple and live with the tensions, if not contradictions, that by definition arise from human society. It is in this sense that Strauss's use of the theologico-political problem is reconstructive. Part One of this essay focuses on Strauss's diagnosis of the theologico-political predicament, whereas Part Two turns to his reconstruction of the theologio-political problem. The conclusion considers the contemporary implications of Strauss's analyses.

PART ONE: THE MODERN CRITIQUE OF RELIGION

The immediate context of Strauss's use of "theologico-political predicament" in his autobiographical preface is the title of Spinoza's *Theologico-Political Treatise*, the subject of *Spinoza's Critique of Religion*. Like many German-Jewish intellectuals of his and the previous generation, Strauss came to define himself in terms of his relation to Spinoza. Both biographically and philosophically, Spinoza set the conceptual framework that occupied and still occupies modern Jewish thinkers. Spinoza's ability to live an independent life free of any religious community anticipated liberal modernity in which, to quote Strauss, "the bond of society is universal human morality, whereas religion (positive religion) is a private affair."[4] But Spinoza also raised a profound problem for modern Judaism when he declared that the laws of the Hebrews were pertinent only in the context of their original, political meaning: "ceremonial observances ... do not pertain to the Divine law, and therefore do not contribute to blessedness and virtue," but "have regard only to the election of the Hebrews, that is ... to their temporal and material prosperity and their peaceful government, and ... therefore could have been of practical value only while their state existed."[5] Because the ceremonial law no longer corresponded to a political kingdom, Spinoza concluded that Jewish law is no longer the divine law, and that postbiblical Jewish law is meaningless.[6] Late nineteenth- and early twentieth-century political Zionist thinkers often drew on Spinoza as Jewish inspiration for the dream of reestablishing a Jewish state.[7] Like Spinoza, political Zionists understood the possibility of a Jewish state not in religious but in solely political terms. Although the Zionist use

---

[4] Strauss, "Preface to *SCR*," in *LAM*, 226.
[5] Benedict de Spinoza, *Theologico-Political Treatise*, trans. Samuel Shirley (Indianapolis, IN: Hackett, 1998), 69.
[6] Spinoza, *Theologico-Political Treatise*, 59–70; see also Strauss, "Preface to *SCR*," in *LAM*, 229.
[7] See for instance Moses Hess, *Rome and Jerusalem* (1862), trans. Meyer Waxman (Whitefish, MT: Kessinger Publishing, 2005).

of Spinoza was anachronistic at best, for the Zionists and Spinoza alike, the return to Jewish politics could only be a return to state sovereignty.

Strauss initially found himself responding to the Jewish neo-Kantian Hermann Cohen's trenchant attack on Spinoza, which itself was the result of the Zionist embrace of Spinoza. Claiming that Spinoza's "pantheism" was incompatible with the truth of pure monotheism, Cohen criticized Spinoza on philosophical grounds. But Cohen also attributed a personal, political motive to Spinoza's arguments, labeling him a betrayer of the Jewish religion and of the Jewish people. Against both Spinoza and Zionism, Cohen maintained that Judaism's truth was found in its nonpolitical, indeed in its wholly religious, constitution.[8] Cohen strongly endorsed precisely what Zionism rejected: the promises of the modern liberal state. In many respects, Cohen followed Moses Mendelssohn in relegating Judaism to the status of religion and in deeming Judaism deeply compatible with a modern liberal political order.[9] Cohen's attack on Spinoza thus brought full circle an argument for liberal Judaism and politics that began in the eighteenth century with Mendelssohn but that, in the early twentieth century with the rise of antisemitism and disillusionment with modern rationalism generally, seemed untenable to many German-Jews, including the young Leo Strauss.

After defending his dissertation in 1921, Strauss worked under Julius Guttmann at the Academy for the Science of Judaism [*Akademie für die Wissenschaft des Judentums*], co-editing Mendelssohn's papers. It was in this context that he began to engage with Spinoza, first in attempting to defend Spinoza against Cohen's attack, essentially contending that Spinoza's arguments were not, contra Cohen, the result of personal malice but were historically justified, although not necessarily philosophically correct, and then in writing what would become *Spinoza's Critique of Religion*. The theologico-political predicament in which Strauss found himself in the early 1920s was simply, though profoundly, whether to choose liberalism or Zionism, the former representing the culmination of Spinoza's separation of theology from politics, the latter representing the utter failure of this project.[10] The young Strauss chose Zionism.

---

[8] Hermann Cohen, "Spinoza über Staat und Religion, Judentum und Christentum," (1915) *Jüdische Schriften*, ed. B. Strauss, (Berlin: C. A. Schwetschke, 1924) 3: 290–372.

[9] Moses Mendelssohn, *Jerusalem or on Religious Power and Judaism* (1783), trans. Allan Arkush (Hanover and London: University of New England Press, 1983).

[10] Strauss regarded cultural Zionism as another form of liberalism; see "Preface to *SCR*," in *LAM*, 229–230.

In his early writings on Spinoza, Strauss focused on epistemological questions such as on Spinoza's criticism of Maimonides's account of the status of prophetic knowledge. So, too, Strauss also thought about Zionism in epistemological terms. As he put it in a 1928 review of Freud's *The Future of an Illusion*: "in the age of atheism, the Jewish people can no longer base its existence on God . . . Political Zionism, wishing to ground itself radically, must ground itself in unbelief."[11] The young Strauss thus saw the theologico-political predicament in epistemological terms, that is, in terms of the modern political results that followed from a philosophical claim. The question became whether or not Spinoza's critique of religion was epistemologically true. Was his argument philosophically successful?

Strauss stresses that Spinoza's critique of religion, and more generally the Enlightenment's critique of religion, could only be thought successful because religion, or revelation, had been dismissed from the conversation. Religion's modern critics used mockery and not rational argument to make their case, and for this reason the seeming victory of modern philosophy over religion is rhetorical and not philosophical, especially as religion's modern critics caricature religious belief as wholly dogmatic and irrational. Spinoza epitomizes this tendency by arguing that Maimonides was "the first among the Pharisees who openly maintained that Scripture must be made to conform to reason,"[12] thus incorrectly depicting Maimonides as a dogmatist with no regard for philosophical reason. As Strauss would argue in his work on medieval Jewish rationalism (to be discussed further later), belief by definition is not certain knowledge. Lack of certainty is therefore not a weakness for the believer.

Worse than this pseudocritique, argues Strauss, modern defenders of religion accepted these caricatures and built a "defense" of religion upon them. Rather than questioning the terms of the argument, modern defenders of religion capitulated to the Enlightenment's assertion that religious truth simply could not hold up to the standard of scientific truth, maintaining instead that religion never made scientific truth claims in the first place. Strauss calls this strategy "internalization" (*Verinnerlichung*): "all 'internalizations' of the basic tenets of the tradition rest at bottom on this: from the 'reflexive' premise, from the 'higher' level of the post-Enlightenment synthesis, the relation of God to nature is no longer intelligible and thus is no longer even interesting."[13]

[11] Strauss, "Die Zukunft einer Illusion," in *GS*, 1: 431–439; translated in Michael Zank, *EW*, 203–204.
[12] Spinoza, *Theologico-Political Treatise*, 165.
[13] Strauss, *PL*, 24.

Cohen's neo-Kantian defense of Judaism exemplifies this approach by claiming that God's creation of the world refers not to a metaphysical doctrine but to the human being's capacity to reason in the world.[14]

In criticizing modern theological apologetics, Strauss draws upon the theologies of Karl Barth and Franz Rosenzweig, who understood revelation not in apologetic terms but as "the experience of an unequivocal command addressed to me here and now as distinguished from general laws or ideas."[15] As Strauss put it, "The reawakening of theology, which for me is epitomized by the names of Karl Barth and Franz Rosenzweig, appeared to make it necessary to investigate how far the critique of orthodox theology – Jewish and Christian – deserved to be victorious."[16] For Strauss, Barth's and Rosenzweig's theology exposed the lie at the heart of the modern criticism and defense of religion: that modern scientific knowledge is the only form of and standard for truth.

Strauss's early musings on the theologico-political predicament led him to a theme upon which he would insist again and again: the irreconcilability between revelation and philosophy (or the irreconcilability of what he would call elsewhere Jerusalem and Athens, or the Bible and Greek philosophy). Strauss maintains that because belief in revelation by definition does not claim to be self-evident knowledge, philosophy can neither refute nor confirm revelation:

> The genuine refutation of orthodoxy would require the proof that the world and human life are perfectly intelligible without the assumption of a mysterious God; it would require at least the success of the philosophical system: man has to show himself theoretically and practically as the master of the world and the master of his life; the merely given must be replaced by the world created by man theoretically and practically.[17]

Revelation and philosophy are incommensurable starting points to truth. In the following, we will turn in more depth to the substance of Strauss's understanding of why revelation and philosophy are incommensurable. But first, we must consider Strauss's further diagnostic claim that the modern denial of the incommensurability between revelation and philosophy – a denial that is at the core of the modern critique of religion – is fatal not only for revelation but also for modern philosophy.

We have seen that according to Strauss, the modern critique of religion shows that the notion that revelation and philosophy should answer

---

[14] See Strauss's discussion of Cohen and internalization in the Introduction to *PL*, 24–25.

[15] Strauss, "Preface to *SCR*," in *LAM*, 232.

[16] Strauss, "Preface to 'Hobbes Politische Wissenschaft,'" in *JPCM*, 453.

[17] Strauss, "Preface to *SCR*," in *LAM*, 254–255.

to the same scientific criteria brings meaningful talk of revelation to an end, either in the form of banishing revelation from the conversation or in the form of so-called modern defenses of religion that can only internalize this banishment. But Strauss argues that the Enlightenment's critique of religion ultimately also brought with it, unbeknownst to its proponents, modern rationalism's self-destruction. Strauss does not reject modern science[18] but he does object to the philosophical conclusion that "scientific knowledge is the highest form of knowledge" because this "implies a depreciation of prescientific knowledge."[19]

Strauss reads the history of modern philosophy as beginning with the elevation of all knowledge to science, or theory, and as concluding with the devaluation of all knowledge to history, or practice. As he put it to Eric Voegelin in a letter of 1950: "the root of all modern darkness from the seventeenth century on is the obscuring of the difference between theory and praxis, an obscuring that first leads to a reduction of praxis to theory (this is the meaning of so-called rationalism) and then, in retaliation, to the rejection of theory in the name of praxis that is no longer intelligible as praxis."[20] Whereas in the seventeenth century, like Spinoza would after him, Hobbes depreciates prescientific knowledge in the name of science, Heidegger in the twentieth century depreciates scientific knowledge in the name of historicity. Modern rationalism thus implodes upon itself: what starts as a modern quest for delineating scientific standards in the name of certain knowledge leads to the conclusion that there are neither such standards nor such truths.

Strauss would draw out this analysis in a number of contexts – culminating in *Natural Right and History* – in which he attempted, among other things, to show the direct line that leads from positivism to historicism. But we leave aside these issues to focus on the connection between Strauss's diagnosis of the demise of philosophy and his analysis of the modern critique of religion. In the early 1930s, Strauss had not yet developed his view of esoteric writing but he already saw that the readings of the Bible offered by early modern political philosophers did not reflect defenses of Christianity, as his contemporaries would have it, but subversive criticism of revealed religion. Cohen's criticism of Spinoza was predicated on the assumption that Spinoza defended Christianity while attacking Judaism. At the same time, nineteenth- and

---

[18] Strauss "Progress or Return?" in *RCPR*, 240: "Science is the successful part of modern philosophy or science, and philosophy is the unsuccessful part – the rump."

[19] Strauss, "What is Political Philosophy," in *WPP*, 23.

[20] Letter to Eric Voegelin March 14, 1950, in *FPP*, 66.

twentieth-century readers of Spinoza could see him as a "God-intoxicated man" only because they had ceased to take religion seriously. As Strauss put it in his 1936 study of Hobbes: "Exactly as Spinoza did later, Hobbes with double intention becomes an interpreter of the Bible ... to make use of the authority of the Scriptures for his own theory, and then ... to shake the authority of Scriptures themselves."[21]

For our purposes, we need not focus on the particularities of Strauss's reading of Hobbes (or on his subsequent reading of Machiavelli and others) but only on the trajectory that his intellectual history of political philosophy takes as he diagnoses the theologico-political predicament. The structure of Strauss's account of the history of modern political philosophy parallels the structure of his account of the history of philosophy. Just as modern philosophy begins with an overinflated sense of reason that privileges theory over practice and ends with a radical historicism that denies any meaning to reason outside of history, Strauss suggests that modern political philosophy begins with the attempt to make the human being wholly part of nature as defined by science and ends by denying any notion of nature altogether.[22] For Strauss, these trajectories come together in the coincidence of Heidegger's philosophy and political misadventures:

The crucial issue concerns the status of those permanent characteristics of humanity, such as the distinction between the noble and the base ... It was the contempt for these permanencies which permitted the most radical historicist in 1933 to submit to, or rather to welcome, as a dispensation of fate, the verdict of the least wise and least moderate part of his nation which it was in its least wise and least moderate mood, and at the same time to speak of wisdom and moderation. The biggest event of 1933 would rather seem to have proved, if such proof was necessary, that man cannot abandon the question of the good society, and that he cannot free himself from the responsibility for answering it by deferring to History or to any other power different from his own reason.[23]

We saw previously that Strauss suggests that the Jewish Question, as reflected by the choice of liberalism or Zionism, epitomized the theologico-political predicament. At its most extreme, the theologico-political predicament is illustrated by the complicity of intellectuals in the Nazi genocide.

Liberal democracy had originally defined itself in theologico-political treaties as the opposite of ... "the kingdom of darkness," that is, of medieval society ... [The

[21] Strauss, *PPH*, 71.
[22] For a concise statement of this point in regard to Hobbes, see Strauss, "On the Basis of Hobbes's Political Philosophy," in *WPP*, 176, note 2.
[23] Strauss, "What is Political Philosophy," in *WPP*, 26–27.

German Jews] were given full political rights for the first time by the Weimar Republic. The Weimar Republic was succeed by the only German regime – by the only regime that ever was anywhere – which had no other clear principle except murderous hatred of the Jews.[24]

Strauss does not mean to imply that National Socialism was inevitable. Rather, he means to investigate why there was no adequate rational, moral response to the rise of National Socialism. It is here that the modern crises of philosophy and theology meet in the modern crisis of politics. Neither modern political philosophy, theology, nor philosophy had the critical resources to respond to the disintegration of the liberal state, the very political structure that was touted as "the opposite of... 'the kingdom of darkness,' i.e., of medieval society."

It would become the mature Strauss's task to consider how political philosophy, theology, and philosophy could each once again have the critical resources to make the most basic distinction between the noble and the base. To do so, Strauss would have to overcome what he called the "powerful prejudice, that a return to premodern philosophy is impossible."[25] As we have seen, Strauss's diagnosis of the theologico-political predicament began with and remained centered on the question of revealed religion and its relation to philosophy. As we will see, the status of revelation remains critical to Strauss's reconstruction of the theologico-political problem.

PART TWO: REVELATION REVISITED

We saw previously that Strauss credited Rosenzweig and Barth for making him rethink the modern critique of religion. Yet for all his respect for Rosenzweig – to whose memory he dedicated *Spinoza's Critique of Religion* – as well as for Barth, Strauss recognized that their approach to theology was still embedded within the prejudices of modern philosophy and subject to the same fate as modern philosophy, despite their attempts to overcome precisely these prejudices. At bottom, the early twentieth-century reawakening of theology did not revive reason's critical potential but left reason behind. As such, this reawakening of theology did not ultimately provide any resources for theological, philosophical, or political rationalism.[26]

With his second book, *Philosophy and Law*, Strauss already realized that a return to rationalism required reconsidering medieval thinkers and their approaches to philosophy and revelation. Julius Guttmann

---

[24] Strauss, "Preface to *SCR*," in *LAM*, 226.
[25] Strauss, "Preface to *SCR*," in *LAM*, 257.
[26] Strauss, "Preface to *SCR*," in *LAM*, 256–257.

had considered this subject in depth, and despite the fact that Guttmann happened to be his supervisor Strauss began his own work on medieval rationalism by attacking Guttmann. According to Strauss, Guttmann had argued that "'philosophy of religion' is actually the original achievement of medieval philosophy."[27] Against this view, Strauss points out that within the historical context of medieval Jewish rationalism, the law existentially preceded the possibility of philosophizing. This fact is not merely historically important but also philosophically significant, as Strauss suggests in the first sentence of the first chapter of *Philosophy and Law*: "There is no inquiry into the history of philosophy that is not at the same time a *philosophical* inquiry."[28]

In keeping with his own neo-Kantian model, Guttmann understood medieval Jewish rationalism primarily in modern epistemological terms, that is, in terms of "science," in this case what was known as the historical science of Judaism (*Wissenschaft des Judentums*).[29] Strauss contends that it is only because Guttmann begins with a modern conception of philosophy that he can understand medieval Jewish rationalism in terms of "philosophy of religion." In a footnote, Strauss concisely sums up his argument against Guttmann: "We do not deny . . . that the problem of 'belief and knowledge' is the central problem of medieval rationalism. Our quarrel with Guttmann is only about the meaning of 'belief' here, and it seems to us more precise to say 'law and philosophy' rather than 'belief and knowledge.'"[30] The phrase "law and philosophy" represents the complex but necessary relation between prescientific and scientific knowledge. On the other hand, "belief and knowledge" represents the attempt to fuse two sources of truth into a scientifically respectable whole that Guttmann calls "philosophy of religion."

The difference between Strauss and Guttmann is surely about the meaning of revelation for Maimonides and his predecessors. But it is also about the meaning and scope of "philosophy." According to Strauss, once revelation is understood primarily as revealed law and not as philosophical knowledge, it is necessary to rethink, from a modern perspective, the medieval Jewish and Islamic conception of philosophy. Although Strauss's focus in *Philosophy and Law* is on the status of Jewish (or religious) law, he looks back from medieval Jewish and Islamic philosophy to Plato. Focusing on the significance of Plato's *Laws* and its Islamic reception, Strauss suggests that the classical conception of law

---

[27] Strauss, *PL*, 55.
[28] Strauss, *PL*, 41.
[29] Julius Guttmann, *Die Philosophie des Judentums* (München: E. Reinhardt, 1933).
[30] Strauss, *PL*, 141, n. 24.

concerns and also anticipates the tense yet necessary relation between philosophy and law in medieval rationalism:

The necessary connection between politics and theology (metaphysics)... vouches for the fact that the interpretation of medieval Jewish philosophy beginning from Platonic politics (and not from the *Timaeus* or from Aristotelian metaphysics) does not have to lose sight of the metaphysical problems that stand in the foreground for the medieval philosophers themselves. And this procedure, so far from resulting in the underestimation of these problems, actually offers the only guarantee of understanding their proper, that is their human, meaning. If, on the other hand, one begins with the metaphysical problems, one misses... the political problem, in which is concealed nothing less than the foundation of philosophy, the philosophic elucidation of the presupposition of philosophizing.[31]

Although philosophy can clarify its meaning, on Strauss's reading of medieval rationalism the law is not derived through philosophical activity. Instead, the law is the prephilosophical context of and framework for philosophy. As Strauss puts it, *"freedom depends upon its bondage. Philosophy is not sovereign. The beginning of philosophy is not the beginning simply."*[32]

Although he had not yet developed his view of esoteric writing, Strauss already in *Philosophy and Law* had sewn the seeds for what would become his mature understanding of revelation, philosophy, and politics. As we saw previously, Strauss's diagnostic view of the theologico-political predicament began with and remained centered on his conception of revelation. Strauss's reconstructive view of the theologico-political problem – that is, his view of what the relations between philosophy, theology, and politics actually are – also begins with and remains centered on his notion of revelation. In *Philosophy and Law*, Strauss defines revelation as law, and not knowledge. So, too, Strauss defines philosophy as dependent on law, not in an epistemological sense but in a political sense.

These premodern conceptions of revelation and philosophy would be decisive for Strauss's attempt to rethink the possibility of rational politics. In a 1936 essay on the political science of Maimonides and Alfarabi, Strauss reconsiders the meaning of prophecy for Maimonides. While most interpreters, including Strauss in *Spinoza's Critique of Religion* and in parts but not all of *Philosophy and Law*, viewed Maimonides's conception of prophecy in epistemological terms, Strauss now argues that Maimonides's innovation was to think of prophecy in political terms. According to Strauss, Maimonides "neither wished nor was able, nor had any need, to lift the veil which conceals the origins of

[31] Strauss, *PL*, 78–79.
[32] Strauss, *PL*, 88.

the Torah, the foundation of the perfect nation."[33] Yet the attentive reader will notice that Maimonides distinguishes between Moses, the law giver, and all other prophets. Maimonides stresses Moses's exalted status, argues Strauss, because for Maimonides Moses is the Platonic philosopher-legislator. This emphasis on the uniqueness of Moses is the core of Maimonides's political philosophy because "Not the mystery of its [the Torah's] origin, the search for which leads either to theosophy or 'Epicureanism,' but its end, the comprehension of which guarantees obedience to the Torah, is accessible to human reason."[34]

Obedience to the law and the philosophical meaning of the law are two different matters that are reflected in what Strauss argues is Maimonides's dual conception of law. The exterior, literal meaning of the law serves to uphold the political community in which certain forms of behavior and belief are required while the ideal meaning of the law is a matter of philosophical speculation only for those who are capable of such speculation. This dual conception of law parallels the dual character of Maimonides's writing, which offers a "moderate" reading meant for the masses and a "radical" reading meant for the philosophical reader.[35] As Strauss would later elaborate in greater detail, this dialectical tension lies at the heart of Maimonides's style of writing and argumentation. Maimonides is able to balance properly the relation between praxis, obedience to the law, and theory, the mystery of the law's origins, not by conflating them but by keeping them in continual dialectical tension. These dualities evidence Maimonides's political moderation and indeed his theological and philosophical radicalism. This tension also offers an important intellectual antidote to the theologico-political predicament of modernity in which the different and complex relation between theory and praxis has been obscured with disastrous consequences for both reason and morality.

Strauss credited Alfarabi's interpretation of Plato for his rethinking of the political dimension of medieval rationalism: "Farabi had rediscovered in the politics of Plato . . . a golden mean which is neither a compromise nor a synthesis, which is hence not based on the two opposed positions, but which suppresses them both, uproots them by a prior, more profound question, by raising a more fundamental problem, the work of a truly critical philosophy."[36] Strauss argues that a truly critical

---

33 Strauss, "Some Remarks on the Political Science of Maimonides and Farabi," trans. Robert Bartlett, *Interpretation*, 18 (1990): 15–16.
34 Strauss, "Some Remarks," 16.
35 Strauss elaborates on this issue in a 1937 essay, "On Abravanel's Philosophical Tendency and Teaching" in *Isaac Abravanel*, ed J. B. Trend and H. Loewe (Cambridge, UK: Cambridge University Press, 1937), 93–129.
36 Strauss, "Some Remarks," 6.

philosophy is not one that finds final answers but one that continually asks questions. Alfarabi, and Maimonides who followed him, came to a golden mean by which both revealed law and philosophy were given their due, and by which a good society and the philosophical freedom to question were properly balanced. Strauss suggests that a compromise or synthesis between revealed law and philosophy makes this balance impossible.

On the basis of Strauss's interpretation of the golden mean achieved by Alfarabi, Maimonides, and Plato, we can return to Strauss's recurrent theme that Jerusalem and Athens are irreconcilable while also touching upon another recurrent theme of Strauss's work: "the quarrel between the ancients and the moderns." Strauss stresses that the relation between "Jerusalem and Athens" admits of neither compromise nor synthesis without destroying the meaning of one for the sake of the other. Instead, as Strauss's reading of Alfarabi and Maimonides suggests, Jerusalem and Athens together raise the problem of "a truly critical philosophy." And Strauss insists that the irreconcilability of Jerusalem and Athens corresponds to his conception of the quarrel between the ancients the moderns: "A Philosophy which believes that it can refute the possibility of revelation – and a philosophy which does not believe that: this is the real meaning of *la querelle des anciens et des modernes.*"[37]

Most fundamentally, the quarrel between the ancients and the moderns for Strauss is about the excesses of the moderns and the moderation of the ancients. As we saw in Part One of this essay, according to Strauss the trajectory of modern philosophy's demise begins with the belief that modern philosophy has refuted revelation once and for all. This false belief is based on an overreaching view of what philosophical reason in and of itself can accomplish, and it leads to the equally false belief that there are no rational standards because reason is always imbedded within and determined by history. In contrast to the excess of modern philosophers, Socrates "did not separate wisdom from moderation."[38] According to Strauss, Socratic moderation is not merely a political concession but bears upon the question of how we come to truth: "Socrates implied that disregarding the opinions about the nature of things would amount to abandoning the most important access to reality which we have, or the most important vestiges of truth which are within our reach."[39] But even though truth is within our reach, philosophy begins

---

[37] Strauss, "Reason and Revelation" (1948), in Heinrich Meier, *Leo Strauss and the Theologico-Political Problem*, trans. Marcus Brainard (New York: Cambridge University Press, 2006), 177.

[38] Strauss, *NRH*, 123.

[39] Strauss, *NRH*, 124.

and ends with the quest for truth: "philosophy is meant – and that is the decisive point – not as a set of propositions, a teaching, or even a system, but as a way of life, a life animated by a peculiar passion, the philosophic desire, or *eros*. Philosophy is not understood as an instrument or a department of human self-realization."[40] As a way of life, "the problems are always more evident than the solutions. All solutions are questionable... Therefore, the right way of life cannot be established metaphysically except by a completed metaphysics, and therefore the right way of life remains questionable."[41] That the right way of life remains questionable brings us back to philosophy's relation to revelation. Without a completed metaphysics, philosophy cannot refute revelation. This inability to refute revelation has serious consequences for philosophy's self-understanding. As Strauss puts it in *Natural Right and History*, in what is probably his best-known statement on the topic:

Philosophy has to grant that revelation is possible. But to grant that revelation is possible means to grant... that the philosophic life is not necessarily, not evidently, *the* right life. Philosophy, the life devoted to the quest for evident knowledge available to man as man, would itself rest on an unevident, arbitrary, or blind decision. This would merely confirm the thesis of faith, that there is no possibility of consistency, of a consistent and thoroughly sincere life, without belief in revelation. The mere fact that philosophy and revelation cannot refute each other would constitute the refutation of philosophy by revelation.[42]

Here we see that the tension between revelation and philosophy is not one between irrationality and rationality but between fundamentally irreconcilable criteria for what constitutes the rational starting point of truth. Philosophy begins and ends for Strauss with the philosopher's sense of wonder, whereas revealed religion begins and ends with adherence to the divine law. Yet as Strauss suggests, this situation puts philosophy at a disadvantage and revelation at an advantage. Never claiming to rest on evident knowledge, revelation can rationally approach its truth claims, not to prove them but to understand them. But philosophy, which values reason first and foremost, is led to the unpleasant truth that it is, in fact, predicated on something that is and remains unevident: that the human quest for knowledge is the right life.

Some interpreters (most notably Heinrich Meier) have concluded that Strauss purposely overstates the problem posed by revelation for philosophy to inspire philosophical readers in their quest for the philosophical life. Meier further understands the theologico-political problem in terms of what he claims is Strauss's lifelong effort to create a philosophical school. Meier's basic contention is that the quarrel between

---

[40] Strauss, "Progress or Return," in *RCPR*, 259.
[41] Strauss, "Progress or Return," in *RCPR*, 260.
[42] Strauss, *NRH*, 75.

revelation and philosophy, as Strauss describes it, leaves the careful reader many opportunities to consider whether revelation really does constitute the refutation of philosophy and to realize that philosophy does, in fact, have philosophical and moral resources from which to respond to revelation.[43]

It is true that some of Strauss's sketches of revelation, such as the one just described, do not make revelation compelling from a philosophical point of view. If the question about the relation between revelation and philosophy pertains to a decision for faith or philosophy, Strauss's conception of revelation sounds very much like Kierkegaard's, in which a leap of faith defines revelation. This theological vantage point is similar to Strauss's description of Rosenzweig and Barth's reawakening of theology. Yet as we saw in Part One, Strauss rejects this view of revelation as unable to offer a way toward rationality. By assuming that Strauss defines revelation as blind faith, many of Strauss's interpreters have concluded that he does not in the end take revelation seriously from a philosophical point of view. In support of this position, Meier in fact quotes Guttmann's critical response to Strauss, which is that Strauss shows an "indifference towards the content of revelation . . . Whether Jewish or Christian revelation is of concern makes no difference whatsoever."[44] For Guttmann, this supposed indifference to revelation's content means that Strauss gets medieval Jewish rationalism wrong. For Meier, this supposed indifference means that despite what seems to be Strauss's defense of revelation's capacity to criticize philosophy, revelation is in the end for Strauss a straw man. As Meier puts it, "What appears to the believer to be 'indifference' proves on closer inspection to be a conscious dissociation and ultimately a rejection."[45]

Yet Strauss was not indifferent to the content of revelation, and certainly not to the difference between Jewish and Christian notions of revelation. In fact, Strauss strongly criticizes what he regards as a particularly Christian view of revelation not to banish revelation from intellectual conversation once and for all but to suggest that modernity's

---

[43] Meier, *Leo Strauss and the Theologico-Political Problem*, 3–28; see Michael Zuckert, "Straussians," this volume.

[44] Julius Guttmann, "Philosophie der Religion oder Philosophie und Gesetzes?" in *Proceedings of the Israel Academy of Sciences and Humanities* 6 (Jerusalem, 1974), 27, as quoted in Meier, *Leo Strauss and the Theologico-Political Problem*, 20.

[45] Meier, *Leo Strauss and the Theologico-Political Problem*, 20, note 25. Strauss's statement in *SCR* to which Meier refers applies to Spinoza's critique of religion, i.e., Spinoza the philosopher who does not care whether revelation is Jewish or Christian. But Strauss's point is that Spinoza's critique of religion is a caricature of religion.

intellectual ills stem in large part from the legacy of Christian theology. As we have seen, it was on the basis of the Islamic, as opposed to the Christian, reception of classical political philosophy that Strauss turned to reconsider the meanings of philosophy, revelation, and politics. Strauss's very attempt to move beyond modern philosophy is predicated on a distinction between the Jewish and Islamic conception of revelation, on the one hand, and the Christian conception, on the other:

For the Christian, the sacred doctrine is revealed theology; for the Jew and the Muslim, the sacred doctrine is, at least primarily the legal interpretation of the Divine Law (*talmud* or *fiqh*). The sacred doctrine in the latter sense has, to say the least, much less in common with philosophy than the sacred doctrine in the former sense. It is ultimately for this reason that the status of philosophy was, as a matter of principle, much more precarious in Judaism and in Islam than in Christianity: in Christianity philosophy became an integral part of the officially recognized and even required training of the student of the sacred doctrine ... The precarious position of philosophy in the Islamic-Jewish world guaranteed its private character and therewith its inner-freedom from supervision. The status of philosophy in the Islamic-Jewish world resembled in this respect its status in classical Greece.[46]

Strauss problematizes the Christian view of revelation as knowledge as opposed to law. In his early through his mature writings, Strauss contends that the making of revelation into knowledge in scholastic theology ultimately led to modern philosophy's far too overreaching claims. As Strauss puts it rather succinctly, "On the *querelle des anciens et des modernes*: I do not deny, but assert, that modern philosophy has much that is essential in common with Christian medieval philosophy; but that means that the *attack* of the moderns is directed decisively against *ancient* philosophy."[47] Or, as he puts it elsewhere, "modern philosophy emerged by way of transformation of, if in opposition to, Latin or Christian scholasticism."[48]

Strauss's distinction between Judaism and Islam on the one hand and Christianity on the other is decisive for understanding his conception of the relation between Jerusalem and Athens as well as for appreciating his conception of the theologico-political problem, both in its diagnostic and reconstructive senses. On an epistemological level, philosophy may well have good arguments to make in response to revelation. As Strauss states in terms of Rosenzweig and Barth, a decisionist notion of revelation (i.e., revelation as a leap of faith) holds no promise of rationalism.[49]

---

[46] Strauss, "Introduction," in *PAW*, 19, 21.
[47] Letter to Löwith, August 15, 1946, in *CCM*, 106; emphasis in the original.
[48] Strauss, "Preface to Isaac Husik, *Philosophical Essays*," in *JPCM*, 252.
[49] See Strauss, "Preface to *SCR*," in *LAM*, 256–257.

Philosophy understood as a way of life, concerned with problems and unconvinced of promises of absolute solutions, will appear more rational to potential philosophers. Yet the serious argument with which revelation challenges philosophy is not epistemological but moral. This is not to deny the importance of the pursuit of truth for Strauss, but it is to return to his criticism of the modern depreciation of prescientific or prephilosophical knowledge. As we have seen, Strauss is a critic of the Enlightenment's view of the self-sufficiency of reason. Strauss argues if philosophy is to have critical potential, philosophy must be skeptical even of itself. This means that philosophers should not only tolerate religion for their own instrumental purposes but that philosophy is challenged by revelation, understood as law and not as knowledge, on moral grounds. We are now in a position to consider the relation between the diagnostic and reconstructive senses of "the theologico-political predicament." Just as Strauss's diagnostic account comes to its head with the moral indictment of those twentieth-century intellectuals who rejected "those permanent characteristics of humanity, such as the distinction between the noble and the base," so, too, his reconstructive account comes to its head with his moral understanding of divine revelation.

Strauss argues in both his early work on medieval Jewish rationalism and in his mature American work that only revelation, and not philosophy, can provide the basis of a universal morality. To be sure, this universal morality is based on faith and not certain knowledge. Nevertheless, it does underscore a moral weakness in the philosophical position. Nowhere does Strauss highlight this point more than in his seminal 1943 essay on the medieval Jewish thinker Judah Halevi. This essay became an integral part of *Persecution and the Art of Writing*, and far from an obscure relic of an interest in things Jewish and medieval, Strauss's reference to this essay forms a decisive part of his argument in *Natural Right and History*.[50]

Strauss's reading of Halevi centers on the question of what Halevi, in his *Kuzari*, could have meant by the "law of reason." Through a detailed analysis of the Halevi's *Kuzari*, Strauss concludes, "the *iura naturalia* are really not more than the indispensable and unchangeable minimum of morality required for the bare existence of any society."[51] But as Strauss points out, the unchangeable minimum of morality is, from a moral point of view, not very much after all. In explicating Halevi's position, Strauss elaborates on Halevi's comment in the *Kuzari* that "Even a

---

[50] For the importance of Halevi for Strauss, see Laurence Lampert, "Strauss's Recovery of Esotericism," this volume.
[51] Strauss, "The Law of Reason in the *Kuzari*," in *PAW*, 132.

gang of robbers must have a kind of justice among them if their confederacy is to last" (the analogy that refers to, without mentioning, Plato's parable of the robbers in *Republic*, Book 1, 342b–d). Strauss writes:

he [the philosopher in Halevi's *Kuzari*] mentions among the governmental laws of the Divine code the prohibition against murder, e.g., while he does not mention it among the governmental and rational *nomoi* which are known independently of revelation; this again is easily understandable considering that the Bible prohibits murder absolutely, whereas a gang of robbers, e.g., would merely have to prohibit the murder of other members of the gang.[52]

Strauss concludes his study of Halevi by suggesting that "by going so far with the philosophers...he [Halevi] discover[s] the fundamental weakness of the philosophic position and the deepest reason why philosophy is enormously dangerous."[53] On Strauss's reading of Halevi, philosophy leads to the dangerous denial of an absolute morality that is not contingent upon allegiance to a specific group.

   In *Natural Right and History*, Strauss does not deny that we can know right and wrong but he does question strongly whether philosophy in and of itself can defend a universal morality beyond that of a closed city or society.[54] Significantly, Strauss alludes to Halevi's analogy of a gang of robbers when he writes:

But it is unfortunate for the defenders of justice that it is also required for the preservation of a gang of robbers: the gang could not last a single day if its members did not refrain from hurting one another, if they did not help one another, or if each member did not subordinate his own good to the good of the gang.[55]

   Strauss's allusion to Halevi is made all the stronger by a reference to his essay on Halevi in a note to the following sentence: "There exists

[52] Strauss, "The Law of Reason" in *PAW*, 132. In Halevi's words, "The Rabbi said: 'These and others like them are the rational laws. They are prerequisites – inherently and sequentially – to the Divine Torah. One cannot maintain any community of people without these laws. Even a community of robbers cannot exist without equity amongst themselves; if not, their association could not continue," Judah Halevi, *The Kuzari: In Defense of the Despised Faith*, trans. and annotated by N. Daniel Korobkin (New Jersey and Jerusalem: Jason Aronson Inc., 1998), 2:48, 94. The rabbi's comments are in response to the Kuzari's question about why the divine law is necessary to know God.

[53] Strauss, "The Law of Reason," in *PAW*, 140.

[54] See especially Strauss, "Jerusalem and Athens: Some Preliminary Reflections," in *SPPP*, 171–172.

[55] Strauss, *NRH*, 105.

an alternative medieval interpretation of Aristotle's doctrine [of natural right], namely, the Averroistic view or, more adequately stated, the view characteristic of the *falāsifa*, (i.e., of the Islamic Aristotelians) as well as of the Jewish Aristotelians."[56] The context of this comment and note is Strauss's distinction between the Aristotelian view of natural right and the Socratic-Platonic view. For Aristotle, Strauss writes, "there is no fundamental disproportion between natural right and the requirements of political society."[57] In contrast, Strauss maintains, the Platonic-Socratic view of natural right recognizes a fundamental discrepancy between the justice of natural right, which is independent of law, and the justice of the city, which is of necessity dependent on law. The Platonic-Socratic view of natural right points to the philosopher's lack of inner attachment to the laws of society.

For Strauss, the "Averroistic view" that is "an alternative medieval interpretation of Aristotle's doctrine" is based on the Islamic reception of Plato's *Laws*, and hence is Platonic in a way that the Christian reading of Aristotle is not. Strauss insists Plato and the "Jewish Aristotelians" recognize a fundamental tension between philosophy and law, which is also the tension between philosophy and "the city." As Strauss makes clear in *Natural Right and History*, it is the Christian interpretation of Aristotle, and particularly Thomas Aquinas's notion of natural law, that denies this tension: "The Thomistic doctrine of natural right or, more generally expressed, of natural law is free from the hesitations and ambiguities which are characteristic of the teachings, not only of Plato and Cicero, but of Aristotle as well...No doubt is left..."[58] We have seen that for Strauss, leaving doubt behind is the intellectual error that led to the theologico-political predicament of the early twentieth century, with ultimately terrible consequences for reason, morality, and politics.

By repeatedly emphasizing his doubts about philosophy's ability to ground a universal morality, Strauss suggests that revelation remains and must remain a continual moral challenge for philosophy.[59] Strauss

[56] Strauss, *NRH*, 158.
[57] Strauss, *NRH*, 156.
[58] Strauss, *NRH*, 163.
[59] Strauss emphasizes his doubts about philosophy's ability to ground a universal morality not only in the sources cited previously but also in his important essay, "Jerusalem and Athens," in which he states: "the messianic age will be the age of universal peace: all nations shall come to the mountain of the Lord, to the house of the God of Jacob, 'and they shall beat their swords into plowshares, and their spears into pruning hooks: nation shall not lift up sword against nation, neither shall they learn war anymore' (Isaiah 2:2–4). The best regime, however Socrates envisages it, will animate a single city which

models his concept of revelation on Jewish sources when he asserts that "Only by surrendering to God's experienced call which calls for one's loving Him with all one's heart, with all one's soul, and all one's might can one come to see the other human being as one's brother and love him as oneself."[60] These words paraphrase without citing the biblical verses following the Jewish creed, "Hear O Israel, the Lord is our God, the Lord is One" (Deuteronomy 6:4–9). Revelation for Strauss does have a particular content and form. Its content is not blind belief in the grace of God but the prophetic call to care not just for one's neighbor but also for the stranger, and its form is law. Revelation as law prescribes care for the stranger and far from being irrational, revelation, understood as law and not as faith, can be understood by human reason.[61] To repeat Strauss's words quoted previously, "Not the mystery of its [the Torah's] origin, the search for which leads either to theosophy or 'Epicureanism,' but its end, the comprehension of which guarantees obedience to the Torah, is accessible to human reason."[62]

To be sure, Strauss's is not an argument for revelation, and Strauss himself was not a believer. But Strauss's arguments about revelation

as a matter of course will become embroiled in wars with other cities. The cessation of evils that Socrates expects from the establishment of the best regime will not include the cessation of war" ("Jerusalem and Athens," in *SPPP*, 171–172). See also *NRH*, 106–107, and again in the Halevi essay: "only revelation can transform natural man into 'the guardian of his city,' or, to use the language of the Bible, the guardian of his brother" ("Law of Reason," in *PAW*, 140).

[60] Strauss, "Preface to *SCR*," in *LAM*, 232–233.

[61] The view of revelation as care for the stranger may sound more like Cohen than Strauss but note that when Strauss defines what revelation could mean, it is precisely in these terms: again, "Only by surrendering to God's experienced call which calls for one's loving Him with all one's heart, with all one's soul, and all one's might can one come to see the other human being as one's brother and love him as oneself." Strauss's definition of revelation in this late autobiographical essay is consistent with his initial musings on Cohen's conceptions of revelation as law in his 1931 essay, "Cohen und Maimuni" (in *GS*, 2: 393–436) as well as with his introduction to the English translation of Cohen's *Religion of Reason Out of the Sources of Judaism*, published in 1972 (in SPPP, 233–247). For more on Strauss's complex relation to Cohen, see chapter five of Leora Batnitzky, *Leo Strauss and Emmanuel Levinas: Philosophy and the Politics of Revelation* (New York: Cambridge University Press, 2006). Whether this conception of Jewish revelation is adequate or not is a separate matter. In the present essay, we discuss only what we take Strauss's view of revelation to be, without evaluating it further. For a brief evaluation, see the conclusion of *Leo Strauss and Emmanuel Levinas: Philosophy and the Politics of Revelation*.

[62] Strauss, "Some Remarks," 15–16.

do offer the believer intellectual resources with which to challenge the philosopher, and for this reason Strauss is neither indifferent to nor does he reject revelation. As Strauss concludes his essay on Halevi, "One has not to be naturally pious, he has merely to have a passionate interest in genuine morality in order to long with all his heart for revelation: *moral man as such is the potential believer.*"[63]

Of course, revelation's challenge to philosophy is but a challenge and never a victory. At the same time, philosophy always remains a challenge to revelation's ability to make claims about the evidence for revelation's truth. This mutual challenge is ultimately a form of moderation. The theologico-political problem that Strauss wishes to reinstate is not a return to medievalism of any kind but a return to the wisdom of doubt, or put another way, a return to a philosophy, theology, and especially a politics of moderation.

CONCLUSION

We began this essay by suggesting that Strauss uses the term "theologico-political predicament" in both a diagnostic and a reconstructive sense. The former refers to the modern demise of critical reason, which had moral and political consequences expressed in their most extreme by the horrors of the twentieth century. The latter refers to Strauss's attempt to rethink what went wrong by considering alternative premodern resources that modernity has forgotten and that the legacy of modern intellectual life makes difficult to retrieve. In both cases, we have seen that for Strauss a rethinking of the modern critique of religion, and even more particularly the modern definition of revelation, is essential for understanding the "theologico-political problem." Of course, the question that remains is what to make of each of Strauss's analyses. Did Strauss understand the intellectual trajectory of modernity correctly? Is his understanding of medieval rationalism, Jewish, Islamic, and Christian, adequate? Finally, what are the contemporary implications of our answers these questions?

Strauss's continuing influence on the history of political philosophy and the recovery of medieval Jewish and Islamic thought are discussed elsewhere in this volume, and the details of his analyses of modern and premodern intellectual trends have continued and will continue to spark controversy among scholars from many walks of the contemporary academy.[64] So, too, the relationship between Strauss's call for a politics of moderation and American democracy,

---

[63] Strauss, "The Law of Reason," in *PAW*, 140; emphasis added.
[64] See Joel Kraemer, "The Medieval Arabic Enlightenment," this volume.

also discussed elsewhere in this volume, has inspired and will continue to inspire much debate.[65] However, in the context of this essay's discussion of Strauss's notion of "theologico-political predicament," we would suggest that Strauss's continual return to the question of the intellectual and political significance of the modern meanings of revelation constitutes and should constitute the enduring legacy of his thought. Strauss's recurrent attempt to take revelation seriously not only connects many of the seemingly diverse strands of his work together but also allows us to appreciate Strauss's lasting importance as a thinker of modernity, regardless of whether he got all or even most of the details of his historical analyses right or not.

Before turning to the contemporary relevance of Strauss's musings on revelation, it is important to note that in an interesting and especially ironic way, Strauss's analysis of the theologico-political problem is extremely irrelevant to the contemporary world, and for this reason certainly shows the absurdity of the view that Strauss is somehow the intellectual godfather of the Bush administration's policies on Iraq and the Middle East more generally. It is important to underscore the irony that Strauss himself was devoted to revitalizing Islamic philosophy, as opposed to Christian thought, for the very sake of the future of Western civilization.[66]

But Strauss's thought is also extremely relevant to the contemporary world because Strauss perhaps uniquely accounts for the inability of intellectuals (and twentieth-century intellectuals, in particular) to conceive of the enduring power of religious belief, an enduring power that no one could deny today. As I have stressed, Strauss's conception of revelation must be understood in Jewish as opposed to Protestant terms, which means that religion should be understood as public practice rather than private faith. In Strauss's day, what may have seemed a narrow academic point about revelation as public law versus revelation as private belief or knowledge could not be more pertinent today, as we continue to witness the breakdown of the boundaries of what had been a dominant conception of private religion in modern political orders, in both the United States and abroad. What Strauss would have said

---

[65] See William A. Galston, "Leo's Strauss's Qualified Embrace of Liberal Democracy," this volume.

[66] Strauss's profound disdain for Christianity can only be understood within the context of the legacy of German-Jewish thought and the political debates that took place in Germany about the academic study of Islam and Judaism. For more on this issue, as well as on Strauss's approach to Christianity, see Chapter Six of *Leo Strauss and Emmanuel Levinas: Philosophy and the Politics of Revelation*.

about all of this, no one knows. But what matters from the perspective of his thought is our clear grasp of the problem, rather than any particular solution. The enduring relevance of Strauss's conception of the theologico-political problem is his grasp of the challenge posed by revelation, not just for believers but equally, if not more importantly, for nonbelievers.

4   Strauss's Recovery of Esotericism

Leo Strauss presented himself as a partisan of ancient and medieval Platonic political philosophy while emphasizing the esoteric character of that philosophy and its artful sheltering of the true teaching in a moral or edifying teaching it judged necessary. It is reasonable to suspect that a partisan of esoteric philosophy would himself write esoterically. The following essay aims to confirm that suspicion by looking first at Strauss's recovery of esotericism and then at his restoration of esotericism, his redeployment of the classical strategy for philosophic communication.[1]

1938–39: RECOVERY

Strauss's actual recovery of esotericism, caught in the act as he discovers just what it is, can now be read in letters to Jacob Klein from January 1938 to November 1939.[2] The letters surge with the exhilaration, even the hilarity of serial discoveries spread across twenty-two months of precarious living for Strauss. In Heinrich Meier's metaphor, they contain "a whole series of philosophical supernovas" that can serve Strauss's readers as orienting points for renewed study of his writings.[3]

Strauss's letters on esotericism begin with his first letter from New York on January 20, 1938. Amid the rigors of travel and failure to find a teaching position, Strauss reports that "Maimonides is getting more and more exciting" (545). Maimonides had been a subject of his study for most of his adult life, and now took on new significance: Strauss had once called him "a believing Jew"[4] but could now say, "He was a truly

---

[1] This essay uses the now-common term "esotericism" for what Strauss more properly called "exotericism": a philosopher "could expound only such opinions as were suitable for the non-philosophic majority: all of his writings would have to be, strictly speaking, exoteric" (Strauss, *PAW*, 35).

[2] See Strauss, *GS*, 3: 544–587; the relevant letters are written in German with some Greek, Latin, French, and English; subsequent references will be to page numbers in the text.

[3] Meier, *GS*, 3: xxxiii.

[4] Strauss, *SCR*, 185, written from 1925 to 1928 but published in 1930.

free mind... The crucial question for him was *not* world-creation or world-eternity (for he was persuaded of world-eternity), instead, it was whether the ideal lawgiver must be a prophet" (545). The crucial question had become political because the ontological issue had been settled: world-creation he "denied, as Farabi had before him and Averroes did in his own time." Strauss adds something almost poignant, given the difficulties his own eventual art of writing would hand his readers: "It's very difficult to prove that because he discusses the question in an exegetical form" (545).

His next substantial letter (February 16) reports the decisive discovery: "You can't imagine with what infinite refinement and irony Maimonides handles 'religion.'... One misunderstands Maimonides *simply* because one does not reckon with the possibility that he was an 'Averroist': consider it and all the difficulties in principle just dissolve" (549). Before stating what his discovery means, Strauss looks to its consequences: "When in a few years I explode this bomb (in case I live so long), a great battle will be kindled." Strauss suggests the destructiveness of the bomb by relating what an acquaintance[5] said to him: "for Judaism Maimonides is more important than the Bible." Therefore, "to pull Maimonides out of Judaism is to pull out its foundation" (549). Strauss comments coolly, "This will yield the interesting result that a simply historical determination – the determination that Maimonides in his beliefs was *absolutely* no Jew – is of considerable present-day significance: the incompatibility in principle of philosophy and Judaism ('clearly' expressed in the 2nd verse of Genesis) would be demonstrated *ad oculos*" (550).

The thinker more important to Judaism than the Bible was absolutely no Jew; he was a philosopher, and philosophy and Judaism are incompatible – that is the bomb. How will Strauss explode it? "[F]or now," he says, he is a long way away "from such important matters;" what concerns him meanwhile is "collecting a lexicon of secret words" – the patient piece-work that will always be foundational to his writing. But "secret words" is misleading: "An essential point in Maim[onides]'s technique is *of course* that he says *everything* completely openly, if in the places where an idiot doesn't look" (550). Maimonides's esotericism is not a matter of curtained enclosures: everything essential is hidden in plain sight. What is needed is the proper perspective for viewing the surface of the text in its planned complexity. Strauss ends: "The reading is an unbelievable pleasure that compensates me for so much." He signs off but cannot let go, adding a note that confirms how his discovery burdens him: "There's an aphorism in N[ietzsche]: when I hold the truth in

5 Nahum Glatzer, (1903–1990) who became a noted scholar of Judaism.

my fist, dare I open my fist?" (550). Strauss holds a bomb in his fist and thinks of Nietzsche who said, "I'm dynamite."

The next letter to take up esotericism comes five months later (July 23) from England. Maimonides occupies him, and he reports being "deeply immersed in my work, that is, in the completion of that mystical treatise which you partly already know. Yesterday I finally finished it" (553). The "mystical treatise" is the essay on Maimonides published three years later and republished as the third or central chapter of *Persecution and the Art of Writing*: "The Literary Character of the *Guide for the Perplexed*."[6] Strauss briefly describes this first writing after his discovery of Maimonides's esotericism: "There are six little chapters from which the exacting reader will understand *everything* and which will give the superficial reader a sheaf of useful information" (553). Strauss holds two audiences in view, those who will understand and those who can profit without understanding – he has already concluded that his own writing will bear the single most important feature of the writing he has just understood. He continues: "The view I succeeded in coming to in N.Y. has confirmed itself even more: the *Guide* is the most amazing book that I at least know. What N[ietzsche] had in mind with his *Zarathustra*, namely a parody of the Bible, succeeds in the *Guide* in far greater measure... The guide of the perplexed, or the instruction of the perplexed is a repetition of the Torah (= instruction) for the perplexed, i.e., for the philosophers – i.e., an imitation of the Torah with 'little' 'additions' which only the expert notices and which imply a radical critique of the Torah" (553). Strauss can speak with a modesty that hardly fits what he knows is an historic advance: "I could actually be a bit proud that I've solved this riddle." But personal pride pales with the thought of what he holds in his fist: "But maybe my nerves aren't strong enough – or I lack '*scientia*' – or both are the case. In short, at times I shudder in the face of what I may cause by my interpretation." His shudder cannot extinguish his high-spirits: "The upshot will be that I, poor devil, have to spoon up the soup in which this diabolical sorcerer of the twelfth century landed me" (554).[7]

---

[6] Strauss, *PAW*, 38–94; first published in Salo Baron, ed., *Essays on Maimonides* (New York: Columbia University Press, 1941), 37–91.

[7] There is a long prehistory to these discoveries about Maimonides's esotericism. Its beginnings can be traced in the difference between Strauss's extensive accounts of Maimonides in *SCR* and *PL*. Two essays published after *PL* record important advances in Strauss's appreciation of Maimonides's esotericism: "Some Remarks on the Political Science of Maimonides and Farabi," (1936) *Interpretation* 18/1 1990: 3–30; see esp. pp. 12–15, 21–24, and "On Abravanel's Philosophical Tendency" (1937) in *GS*, 2: 195–227). In this last essay to be published before the discoveries in the letters, Strauss refers to

In the next relevant letter (October 15), Strauss is back in New York and the gains he made with Maimonides he now begins to make with Maimonides's ultimate teacher, Plato. His report is laconic: "I'm starting to work: *Nomoi.*" Plato's *Laws* has begun to open itself to him: "Above all, understanding the meaning of 'ambiguous speech' *polynoia* in the work." He has help in reading Plato: "I'm now reading Herodotus, who – I swear it as a Catholic Christian – is also an esoteric writer and one in perfection. In short, it's happening again" (556). What happened with Maimonides is happening with a Greek, and will happen repeatedly until Strauss has the whole tradition of Greek esotericism in view. He signs off his brief letter with a fine little joke: "Cordially greeting you, also in the name of his wife, your friend, Leo Strauss" (556). A numeral "*1*" affixed to *Frau* leads to a footnote, three lines of Greek from the first full story in Herodotus, Candaulus's offer to Gyges to view his wife naked to confirm that she is the most beautiful of women.[8] Strauss explains the esoteric meaning of the "clever story": "the wives are the 'patriarchal laws' which everyone holds for the most beautiful. Woe to Gyges, who views a 'wife' who is not his own. Therefore: esotericism" (556).

Five days later (October 20), Strauss reports further on Herodotus: "I'm really stunned, and prostrate myself before such artistry (= capability)" (557). Bowled over as he is by Herodotus, his focus lies elsewhere: "My lucky star wants it that his work is really the single model for Plato known to me." That singleness may stem from his own ignorance: "(But then maybe all we learned about the tragedians, for example, is completely false)." What Herodotus points Strauss to in Plato is by any measure a supernova: "I can therefore show that what is nearest my heart about Plato is independent of the specifically platonic philosophy" (557). Plato is separable from Platonism, and the separated Plato is the one dear to Strauss. He makes one Herodotus-Plato connection explicit: "Herodotus: a book of *logoi* (histories, stories) with the antidote to *logoi*.

Maimonides's "thoroughgoing rationalism" (203) and describes his distinction between "an exoteric, literal meaning, addressed to the vulgar ... and a secret meaning of a purely philosophical nature" (199; see also 200). Strauss showed just how decisive the advance recorded in the letters is with the first sentence of his 1963 essay, "How to Begin to Study *The Guide of the Perplexed*": he refers to "the plan of the *Guide* as it has become clear to me in the course of about twenty-five years of frequently interrupted but never abandoned study." Heinrich Meier reports that on the manuscript Strauss struck the number that would have dated the beginning of his study of the *Guide* in 1924 (the year he published "Cohens Analyse der Bibel-Wissenschaft Spinozas") and replaced it with twenty-five, which put the beginning around 1938: fourteen years of work on Maimonides recorded in two books and many articles erased to place the beginning at the time of the letters (*GS*, 2: xxiii).

[8] Herodotus, *Histories*, 1.8.1–2.

Nomoi: a book of *nomoi* with the antidote to *Nomoi*." He then adds a parenthetical remark that reveals how he now reads Plato: "(Besides, the *Phaedrus* passage on Egyptian *logoi* was certainly not written without an express relation to a very particular paragraph in Herodotus.)" Esoteric Plato is fully aware of esoteric Herodotus and responds in kind. Strauss expresses his great pleasure: "With my customary naiveté and modesty I declare that the riddle of Herodotus is solved!" (557).[9]

Two weeks later (November 2), there is more: "I find myself in a state of frenzy that's consuming me: after Herodotus now Thucydides too!" (558). The frenzy involves Plato: Pericles' funeral speech is "a pure parody – exactly like the Protagoras speech in the *Protagoras*." Thucydides's esotericism includes conveying his meaning through silences: "the word *sophrosune* does *not* appear in the funeral speech: *that* is Thucyd.'s critique of Periclean Athens and of Pericles *himself*." His esotericism is more systematically present in his mix of speeches and deeds: "His history is no 'history' but an attempt to show by *deeds* those who are unteachable by speeches just where ignorance of *sophrosune* leads." Strauss is certain about where the "historian" Thucydides stands: "but it's settled for Thuc. that the speeches are more important than the deeds." Strauss had inserted Plato parenthetically into his sentence – "(a completely Platonic theme – cf. *Apology* and *Crito*)" – and he shows how he reads Plato esoterically: "Moreover, the *Apology* ends with the word *theos*, i.e., with the word with which the *Laws* begins, i.e., the problem intentionally conjured away in the *Apology* – the gods in which the city believes – becomes *the* theme of the *Laws*. The *Laws* are Plato's *greatest* work of *art*." Strauss adds a sentence after signing off: "It's beginning *to dawn* on me *how* misunderstood the ancients are" (558).

---

[9] Strauss was evidently led back to Plato (who is not mentioned in *SCR* or the publications of the 1920s) by Maimonides and his Islamic predecessors. The importance of Plato becomes visible in lectures and papers from 1930 to 1932 as part of the first indications of what Strauss later called his "change of orientation" (*LAM*, 257). The themes of particular importance are the cave image of the *Republic* (whose account of the natural impediments to philosophy becomes the basis for Strauss's understanding of the additional or historical impediment added by revelation and by modern philosophy); Socrates's question of the right life; and the philosopher king as the foundational teaching for the prophetology of Maimonides and his predecessors. See "Religiöse Lage der Gegenwart," (1930), *GS*, 2: 385–389; "Cohen und Maimuni," (1931), *GS*, 2: 411–413, 426; "Die philosophische Begründung des Gesetzes," (1931), later republished as the final Part of *PL*; and "Die geistige Lage der Gegenwart," (1932), *GS*, 2: 455–456, 461–462; see also the later remarks on Plato in *PL*, 73–78; "Some Remarks," 6, 10–11, 21–24; and "Abravanel," 196–199.

Three weeks later (November 27), Strauss reports that he has started a new essay, "On the Study of Classical Political Philosophy." He intends it to show that "Herodot, Thucyd, and Xenophon are *no* historians – of course not – but authors of exoteric, protreptic writings" (559). Thus does Xenophon enter Strauss's letters on the misunderstood ancients and will soon occupy a favored place, though always in a way that points to Plato's still greater importance. "Their history books," he says of all three Greek historians, "are exactly those readings for youths that Plato recommends in the third book of the *Republic*: *prose* writings in which what is *between the speeches* (i.e., the presentation of deeds) is outweighed by the *speeches* (i.e., the *logoi* which are inserted into the historical-works)." He offers a parenthetical remark: "(The Platon. dialogues in which the author *fully* hides himself belong after Plato to a higher plane.)" The whole history of Greek esotericism is coming into view with Plato the crowning figure; his art of philosophic esotericism surpassed all previous efforts at esoteric communication. Strauss then reports just what Xenophon aimed at in *The Education of Cyrus*. Calling it "a wholly great book of sublime irony," he says that "what Socrates is is shown through his caricature of Cyrus. Only through that medium does Xenophon show the true, hidden Socrates whereas he shows the manifest Socrates in his *Memorabilia*." Distinguishing this way among Xenophon's writings leads Strauss to one of his greatest insights into the Socratic circle: "His Socrates-image is therefore *not fundamentally* different from that of Plato" (559).

Five days later (December 2), Strauss can say that "The history of Greek political philosophy still remains most highly exciting" (560). Beginning from Aristotle, he can see that "the 'inferiority' of ethics and politics ... was of course shared by Plato who ... wrote only ironically about politics." Then comes the first notice of what will become the most explosive bomb: "Socrates too was no 'ethicist': he simply replaced the myths (Herodotus') and the history (Herodotus' and Thucydides') with *dialogues about the human things*." Strauss does not elaborate his stunning conclusion except to say, "One can prove this from – Xenophon's *Memorabilia*" – that is, from the very book that seems most to prove that Socrates was an "ethicist" and nothing but. Strauss wants to know more: "I'm curious about what is hidden in Sophocles who, according to tradition, was a friend of Herodotus – I'm afraid that here too it's philosophy and *not* the *city and the ancestors*." "I already wrote you that the correct translation of *daimonion* is: *nous* [mind]." The Socrates who is not an "ethicist" piously called what guided him a personal "daimonion" while actually guiding himself by mind alone. Strauss expands on this Socrates: "science is the true *Mantik* [art of divination], the true knowledge of the *teleute* [end] because [it is] of the *arche* [principle or cause]" (560).

Ten days later (December 12), Strauss reports that he is working on the problem of the dialogue "as the ideal form for the *disguised* presentation of the truth" (561). A comment on the *Laws* conveys his new way of reading the Platonic corpus as a whole. "The *Laws* rests on the fiction that Socrates escaped from the prison! The opening for the *Laws* (the opening through which Socrates slipped off to Crete) is clearly shown in the *Crito*!" (562). Then comes a little sentence that most demands an exclamation mark: "There is therefore no 'earlier and later' in Plato's authorship." Strauss thus suspends perhaps the largest scholarly preoccupation with Plato's writings, arranging them chronologically as early, middle, late: in the "early" *Crito*, the Laws of Athens present Socrates with the options for his escape, but although their disjunction persuaded Crito it was not exhaustive, for it left open escape to a law-abiding place far away, an escape to Crete, say, as portrayed in the "late" *Laws*. An "early" dialogue sets the scene for a "late" dialogue – Strauss's refusal of scholarly orthodoxy allows him to view the Platonic corpus as a unified whole.

Over two months pass before Strauss again mentions his work in his letters, but the letter in which he does (February 16, 1939) is the most explosive of them all. He announces his intention to write the essay that appeared nine months later as "The Spirit of Sparta or the Taste of Xenophon"[10]: "I plan to prove in it that his apparent praise of Sparta is in truth a satire on Sparta and on Athenian Laconism." "Xenophon is my special *Liebling*," he says, "because he had the courage to clothe himself as an idiot and go through the millennia that way – he's the greatest con man I know" (567). The clothing, the con that so endears Xenophon to Strauss, leads him to conclude that what Xenophon does his teacher did: "I believe that he does in his writings exactly what Socrates did in his life." Socrates was a great con man who taught his best students to be con men – about what? Strauss elaborates the most radical aspect of his recovery of esotericism and revels in it: "In any case with [Xenophon] too morality is purely exoteric, and just about every second word has a double meaning." Socrates and his circle stand beyond good and evil. Strauss gives two examples of words with double meanings: *kalokagathia*, the word for "gentleman" that joins "beautiful" (or "noble") to "good" to name the model of aspiration for young Greek males, and *sophrosune*, the word that gathers the total of Greek virtue into thought-guided sound-mindedness or wise self-control. Together,

---

[10] *Social Research* 6/4 (1939): 502–536; Strauss never republished the article.

these words name the pride of the Greek gentleman, that pillar of civic rectitude and public-spirited generosity who made the polis both possible and great – the gentleman for whom Xenophon is customarily taken to be the tedious spokesman, the Colonel Blimp, the idiot for whom he wanted to be mistaken. Strauss supplies only the esoteric meaning of the words: "*Kalokagathia* was, in the Socratic circle, a swear-word, something like '*philistine*' or '*bourgeois*' in the 19th century. And *sōphrosunē* is essentially self-control in the expression of opinions" (567). Socrates's *sōphrosunē* was his exotericism, self-control in hiding what he meant in words of praise for what he judged socially necessary; morality was merely a means for an immoralist who understood society's need to believe in morality.

Strauss adds a final clause: "in short, there's a whole system of secret words here exactly as in Maimonides, therefore a found feast (*Fressen*) for me" (567). Strauss's recovery one year earlier of the esotericism of Maimonides put him in a position to recover – feast on – the esotericism of Maimonides's great Greek teachers: what Maimonides did, Socrates had done. The "secret" words are no hocus pocus; they are the most honored words of everyday use supplied with a meaning very different from their everyday sense, turning them ironic when used by artful speakers like Socrates or Maimonides. There is more than an artful practice here. If Maimonides carried into his setting of the one true revealed religion the ironic or esoteric practices that Socrates generated in the different context of Athens, then the differences between Athens and Jerusalem with respect to religion are not essential differences. Socrates/Xenophon/Plato stood beyond morality and gained insight not only into morality but into religion as morality's support; to move from the esotericism of Maimonides to the esotericism of the Socratic circle is to see that they gained insight into the nature of the revealed religions or the monotheisms without direct experience of them. The bomb about Maimonides becomes a bomb about Platonic political philosophy as a whole.

Xenophon may be Strauss's *Liebling* but Plato is the massive presence offering the greatest challenge and greatest reward. In this same letter, Strauss reports that the first book of the *Laws* contains a hidden reference to the closing scene of the *Phaedo*, where Phaedo narrates that Socrates "covered himself" as the effect of the poison moved up his body. Again, treating Plato's works as a single whole offers insight: "even Socrates fails in the face of death, *all* humans suffer defeat in the face of death."[11] By going outside the *Phaedo* to understand Socrates's desire

---

[11] Strauss refers to *Laws* 1.648d5–1.648e5 together with 647e; the whole context is relevant but the decisive words are "fear of the defeat inflicted on all men by the wine-cup" – "the fear-drink," Strauss says, "is of course death!"

to cover his face as death approaches, Strauss can see Plato's artfulness in making the *Phaedo* a narrated dialogue: "it characterizes Phaedo as narrator that he didn't notice this and *for that reason* also accepted the proofs of immortality" (567). What Phaedo did not notice, almost every hearer and reader of his narration will not notice: the *Phaedo* is a faithful record of Socrates's last day transmitted through a literalist disciple who loves to recite Socrates's words. He transmits Socrates's speeches and deeds to a posterity that will resemble him; only a rare reader will reassemble what Plato so artfully scattered between the *Phaedo* and the *Laws*. Strauss can conclude with every confidence that Socrates's proofs of immortality were exoteric; Socrates's fear of death required that he cover his face in the presence of those he had encouraged, made courageous, by his arguments for immortality. Strauss ends his report on the *Laws*: "The *Laws* are now, I believe, clear to me (the theology of the 10th book is part of penal law!)" (567). That exclamation mark – theology is part of politics! – is the part that concerns itself with the laws of punishment; punitive gods guarantee obedience to mere laws. Belief in immortality, secured by the mortal Socrates, is an especially effective part of penal law.

If the *Laws* is now clear to him, "The *Republic* is *beginning* to become clear to me." Growing clarity about it yields these results: "My suspicion from last year that its actual theme is the relation between the *bios polit.* and the *bios philos.* and that it is dedicated to a radical critique and rejection of the political life, has been fully confirmed." Strauss adds a third indispensable word with a double meaning for Socrates's circle: *dikaiosunē*, justice. Again he gives only its esoteric meaning: "And [my suspicion] has gained precision in this, that it is dedicated to a critique of *dikaiosunē*: the *Republic* is an ironic justification precisely of the *adikia* [unjust], for philosophy *is adikia* – that comes out beautifully in the Thrasymachus discussion – *dikaiosunē loses* the trial, it wins it *only* through the myth at the end, that is, through a *kalon pseudos* [beautiful lie], that is, through a deed that is strictly speaking *adikon*" (568). The whole of the *Republic* from Book 1 through the final myth lies open to Strauss as an exoteric defense of justice to shelter philosophy, which is in its very nature unjust, the judge and critic of justice that, with Socrates, learns to speak well of practical life and the justice it requires.[12]

---

[12] A forerunner of this discovery can be read in Strauss, *PPH*, 147, where Strauss outlines Plato's account of virtue as presenting a hierarchy in which "wisdom stands supreme, but justice stands supreme from an exoteric point of view." The whole of Chapter 8, "The New Political Science," casts light on Strauss's view of Plato before the discoveries of 1938–1939.

Strauss is not finished: in beginning to come clear to him, the *Republic* offers another primary insight with a fourth primary word, *thumos*, the spirit or heart that is the key word for the *Republic's* new teaching on the soul: "And *thumos* too is purely ironic! The distinction between *epithumia* [desire] and *thumos* is permissible *only exoterically*, and with that *'Glaucon's' kallipolis* breaks apart" (568). It is *Glaucon's* beautiful city, not Socrates's; Socrates built it in speech for Glaucon and his thumotic like. Here are whole slabs of Strauss's mature interpretation of the *Republic* published in less explicit language in *The City and Man* and the Plato chapter of the *History of Political Philosophy*. After these stunning sentences, Strauss collects himself: "But now back to so-called life" (568).

Two weeks later (February 28), Strauss can report that "[t]here's no question anymore that Xenophon's Socrates is *identical* to the Platonic – only Xenophon shows Socrates *still* more disguised, *still* more *as he visibly was* than Plato. And besides, he's far more aristocratic (= more obscene) than Plato." His discoveries allow him to add, "The philologists are indescribable idiots!" (569).

On July 25, Strauss reports that he had withdrawn his Xenophon essay to rewrite it, and he is defiant about it: "As far as Xenophon is concerned, I have not, by Hera, exaggerated: he's a very great man, not inferior to Thucydides and even Herodotus. The so-called deficiencies of his histories are in the end the result of his sovereign contempt for the laughable *erga* [deeds] of the *kaloikagathoi*" (574). And he adds about Xenophon's esoteric technique: "Furthermore, he says all of that when one takes the trouble to open one's eyes, or as he calls it, when one is not satisfied with *hearing* but is also willing to *see*." Strauss restates his already expressed judgment, "The identity of the Xenophonian and Platonic Socrates is beyond doubt, it's the same Socrates-Odysseus in both, the *teaching* too." He elaborates his claim by stating that "[t]he problem of the *Memorabilia* is identical to that of the *Republic*: the problematic relation between justice and truth, or between the practical and theoretical life." Moreover, "The technique of Plato and Xenophon is largely identical: neither writes in his own name; the author of the *Memor[abilia]* likewise of the *Anabasis* is *not* Xenophon but an anonymous ego; in the *Memor[abilia]*. Xenophon is the single associate whom Socrates labels 'Wretch.' As for *ne kuna* [by the dog], Xenophon treats it this way: he lets Socrates tell a fable in which a dog swears by Zeus! This example shows most clearly what a dog Xenophon is. In short, he's completely wonderful and from now on my undisputed *Liebling*" (574).

Two weeks later (August 7), Strauss reports that he has begun to make notes on the *Memorabilia* and states "the greatest problem" he finds with it: "in what sense the principle that Socrates concerned himself only with the ethical things – in what sense this thoroughly false principle is nevertheless also correct" (575). Strauss's reading of esoteric texts requires that the false must in some sense be true as well, if from a perspective different from that of the typical reader. Most readers will be pleased to read that Socrates concerned himself only with the ethical, but some few will want to learn in what way this esoterically false statement can be true. Strauss says the general answer is clear: "*anthropos – logos – on*" [human – speech – being]. And he adds: "Of special meaning is the problem of *philia*, insofar as the understanding of what *philia* is destroys the theology of mythos: the higher can not be 'friend' to the lower; ergo: denial of providence. This is, I believe, the central thought of the *Memor[abilia]*" (575–576). The truth in the false claim that Socrates concerned himself only with the ethical resides in its ontological implication in moving from human beings to the highest beings. Strauss can end saying, "I believe I've essentially understood Xenophon's Socratic writings, also *Anabasis, Hellenica, Cyropedia,* and some of the shorter writings" (576).

Strauss reports on August 18 that despite the heat that keeps him from his "*Xenophonstatistik*," his noting words like *dialegesthai* and *philoi*, "I have in the meantime understood the *Memor[abilia]* completely, if to completely understand with such books is identical with understanding the plan. The agreements with Plato are simply astounding, at times so astounding that one asks oneself astounded: are Xenophon and Plato at all different people?" (579–580). Strauss draws a conclusion about Socrates: "The relatedness is doubtless connected with the fact that a considerable part of the teaching as also the tricks goes back to Socrates himself" (580). This teacher-trickster Socrates is not the moralist of the "Socratic dialogues or the *Memorabilia*" but a Socrates immeasurably more radical and more an ontologist than all but the fewest have imagined.

Strauss opens his next letter (October 10) with a "poetic" phrase, and his letter will report that he has traced Greek esotericism to the founding poetry of Greece, the last great advance in the recovery of esotericism these letters record. Strauss enters Hesiod's *Theogeny* through Plato, through the cosmology of the *Timaeus*. "The poem is no theogeny as the title proves (for what good author shows the theme in his title instead of letting his reader find it)" (581). Strauss reports the theme in three laconic judgments: "instead, it is an answer to the question of what the first, the unborn things are; further, an illumination of the Olympian through this question; and finally, an enlightenment of what this question and answer, that is, what wisdom, means. The first things are not the gods but such things as earth, sky, stars, ocean which at one place are expressly distinguished from the gods simply." Strauss has again found "the key" to a fundamental Greek book by reading its meaning in its exoteric details: "The key to the book are – the Muses." The "two-fold genealogy" of the Muses shows the book's exoteric and esoteric character: "1) exoterically [the Muses] stem from Zeus and Mnemosune; 2) esoterically they are the progeny of Ocean. How this hangs together you will guess immediately on the basis of the opening of the *Odyssey*, as from the remarks in the *Theaetetus* and the *Metaph.* about the origin of Thales's principle" (582). Strauss's discoveries in esotericism led him to an insight into the overarching unity of Greek thought: the esoteric meaning of Hesiod's Muses springing from the ocean can be read in Homer and in the comments of Plato and Aristotle on Thales's principle that water is the element from which everything springs – each of the great Greeks knew what the others were saying and each responded in kind.

Strauss turns to Hesiod's other main poem:

What Hesiod himself really thought of the first things, I don't know: Plato says in the *Cratylus* when he comes to speak about this question: 'I think.' But what I know with certainty is what *Works and Days* has to do with. You once raised the question of what the title means. The answer: just replace each element with its provable opposite from the poem itself: *words and nights*, that is, disguised speech. The theme is: a contest between nightingale and falcon, that is, singer and king, with an exoteric morality for *hoi polloi* (the last point, the exoteric character of the praise of work lies almost on the surface). And Hesiod is expressly the singer. (582)

As always, Plato is present: "what Plato in the *Theaetetus* says about the poets of the past age, namely, that they disguised philosophy in poetry, can, as far as Hesiod is concerned (who also appears in the *Republic* somewhere in the middle of a story)[13] be really *proven*." Strauss looks beyond Hesiod: "I'm convinced it's not different in Homer. Just read the shield of Achilles! And the self-identification with Odysseus in the *Odyssey* and the remarkable fact that Thersites *speaks* the truth" (582). Finally, Strauss turns to Parmenides, remarking on just how he fits into the esoteric whole Strauss is discovering Greek wisdom to be: "the relationship to Hesiod backwards and to Plato forwards jumps to the eye." Noting the role of the female in Parmenides and the fragment that says "women are 'warmer' (that is, more light-like) than men," Strauss calls it: "A milestone in the criticism of the *andreia* [manly]." Plato again: "The sentence is as ironic as what is said in the *Rep*[*ublic*] about the equality of women – the background is in both cases the same. And

[13] The only candidate seems to be the appearance of "Hesiod's races" in Socrates's account of the decline of the city in speech (546e).

yet something one can see only when one believes not in 'the Greeks' but in philosophy" (583). Maleness and femaleness combined with a critique of the manly: here is a major theme of Strauss's maturity that receives its most impressive statement at the center of his late commentary on *Xenophon's Socratic Discourse.*

Strauss ends his report with a parenthetical remark: "(Don't laugh at your little friend who has in the meantime stepped into *Schwabenalter* [583])" – into age forty, ten days away for Strauss, when according to an old Schwabian ritual one entered the age of wisdom. Strauss is joking but he is not wrong: at age forty he has stepped into the most breathtaking wisdom, the wisdom gained by Homer and Hesiod, and passed on in an esoteric way to future generations of Greece. Recovered and repeated in a different way by Herodotus and Thucydides, it was recovered and repeated in a still different way by Socrates and the two greatest writers of the Socratic circle. Secured in their writings, Greek enlightenment was passed on to non-Greek peoples.

On November 28, Strauss reports on Plato's *Letters*: "I'm convinced that *all* the Platonic letters (also the first) are genuine: they're the Platonic counterpart to Xenophon's *Anabasis*: they are meant to show that the author was not corrupted by Socrates: while the author constantly disguises himself in the dialogues, it's the goal of the *Letters* as of the *Anabasis* to show that the one disguised is absolutely harmless, absolutely *normal.*" Strauss suggests that Plato's letters are a coherent whole, thirteen in number, with the seventh or central letter dealing with the central matter. "How I can make this believable to anyone but you – that I certainly don't know" (586). He ends: "Johnson formally struck me from the list of faculty members of the New School.[14] So I again stand right there where I stood in January of 1938" (587). This is the last of Strauss's letters dealing with his discoveries in esotericism, and its remark that he stands where he stood in January 1938 puts an accidental closing exclamation mark on his private report of his recovery of esotericism. Strauss stands where he stood almost two years before in all respects but the essential one: in the intervening months, he recovered the esoteric riches of Western philosophy and poetry in its Greek origins.

As rich as these letters are in tracing Strauss's recovery of esotericism, their limitations must be recognized. The gains reported in the letters have a prehistory that can be traced in Strauss's published and unpublished writings. But more important than the longer trajectory of discovery is the fact that the letters do not mention the great theoretical

---

[14] Alvin Johnson was President of the New School; for Johnson's role in the New School, see Steven B. Smith, "Leo Strauss: The Outline of a Life," this volume.

gain implied in the recovery of esotericism. In the face of the most powerful sophism of the present age, the belief that philosophy itself is bound
to its time and place in what it thinks – that philosophy in its classical
sense is impossible – Strauss's recovery of the philosophers' esotericism
proves philosophy to be possible by showing it to be actual. Insight into
the philosophers' esotericism makes it evident that the great philosophers transcended their time and place in thought and then descended,
as it were, reporting their gains exoterically by accommodating them to
the prevailing prejudices of their time. Strauss's recovery of esotericism
is nothing less than the recovery of the possibility of philosophy.[15]

1943: RESTORATION

Strauss's letters to Klein record his recovery of esotericism; his subsequent life work displays its omnipresence in Western philosophy up to
the Enlightenment. However, the way he chose to display it differs from
the open declarations of his letters, for Strauss chose to restore esotericism. "The Law of Reason in the *Kuzari*" marks a special occasion
in that restoration for in showing "what a philosopher is" in relation
"to social or political life," as this essay indicates both Halevi's esotericism and Strauss's own. Here Strauss mounted the stage to show
who he intended to be. "The Law of Reason in the *Kuzari*" is the only
essay Strauss published on what he called "the other classic of medieval
Jewish philosophy,"[16] and the only time he discussed Yehuda Halevi in
print.[17] It appeared in 1943, five years after the letters on esotericism
began; Strauss republished it as the fourth of five chapters in *Persecution and the Art of Writing*.[18] The *Kuzari* itself is a dialogue that
opens with the Kuzari, king of the Khazars, having dreamed that God

[15] This philosophical gain is the theme of Heinrich Meier, "The History of
Philosophy and the Intention of the Philosopher," *Leo Strauss and the
Theologico-Political Problem* (Cambridge, UK: Cambridge University Press,
2006), 55–73, and Arthur Melzer, "Esotericism and the Critique of Historicism," *American Political Science Review*, 100/2 (2006): 279–295.
[16] "Plan of a Book Entitled *Philosophy and the Law: Historical Essays*," in *JPCM*,
469.
[17] Yehuda Halevi (1075–1141) is now commonly described as a poet and philosopher, but his *Kuzari* appears to be opposed to philosophy; his poetry survives
as part of the liturgical tradition of Judaism. Strauss gives the actual title of
the *Kuzari* as "Book of Argument and Demonstration in Aid of the Despised
Religion"; see also Leora Batnitzky, "Leo Strauss and the Theologico-Political
Predicament," this volume.
[18] *Proceedings of the American Academy for Jewish Research*, 13 (1943), 47–96.
In *PAW*, two typos are corrected and the internal page references in foot-
notes changed; everything else is left as it was, including British spellings

was displeased with his religious practice. To determine what to do, he consulted in turn a philosopher, a Christian, and a Muslim; dissatisfied with each, he turned last to a Jewish scholar who persuaded him that the Jewish religion, a religion he despised, is the true religion for him and thus for his people.

In his first paragraph, Strauss indicates that the theme of his essay is the great theme of political philosophy, "what a philosopher is," or "the relation of philosophy to social or political life," a relation "adumbrated by the term 'Natural Law.'" Because Strauss uses Natural Law as a virtual synonym of the Law of Reason, the title of his essay can be read as "The Philosopher's Relation to Society in the *Kuzari*." Appearances aside, his essay will show that Halevi holds "*the* philosophic view." As for Strauss, his opening paragraphs indicate who he, the author, is. His first use of the first person pronoun says, "If we follow the advice of our great medieval teachers" (95); he soon indicates that "our" refers to the "Jewish Aristotelians" (96). Strauss comes forward in this essay as a Jewish scholar following the advice of his great medieval teachers.

Strauss opens the first of five numbered sections, "The Literary Character of the *Kuzari*," speaking of safety, and safety is its sustained theme. He says the literary setting of the *Kuzari* looks ideal as a defense of the despised religion, for the Jewish scholar persuaded the king and his rivals failed. But he notes that it is less than ideal: the king is not "an exacting adversary." Why did Halevi not choose the ideal setting and show the Jewish scholar defeating the most exacting adversary, a philosopher, in the presence of the king? Asking that question in the central paragraph of his section, Strauss comically magnifies what Halevi would have achieved by staging a debate "which would culminate in the conversion, not merely of the king, but above all of the philosopher himself: a greater triumph for the scholar, for the author, for Judaism, for religion could not be imagined" (104). Halevi arranged his dialogue to lead a reader to imagine an achievement more supreme than the one described and wonder why he did not choose it. Strauss ends his central paragraph on a question dictating the rest of the section: "What was his reason?"

The first of two reasons begins this way: "Halevi knew too well that a genuine philosopher can never become a genuine convert to Judaism or to any other revealed religion. For, according to him, a genuine philosopher is a man such as Socrates who possesses 'human wisdom' and is invincibly ignorant of 'Divine wisdom'" (104–105). Strauss attaches to

(e.g., defence), mistakes in English (e.g., "informations," "as" as a conjunction without a verb, German punctuation), and the footnote numbering that includes a 7[a] and a 103[a]. References to the essay will be to page numbers given in parentheses in the text.

this claim the central footnote of the section and relegates to it a central matter: philosophy is less a set of dogmas than "a method, or an attitude" whose classic representative is Socrates. Moreover, his footnote raises the key issue of the possibility of "adherents of philosophy who belong to the adherents of the religions" (105, fn. 29). What was Halevi's reason for omitting the disputation? "We may say" what Halevi said Socrates said, that a disputation is impossible because the philosopher lacks the experience of religion.

But claiming ignorance as the reason is "not fully satisfactory" (106) because it is not true – an untrue reason can be satisfactory but not fully satisfactory, for some will want the true reason. Before giving the true reason, Strauss states why the first reason is false: a philosopher's "alleged ignorance is actually doubt or distrust" (107). The footnote he appends to this remark says that Socrates's claimed ignorance of the divine wisdom of those to whom he talked at his trial "is evidently a polite expression of his rejection of that wisdom." This is relevant only if Halevi read the *Apology* this way. Did he? "Those who do not think that Halevi noticed Socrates' irony, are requested to disregard this paragraph which is based on the assumption, in itself as indemonstrable as theirs, that he did notice it." This amusing little politeness is also a promise: you who think that Halevi might have noticed Socrates's irony, study this paragraph for the true reason Halevi did not present the dispute between the philosopher and the scholar. Strauss adds an aid to study: "the attitude of the philosophers is not altered if the people of Socrates' time are replaced by adherents of revealed religion" (107, fn. 33).

Philosophers do not just doubt claims to religious experience, "the philosophers whom Halevi knew, went so far as to deny the very possibility of the specific experiences of the believers as interpreted by the latter, or, more precisely, the very possibility of Divine revelation in the precise sense of the term" (107). They presented their denial "in the form of what claimed to be a demonstrative refutation."[19] The defender of religion then "had to refute the refutation by laying bare its fallacious character." Is this important? "On the level of the refutation and of the refutation of the refutation, i.e., on the level of 'human wisdom,' the disputation between believer and philosopher is not only possible, but without any question the most important fact of the whole past" (107). Composing a dialogue on a past debate in religion, Halevi chose to omit the most important fact of the whole past. The footnote appended to this arresting claim quotes in German a statement by Goethe that

[19] Strauss presented such a refutation in a talk to theologians five years later that he never published, "Reason and Revelation;" it was first published in Meier, *Leo Strauss and the Theologico-Political Problem*, 141–167, esp. 166–167.

Strauss introduces with an exhortation, "One cannot recall too often this remark by Goethe: 'The genuine, single, and deepest theme of world-history and human-history, to which all the others are subordinate, remains the conflict between unbelief and belief'" (107, fn. 35). While omitting the disputation, one cannot recall too often that Halevi "draws our attention most forcefully to the possibility of such a disputation": he has his scholar invent a fictitious disputation in which he says "O philosopher" as if the philosopher were present. Strauss's footnote says, "In a sense, the philosopher is always present in the *Kuzari*" (108, fn. 36). Is the scholar's refutation of the refutation persuasive? It "evidently satisfies the king, but perhaps not every reader" (108).

Why omit the most important disputation of the whole past while giving a defective fictitious version of it? "If Halevi were a philosopher, the absence of an actual conversation could be accounted for precisely on the ground of the doubt just expressed" (whether and how far a philosopher would be impressed by the scholar's refutation) (108). If Halevi were a philosopher, his purpose in omitting a dialogue between scholar and philosopher "would be to compel the reader to think constantly of the absent philosopher, i.e., to find out, by independent reflection, what the absent philosopher might have to say" – to remedy his absence by making him present in a substitute, a reader reasoning on behalf of the absent reasoner. So it is that Strauss suggests that Halevi, the author of a dialogue opposing philosophy, was a philosopher: he omitted the disputation that matters most in history to invite the philosophically inclined to enter the conflict between unbelief and belief prepared to settle it by reason alone. "This disturbing and invigorating thought" – this thought that gives life by stirring up – "would prevent the reader from falling asleep" – from being prey to dreams – "from relaxing his critical attention for a single moment" (108). Disregard this paragraph? Only if you fear disturbance. Strauss ends with calming disturbance: "But Halevi is so much opposed to philosophy, he is so distrustful of the spirit of independent reflection, that we are obliged not to lay too strong an emphasis on this line of approach" (108). "We" declares Strauss's presence: as a reader invigorated by Halevi's treatment of the conflict between philosophy and religion, we find ourselves obliged to follow Halevi and "not lay too strong an emphasis on this line of approach" (108). To not lay too strong an emphasis on this approach is to take this approach.

Obliged "[t]o return to safer ground," Strauss shows how philosophy worked its "influence" on Halevi. For most, influence is governed by one's "previous notions." "In the case of a man such as Halevi, however, the influence of philosophy consists in a conversion to philosophy" (109). Strauss uses Plato's word from the *Republic* where Socrates's lesson after his cave image describes the genuine education of the cave-dweller as a conversion (*periagogē*). Strauss does not have to say what conversion would mean for Halevi because he had just stated what influence is not for most: Halevi would "be induced by the influencing force to take a critical distance from his previous notions" – his Judaism – "to look at things, not from his habitual point of view, but from the point of view of the center, clearly grasped, of the influencing teaching" – of philosophy – "and hence he will be [capable] of a serious, a radical and relentless, discussion of that teaching" (108–109).

Strauss inserts himself into the judgment on Halevi's conversion: "for some time, we prefer to think a short time, he was a philosopher." Dreaming of a brief conversion leads Strauss to the most amusing phrase in his whole essay: "After that moment, a spiritual hell, he returned to the Jewish fold" (109). Safe ground obliges Strauss to follow his great medieval teacher and slander philosophy from a believer's point of view. Because of "what he had gone through," descent to a spiritual hell, "he could not help interpreting Judaism in the manner in which only a man who had once been a philosopher, could interpret it" – from the point of view of the center of the influencing teaching. Strauss does not say the converted philosopher converted back to Judaism: he "returned to the Jewish fold," returned irremediably different, viewing Judaism from the perspective of philosophy. Strauss indicates what that means: "For in that moment he had experienced the enormous temptation, the enormous danger of philosophy" (109). The footnote to the previous passage explains that the danger of philosophy lies in its "pernicious" fruit, the eternity of the world that contradicts the Jewish teaching of God's creation of the world, whereas the temptation of philosophy lies in its "beautiful" blossoms. Persuaded by reason of the eternity of the world, made a lover of the beauty of philosophy's blossoms, the philosopher Halevi returns to the Jewish fold knowing the enormous temptation and danger of its greatest adversary.

Had Halevi staged the disputation between philosopher and scholar, "he would have been compelled to state the case for philosophy with utmost clarity and vigor, and thus to present an extremely able and ruthless attack on revealed religion by the philosopher" (109). Because Halevi returned to the Jewish fold, "the arguments of the philosopher could have been answered by the scholar." Knowing the inadequacy of that answer, the philosopher composing it would know that "one or the other" reader might have been more impressed by the philosopher's argument than the scholar's. From the perspective of the Jewish fold, "The *Kuzari* would thus have become an instrument of seduction, or at least of confusion" (109). As Strauss is showing, it is an instrument of seduction but, from the perspective of the Jewish fold, invisibly. Halevi offered more aid: "[n]othing is more illuminating than the way in which Halevi demonstrates *ad oculos* the danger of philosophy:" even the king, "in spite of all that men and angels had done to protect him," finds an "unimpressive sketch of philosophy" impressive, and the scholar "has to repeat his refutation of philosophy all over again." Strauss ends his paragraph: "Only by elaborating the philosophic argument which Halevi, or rather his characters merely sketch, can one disinter his real and inexplicit objection to, and refutation of, that argument" (110). The paragraph written from safer ground assigns the tempted reader a promising task: elaborate the philosophic argument merely sketched in Halevi's dialogue and dig up what Halevi buried, his real, inexplicit objection to the philosophic argument.

Strauss's argument flowing out of his central paragraph – what was his reason? – is complete. The explanation that Halevi was a philosopher who recognized philosophy's temptation and danger compels a question: Why was Halevi so timid about philosophy? Defending Halevi against the charge that he lacked courage allows Strauss to end his section on the literary character of the *Kuzari* defending esotericism. He invokes a "line of demarcation between timidity and responsibility," a line "drawn differently in different ages," and makes his defense rely on what "most people today would readily admit," that "we have to judge an author according to the standards which prevailed in his age." Halevi's seeming timidity accords with the standards of an age in which "the right, if not the duty, to suppress teachings, and books, which are detrimental to faith, was generally recognized" and "philosophers did not object to it" (110). The philosophers took over "the traditional distinction between exoteric and esoteric teachings, and they held therefore that it was dangerous, and hence forbidden, to communicate the esoteric teaching to the general public. They composed their books in accordance with that view" (110). Halevi composed his book in accord with the philosophers' view in an age that sanctioned destruction of philosophers' books. Strauss refers explicitly only to the danger of philosophy. But he introduced as the model of the genuine philosopher the Socrates of the defense speech preceding his conviction and execution for not believing in the gods the city acknowledged: Strauss also means the danger to philosophy, a situation not altered if the people of Socrates's time are replaced by the adherents of revealed religion. Halevi returned to the Jewish fold an unbeliever, measuring belief from the point of view of philosophy and therefore seeing the great danger philosophy faced from belief.

Strauss ends his section identifying the audience for "Halevi's defense of Judaism against its adversaries in general, and the philosophers in particular": it "is addressed to naturally pious people only," those

naturally pious who are prey to doubts that can be settled only by arguments. "Halevi refrained from refuting the argument of the philosophers
on its natural level out of a sense of responsibility" (111–112). Strauss
emphasizes responsibility to the pious, but he has made Halevi's genuine responsibility apparent: the presence of Socrates, the quotation
from Goethe, the audience of the naturally pious, and the point of view
of the center of the influencing teaching indicate that Halevi acted out
of responsibility to philosophy. He stands with the philosophers who,
in adopting esoteric writing, exercised responsibility toward philosophy
in an age in which the duty to suppress teachings detrimental to faith
was generally recognized. Halevi drew the line between timidity and
responsibility where responsibility to philosophy dictated. That was his
reason. Reason was his reason.

The literary character of Strauss's essay is to take to safer ground
while allowing recovery of disturbing and invigorating thoughts.
Strauss's main argument on the *Kuzari* enacts this literary character
as it unfolds in the four remaining sections. Section II outlines what
Halevi's philosopher says and does with respect to religion; Sections III
and IV show how Halevi innovates in what philosophers say and do;
Section V traces that innovation back to Plato – and issues a warning.

The advice Halevi's philosopher offers the king is "the only authentic
declaration, occurring in the *Kuzari*, of the intentions of the philosophers" (115). His advice – decide the religious question on grounds of
expediency alone – shows that the "religious indifference of the philosopher knows no limits": it is based solely on reason to serve his way of
life. The philosopher requires neither that their religious indifference be
revealed nor that the religion of their fathers in which they no longer
believe be criticized; and they consider it perfectly legitimate to adhere
to a religion, complying in deed and speech with its requirements and
even defending what "he cannot but call the true faith, not only with
the sword, but with arguments, viz., dialectical arguments, as well"
(115). The philosopher offers three alternatives; the first is to choose
open indifference to religion. The second contains a unique element:
the philosopher may invent a religion to guide themselves, their household, and their city: they may choose to rule through a religion of their
own devising. The third is to choose to follow the rational *nomoi* set
up by philosophers who chose the second. The philosophers' rational
nomoi are a complete theologico-political code, noncompulsory to them
and ambiguous, both a political code and apolitical rules of solitude.
How does Halevi's Jewish scholar stand to the philosophers' rational
nomoi? He opposes them and approves of them. Out of that contradiction, Strauss disentangles Halevi's innovation in philosophy's stance
toward religion.

The scholar opposes the philosophers' rational *nomoi* as theologico-political codes. An adherent of a religion based on revelation and opponent of the philosophers, they can be more open about the purpose of the philosophers' codes: they are exoteric teachings using partly sophistical arguments for the purpose of rule. Strauss devotes the central sentence of his central paragraph to the scholar's opposition to "the religion...to which speculation leads": "He objects to it because it leads to doubt and anarchy," not because of its truth or falsity (119). Aiming at belief and order, philosophers' codes led to their opposite. Consequently, being indifferent to the particular religion that rules the philosophers must consider Halevi's argument regarding religion. In the central paragraph of his central section, Strauss shows that the philosophers, while seeming not to agree on a single action or belief, agreed on "the most fundamental point": "governmental religion" is a product of practical reason and is useful "to strengthen the people's willingness to obey the purely political laws" (122). Could any conclusions of theoretical reason have played a part in generating the philosophers' rational *nomoi*? Their rational *nomoi* were species of a genus whose species traits include explicit denial of divine revelation; Maimonides intimates that their rational *nomoi* opposed revealed religion partly on grounds of theoretical reason. Theoretical reason judged a religion based on revelation less favorable in principle to philosophy than a superstitious religion that divinized the heavens. As a conclusion of theoretical reason, this belongs to "the point of view of the center, clearly grasped, of the influencing teaching" from which Halevi judged revelation (109). Yet he opposed their rational *nomoi*.

Strauss turns to the rational *nomoi* of which the scholar approves in the fourth section on "The Law of Reason as the Framework of Every Code." He must disentangle the scholar's "strange elusiveness" (129) to isolate those "governmental laws" that are the framework of every code, the indispensable minimum of morality required for the preservation of any society. The scholar was elusive on two questions about the moral minimum: Do they include duties toward God? Can they be called rational? Strauss catches Halevi giving a double answer to the double question, hiding one answer in the scholar's three scattered statements approving the rational *nomoi*. To find out that moral minimum, Strauss compares the last two statements – lists – each of which mixes that moral minimum with a separate set of items: laws that occur in both "are without any doubt" the moral minimum, the governmental laws, the framework of every code. Performing that delicate operation on Halevi's text to discover what it covertly communicated, Strauss disentangles two laws only and concludes that the framework of every code does "not comprise any duties toward God, [does] not go beyond delimiting the essential elements of any 'Binnenmoral,' and ... cannot be called rational" (133).[20] Strauss calls this "the philosophic view," but then seems to argue that the scholar cannot have accepted the view they disentangled "although it is one alternative interpretation of his statements" (134). Strauss ends the section arguing that the scholar held that the preservation of any community depends on duties toward God and laws called rational: he rehid Halevi's hidden view that a community may preserve itself with no duties toward God and a *Binnenmoral* that cannot be called rational. Why?

Strauss spoke early of "those elementary rules of social conduct which have to be observed equally by all communities" (116), placing at one extreme "the most noble community," and at the other, "a gang of robbers." Robbers appear again when Strauss quotes the scholar's first approval of the rational *nomoi*: "even a community of robbers cannot dispense with the obligation to justice in their mutual relations: otherwise their association would not last" (127). Strauss points out a subtlety in this statement: "When speaking explicitly of the community of robbers, he mentions the obligation to justice only, while when speaking of the smallest and lowest community, he mentions justice, goodness, and God's grace" (129): Halevi separated the community of robbers from the smallest and lowest community. When Strauss next mentions robbers, he says "the proverbial gang of robbers, or the lowest and smallest community" (130): if Strauss is not careless, he identifies the lowest and smallest community with the gang of robbers to differentiate his gang from Halevi's community. To what end?

The gang of robbers plays a decisive role in Strauss's disentangling of the moral minimum from the scholar's two lists. In what seems an unnecessary complication, he mentions first two items that each appear on one list only. The duty to train one's soul by fasting and humility is on only one: "this is not surprising, since it is fairly absurd to imagine a gang of robbers training their souls by means of fasting and humility in order to guarantee the preservation of their gang" (132). The prohibition on murder is on only one: "this again is easily understandable considering that the Bible prohibits murder absolutely, whereas a gang of robbers, e.g., would merely have to prohibit the murder of members of the gang" (132). Then comes the first item on both lists: "This explains also why he mentions in both enumerations the prohibition against deceit or lying; for the Bible itself speaks on the occasion of that prohibition merely of

---

[20] *Binnenmoral* was used by Max Weber to denote a morality internal to a particular group, a nonuniversal morality by definition, group-loyalty that explicitly took priority over the *Aussenmoral*-prescribing behavior toward outsiders.

the neighbor" (132). No robbers. Why not? They return for the second item on both lists, a duty to honor parents, which Strauss makes the duty to honor fathers understood as advisers or teachers; "even a gang of robbers cannot last if they do not respect those of their fellows who are their intellectual superiors" (132). A prohibition on deceit and honoring one's advisers is the moral minimum needed for any community to survive – but Strauss ends this section acting, as Halevi's scholar did, as if the moral minimum includes duties to God (134–135).

Did Strauss do all his disentangling for nothing, or did he uncover a specific community with no duties toward God? Omitting robbers from the prohibition on deceit helps. The essay is about what a philosopher is in relation to society, and Strauss showed that philosophers practice deceit in principle about society's religion – how do those who are the topic of the essay stand toward a prohibition on deceit? The Bible applies that prohibition only to the neighbor. Strauss invites the reader to apply the prohibition to the omitted gang – no, community of robbers, understood as the community of philosophers who practice deceit to survive but honor a prohibition on deceiving one another. But philosophers are solitaries. Yes, but they are a community across time, and whereas their individual surviving depends upon deceit, their lasting as a community depends upon a prohibition on deceiving one another, upon truthfully supplying their reasoning to one another. Halevi did this in his dialogue; he is a model community member; obliged by justice to his own kind, he addresses them out of his implications and silences while addressing his defense of Judaism "to naturally pious people only" (111).[21]

The purpose of esotericism is to preserve the community of philosophers across time. Such preservation implies esotericism's second purpose: to enlarge that community one fit reader at a time. Reading the *Kuzari* as he did, Strauss found it enlisting him in the community of philosophers, robbing him from inner attachment to the community in which he was brought up, assigning him a *Binnenmoral* prohibiting

---

[21] Strauss never mentions that the necessity of justice in a community of robbers is Socrates's central argument in gentling Thrasymachus. That argument leads Thrasymachus to treat him more justly as one who shares an enterprise with him: think of us, Socrates advises Thrasymachus, as a community of robbers aiming to steal young men from the ways of their fathers; our strength – you who hold that justice is the interest of the stronger party – depends on treating one another justly (*Republic* 351a–352d). Socrates made a similar argument for community with Protagoras: his fable of Spartan philosophy turns thinkers into family members with responsibilities toward kin (*Protagoras* 342a–343b); his exegesis of Simonides's ode gives him permission to blame a kinsman for putting the whole family at risk (343b–347a).

deceit in honoring his advisers. Writing "The Law of Reason in the *Kuzari*" as he did does justice to the community to which his reading of the *Kuzari* helped gain him membership.

Halevi did justice to his community past and future by allowing its moral minimum to be disentangled. But are the two laws of the most rational not rational? Strauss says they "cannot be called, in the last analysis, rational laws": they are not universally valid conclusions of theoretical reason but conclusions of practical reason, which are "in a sense more rational" for they solve justly problems that exist in a given country at a given time (133). Halevi solved a problem for philosophy that existed in his place and time. True to a *Binnenmoral* prohibiting deception among its kind and honoring its advisers, he developed an innovative *Aussenmoral* for philosophy that seems to dishonor its advisers. Keeping to the two essentials, he reasonably replaced the rational *nomoi* that led to doubt and anarchy with adherence to a living religion that counts itself eternal (134). Having intimated the connection of religion and morality for one society, the philosophers' moral minimum, Strauss does what Halevi did: submerge this true conclusion about one society in a different conclusion about all other societies – their moral minimum includes duties not just toward God but toward the God of revelation whose rules must be called rational; the connection between religion and morality for them is morality's dependence on religion. Strauss honors his adviser by submitting ("we find ourselves driven") to his exoteric claim about all societies that hides the esoteric truth about one: "We shall say then," and so on.

Strauss puts "Natural Law" in the title of Section V after omitting it since the introduction, where it named the relation of philosophy to social or political life. His final two paragraphs convey Halevi's judgment that revelation so altered the situation for philosophy in comparison with Plato's time that innovative action was required. The summary clarifications of the penultimate paragraph answer the question with which the essay began: Halevi shares "*the* philosophers' view" of the Natural Law. The rules governing the social part of the Law of Reason, or "philosophy's relation to social or political life" (95), are means to the end of contemplation, are not obligatory, and "are rules of 'prudence' rather than rules of morality proper" (139). The Natural Law is therefore addressed to philosophers, "rugged individualists" with no inner attachment to society. In contrast to these solitaries, "the truly good or pious man is called 'the guardian of his city'" (139). Strauss uses Greek words going back to Plato's *Republic* (414a–414b) as the source of the distinction made by medieval philosophers – words that Plato put immediately before the noble lie necessary for securing the goodness and piety of the guardian of the city. Having separated the philosophers and the guardians by noting that philosophers govern themselves by prudence rather than the rules of morality proper, Strauss shows in his final paragraph how the philosopher Halevi acted toward his societies – that of the philosophers and that of the religion in which he was brought up.

By going as far as he does with the philosophers, the scholar discovers "the fundamental weakness of the philosophic position and the deepest reason why philosophy is so enormously dangerous" (140). That reason is that "natural morality is, strictly speaking, no morality at all: it is hardly distinguishable from the morality essential to the preservation of the gang of robbers" – it is as weak as the morality guiding philosophers. Society needs more than philosophers need: "only a law revealed by the omnipotent and omniscient God and sanctioned by the omniscient and omnipotent God can make possible genuine morality, 'categoric imperatives'" (140). As if speaking for the scholar, Strauss states the case for revelation: "only revelation can transform natural man into 'the guardian of his city,' or, to use the language of the Bible, the guardian of his brother" (140). Plato buttressed guardian-morality with the noble lie; the scholar goes him one better, buttressing guardians of the brothers with the all-seeing, all-powerful rewarder and avenger.[22]

Having indicated that Plato's city in speech had become actual with the help of God, Strauss inserts a warning that recalls what one cannot recall too often: "One has not to be naturally pious, he has merely to have a passionate interest in genuine morality in order to long with all his heart for revelation: moral man as such is the potential believer" (140). Moving from the scholar to Halevi, Strauss reviews the connection between religion and morality: the alternative represented by the philosophers was that their community had no duties toward God and a morality that cannot be called rational; the "*vice versa*," the other alternative, is what the philosopher Halevi advocates for nonphilosophers. Strauss represents Halevi as morality's champion. "In defending Judaism . . . he was conscious of defending morality itself and therewith the cause, not only of Judaism, but of mankind at large" (141). As a philosopher, as transmoral, he consciously defended a morality for guardians of mankind at large. "His basic objection to philosophy" – Strauss nearly ends acting as if the philosopher Halevi could have an objection to philosophy from somewhere transcendent to philosophy – "was then not particularly Jewish, nor even particularly religious, but

---

[22] Plato prepared the way in the *Republic*: he had Socrates buttress the noble lie with arguments that the whole is ruled by a unitary Good and at the end with an argument for all-seeing moral gods who, according to the story, reward and punish in the next life. Plato initiated the dangerous game.

moral" (141). Strauss placed in the introduction of the book within which "The Law of Reason in the *Kuzari*" would permanently reside the measure of this moral objection to philosophy: the philosophers "defended the interests of philosophy and nothing else. In doing this, they believed indeed that they were defending the highest interests of mankind."[23] Halevi's objection to philosophy is philosophical, it is the prudential judgment that philosophy in his age must abandon the philosophers' rational *nomoi* and go underground, sheltering itself within a living religion that theoretical reason knows to be more dangerous than a religion that divinized the heavens. Halevi's ostensibly moral objection to philosophy signals the deepest reason why philosophy is so enormously dangerous: the moral have an objection to philosophy and the moral in his place and time could call in the All-Powerful.

Strauss ends on Halevi's "remarkable restraint" and gives its reason: "not being a fanatic" – ruled by his mind not by a longing heart – "he did not wish to supply the unscrupulous and the fanatic with weapons which they certainly would have misused" (141). There are two weapons: the weapon of the unscrupulous is the truth about philosophy in its relation to society, which they could have betrayed by not observing the moral minimum for the preservation of any community; the weapon of the fanatic is the truth about Halevi, whom they would have punished with the wrath of God. Strauss ends: "But this restraint cannot deceive the reader" – observing a prohibition on deceit Halevi deceives all but "the reader," that singular precipitated out of the plural named in the first words of the essay ("Every student") by reading alone – "about the singleness of his primary and ultimate purpose" – assimilation to the God of Aristotle, which he made seem assimilation to the God of Abraham (141).

RECOVERY WITHOUT RESTORATION

Five years had passed since Strauss reported to Klein that Maimonides was absolutely no Jew in his beliefs – the bomb that would, when he opened his fist, ignite a great battle in the one conflict that always counted. This is how he opened his fist: not stating that Halevi is absolutely no Jew in his beliefs but intimating it from safer ground prepared by Halevi. In 1943, Strauss showed by enactment, not announcement, the literary character his own writings would take. Yet Strauss made no pretense to follow Halevi as an adherent of a living religion strategically sheltering philosophy. Instead, his life work from this point on represents a great innovation in the history of esotericism: Strauss was

[23] Strauss, *PAW*, 18.

the first ever to display openly the esoteric practices of the philosophers and to describe in detail esotericism's principles; yet while publicizing esotericism he restored esotericism in the restraint with which he spoke about the ultimate reason for philosophy's esotericism gained from its stance beyond good and evil. What were Strauss's grounds for his novel mix of disclosure and restraint? He seems to present the general ground for such political decisions about philosophy when he defends Halevi's esoteric strategy: "the line of demarcation between timidity and responsibility is drawn differently in different ages" (110). Halevi's responsibility to philosophy required a seeming timidity because in his age, the suppression of books detrimental to faith was a right and even a duty. Strauss's history of esotericism, of "Platonic political philosophy," is a history of responsibility: political philosophers exercised their practical reason to judge the degree and manner of restraint appropriate to their age for the public presentation of philosophy. What was it about our age that led Strauss to judge that an innovative mix of disclosure and restraint was his responsibility?

The judgment about our age underlying Strauss's innovations in esotericism seems previewed in his Zionist writings of the 1920s and his essays and letters of the early 1930s: they attest to his extreme opposition to the modern Enlightenment, his contempt for it, and his judgment that its disastrous failure, most visible intellectually in the radical historicism of Heidegger, required a new beginning for philosophy. Strauss judged his age the logical completion of the modern Enlightenment, its theoretical self-destruction. That judgment sent him back to the medieval enlightenment and then to the Greek enlightenment to investigate, as a man of enlightenment, their treatment of philosophy. Strauss's innovations in esotericism seem to be what he judged a responsible preparation for philosophy's place in a postmodern, post-Enlightenment world.

In his Introduction to *Persecution and the Art of Writing*, Strauss spoke of "the eventual collapse of philosophic inquiry in the Jewish and Islamic world, a collapse which has no parallel in the Western Christian world," yet he could go on to say that "the precarious status of philosophy in Judaism as well as Islam was not in every respect a misfortune for philosophy" because it guaranteed the private character of philosophy.[24] Strauss's esoteric strategy seems calculated for philosophy's survival in private after the collapse of the Enlightenment. In an essay of the 1950s, at the height of the Cold War, Strauss described a quite particular collapse of the Enlightenment that would doom philosophy. Arguing against Kojève's view of the fulfillment of the Enlightenment in the

---

[24] Strauss, *PAW*, 19, 21.

universal and homogeneous state, Strauss's final argument raised the specter of the "Universal and Final Tyrant" at the end of history as the new persecutor of philosophy. Facing that global Tyrant, philosophy could not survive as it had done in former ages by going underground to escape the tyranny of thought through exoteric writing. The end of history in the Universal and Final Tyrant would be "the end of philosophy on earth."[25]

Strauss's strategy for esotericism seems to be based on an alternate possibility to this nightmare end of the modern Enlightenment: restored authority for revelation in public belief. Public restoration of faith in revelation seems the precondition for the debate between philosophy and revelation that Strauss seemed to think could be perpetual, desirably perpetual. Strauss even devised his own novel strategy for the renewal of the old debate. Contemptuously rejecting philosophy's historic compromises in the face of revealed religion (such as Maimonides's exoteric claim that reason and revelation ultimately maintain the same things, or Bacon's that reason and revelation operate in separate, nonoverlapping domains), and having abandoned the ongoing Enlightenment effort to marginalize revelation as an obsolete and laughable account of the world, Strauss made philosophy and revelation irreconcilable warring opposites whose opposition was a boon for philosophy. That boon was strictly private and pedagogical: as philosophy's allegedly most serious and demanding opponent, revelation had to be refuted by the budding philosopher both to prove his strength and to confirm to him the viability and consistency of his desired life of reason. To enhance that opposition, Strauss gave hope to revelation: he went so far as to make reason look weaker than it is, less capable than it is, both of grounding itself rationally and of refuting revelation; and he made revelation look stronger than it is, both in its supposed self-consistency and in its capacity to refute philosophy as self-contradictory, as a denial of faith based on a faith.[26] It is no accident that Strauss, an unbeliever from beginning to end, is believed by many of his adherents to be a believer if an odd one: he acted as if the conflict between unbelief and belief was less a stalemate than tipped in favor of revelation.

Two grave questions rise against Strauss's restoration of esotericism. First and with respect to Strauss's novel strategy regarding philosophy

---

[25] Strauss, "Restatement on Xenophon's *Hiero*," in *WPP*, 132–133. Strauss gave greater prominence to this argument by choosing to delete what had been the final paragraph of the first publication of this essay, a French translation in 1953; he chose to let the Final Tyrant and the end of philosophy appear as the last thought of the English versions of the essay in *WPP* (1959) and *OT* (republished 1963).

[26] See Strauss, *NRH*, 74–75; Meier, *Leo Strauss and the Theologico-Political Problem*, 15–24.

and revelation: Can it be wise in our age, given the rise of fundamentalisms in the last half-century, for philosophy to give heart to fundamentalism, to encourage the belief that the virulent orthodoxies of Judaism, Christianity, and Islam occupy an unassailable intellectual position, that reason is too weak to refute them and contradictory in itself?

Second and with respect to Strauss's eagerness to abandon the modern Enlightenment: Are we living the end, welcome or not, of the modern Enlightenment, where responsibility to philosophy requires making philosophy timid again? The most powerful recent advocate of enlightenment and strategist of its advancement, Nietzsche, understood the esoteric tradition that began with Plato. He could therefore warn "you who understand," that "soon the time will be past when you could be content to live hidden away in forests like shy deer."[27] Nietzsche's openness about philosophy's secrets was based on his prudential judgment on our age. His early writings counseled restoration of philosophy's esotericism to facilitate healthy if false horizons within which alone humanity could flourish. But over time, he came to view the modern enlightenment as so deeply established and so potentially edifying that he judged the only viable politics for philosophy to be one that furthered the enlightenment.[28] He recognized our age as the forward edge of centuries of the Baconian advancement of science; its ongoing achievements in cosmology, biology, and the history of human culture placed before the public the truths that ancient and medieval philosophy surmised but about which the beliefs of their age dictated nearly total silence, including most decidedly the genealogy of morality. In Nietzsche's view, the great event of our age was an experiment with the truth that the age simply handed to the thinker and about which Nietzsche could say: "Perhaps humanity will perish of it! On with it!"[29] Strauss's anti-Enlightenment fostering of fundamentalism seems a less wise strategy for philosophy in our age than Nietzsche's reinvigoration of the enlightenment.[30]

Strauss's restoration of esotericism, his refusal to endorse the modern enlightenment while acting as if it had poor weapons, seems a

---

[27] Nietzsche, *The Gay Science*, 283.
[28] Nietzsche recognized that a certain type of esotericism is both indispensable and beneficial, a pedagogical esotericism that invites the capable to investigate public truths that can always only be beliefs even if they accord with or image what is true.
[29] *Kritische Studienausgabe* 11.88 (a notebook of 1884).
[30] For an elaboration of this argument, see Laurence Lampert, "Nietzsche's Challenge to Philosophy in the Thought of Leo Strauss," *Review of Metaphysics* 58 (2005): 585–619, and Laurence Lampert, *Leo Strauss and Nietzsche* (Chicago: University of Chicago Press, 1996).

misreading of the age with bad political consequences for philosophy. But Strauss's recovery of esotericism is of permanent importance precisely for furthering the modern enlightenment. Recovering esotericism recovers the history of enlightenment beginning with the Greek paradigm and its provision for alterations by practical reason. Understanding this history immeasurably strengthens the intellectual ground of the modern enlightenment; its founders such as Bacon and Descartes were no more Christians in their thinking than Halevi was a Jew; they were strategists for the rational acting to crush an irrationalism, Christianity, whose wars threatened to make their age a new dark age. They were wise men who, in judging their age, judged it wise not to dissolve their responsibility to philosophy into timidity but instead to act on behalf of philosophy, to alter the social conditions of philosophy fundamentally by changing the direction of their age. Thanks to Strauss's recovery of esotericism, the history of philosophy – including modern philosophy – can now come into the light as the history of the highest spiritual achievements of our species, a history of political philosophy that changed the world and can go on changing it in the time-honored way that adds poetry to philosophy.

5 Strauss's Return to Premodern Thought

In an essay entitled "Progress or Return? The Contemporary Crisis in Western Civilization," Leo Strauss argued that the characteristically modern notion of "progress" is both empirically and conceptually problematic.[1] Having analyzed the problem with the modern notion of progress, he then suggested that his readers ought to consider a return to "premodern" ways of thought. In calling for such a return, Strauss appeared to be an incredible reactionary. However, examining the type of "return" Strauss proposed as well as the reasons he gave for proposing it shows that the "return" consists as much, if not more, in a new understanding of both of the "roots" of Western civilization: biblical morality and ancient Greek rationalism.

Why did Strauss think such a return was needed? Why not just continue on as we are? Recognizing the "progressive" prejudices of his American audience, Strauss began his essay by noting that the evidence of progress was questionable, especially with regard to human beings themselves. But then he broadened the scope of his inquiry greatly by suggesting that the belief in progress itself involves a fundamentally contradictory combination of ideas drawn from the two "roots" of Western civilization, ancient rationalism and biblical morality. Indeed, he observed, the entire history of Western civilization appears to consist in a series of attempts to harmonize, if not synthesize, these essentially conflicting roots. However, because ancient philosophy is fundamentally incompatible with belief in the Creator God, these attempts necessarily failed. The attempt on the part of modern philosophers to destroy irrational belief in the Creator God but to retain biblical morality culminated in despair over the possibility of knowledge and of all moral standards. These modern philosophers appeared to be reacting, at least in part, against the attempt of medieval philosophers to combine reason and revelation. But Strauss discovered when he turned to study medieval

---

[1] Strauss, "Progress or Return," in *RCPR*, 227–270. The three parts of this essay were first delivered as lectures at the Hillel House, University of Chicago, in November, 1952; all references to this text will be given in parentheses.

philosophy that Christian "scholastics" had "reconciled" reason and revelation only by making philosophy the "handmaid" of theology. By using reason to "prove" the truth of articles of faith, they had fundamentally changed the character of philosophy. Although the Islamic philosopher Alfarabi and his Jewish student Maimonides appeared to be trying, like Aquinas, to reconcile the morality of the Bible with Aristotelian philosophy, further study had convinced Strauss that these philosophers not only understood the fundamental opposition between faith and reason but also recognized the superiority of reason. On the basis of his studies of Maimonides and Alfarabi, Strauss himself then developed new readings of both of the "roots" of the Western tradition in the Bible and Plato.

Strauss admitted that the discovery that the two roots of Western civilization are fundamentally incompatible might initially be disconcerting. But he emphasized, "if the very life of Western civilization" arises from this "fundamental tension, there is no reason inherent in the Western civilization itself... why it should give up life" (270). However, if that civilization is to persist advocates of the two incompatible roots would have to recognize the irresolvable tension between them. Theologians would have to credit the philosophers' testimony that they are able to live happily without revelation, and philosophers would have to recognize their own inability to disprove the possibility of revelation. Neither would be able to refute the other; but by continually confronting the challenge posed by the other, each would be forced to recognize its own character and limits.

When Strauss gave his lectures on "Progress or Return?" in 1952, few scholars would have credited his claim that the millennia-long effort of the two opponents to refute the other "is continuing in our day, and in fact it is taking on a new intensity after some decades of indifference" (260). Most scholars then thought that the world was becoming ever more rationalized, tolerant, and secular. Confronted with the rise of the Christian Right in the United States and fundamentalist Islam in the Middle East, few people now would challenge Strauss's contention about the continuing conflict between reason and revelation. However, few have recognized the broader implications or potentially positive outcomes of the conflict that Strauss points out. Therefore, we have something to learn from a more thorough look at Strauss's argument.

THE PROBLEMATIC FOUNDATIONS OF OUR BELIEF IN PROGRESS

Strauss recognized that advocating a "return" to "pre-modern" thought was apt to sound bizarre, if not simply preposterous, to his American audience. We may not think our government is the best imaginable, but we tend to believe that it is the best form of government yet established. And we continue to expect that the acquisition of more knowledge will enable us to live better as well as longer lives. Therefore, Strauss began his essay by challenging the validity of these widespread beliefs. Modern natural science has given human beings much more control over their environment than people had earlier, Strauss acknowledged; but he also pointed out that knowledge, much less control of nature, is far from complete. And most important of all, the human beings who exercise that control are demonstrably no better than human beings in the past.

Strauss was not content to remind his audience of the at best ambiguous empirical evidence for the claims made on behalf of progress. On the contrary, he argued, the concept of progress itself was an example of the failure of the past attempts to combine elements from the two fundamentally incompatible roots of Western civilization that had given rise to the current crisis.

Strauss noted that to make or mark one's progress one must have a goal toward which one is moving. Moreover, that goal must be attainable lest all "progress" toward it appear, in the end, to be vain. In this respect, he observed, ancient Greek philosophy was progressive insofar as it contained the promise of some gain in wisdom (249–250). But, he emphasized, Greek philosophy was not simply progressive. Not all ancient Greek philosophers thought that the world is eternal (and if the world came to an end, so obviously would "progress"); but even those, like Aristotle, who thought the world was eternal, observed that there were periodic or cyclical destructions of the gains human beings had made, both as individuals and societies, in floods or other natural disasters. Perhaps even more fundamental, ancient Greek philosophers thought that only a few people – at most – would ever attain the desired wisdom. Moreover, these few could not simply transmit that wisdom to their successors; not merely each generation but each individual had to acquire it for themselves.

The modern conception of progress thus differs from ancient rationalism in two decisive respects. First, modern progress is supposed to be cumulative. Second, as a result of the accumulation and spread of knowledge through popular enlightenment, there are to be social as well as scientific gains.

If there is to be continuing progress, as some modern thinkers say, the accumulation of knowledge must go on interminably or infinitely. Strauss observed such a notion is compatible with the hypothetical character of modern natural science, but it produces a fundamentally incoherent notion of "progress." If there is to be progress, there must be movement from a defective beginning to a better condition. In ancient philosophy, such progress was marked in terms of a goal that could be attained by a few rare individuals, but their efforts had to be repeated by other individuals who wished to achieve the same goal. The notion of "infinite" progress or improvement in human life over an infinite amount of time is taken from the Bible, which promises human beings massive improvement in their condition in the form of eternal salvation in the indefinite future. It is not clear in the Bible exactly how or when that redemption will be achieved; but it is clear that salvation cannot be achieved solely by human means, and that when it is achieved, it will constitute a return to the good beginning of everything, which is God. However, if the beginning to which human beings return in the end is and was good, it does not make sense to talk about "progress" toward an end we cannot attain through our own efforts.

Strauss concluded that without a source or basis in God there is, in fact, no ground or reason to hope for neverending improvement or progress. If there is always something further to learn, no data or generalizations we draw on the basis of that data can be considered to be knowledge, strictly speaking. Our views of everything could change as a result of a future discovery. Moreover, if we are to believe modern physics, there will be a terminus to all human life, knowledge, and "progress" because the world is necessarily going to come to an end.

THE FAILURE OF THE MODERN PROJECT

Strauss thought that the problematic character of the modern concept of progress was "only a part, or an aspect, of a larger whole" he would "not hesitate to call modernity" (239). Strauss explained that by modernity, he did not refer simply to recent events. The distinction Strauss often drew between the "ancients" and "moderns" was not a matter of time and place so much as between ways of thought. Indeed, he argued, "because premodern traditions of course survived and survive throughout the modern period, there has been a constant movement against this modern trend" (242–243).[2]

---

[2] Because each of the three "waves" of modernity Strauss identifies begins with an attempt to recapture elements of ancient virtue, Frederick G. Lawrence argues in "Leo Strauss and the Fourth Wave of Modernity," *Leo Strauss and Judaism*, ed. David Novak (Lanham, MD: Rowman & Littlefield, 1996), 111–130, that Strauss's own work constitutes a "fourth wave" that brings even greater dangers of nihilism. As we shall see, Strauss attempts to forestall just such a development with his emphasis on "return" rather than "new beginning," and his critique of the historical notion that human thought and existence changes fundamentally in time as opposed to the older notion of the perennial problems that philosophers confront, in principle, at all times and places.

Strauss admitted that it would be difficult to define "this modern trend" completely in a single essay, but he thought that he could point out the most salient and defining features of what he called "modernity."

Anti-Theological Ire

Since human beings would not seek knowledge in order to transform the world so long as they regarded that world as the creation of a good and omnipotent God, Strauss argued, an "anti-theological ire" lay at the bottom of the modern philosophical enterprise. Modern philosophers saw widespread belief in a Creator God as *the* obstacle to the human attainment of knowledge that would massively improve their condition. Resting on indemonstrable claims to divine revelation or "miracles," these philosophers maintained, Biblical religion was fundamentally irrational. But, as Strauss often pointed out, neither revelation nor miracles claim to be based on reason. The truth of revelation cannot be "disproved," therefore, simply by showing that revelation is not reasonable.[3]

Retention of a Biblical Notion of Morality Without the Biblical God

Modern rationalism rejected biblical theology and replaced it by such things as deism, pantheism, atheism. But in this process, biblical morality was in a way preserved. Goodness was still believed to consist in something like justice, benevolence, love, or charity (239–240).

Many other commentators on the works of modern political philosophers like Spinoza, Hobbes, and Locke have objected to Strauss's readings of them as, fundamentally, atheists who sought to cover up their atheism with obfuscating references to traditional Jewish or Christian beliefs.[4] Strauss responded to the critics who maintained that these modern philosophers were in some sense "believers" by pointing out that, as the lives of Spinoza and Hobbes demonstrate, it was dangerous to appear not to accept the tenets of the established religion. Many critics at the time that these philosophers wrote objected to their "unconventional" views despite the philosophers' gestures toward orthodoxy. It was only in the nineteenth century that commentators began to insist that repeated references to the Bible meant that authors were believers.[5]

---

[3] See Leora Batnitzky, "Leo Strauss and the Theologico-Political Predicament," this volume.

[4] See John Yolton, "Locke on the Law of Nature," *Philosophical Review* 67 (1958): 478ff; John Dunn, *The Political Thought of John Locke* (Cambridge, UK: Cambridge University Press, 1968); Martin Seliger, *The Liberal Politics of John Locke* (New York: Praeger, 1969).

[5] Strauss, "Persecution and the Art of Writing," in *PAW*, 26–28.

Strauss nonetheless thought that these philosophers retained ideas that had a biblical foundation (265). However, he agreed with Nietzsche, who had insisted on the impossibility of maintaining biblical morality without biblical faith. And Strauss argued it was impossible for modern philosophers to be true believers for two reasons. As philosophers, they insisted that nothing should be held to be true that could not be shown to be in accord with reason. Moreover, insofar as they thought that human life and the world needed to be fundamentally transformed if human beings were to live peacefully in prosperity, these philosophers did not accept the biblical idea that life is good or think that God's providence could be relied upon.

THE ELEVATION OF FREEDOM AND HISTORY
AS THE ESSENTIAL HUMAN TRAITS

Strauss thought that modern political philosophy retained a biblically based notion of morality, especially in its desire to relieve the condition of the poor and oppressed. Nevertheless, he pointed out, the works of modern philosophers expressed a fundamental shift in moral orientation. Rather than emphasize human subordination to God or an impersonal fate, modern philosophers increasingly emphasized human freedom understood as the capacity to control nature and make it serve our ends.

Second, because human beings did not have any reliable knowledge of a divine or natural order, modern philosophers concluded a good or virtuous form of human existence could no longer be defined in terms of duty, that is, seeking to know and then abide by the precepts of a natural or divine order. Therefore, morality was increasingly defined in terms of "rights" rather than right. Beginning with Hobbes, these "rights" were also seen to consist, fundamentally, in liberties. Indeed, human beings were increasingly seen to be distinguished from other living things not by their reason but by their freedom. Strauss concluded that in modern political philosophy, "freedom gradually takes the place of virtue" as the definition of the good life. "The good life does not consist, as it did according to the earlier notion, in compliance with a pattern antedating the human will, but consists primarily in originating the pattern itself... Man has no nature to speak of. He makes himself what he is; man's very humanity is acquired" (244–245).

Unfortunately, the philosophical development that seemed initially to celebrate human knowledge and power culminated in demonstrating their fundamental limits. Having accepted the natural scientific view of the world as composed merely of matter in motion, modern philosophers gradually came to see that they could not consistently posit the existence of a distinctively human nature. How, then, could they explain how human beings acquired their distinctive moral and cognitive abilities?

The answer that emerged to that question, beginning with Rousseau but coming to its full fruition in the works of a series of German philosophers – Hegel, Marx, Nietzsche, and Heidegger – was "history."[6] Human beings had acquired their distinctive traits and abilities as the unintended results or effects of their own actions. Their actions were products of their passions, especially the desire to preserve and then to distinguish themselves as individuals. But the arts and institutions they developed to preserve and enhance human existence gradually changed the human beings that were their origin.

Strauss insisted this modern philosophical understanding of history had to be distinguished from the simple recording of what had happened, characteristic of ancient "historians" like Herodotus and Thucydides, or the record of God's works to be found in the Bible.[7] Unlike ancient records, the modern conception of "history" entailed a fundamental "progress" in human events. However, whether the changes were truly fundamental depended on what the end or ultimate result of the "process" was. Hegel claimed that he had replaced philosophy or the mere search for wisdom with the possession of *Wissenschaft*, but his claim to complete knowledge was immediately challenged by his successors, who showed that neither Hegel nor anyone else could give an entirely rational explanation of everything that happened. Marx's claim that the practical application of modern scientific knowledge or technology, broadly understood to include social organization, would relieve human beings of need and allow them to live as they wished in an economy of abundance also appeared to be obviously false. The capacity of the human imagination to generate new desires far outstripped the development of the means of satisfying them. Rather than ushering in an era of unprecedented human freedom, historical "dialectics" became the source of an ideological justification for the imposition of an unprecedented kind of world dominion or tyranny.[8]

---

[6] Strauss traces the development of this thought both in *NRH*, 252–323, in a chapter titled "The Crisis of Modern Natural Right" and in his essay "What is Political Philosophy," in *WPP*, 40–55, in the section titled "The Modern Solutions."

[7] For Strauss's thoughts on some of the differences between ancient and modern historiography, compare his "On Collingwood's Philosophy of History," *Review of Metaphysics*, 5 (1952): 559–586, to "Thucydides: The Meaning of Political History," in *RCPR*, 72–102.

[8] This is the thesis of Strauss, *OT*, especially his "Restatement on Xenophon's Hiero," in *OT*, 177–212.

The extreme claims made with regard to historical and scientific progress had provoked an equally extreme philosophical and political response. As Nietzsche pointed out, the life of a middle class burgher, much less of a proletarian worker, was by no means obviously better – greater, nobler, more just or more moral – than the life of any of Hegel's "world historical figures." Although these "figures" suffered from the delusions associated with great passions, they had not merely founded nations, created beautiful works of art, and discovered fundamental scientific truths. They showed themselves to be noble, and thus provided others with examples of human lives truly worth living. Nor was it clear, Nietzsche argued, that modern scholars or "scientists" knew more than the sages of old. Modern scholars had acquired much more information but their "knowledge" had been fragmented into so many specializations or "disciplines" that it was impossible to achieve a comprehensive view. Indeed, Nietzsche pointed out that if all human knowledge is a product of the will, then modern natural science is no better than Greek science. It simply expresses a more successful will to power. All forms of order – scientific as well as moral – are merely manifestations of a universal desire to impose one's own order on things that he called the "will to power."[9]

Heidegger drew the ultimate conclusion from the modern conception of human life as essentially historical. If all knowledge originates and is based on human beings, all knowledge is finite and temporal. Human beings do not and will never have knowledge of anything eternal. Strauss concluded: "Oblivion of eternity, or, in other words, estrangement from man's deepest desire and therewith from the primary issues is the price modern man had to pay, from the very beginning, for attempting to be absolutely sovereign, to become the master and owner of nature, to conquer chance."[10]

---

[9] "Nietzsche's creative call to creativity was addressed to individuals who should revolutionize their own lives, not to society or his nation. But he expected or hoped that his call . . . would tempt the best men of the generations after him to become true selves and thus to form a new nobility which would be able to rule the planet. He opposed the possibility of a planetary aristocracy to the alleged necessity of a universal classless and stateless society . . . He preached the sacred right of 'merciless extinction' of large masses of men with as little restraint as his great antagonist had . . . After having taken upon himself this great political responsibility, he could not show his readers a way toward political responsibility . . . He thus prepared a regime which, as long as it lasted, made discredited democracy look again like the golden age" (Strauss, "What is Political Philosophy," in *WPP*, 55).

[10] Strauss, "What is Political Philosophy," in *WPP*, 55.

THE FLAWS IN THE TRADITIONAL UNDERSTANDING
OF THE "TRADITION"

Moreover, it was not merely the modern attempt to wed science, which had been the preserve of the few, to the moral project of relieving the estate of the poor and downtrodden that was fundamentally flawed. "The whole history of the West presents itself at first glance as an attempt to harmonize or to synthesize the Bible and Greek philosophy. But," Strauss had concluded, "a closer study shows that what happened and has been happening in the West for many centuries, is not a harmonization but an attempt at harmonization" (245).

The failure of the explicit attempts on the part of medieval thinkers to show that ancient philosophy and scriptural revelation were compatible was perhaps not as obvious as the antagonism between modern science and the Bible. But, Strauss argued, the medieval attempts to synthesize biblical revelation with ancient philosophy were also doomed to fail because "faith" and "reason" are fundamentally incompatible.

Strauss conceded that at first glance, Christian thinkers like Thomas Aquinas seemed to have succeeded in achieving a state of peaceful co-existence, if not synthesis or harmony, between revelation and reason by making philosophy explicitly subservient to theology. Philosophy could and should provide arguments in support of faith that faith could not provide on its own. But Strauss observed, as a result of its subordination to revealed truths, philosophy lost its defining characteristic as a life of questioning and became rather a source of arguments, a discipline or university department. As exemplified by Socrates, Strauss objected:

[P]hilosophy is . . . not a set of propositions, a teaching, or even a system, but . . . a way of life, a life animated by a peculiar passion, the philosophic desire or *eros*, not . . . an instrument or a department of human self-realization. Philosophy understood as an instrument or as a department is, of course, compatible with every thought of life, and therefore also with the biblical way of life. But this is no longer philosophy in the original sense of the term. The original meaning of philosophy had been lost in "the Western development," because philosophy was certainly in the Christian Middle Ages deprived of its character as a way of life (259–260).

Strauss discovered that in contrast to Christian theologians, medieval Jewish and Muslim philosophers retained the original understanding of philosophy as a way of life. The conflict between scriptural revelation understood in terms of law, which requires unquestioning obedience on the part of human beings, and philosophy, which just as unambiguously and absolutely requires questioning, was obvious. Christian theologians could demonstrate the compatibility of philosophy with faith by making arguments to support propositions based, ultimately, on faith, but Jewish and Muslim philosophers could not raise questions about the basis or meaning of the law without seeming to challenge the law itself.[11]

Strauss emphasized two results of the Islamic and Jewish understanding of revelation in terms of law rather than faith. First, when Islamic and Jewish philosophers reflected on the law, what came to sight "was not a creed or a set of dogmas, but a social order, if not an all-comprehensive order, which regulates not merely actions but thoughts or opinions as well."[12] Understanding revelation as law, the *falasifa* (the Arabic translation of the Greek word for philosophers) thus took revelation to specify the most perfect political order. Arguing that revelation is intelligible to human beings "only to the extent to which it takes place through the intermediacy of secondary causes, or to the extent to which it is a natural phenomenon," the *falasifa* then attempted to justify their own study of philosophy by arguing that "the founder of the perfect order, the prophetic lawgiver, was not merely a statesman of the highest order but at the same time a philosopher of the highest order."[13] In other words, in attempting to justify the study of philosophy before the law, the *falasifa* employed the Platonic conception of a "philosopher-king" rather than the Aristotelian conceptions of causation or being that became so prominent in Christian theology.

Strauss acknowledged on first reading that both the Jewish philosopher Maimonides and his Islamic teacher Alfarabi appeared to be arguing that an essentially Aristotelian understanding of the cosmos is compatible with the law. However, closer study of their works convinced Strauss that this first impression was mistaken.

Therefore, the second feature of the writings of medieval Jewish and Islamic thinkers, Strauss emphasized in his new and very controversial readings of their works, was their esoteric character. Understanding the obvious conflict between philosophical questioning and obedience to the law, philosophers like Maimonides and Alfarabi could not present their thoughts or conclusions openly and directly. They thus employed a certain "art of writing," analogous in some ways to the Platonic dialogues, designed to communicate the questions they were raising to their most discerning readers while appearing to support the teachings and requirements of the law. Rather than demonstrating the way in which their philosophical investigations supported the law, the works of these

---

[11] This argument was first developed in Strauss, *PL*; see Joel Kraemer, "The Medieval Arabic Enlightenment," this volume.

[12] Strauss, *PAW*, 9–10.

[13] Strauss, *PAW*, 10.

philosophers revealed *sotto voce* the fundamental conflict between reason and revelation.

In his studies of Maimonides's *Guide of the Perplexed*, Strauss thus emphasized its "literary" character. Addressed to a young disciple named Joseph, a student of theoretical philosophy who wanted to learn the secrets of the Torah from Maimonides, Strauss suggested, Maimonides's "speeches" shared the *ad hominem* character of Socratic arguments.[14] In deciding whether and what to teach Joseph, Maimonides faced two difficulties. First, teaching the secrets of the Torah was expressly forbidden by the law, except according to the ordinance of the Talmudic sages – if it were to one man who was wise and able to understand by himself. But second, Maimonides did not know if Joseph is such a man, nor did he have an opportunity to test him because Joseph had to leave. Strauss argued that as a result of the Diaspora, which threatened the future existence of the law, Maimonides was forced to disobey the letter of the law by writing this book. Maimonides nevertheless preserved the spirit of the law by making his explication of the "secrets" far from clear.[15] He tested his readers' acumen by presenting both an exoteric teaching supporting the law and an esoteric questioning of the truth of its foundations or "roots."

In his introduction to the *Guide*, Maimonides said that he had given only the "chapter headings" of his teaching and that these were "not presented in an orderly fashion, but are scattered throughout the book." Strauss thus began his explanation of "how to begin to study the *Guide*" with an outline of its contents.[16] In the order indicated by Maimonides's own chapter and section headings, we see that "the account of the Chariot" (III, 1–7) is central. *Ma'aseh merkabah* (or the account of the chariot in Ezekiel 1 and 10) is the secret the Talmudic sages declared should not be revealed, unless to one wise man. On the basis of the outline of the content of the sections, Strauss juxtaposed with the order of

---

[14] See Strauss, "The Literary Character of the *Guide for the Perplexed*" in *PAW*, 42–48; "How to Begin to Study *The Guide of the Perplexed*," introductory essay to Maimonides, *The Guide of the Perplexed*, trans. Shlomo Pines (Chicago: University of Chicago Press, 1963), xi–lvi; reprinted in *LAM*, 145–149. For a good introduction to Strauss's view of Maimonides, see Hillel Fradkin, "A Word Fitly Spoken," and for a more traditional nonesoteric reading, see Kenneth Seeskin, "Maimonides' Conception of Philosophy," *Leo Strauss and Judaism*, 55–86, 87–110.

[15] For Maimonides's strategy in composing the *Guide*, see "How to Begin," in *LAM*, 143–144; see also "The Literary Character," in *PAW*, especially the section titled "The Conflict Between Law and Necessity," 46–55.

[16] Strauss, "How to Begin," in *LAM*, 140–142.

Maimonides's chapter and section headings; however, readers see that the account of the creation (*ma'aseh bereshit*) is central. According to Strauss, the only respect in which Maimonides thinks the philosophers and the adherents of the law disagree is whether the world is created or eternal.[17] But, Strauss also pointed out, that disagreement is decisive.

Having detailed the twists and turns of Maimonides's initial demonstration that God does not have the corporeal features suggested by the text of the Bible (which is thus shown to contain traces of Sabianism [idol worship]) that would make it impossible for him to be One, Strauss brings out the problematic character of Maimonides's central discussion. "The Kalam proves that God as the Creator is, is one, and is incorporeal by proving first that the world has been created; but it proves that premise only by dialectical or sophistical arguments. The philosophers prove that God is, is one, and is incorporeal by assuming that the world is eternal, but they cannot demonstrate that assumption. Hence both ways are defective."[18] However, Maimonides suggests that the two defective arguments can be combined to prove that God is one, incorporeal, and eternal. "For, he argues, 'the world is eternal – the world is created' is a complete disjunction; since God's being, unity, and incorporeality necessarily follow from either of the only two possible assumptions, the basic verities have been demonstrated by this very fact (I, 71; II, 2)." But Strauss points out, "the results from opposed premises cannot be simply identical ... The God whose being is proved on the assumption of eternity is the unmoved mover, thought that thinks only itself and that as such is the form or the life of the world. The God whose being is proved on the assumption of creation is the biblical God who is characterized by Will and whose knowledge has only the name in common with our knowledge."[19] Moreover, there is an even more fundamental difficulty: "The belief in God's unity, being, and incorporeality, required by the Law, [while] being compatible with the belief in the eternity of the world, is compatible with the unqualified rejection of the Law: the Law stands or falls by the belief in the creation of the world."[20]

---

[17] By confining his own discussion to the text leading up to Maimonides's discussion of the difference between the adherents of the law and the philosophers regarding the question as to whether the world was created or is eternal, Strauss himself may be said to be adhering to the law in a way analogous to the way he argues Maimonides did. Cf. Steven B. Smith, *Reading Leo Strauss: Politics, Philosophy, Judaism* (Chicago: University of Chicago Press, 2006), 38–40.

[18] Strauss, "How to Begin," in *LAM*, 180.

[19] Strauss, "How to Begin," in *LAM*, 180.

[20] Strauss, "How to Begin," in *LAM*, 182.

Rather than showing that the arguments of the philosophers concerning the eternity of the world are compatible with the biblical assertion of its Creation, it therefore became "incumbent on Maimonides to show that Aristotle or Aristotelianism is wrong in holding that the eternity of the world has been demonstrated."[21] Maimonides was thus led to assert that "Aristotle had indeed perfect knowledge of the sublunar things, but ... that man as man ... has knowledge only of the earth and the earthly things."[22] This conclusion is supported by Psalm 115:16: "The heavens, even the heavens, are the Lord's; but the earth hath he given to the children of Man." But Strauss reminded his readers, "it was knowledge of heaven that was said to supply the best proof, not to say the only proof, of the being of God (II, 18)."[23]

Strauss concluded that according to Maimonides, the God of the Bible is fundamentally mysterious, which is to say that He is fundamentally different from Aristotle's purely intelligible first mover or thought thinking itself. Writing the *Guide* "as a book written by a Jew for Jews," Maimonides seemed to adhere to the "old Jewish premise that being a Jew and being a philosopher are two incompatible things."[24] But Strauss pointed out, Maimonides also wrote at least one philosophical book.[25] And in that "philosophical book," Maimonides indicated that the function of the law (or religion) was fundamentally political.

Strauss observed that unlike the *Guide*, the *Treatise on the Art of Logic* was written by Maimonides "in his capacity as a student of logic" to "a man of high education in the Arabic tongue who wished to have explained to him as briefly as possible the meaning of the terms frequently occurring in the art of logic."[26] In other words, Maimonides did not write his *Treatise on Logic* as a Jew to a Jew but as a philosopher to a student of logic. In commenting on the last chapter of the *Logic*, Strauss observed that Maimonides first distinguished theoretical philosophy – mathematics, physics, and theology – from practical philosophy – man's governance of himself, governance of the household, governance of the city, and governance of the great nation or of the nations. Noting that many of the books of the philosophers on these subjects have already been translated into Arabic, Maimonides commented that

---

[21] Strauss, "How to Begin," in *LAM*, 182.
[22] Strauss, "How to Begin," in *LAM*, 183.
[23] Strauss, "How to Begin," in *LAM*, 183.
[24] Strauss, "How to Begin," in *LAM*, 142.
[25] See Strauss, "Maimonides' Statement on Political Science," *WPP*, 155–169; "Note on Maimonides' *Book of Knowledge*," "Note on Maimonides' *"Letter on Astrology,"* and "Note on Maimonides' *Treatise on the Art of Logic*," in *SPPP*, 192–204, 205–207, 208–209.
[26] Strauss, "Note on Maimonides' *Treatise on the Art of Logic*," *SPPP*, 208.

"the books of the philosophers on politics proper" are "useless for 'us' 'in these times.'" If the "us" refers to "us Jews," Strauss suggested, "of all genuinely philosophic books, only the books on politics... have been rendered superfluous by the Torah." Because the Torah antedates Greek philosophy by centuries, the operative phrase becomes "in these times."[27] It is "not the Jews as such, but the Jews in exile, the Jews who lack a political existence [who] do not need the political books of the philosophers." And "the Torah is not sufficient for the guidance of a political community." Moreover, the "we" to whom Maimonides refers in the *Treatise* appears not to be "we Jews" so much as "we men of theory," who do not need the books of the philosophers on politics "in these times" because of the dominance of divinely revealed laws. Because the need for the books of the philosophers "on ethics and, especially, on theoretical philosophy has not been affected by the rise to dominance of revealed religions," Strauss concluded, Maimonides "suggests that the function of revealed religion is emphatically political... [And] if only the most practical part of the political teaching of the philosophers is superfluous 'in these times' because its function is at present fulfilled by revealed religions... political philosophy is as necessary 'in these times' as in all other times for the theoretical understanding of revealed religion."[28]

Strauss thought that Maimonides himself took such a "theoretical" view of the Law.[29] In the *Guide*, Maimonides showed how the traditional understanding of the Law needed to be purified and improved with knowledge that could be obtained only through the study of philosophy. He did not show that Aristotelian philosophy was compatible with the teaching of the Bible; and in his only truly "philosophical" work, Maimonides suggested that the Law itself should be understood primarily in terms of its political function. In his "Note on Maimonides' *Letter on Astrology*," Strauss concluded that Maimonides did not think that the Law, as traditionally understood and practiced, had performed its political function well because it did not promote the art of war.[30]

---

[27] Strauss, "Maimonides' Statement on Political Science," in *WPP*, 156–157.

[28] Strauss, "Maimonides' Statement on Political Science," in *WPP*, 158–159.

[29] Strauss was more open in his letters. On January 20, 1938, he wrote Jacob Klein that Maimonides had "a truly free mind," and on February 16, that "Maim[onides] was *absolutely* not a Jew in his belief." *GS*, 3: 545, 549. On May 20, 1949, Strauss wrote to Julius Guttman that "Maimonides was a 'philosopher' in a far more radical sense than is usually assumed today," quoted in Heinrich Meier, *Leo Strauss and the Theologico-Political Problem* (Cambridge, UK: Cambridge University Press, 2006), 23–24n); see Laurence Lampert, "Strauss's Recovery of Esotericism," this volume.

[30] See Strauss, "Note on Maimonides' *Letter on Astrology*," in *SPPP*, 207.

Strauss found the same political view of religion in the works of Alfarabi whom Maimonides regarded as "the greatest among the Islamic philosophers, and indeed as the greatest philosophic authority after Aristotle." Wishing to restore philosophy "after it ha[d] been blurred or destroyed," Alfarabi followed Plato's example in the *Republic* by presenting his own philosophy in an emphatically political context.[31]

Like Plato, Alfarabi wanted to show the utility of philosophy to non-philosophers. In the first part of his treatise *On the Attainment of Happiness*, Alfarabi "discusse[d] the human things which are required for bringing about the complete happiness of nations and of cities. The chief requirement prove[d] to be philosophy, or rather the rule of philosophers."[32] But at first glance, philosophy and rule appeared to require two different types of "arts," the science of the essence of every being or philosophy, and the royal or political art. However, upon further reading "the philosopher and the king prove[d] to be identical...; philosophy by itself is not only necessary but sufficient for producing happiness."[33] Indeed, Strauss concluded, "Farabi's Plato eventually replace[d] the philosopher-king who rules openly in the virtuous city, by the secret kingship of the philosopher who, being 'a perfect man' precisely because he is an 'investigator,' lives privately as a member of an imperfect society which he tries to humanize within the limits of the possible."[34] Not merely does a philosopher not need to know how to rule, much less rule, to be happy; he does not need to possess knowledge. Like Socrates, he only need seek it.

Strauss argued that Alfarabi's "praise of philosophy is meant to rule out any claims of cognitive value that may be raised on behalf of religion in general and revealed religion in particular. For the philosophy on which Farabi bestowed his unqualified praise, is the philosophy of the pagans Plato and Aristotle."[35] Taking advantage of "the specific immunity of the commentator or historian," Alfarabi declared through the mouth of Plato "that religious speculation, and religious investigation of the beings... do not supply the science of the beings, in which man's highest perfection consists, whereas philosophy does."[36] Because he proceeded with some caution, Alfarabi distinguished "the happiness of this world in this life" from "the ultimate happiness in the other life" at the beginning of his treatise *On the Attainment of Happiness*, with which he prefaced his summaries of the philosophies of Plato and Aristotle.

[31] Strauss, *PAW*, 9, 12.
[32] Strauss, *PAW*, 12.
[33] Strauss, *PAW*, 12–13.
[34] Strauss, *PAW*, 17.
[35] Strauss, *PAW*, 13.
[36] Strauss, *PAW*, 13.

But in his account of *The Philosophy of Plato* in the central, hence least exposed and shortest part of the work, Strauss observed Alfarabi altogether neglected to mention life after death. "Proceeding in accordance with the same rule," Alfarabi "pronounces more or less orthodox views concerning life after death in *The Virtuous Religious Community* and *The Political Governments*, i.e., in works in which he speaks in his own name... But in his commentary on the *Nicomachean Ethics* he declares that there is only the happiness of this life, and that all divergent statements are based on 'ravings and old woman's tales.'"[37] A skeptic might object that in his commentaries, Alfarabi was merely presenting the views of the pagan philosophers, not his own. But Strauss emphasized, Alfarabi very obviously did not simply report Plato's views. "Precisely as a mere commentator of Plato, Alfarabi was compelled to embrace the doctrine of a life after death. His flagrant deviation from the letter of Plato's teaching... proves sufficiently that he rejected the belief in a happiness different from this life, or the belief in another life."[38]

In sum, Strauss's study of Maimonides and Alfarabi convinced him that these thinkers had not tried to reconcile or combine ancient philosophy with revealed truth because they recognized that philosophy and law were fundamentally opposed. Their arguments in support of the law were designed to preserve the political communities that made the pursuit of wisdom by a few rare and fortunate individuals possible. Moreover, if reason and revelation were as fundamentally opposed as the medieval Jewish and Islamic philosophers suggested, later modern philosophical attempts to synthesize rational natural science with biblical morality or ancient virtue were also fundamentally misguided. Each of the parts was more tenable than the attempted combinations. Strauss's studies of Maimonides and Alfarabi thus led him to give new and more original readings of the Bible and ancient philosophy that emphasized the conflict between them.

---

[37] Strauss, *PAW*, 13–14.

[38] Strauss, *PAW*, 14–15. In his essay on "How Farabi Read Plato's *Laws*," in *WPP*, 134–154, Strauss points out many other examples of ways in which Farabi inserted discussions that are not to be found in Plato's dialogue and ignored topics or whole parts (like the discussion of piety in Book 10) that are, in what appears at first glance, to be merely a boring "summary." In claiming that Strauss availed himself of the same "immunity of the commentator" in relating his own views through the mouths of Thrasymachus, Machiavelli, and Nietzsche, Shadia Drury fails to show the way in which Strauss's accounts of these thinkers obviously contradict what they say or wrote. *The Political Ideas of Leo Strauss* (New York: St. Martin's Press, 1988). See Catherine and Michael Zuckert, *The Truth about Leo Strauss* (Chicago: University of Chicago Press, 2006), for a more complete response to her claims.

According to Strauss, "what has taken place in the modern period has been a gradual corrosion and destruction of the heritage of Western civilization" (242). Modern political philosophy culminated in Nietzsche's declaration that "God is dead," and Heidegger's conclusion that the history of philosophy had come to an end. The "historical" turn in philosophy had not merely destroyed belief in human freedom and progress; the foundations of all moral standards had been erased along with belief in the biblical God and the possibility of knowledge.

The soul of the modern development... is a peculiar "realism," [which insists] that moral principles and appeal to moral principles... is ineffectual, and therefore that one has to seek a substitute...[first] in institutions and economics,... [but ultimately in] what was called "the historical process"... Once it became clear, however, that historical trends are absolutely ambiguous and, therefore, cannot serve as a standard,... no standard was left. (242)

However, Strauss's studies of medieval Jewish and Islamic philosophy had persuaded him that neither the end of rational inquiry nor the undermining of morality was an inevitable consequence of the history of philosophy. There was a "solution" to the "crisis of Western civilization." That was to "return" to its opposed "roots" and to live the tension between them. "This unresolved conflict... between the biblical and the philosophic notions of the good life is the secret of the vitality of Western civilization" (270) (for example, as opposed to "the market," the worldwide spread of liberal democracy or technological advancement). Strauss admitted that "the recognition of two conflicting roots of Western civilization is, at first, a very disconcerting observation." But he pointed out, "this realization has also something reassuring and comforting about it." If "the very life of Western civilization" arises from this fundamental tension, "there is no reason inherent in the Western civilization itself,... why it should give up life" (270). However, Western civilization would persist "only if we live that life, if we live that conflict." And preserving that life or tension at the core of Western civilization required a new understanding of its history.

Strauss admitted that "the whole history of the West presents itself at first glance as an attempt to harmonize, or to synthesize, the Bible and Greek philosophy" (245). Strauss suggested the opposition between the two roots had not been perceived or fully appreciated, partly because the Bible and the Greek philosophers agree on many of the core propositions of traditional morality (e.g., that murder, theft, and adultery are unqualifiedly bad). Further, both agree "that the proper framework of morality is the patriarchal family, which... forms the cell of a society in which the free adult males, and especially the old ones, predominate" (247). Both thus "insist on the superiority of the male sex." Both also deny the legitimacy of worshipping any human being. Finally, and most importantly, both "agree in assigning the highest praise among the virtues, not to courage or manliness, but to justice" (247). Because the unjust often appear to succeed better than the just, both the Bible and Greek philosophy agree, justice requires suprarational or suprasocietal support. But Strauss emphasized that the Bible and Greek philosophy disagree fundamentally about the character of the necessary support.

If everything that happens occurs because God or the gods will it, the composers of the Bible saw, the true God has to be one and omnipotent. Otherwise, this God will not be simply responsible for or the cause of what happens. If there is more than one god, the others will check and confound each other's wills. But an omnipotent God is not intelligible or predictable (and thus potentially controllable by those who come to understand Him). Especially if the law He gives to one particular people is to be understood to be the divine law, God must be understood to be essentially free to be as He shall be and do as He shall will. As Maimonides recognized, God and His will thus remain essentially mysterious. Right will prevail, if God wills it, but human beings will never be able to see how or to fathom the reasons why.

On the other hand, according to the Greek philosophers the source of justice and injustice, order and disorder, right and wrong must be sought in the impersonal forces that determine the character of the cosmos. As presented in Maimonides's *Guide* (and as more generally traditionally understood), the difference between the Bible and philosophy concerns the creation or eternity of the world. If the world is created, it is not and never can be made fully intelligible because everything depends ultimately on God's will. It is possible that someday swords may be made into plowshares (i.e., that human nature will change) so that wars will no longer occur. Everything is contingent (on the will of God); nothing exists necessarily or in itself. However, according to Greek philosophy the gods, like everything else, are subject to higher, more impersonal forces.[39] Although they disagreed about the specific character of these forces – be they the fates, properties of matter, or purely intelligible ideas – in no case did Greek philosophers think that anything could be fundamentally changed or altered. "What distinguishes the Bible from Greek philosophy is the fact that Greek philosophy is based on this

[39] In "Jerusalem and Athens," in *SPPP*, 165–166, Strauss argues that the demiurge in Plato's *Timaeus* is the closest ancient Greek figure to the biblical God. But, the demiurge follows the models of the eternal ideas (i.e., he does not create out of nothing).

premise: that there is such a thing as nature, or natures – a notion which has no equivalent in biblical thought" (253).

Strauss insisted the difference between "revelation" and "reason" cannot be settled at this "metaphysical" level because revelation does not rest on reason. The One Omnipotent God of the Bible is beyond human ken. Human reason is not capable of showing that it is impossible for such a God to exist because human reason cannot give a completely rational account of the whole, and so prove that there is no room for this God. Nor can the difference be decided on the basis of an argument about "human nature" because "the nature of man cannot be fully clarified except by an understanding of the nature of the whole," and such an understanding is not – and probably never will be – available (260).

How then are human beings supposed to live? The instinctively based Hobbesian war of all against all for self-preservation and recognition is surely not appealing. Nor are contracts or conventions based solely on self-interested calculations lasting or effective. Is the alternative then pious obedience from fear and love of the Lord? Or are we forced to rely on autonomous human reason, however faulty? Human beings appear to be confronted with an "abysmal" ungrounded choice.

In fact, Strauss suggests the "choice" between "faith" and "reason" cannot be made as such. It is not clear that one can "choose" to believe or to love God; one can at most act as if one does. Mere adherence to the law does not give one a righteous heart. Nor can one ground a life of pure reason on a choice without reason; such a "choice" would constitute "an act of will, of belief [in the superiority of reason to revelation], and that being based on belief is fatal to any philosophy."[40]

Strauss suggests what we see at the heart of "Western civilization" is a conflict between two understandings of the best form of human existence. Most human beings vacillate between the two. In their pure form, these two understandings belong to relatively small numbers of people – a few extremely reflective readers of the Bible and a few ancient philosophers.

The first is to be found in the Hebrew Bible or Torah. Rather than approach the Bible literally as the word of God, Strauss suggests that we can read the Bible as the compilation of many generations of compilers of "memories of ancient histories." Such "memories of memories are not necessarily distorting or pale reflections of the original; they may be re-collections of re-collections, deepening through meditation of the primary experiences."[41] The Bible begins reasonably at the beginning,

---

[40] Strauss "Preface to *SCR*," *LAM*, 256.
[41] Strauss, "Jerusalem and Athens," in *SPPP*, 151.

and one sees that there is an intelligible order to the events recounted. A modern natural scientist may think it strange, if not "irrational," that "light" is created before the sun. However, believing in the goodness of the One God and his Creation, the compilers of the Bible recognized that creation proceeded in stages, marked by distinctions (like Platonic *diareses*) or separations of different types of beings. The most important such distinction is between those things that do not move themselves (created in the first three days) and those which do (created in the last three days). (Not depending upon the sun, biblical "days" are, obviously, not like our days.) All stages of creation are said by God to be good except for the heavens and man. The creation of the heavens was not unambiguously good because the compilers of the Bible knew that many peoples worshipped the heavenly bodies rather than the one true God. As the second creation story shows, human beings were not simply obedient. Our nature is, or was, such that we had to learn about good and evil. We did not simply or automatically do good. Indeed, it took many generations and much suffering – continuing suffering – to teach human beings that they should obey, of their own free will, the covenant or law freely offered to them by God.[42] That God, we have already seen, is essentially mysterious because He is omnipotent – pure Will and absolutely Free. Human beings are images of the ruling principle of the world insofar as we are free, free to choose to do good or evil. In other words, the Bible is an expression of the view of human life and the world developed by those who meditated on the fact of human freedom and consequent morality, as not only the most distinctive but also the most distinguished feature of human life.

Precisely because human beings are free, it is not clear how we must or should live our lives. Greek philosophers, Plato and Aristotle in particular, thus suggested that we needed to use our reason, our most distinctive faculty, to find out. The alternative to the life of freedom or morality, as the highest human possibility, thus becomes the life of reason. That life is not based on the knowledge that everything is reasonable. Such knowledge is not available to human beings. Rather, the philosophical life is based on the perception that the right way of life is and remains a question, the "quest for knowledge [is] the most important thing, and therefore a life devoted to it the right way of life" (260). Like Alfarabi, Strauss identifies this original understanding of philosophy with Socrates. In Plato's *Apology of Socrates*, the philosopher admits that he does not know whether there is life after death; however, he is convinced that if there is, it will constitute a continuation of the life he has lived. His choice is not based on an arbitrary conviction or "faith";

[42] Strauss presents his most detailed reading of *Genesis* in "On the Interpretation of Genesis," in *JPCM*, 359–405.

it is based on his perception of the most pressing need. The philosopher "refuses assent to anything which is not evident to him and revelation is for him not more than an unevident, unproven possibility" (258–259).

Greek philosophers did not know the Bible, nor did the compilers of the Bible know Greek philosophy. But Strauss observed each nevertheless indicates awareness of the alternative. According to the Bible, the sin to be avoided is worship of the heavenly bodies. Human beings should not contemplate the motions of these bodies with wonder, much less seek the intelligible source of life on earth in them. On the other hand, according to the Greek philosophers tragedy presents a popular but ultimately false view of human existence as fundamentally "guilty," arousing pity (or piety) and fear (257).

Just as Maimonides took a "theoretical" view of the Law, so it seems that Strauss took a philosophical view of the tension between reason and revelation. He emphasized that "philosophy is quest for knowledge regarding the whole. Being essentially quest and being not able ever to become wisdom, as distinguished from philosophy, the problems are always more evident than the solutions" (260). Thus Strauss himself always emphasized the perennial problems. Although he repeatedly argued that reason could not refute revelation because revelation did not base its claims on reason, he himself clearly did not adopt an orthodox way of life.[43] He also insisted that "revelation, or rather theology" has never refuted philosophy. "For from the point of view of philosophy, first, revelation is only a possibility; and secondly, man, in

---

[43] In "Progress or Return?" Strauss concludes, "Philosophy is victorious as long as it limits itself to repelling the attack which theologians make on philosophy with the weapons of philosophy. But philosophy in its turn suffers a defeat as soon as it starts an offensive of its own, as soon as it tries to refute, not the necessarily inadequate proofs of revelation, but revelation itself" (266). In arguing that Strauss thought that philosophy could and did refute revelation by giving an account of its origin and historical development, Meier does not appear to pay sufficient attention to the distinction he himself quotes from Strauss, between "a philosophy which believes that it can refute the possibility of revelation – and a philosophy which does not believe that: this is the real meaning of *la querelle des anciens et des modernes*" (Meier, *Strauss and the Theologico-Political Problem*, 5). According to Strauss, ancient philosophy recognized the limits of its knowledge (marked in a way by revelation), whereas modern philosophy did not; and it was modern philosophy that Strauss thought was fatally based on a belief. Also abstracting from the difference between ancient and modern philosophy, Smith (*Reading Leo Strauss*) thinks that Strauss saw "the alternatives of reason and revelation as resting on an act of choice or faith" (17). However, in contrast to Meier, Smith (1) sees that Strauss equated "Jerusalem and Athens" with the "theologico-political problem" Strauss said was the theme of his work. Smith also recognizes that Strauss "denies that philosophy has or perhaps ever can refute the premises of the Bible" (126).

spite of what the theologians say, can live as a philosopher, that is to say, untragically" (269).

Precisely because the two understandings of the best form of human life were fundamentally opposed, Strauss argued that "no one can be both a philosopher and a theologian, or, for that matter, some possibility which transcends the conflict between philosophy and theology, or pretends to be a synthesis of both. But every one of us can be and ought to be either one or the other, the philosopher open to the challenge of theology, or the theologian open to the challenge of philosophy" (270). As a philosopher open to the challenge of theology, Strauss thought that he and anyone else who took such a position would be reminded that philosophy is and always will be only the search for wisdom because they would be reminded of the limits of human knowledge. Philosophy consists in a way of life whose mission is never completed or ended. On the other hand, theologians who opened themselves to the challenge of philosophy would be reminded that the inability of reason to refute revelation does not establish the truth of any particular form of revelation. To demonstrate the superior morality, much less truth, of any particular religion, one has to use reason. Recognizing the conflict would thus keep both traditional sources of human morality, nobility, and happiness alive.

Strauss's own position on reason and revelation could thus be described as a mirror image of Maimonides, the philosopher Strauss most admired. Like Maimonides, Strauss reasserts the traditional Jewish conviction that "being a Jew and being a philosopher are mutually exclusive."[44] But like a mirror image, Strauss's position also reversed certain aspects of Maimonides's argument. Where Maimonides emphasized the common conclusion from the two fundamentally different "metaphysical" arguments for the existence of God, Strauss insisted upon the fundamental incompatibility of their grounds. Likewise, whereas in his *Mishnah Torah* Maimonides clearly acknowledged the differences between ancient political and philosophical ethics on the one hand and Jewish law on the other, Strauss showed that the Bible and Greek philosophy converge at a practical level, not only in their moral teachings but also in insisting that human beings ought to obey the law (246–248).

In contrast to Maimonides, who wrote books primarily as a Jew for other Jews, Strauss wrote almost exclusively philosophical books for non-Jews.[45] And in these books, Strauss emphasized two other dichotomies or perennial problems as much, if not more, than the

[44] Strauss, *PAW*, 19.
[45] Strauss's lecture, "Why We Remain Jews," in *JPCM*, 311–356, might constitute an exception. Strauss himself did not publish this lecture.

difference between reason and revelation – the difference between the ancients and the moderns, and the tension between city and man. In "What Is Political Philosophy?" Strauss declared that the sole difference between the ancients and the moderns with regard to democracy could be traced to their different views of technology.[46] That difference is obviously linked to the conviction on the part of modern philosophers that nature must be transformed if human beings were to live safely and prosperously, and their consequent attempt to persuade their readers that the world was not created by a beneficent god. Modern philosophers hoped that people could be persuaded to adopt true opinions and thus become "enlightened." Ancient authors – both biblical and philosophical – did not think that the tension between the necessary and the desirable that gave rise to the contradictory opinions most human beings hold about what is just could be resolved. In this respect, Strauss himself appears to have agreed with the "ancients" – both biblical and philosophical.

Explaining why he had not returned to orthodoxy in the "Preface" he wrote to the English translation of *Spinoza's Critique of Religion*, Strauss admitted that as a youth he had been a Zionist. Like the young Germans he describes in his lecture on "German Nihilism," Strauss seems to have believed that the courage to unite and fight to defend the existence of one's own people constitutes the absolute minimum, if not definition, of human virtue.[47] However, under the influence of Franz Rosenzweig, Strauss came to see that the formation of a Jewish state, like any other state, would represent the effective destruction of what is distinctive about the Jewish people. They are the "chosen people," defined by the law they had received and obeyed as a result of their covenant with God. Strauss was not dissuaded from returning to the ways – and beliefs – of his fathers by modern critiques of the Bible or the findings of modern natural science. On the contrary, he had concluded relatively early that neither the claims of the "higher criticism" that developed on the basis of Spinoza's critique of miracles nor the findings of modern natural science could disprove revelation because revelation was not based on reason. However, Strauss could not leave the "disproof" of the claims of modern science at that because such a "disproof" in principle insulated any and every explicitly irrationally based claim from rational critique.

The problem for someone who was proud of their heritage and wanted to see it preserved was not the external critical or "rational" critique. The problem was that, as Jewish thinkers as different as Maimonides

---

[46] Strauss, "What is Political Philosophy," in *WPP*, 37.
[47] See Susan Shell, "'To Spare the Vanquished and Crush the Arrogant': Leo Strauss's Lecture on 'German Nihilism'," in this volume.

and Hermann Cohen had shown, strict obedience to the law that defined the Jewish people made the survival of a Jewish political community and thus of the Jewish people extremely precarious, if not simply impossible. The end of the community undercut the necessary means, and vice versa.

But Strauss also found the "Jewish" problem was not simply or solely Jewish; it was a human problem. The problem was – or at least at first sight appeared to be – the problem with which the medieval Jewish and Islamic philosophers had struggled. Founding and maintaining a political society required people to obey laws, which are formulated and defended in terms of contradictory opinions about what is just. These opinions are contradictory because they combine recognition of the necessary (e.g., production and war) with recognition of the desirable (e.g., freedom, pleasure, and wisdom).

If political communities are established, as Aristotle argued, not merely to preserve life but to enable their citizens to live well, neither the political communities themselves nor their individual members can achieve that goal without questioning the contradictory opinions that lead to the formation of the communities in the first place. Nor can the contradictions be eradicated merely by showing that they are contradictions. The contradictions reflect the disparate needs and inclinations of beings who have both minds and bodies.

In his famous reading of Plato's *Republic*, Strauss argued that Socrates and his companions never come to a completely adequate definition of justice (or the just in itself).[48] What their conversation shows are the reasons why no actual city will ever be just, that is, the limitations or definition of the political. To have just rule (for the common good), cities must have rulers who have nothing to gain for themselves by ruling. The only such rulers, even potentially, are philosophers, not because they know the ideas of the virtues and can impress them on the souls of their fellow citizens, but simply because they love and thus seek truth or wisdom rather than safety, wealth, glory, or power (which philosophers recognize are at most transient goods). However, precisely because these philosophers have nothing to gain for themselves by ruling, they will not want to rule. Nor would it be just of any community that does not provide them with their philosophical education to force them to rule. After suggesting that a rhetorician like Thrasymachus might persuade the people to accept philosophers as rulers, in his famous description of what would happen if the philosophers returned to the cave Plato then shows how angry people become when a philosopher directly challenges the truth of their opinions. He knew that the Athenians had killed

---

[48] Strauss, "On Plato's *Republic*," in *CM*, 50–138.

Socrates for doing just that, even though Socrates had stayed away from the assembly and did not try to rule.

Strauss did not seek merely to revive or literally to return to medieval Jewish or Islamic, or even to ancient, political philosophy. On the contrary, he explicitly recognized that such a return was neither possible nor desirable. In his introduction to *The City and Man*, he cautions:

We cannot reasonably expect that a fresh understanding of classical political philosophy will supply us with recipes for today's use. For the relative success of modern political philosophy has brought into being a kind of society wholly unknown to the classics, a kind of society to which the classical principles as stated and elaborated by the classics are not immediately applicable. Only we living today can possible find a solution to the problems of today.[49]

Moreover, in his essay on "Machiavelli" Strauss declares that "the restoration of the ancient modes and orders is in all cases, including that of Machiavelli himself [and presumably Strauss], the introduction of new modes and orders."[50]

Strauss sought "merely" to revive the questions that had given rise to ancient political philosophy by showing that neither the "progressive" accounts of the history of philosophy, which claimed that later philosophers solved the problems posed by their predecessors, nor the more "pessimistic" late modern accounts of the end of the history of philosophy were well founded. By reraising the questions or irreconcilable "tensions," Strauss explicitly admitted that none of the previously given answers or solutions was adequate.[51] Like Alfarabi, Strauss understood himself to be attempting to revive philosophy "after it has been blurred or destroyed." Strauss thus presented his philosophy in an explicitly political or "Platonic" framework.[52] Strauss saw that the future of philosophy as a way of life was threatened in an unprecedented way in modern times by the logic of the development of modern philosophy, as well as by the threatened establishment of a totalitarian world-state whose ideology and technology would make all questioning or dissent

---

[49] Strauss, *CM*, 11.

[50] Strauss, "Niccolo Machiavelli," in *SPPP*, 223.

[51] Strauss, "Restatement on Xenophon," in *OT*, 196: "Philosophy as such is nothing but genuine awareness of the problems...It is impossible to think about these problems without becoming inclined toward a solution, ... Yet as long as there is no wisdom but only quest for wisdom, the evidence of all solutions is necessarily smaller than the evidence of the problems."

[52] See Strauss, "On Classical Political Philosophy," in *WPP*, 92–94, for Strauss's definition of "political philosophy," and the reasons why he could give a book containing essays on medieval and modern philosophers as well as ancient the title, *Studies in Platonic Political Philosophy*.

impossible.[53] New circumstances called for new responses, including new readings or critiques of the "Western tradition" and the history of philosophy. Because Strauss was reconceiving the Western tradition from its very inception or "roots" in order to revive old questions and therewith the original understanding of philosophy as a way of life, he could and did describe his own work as a "return."

[53] Strauss, *OT*, 211.

6   Leo Strauss and the Problem
of the Modern*

MODERNITY AS A PHILOSOPHICAL PROBLEM

Because I am going to argue that Leo Strauss's understanding of the problem of the modern has numerous affiliations with the thought of Martin
Heidegger, it would be remiss of me not to begin with an etymology,
a procedure often followed by Heidegger in his ontological (and post-
ontological) musings. The etymology I have in mind also prepares us
to appreciate the links between Hegel and Strauss, despite the relative
silence of the latter concerning the former.

According to the unabridged Oxford English dictionary, the word
"modern" goes back to sixth-century CE Latin, and means "made just
now," by analogy with *hodiernus*, "made" today (i.e., "just recently" but
not just now). Etymologies are not philosophical arguments but they
help us understand what we are arguing about. If only for introductory
purposes, it is helpful to hear the resonances of *modus* – order, measure,
moderation, and *modo* – "just now, lately" and its opposite, "some
time ago."

We may take one more speculative step, in keeping with both the
etymologizing of the ancients and the dialectics of the moderns, to
identify "modern" as a self-contradictory term. Its linguistic ancestry is
both constitutive and dissolute, and it is thus a simulacrum of time. The
term "modern" thus qualifies as an example of what Hegel means when
he speaks of philosophical or speculative words, and it also expresses
the restlessness of the modern spirit, as Hegel refers to it. This comes
very close to the Straussian understanding of the fundamental defect of
the modern spirit. The modern is what is happening in an indeterminate
"now." As such, it is dissolving before our very eyes.

Of course, my point is not that Leo Strauss was a professing Hegelian.
I rather wish to indicate the subterranean connection between Strauss's
approach to the political problem of modernity and what used to be
called "metaphysics." This is all the more necessary because Strauss

* My thanks to David Botwinik for his invaluable help in the preparation of this
manuscript.

tends to avoid extensive metaphysical analyses and presents himself as a historian of political thought. I shall return to this point shortly. But let us first remind ourselves of the most accessible and inclusive features of Strauss's account of the problem of modernity.

Stated with introductory brevity, Strauss sees the problem as arising from the assault by partisans of modern science against *philosophia perennis*, in the service of the attempt to make humankind the masters and possessors of nature.Perhaps the two most important goals of this attempt, to which we may refer for the sake of brevity as the Enlightenment, are to free mankind from the bonds of religion and to employ the methods of mathematical reasoning to resolve ethical and political problems. The attempt to achieve these goals leads to the development of the modern doctrine of subjectivity and the attendant conception of intelligible order as a product of the constructive faculties of human cognition, and in particular of the imagination. In sum, the pursuit of freedom comes to be indistinguishable from the steady dissolution of spontaneity.

Let us be clear from the beginning: Strauss is neither a Luddite nor an irrational reactionary. But neither is he a heterodox eccentric, or for that matter a revolutionary thinker who is misunderstood because of the great originality of his views. This should be obvious from his general response to the two claims or goals of the Enlightenment. Strauss accepts the widely held view that religious faith cannot be refuted by reason, and he holds that the attempt to make mathematics the exclusive paradigm of reason leads to the impossibility of a rational distinction between good and evil, and so to the replacement of the virtues by the passions.[1]

The purpose of the preceding paragraph was not at all to trivialize Strauss's accomplishments but to dispel some of the notoriety that has come to surround him. A large part, but not all, of this notoriety stems from his rediscovery of the tradition of esotericism, or the presentation of dangerous political and religious views under a veil of prudence. I lack the space to discuss this point at length, but I must observe that Strauss himself has published his discoveries very widely. There is not much secrecy remaining about the matter. Erudition to one side, the point is self-evident in actual political practice. One can therefore suggest with great plausibility that in crucial respects, Strauss is a modern rather than an ancient. This is the argument that underlies the approach to Strauss by way of Nietzsche, and sooner rather than later, of Heidegger.

It should be easy to see that the recommendation of a return to the past is the mark of a modern. I can illustrate this by a reference

[1] Compare "Progress or Return," in *RCPR*, 143, and Descartes' *Les passions de l'ame*.

to Husserlian phenomenology, and in particular to the doctrine of de-sedimentation, which played a crucial role in the thinking of both Heidegger and Strauss. Husserl wished to return to the presence of the pure phenomenon (let us call it "being") by removing the various layers of perceptual, historical, and doctrinal detritus that have concealed it from our view. The return to the origin, namely, things in themselves, is thus designed to exhibit the foundation upon which we can build the presupposition-less and absolute starting points of a purified science.

In short, our goal as phenomenologists is the future, not the past, from which we seek to liberate ourselves by employing the proper method. We should note the sense in which this is also true for Strauss, despite all appearances to the contrary. The return from modernity by way of a "deconstruction" of the past is not designed to reinstitute a bogus version of the Greek *polis* but to rehabilitate the present for the sake of the future.

In the case of Heidegger, the situation is quite different. Husserl and Strauss are both secular thinkers. Both accept the primacy of theory over practice, and so too of reason over faith (we note that Strauss uses reason to prove that reason cannot refute faith). However, Heidegger is a prophet, and the scope of his prophecy is that of the entire history of Being, that is, of the concealment of Being by the production of beings. From this standpoint, Husserl and Strauss are provincials in comparison with Heidegger, who follows Nietzsche in this crucial sense: he wishes to destroy the corrupt and hopelessly nihilist values and doctrines, not only of his day but of the entire epoch of the Western tradition. The prophet instructs us to clear the ground of the tradition to make room for the coming of some future God.

STRAUSS AND HEIDEGGER

My intention in the first section of this essay was to situate the problem of the modern in the context of its theoretical presuppositions. Modernity is not simply a historical period but a metaphysical condition of the human spirit.For obvious reasons, I could touch only on the chapter headings. However, it should be clear that for Nietzsche, Husserl, and Heidegger, the content of the first chapter of our investigation of the problem of the modern is not political. The same cannot be said of Strauss. No competent person could question his erudition or the philosophical penetration in which it was grounded. But it is undeniable that there is a certain incongruity between his perception of the depths and his exposition of their content.

No doubt this is partly to be explained as a consequence of his habitual lucidity as a teacher, but that cannot be the whole story. Much more important is that for Strauss, "the problem inherent in the surface of things, and only in the surface of things, is the heart of things."[2] I take this to be a concise expression of his version of the phenomenological method. But is it entirely adequate to the depths?

Heidegger has often been criticized for the obscurity of his philosophical writing. In view of the difficulty of his authorial intentions, one might wish to say that Heidegger's texts are insufficiently obscure. On the other hand, Strauss was for the most part a practitioner of standard academic prose, with certain striking exceptions at the beginning and toward the end of his academic career. With all due acknowledgment of these exceptions, one can fairly say that Strauss's literary style was in general straightforward and professorial. In this respect, it reflected the sobriety of his thinking. From time to time, he would rise from the level of sobriety to the polemical, as for example when denouncing the defects of the communist regime in Russia or defending religion against the unsatisfactory criticism of the modern Enlightenment. I can best express my perception of Strauss as a writer or public lecturer by saying that he was never raucous and even his wit reminded me of Aristotle rather than Plato.

In slightly different terms, Strauss's literary style was attuned, not to the music of the spheres, but to the common sense and equable temperament of what Aristotle called the "serious man" (ho spoudaios). Strauss often spoke of the divine Platonic mania, but his public exhibitions of this attribute, so necessary for philosophy, were few and far between. And so I raise the question again: Is common-sense intelligence adequate to the task of eliciting philosophical mania? In other words, is it possible to discover the beginning of philosophy in the de-sedimented phenomena of everyday life? Incidentally, it is in this context that the question, much discussed by Strauss's students, can best be treated, namely, the question of whether Strauss himself practiced esotericism. I note only that if he did, it was as a modern rather than an ancient form. And we have his testimony to the greater difficulty of the latter.[3]

To return to the main argument, Strauss also practiced a kind of deconstruction or de-sedimentation of the traditional history of philosophy. As we have seen, he did not attempt to demonstrate the defects of traditional rationalism in the Heideggerian manner, but rather to show the disastrous consequences of its misuse in the study of human affairs. I am thinking in particular of Strauss's famous critique of the fact-value distinction of modern social science. But this critique is innocuous compared to Heidegger's deconstruction (more bluntly stated, his destruction) of Western European rationalism. It is quite clear from Strauss's

[2] Strauss, *TM*, 13.
[3] Strauss, *PAW*, 33.

own words that he has no adequate defense against Heidegger's fundamental views, nor does he find any prospect of assistance in the various
philosophical positions of his day.[4]

The question therefore arises: How are we to protect ourselves against
Heidegger? Stated in a more accessible manner, how are we to defend
Greek rationalism of the Socratic type, namely, what Heidegger calls
"Platonism," and thereby avoid the nihilism of our own day? As we
have seen, Strauss himself is not a metaphysician; he takes his bearings
by *doksa* ("opinion") or the everyday, that is to say, by the political
or pretheoretical. Is this anything more than a propaedeutic to theory?
Certainly, it does not seem to be a robust basis for the pursuit of Being.

The late-modern or contemporary philosopher who has been educated
in the Kantian tradition will object to Strauss that Husserl's *Lebenswelt*
("life-world") and Heidegger's "average everydayness" are both theoretically superior to the Straussian appropriation of the Socratic starting
point in *doksa*. Strauss would reply that the methods of both thinkers
are excellent examples of his main thesis, namely, that they exhibit
the triumph of modern science, whether in the form of descriptive phenomenology or Heidegger's ontological method. In both cases, very far
from being transparent analyses of "ordinary language" (to use another
example of scientistic reasoning), these thinkers impose a theoretical
superstructure onto their preferred linguistic phenomena, which are
thereby transformed from the things in themselves to human constructions.

The steady transformation in modern philosophy of the Greek *logos*
into concepts results eventually in the triumph of subjectivity. The
search for conceptual precision leads paradoxically to the identification
of form as a product of the cognitive process. Thinking is now understood as making, and this would of course be true with respect to our
standards of intelligibility, but in the first instance, to our highest values. Rank-ordering is transformed into the expression of personal taste.
De gustibus non disputandum est. The highest form of praise is to say
of some expression of principle, "I can live with that," or "I am com-
fortable with that."

This is what Strauss refers to frequently as "historicism," a pejorative
term for the repudiation of the paradigm of a stable nature on behalf of
the changing philosophical perspectives of human subjectivity.[5] Perhaps
his most important argument on behalf of the advantages of classical
over modern political philosophy is based upon the claim that Plato and
Aristotle are in direct touch with the political phenomena. They see,

---

[4] Strauss, "An Introduction to Heideggerian Existentialism," in *RCPR*, 29–30.
[5] Strauss, "Political Philosophy and History," in *WPP*, 56ff.

or are in a position to see, political things as they are in everyday life, without the distortions of tradition by history, or what we call today "ideology." As Strauss says, "it was only after the classical philosophers had done their work that political philosophy became definitely 'established' and thus acquired a certain remoteness from political life."[6]

This argument is not entirely clear. Strauss seems to assume what requires to be proved, namely, that the classical prephilosophical view of human nature is not the residue of some still earlier and mistaken belief about our direct access to political things. Nor has Strauss shown that some still more adequate conception of human nature will never appear in the future.

The Straussian argument seems to boil down to this: If everything changes its nature, then there is no nature, and so no genuine knowledge, but only transient beliefs. That was evident in the point about the direct access to nature by the classical political philosophers. This thesis is vulnerable to the following objection. We should not overlook the fact that the claim that everything is historical is not equivalent to the claim that everything is permissible. Nietzsche's doctrine of the eternal return of the same is specifically designed to overcome this equivalence. So far as I know, Hegel is the first major philosopher to offer a detailed exposition of the overcoming of history in the traditional sense with the tools of dialectical logic. I cannot develop this point here, but will say only that some truths emerge with the passage of time.

One last observation in this series of remarks. Even if Greek political thought is by nature transparent throughout history, why does this guarantee the superiority of the natural to human creations of a new political organization in postclassical or postmodern times? The argument on behalf of modernity, that is, of the relief of man's estate, can be made by appeal to considerations of nobility, which are equally cogent in comparison to those of classical antiquity. The quarrel between the ancients and the moderns has not been settled, nor is it likely that a conclusion will ever be reached, so long as human nature remains the same.

MODERNITY AND SECULARIZATION

Strauss combats the constructivism of the partisans of modernity by means of the rehabilitation of eternity. Let me clarify this statement with the assistance of a reference to Hans Blumenberg's massive work, *The Legitimacy of the Modern Age.* Strauss's name appears in one passage in this work, which was written primarily to defend against the implicit attack upon modernity instigated by partisans of the

[6] Strauss, "On Classical Political Philosophy," in *WPP*, 78.

secularization thesis (that modernity is a secularized version of medieval Christian Europe).[7] According to Blumenberg, this thesis makes the modern age a derivative of medieval rationalism. To the contrary, for Strauss the rationalism of great medieval thinkers like Maimonides was more reasonable than that of the moderns, who turn reason into a derivative of freedom and spontaneity.

Blumenberg, who was given to the writing of very large volumes, is now out of fashion but his book on modernity achieved a wide currency in Europe and the United States. In it, we find at the foundation of Blumenberg's argument the following response to a criticism of Carl Schmitt, the conservative German political philosopher who played a peripheral but not insignificant role in the thoughts of the young Strauss. Schmitt charges that Blumenberg legitimates modernity through its newness or as a creation *ex nihilo*. Blumenberg denies this and characterizes his central concept as "the principle of a sufficient rationality." "It is just enough to accomplish the postmedieval self-assertion and to bear the consequences of this emergency self-consolidation. The concept of the legitimacy of the modern age is not derived from the accomplishments of reason but rather from the necessity of those accomplishments."[8]

One might refer to Blumenberg's substitution of sufficiency for necessity as feeble Hegelianism. Necessity returns in the immediate sequel, but in the hundreds of pages of this massive volume no explanation is given of how to reconcile necessity and the spontaneity of historical thinking. In Hegelian language, there is no completion of the revelation in human thought of the nature of dialectical reasoning. If Strauss owes us an ontological assessment and defense of eternity, Blumenberg is equally if complementarily remiss in not rescuing his fundamental principle of spontaneity from sheer contingency. Blumenberg is a neo-Kantian tinctured with a diluted form of Hegelian historicism. The necessity of history is for Blumenberg what Strauss calls a "dispensation of fate," which refers above all others to Heidegger.[9] Schmitt uses the language of the will as a surrogate for freedom; his is a philosophy of decisionism.

Strauss speaks relatively little about Hegel, even in the famous reply to Alexandre Kojève's review of Strauss's commentary on Xenophon's *On Tyranny*. But as I have tried to suggest, Strauss uses the Greeks to criticize modernity as Kojève uses Hegel to surpass the ancients. Socrates tells us that he knows nothing, except that he does not know,

---

[7] Hans Blumenberg, *The Legitimacy of the Modern Age*, trans. Robert M. Wallace (Cambridge, MA: MIT Press, 1985), 55.

[8] Blumenberg, *Legitimacy of the Modern Age*, 98–99.

[9] Strauss, "What is Political Philosophy," in *WPP*, 26–27.

whereas Hegel claims to know everything essential. These are the two extreme points of Western European philosophy. The problem of the modern is whether these points can bend back upon themselves, or in other words unite in such a way as to mediate and so resolve the quarrel between the ancients and the moderns. Without such a resolution, each step forward of the modern dialectic is also a step backward: the night in which all cows are black, to use Hegel's definition of nihilism as it arises in Schelling.

I have been arguing that Strauss's critique of modernity, although at its surface is political, takes us directly to the depths, and thus not to politics but to what used to be called metaphysics and is now known as ontology. For example, in the passage of *Natural Right and History* cited by Blumenberg, Strauss says that secularization "is a modification of the traditional belief in Providence": "Secularization is the 'temporalization' of the spiritual or of the eternal."[10] What makes Strauss difficult to understand is his failure to carry through his argument at its own proper level. Too much simplicity is sometimes worse than too little. Strauss's ultimate target is Heidegger, who claims to be preparing a new way of thinking that, once it is accessible, will have as a consequence the authentic contemplation of human being. In other words, political philosophy is not possible so long as we think incorrectly of Being. The first step in the rectification of thinking is the aforementioned destructive analysis of the history of philosophy, a destruction to which we may refer as the temporalization of the eternal.

Strauss sometimes gives the impression that the inoculation of contemporary students against Heideggerian nihilism itself begins with the study of Xenophon. With all due respect, the victory of the moderns is not going to be avoided, or even postponed, under the leadership of Xenophon, even though his name, as Strauss liked to point out, means "Killer of Strangers," and who was himself a general. In Straussian language, we need a frontal attack on Heidegger, not an elusive and playful reference to Xenophon's prose style.

To clarify this remark, Strauss was famous for his admiration for Jane Austen, whose prose style he regarded as a suitable introduction to an appreciation of Xenophon. The point cuts deeper than one may initially suppose, and is worth expanding. In his study of the *Hiero*, Strauss is in the process of explaining the difference between ancient and modern rhetoric:

We are in need of a second education in order to accustom our eyes to the noble reserve and the quiet grandeur of the classics. Xenophon, as it were, limited himself to cultivating exclusively that character of classical writing, which is

---

[10] Strauss, *NRH*, 317.

wholly foreign to the modern reader. No wonder that he is today despised and ignored. An unknown ancient critic, who must have been a man of uncommon discernment, called him most bashful. Those modern readers who are so fortunate as to have a natural preference for Jane Austen rather than for Dostoievski, in particular, have an easier access to Xenophon than others might have.[11]

This passage leads us to wonder whether whatever may be true of Xenophon also holds good for Plato, Strauss's highest authority. However this may be, the passage in question allows us to introduce Strauss's quarrel with modernity in a pleasant way, thereby acting in accord with Xenophon's assertion that "[i]t is both noble and just, and pious and more pleasant, to remember the good things rather than the bad ones." Strauss glosses this assertion as follows: "In the *Hiero* Xenophon experimented with the pleasure that comes from remembering bad things, with a pleasure that admittedly is of doubtful morality and piety."[12] At first glance, Strauss seems to be praising the greater piety of Xenophon in contrast with those moderns who prefer Dostoevsky to Jane Austen. However, a moment's reflection shows us that Xenophon is capable of enjoying impious as well as pious pleasures, namely, those associated with tyranny. Another moment, and the question arises: Who was more pious, Austen or Dostoevsky? Stated more frankly, who exhibits the superior way of life, Austen or Dostoevsky?

What Strauss admires in Jane Austen is her Xenophontic reticence. But reticence with respect to what? Must we not say that Austen's adherence to upper middle-class piety is the exoteric surface of an indictment of the vulgarity and selfishness of modern society? Nor is it entirely clear, to say the least, that Dostoevsky has a narrower and more "modern" insight into the human soul than does Austen. The question can only be raised here: Who has more to teach us about the defects attributed to modern life by Strauss? And finally, is it not the height of romanticism to adopt as one's paradigm for society the exoteric rhetoric of eighteenth-century snobbism?

Strauss's obvious wish to reformulate the style of modernity in accord with Jane Austen (or if worst comes to worst, with the style of Macaulay or even Winston Churchill), if fulfilled, would not lead simply to the excision of Dostoevsky from modern culture. It would also lead to the rejection of Tolstoy, not to mention Henry James, Marcel Proust, and Thomas Mann. Our playful if somewhat impious consideration of Jane Austen may help us to understand the Straussian rhetoric with respect to the quarrel between the ancients and moderns. Of course, Strauss was well aware that there is no actual return to the past. Only moderns wish

[11] Strauss, "Restatement on Xenophon's *Hiero*," in *OT*, 185.
[12] Strauss, "Restatement on Xenophon's *Hiero*," *OT*, 185.

for such a return. Nevertheless, it is interesting to see him forgetting for a moment his own strictures on the interpretation of politics by means of references to literary style.[13] Let us turn now to a less playful but not, we may hope, less pleasant consideration of Strauss's dissection of the problem of modernity. I shall develop my analysis with the initial assistance of brief passages from Strauss's accounts of Machiavelli, Hobbes, Spinoza, and Rousseau.

THE FOUNDING FATHERS OF MODERNITY

We begin with a passage from Strauss's detailed study of Machiavelli:

> Machiavelli addresses his passionate and muted call to the young, to men whose prudence has not enfeebled their youthful vigor of mind, quickness, militancy, impetuosity, and audacity. Reason, youth, and modernity rise up against authority, old age, and antiquity. In studying the *Discourses*, we become the witnesses, and we cannot help becoming the moved witnesses, of the birth of that greatest of all youth movements: modern philosophy, a phenomenon that we know through seeing, as distinguished from reading, only in its decay, its state of depravation and its dotage.[14]

In other words, the modern revolution has already failed. On this central point, Strauss is very close to Nietzsche. The nineteenth century is to the eighteenth century for Nietzsche what the twentieth century is to the nineteenth for Strauss.[15] However, Machiavelli sees himself not, like Nietzsche, as the decadent prophet of creativity but rather as the *consigliere* of the young in heart.

"He who must be a creator always destroys," as Zarathustra expresses it.[16] Strauss's Machiavelli sets into motion the creation of modernity by radicalizing and accelerating the dissolution of antiquity. But this dissolution, intended to liberate humankind from the philosophy and morality of the ancients, dissolves nature instead, thus blocking if not destroying the Cartesian extension of the Machiavellian revolution. In attempting to become "like the masters and possessors of nature," the late moderns succeeded instead in destroying nature. The return to nature has been blocked by the very weapon that allowed us to progress to an amazing degree in the mastery of nature: modern science.

---

[13] Strauss, "Thucydides: The Meaning of Political History," in *RCPR*, 102.

[14] Strauss, *TM*, 126–127.

[15] Friedrich Nietzsche, *Götzen-Dämmerung* in *Sämtliche Werke*, ed. Colli-Montinari (Berlin: Walter de Gruyter, 1989), 6: 152.

[16] Nietzsche, *Zarathustra*, Part I, Section XV, "Of a Thousand and One Goals," in *Sämtliche Werke*, 4: 75.

Our next proof-text is from Strauss's discussion of Hobbes:

I had seen that the modern mind had lost its self-confidence or its certainty of having made decisive progress beyond pre-modern thought; and I saw that it was turning into nihilism, or what is in practice the same thing, fanatical obscurantism. I concluded that the case of the moderns against the ancients must be reopened, without any regard to cherished opinions or convictions, *sine ira et studio*. I concluded in other words that we must learn to consider seriously, i.e., detachedly, the possibility that Swift was right when he compared the modern world to Lilliput and the ancient world to Brobdingnag.[17]

The self-confidence of the modern world stems from the extraordinary achievements of its science and technology. But science and technology speak the language of mathematics. There is no mathematical justification of mathematics. We are forced to look elsewhere, and this blurs our vision. Strauss characterizes these processes as relativism and historicism. Just as for the extreme empiricist, we are in immediate contact with sensations out of which everything else is produced, so too in modern formalism the axioms and deductive procedures of scientific reasoning come to be understood as artifacts. In this case, does not the difference between mathematical universals and subjective constructions from sensation disappear, to be replaced by the history of human production? As the Marxists used to say, "Man makes himself," but how can we keep this view separate from the self-destructive claim that man makes intelligible order?

As seen through Straussian eyes, the problem of the modern is that it devolves into the postmodern. What looks like nihilism with a human face is instead trans-human, and not as far removed from mathematical thinking as one might believe. At the same time, there is a solid stratum of Nietzscheanism in the modern conception of self-construction. Where there is no rank-ordering, power supervenes as the highest, and indeed as the only value. This can be seen in both Hobbes and Spinoza, as the following passage from *Spinoza's Critique of Religion* indicates:

Hobbes rejects the conception of *beatitudo* propounded by the ethical thinkers of antiquity, and replaces it by the prospect of endless progress from desire to desire, from power to ever greater power, and establishes, by reason of this conception of happiness, positive science as foundation of technology. Spinoza stands incomparably closer to original Epicureanism [than does Hobbes,] since he holds fast to the classical view of *beatitudo* and sees science as a means of obtaining to *beatitudo*, a stable condition complete in itself.[18]

---

[17] Strauss, *PPH*, xv.
[18] Strauss, *SCR*, 210.

What Hegel refers to as the restlessness of the modern spirit thus has its source in the Hobbesian conception of power, which prepares the way for modern empiricism (especially in Locke) as well as Nietzsche's creative nihilism. The problem of modernity arises from the steady and combined advance of two opposing forces: the exhilaration of Machiavelli's youth movement and the metaphysical anxiety that is epitomized by Locke's "joyless quest for joy."[19] One thinks here of Hobbes's treatment of death as the source of significance for human life.[20] Nor can we avoid thinking of Heidegger's "Being unto death" as the ostensible replacement of eternal values by a self-projected grounding of finitude. Joylessness is not so far removed from restlessness, alienation, and anxiety. Ironically enough, these attributes emerge from the consequences of the presumed condition for happiness, namely, freedom from nature.[21] This assertion should be made more precise. Whereas Hobbes and Locke replace happiness with pain, fear, and death, Spinoza understands freedom as the self-determination of reason.[22] Strauss is surely correct to see here a repudiation of scripture. Modern philosophy in general replaces the creation *ex nihilo* with the creation out of reason. Despite all talk of eternity, the eternal is replaced by the constructed, and poetry wins its long-standing quarrel with philosophy. However, instead of the happiness of the philosopher, history vindicates the suffering of the artist.

In *Natural Right and History*, Strauss offers the following summary of Rousseau's critique of modernity:

Rousseau attacked modernity in the name of two classical ideas: the city and virtue, on the one hand, and nature, on the other. "The ancient politicians spoke unceasingly of manners and virtue; ours speak of nothing but trade and money." Trade, money, enlightenment, the emancipation of acquisitiveness, luxury, and the belief in the omnipotence of legislation are characteristics of the modern state... Manners and virtue are at home in the city.

By the latter term, Rousseau refers to the ancients, and in particular to Rome. Geneva is the best of the modern cities but its citizens lack "the public spirit or the patriotism of the ancients."[23]

The reference to nature points toward the state of nature, not the *phusis* of natural science. Strauss summarizes Rousseau's thought as the tension between the return to the city and the return to the state of nature.[24] Rousseau's position with respect to natural science, at least in

---

[19] Strauss, *NRH*, 251.
[20] Strauss, *PPH*, 116.
[21] Strauss, *SCR*, 207.
[22] Strauss, *SCR*, 210–211.
[23] Strauss, *NRH*, 253–254.
[24] Strauss, *NRH*, 254.

the *First Discourse*, is quite close to that of Bacon in the *New Atlantis*. Science in the modern sense is allowed to develop, as Bacon puts it, in caves on high mountains and beneath the earth; in other words, its development and publication or concealment depends upon the opinions of the scientific elite.[25] The historical destiny of science in the last two centuries suggests strongly that the hope of controlling science for the sake of political virtue is an illusion. But we shall have to reconsider this point in the following.

MODERNITY'S SELF-OVERCOMING

One does not find this illusion in Strauss's presentation of his own thesis, but he is not exactly forthcoming on his view of the matter. He tells us in the Introduction to *Natural Right and History*:

Natural right in its classic form is connected with a teleological view of the universe. All natural beings have a natural end, a natural destiny, which determines what kind of operation is good for them. In the case of man, reason is required for discerning these operations: reason determines what is by nature right with ultimate regard to man's natural end. The teleological view of the universe, of which the teleological view of man forms a part, would seem to have been destroyed by natural science.[26]

Strauss increases the ambiguity by saying "would seem" rather than "has." We are then left with the need for a nonteleological view of natural science and a teleological science of man. "The fundamental dilemma in whose grip we [modern men] are, is caused by the victory of modern natural science. An adequate solution to the problem of natural right cannot be found before this basic problem has been solved."[27]

Strauss does not say whether a solution is possible. Because he rejects all modern solutions, and in view of the extraordinary progress of modern science, and in particular of technology, we are left to assume that the situation is hopeless. I find this odd because it is substantiated by a tacit and unargued repudiation of the independence from each other of cosmology and the understanding of human nature. To put it crudely but (in my view) correctly, Strauss rejects all available resolutions to the dialectic of man and nature because he rejects all systematic resolutions. But what if the solution is in the reiteration of the problem, as Strauss himself regularly suggests? As Strauss insisted, reason and system are not synonyms. There is also the reason of common sense,

---

[25] Francis Bacon, *New Atlantis*, in *Selected Writings of Francis Bacon*, intro. Hugh G. Dick (New York: Modern Library, 1955), 574–575.

[26] Strauss, *NRH*, 7–8.

[27] Strauss, *NRH*, 8.

not to mention the intuition of pure forms. Otherwise stated, according to Strauss's interpretation of Socrates, the doctrine of the pure forms or Ideas is meant to found the independence of human from cosmological nature, and so the independence of political thought from natural science. Strauss refers to this as the doctrine of noetic heterogeneity. This doctrine goes back to the Socrates of Xenophon and Plato for both of whom "the key for the understanding of the whole is the fact that the whole is characterized by what I shall call noetic heterogeneity" and it seems to overcome the problem of teleology, which can now be said to manifest itself differently in human affairs than it does in pure theory.[28] The Idea of the soul, and so the soul itself, is accessible independently of the Idea of the cosmos.

In this connection, I note that Strauss distinguishes between human things or affairs and human nature.[29] He might thus wish to indicate that the understanding of human nature is for Socrates a part of the understanding of nature as a whole. If this is right, it establishes a dualism of praxis and physics, and once again a teleology of praxis is different from and need not depend upon a teleology of natural science. However Strauss envisioned the solution to this problem, assuming that he did so, the recuperation of classical political philosophy does not seem to depend upon a monotonic conception of nature.

As I noted previously, Strauss knew very well that there is no simple return to the classics.[30] His abiding political concern was to apply an analogue of Husserlian de-sedimentation, that is, of the removal of the dominant strands of the European tradition to return to the natural level of human praxis, not to reinstitute the Greek *polis* but to serve as a paradigm for the mitigation of the modern political problem.

I have in effect been arguing on behalf of Strauss that the entire modern movement, namely, the attempt to free humankind from the scientific and political doctrines of the classical tradition, is self-contradictory. The mathematical paradigm of rationality provides the horizon of progress for modernity. But the paradigm is incapable of certifying its own claims, which gradually deteriorate into free creations of the human spirit. The announcement that we have freed ourselves from the hostility or indifference of nature renders us slaves to nature, that is, to mechanism or chance.

At the same time, I have raised the question whether Strauss has himself triumphed over modernity. Or shall we say, has he shown that the traditional modernity of Jane Austen is inferior to the pure classicism

[28] Strauss, "The Problem of Socrates," in *RCPR*, 132.
[29] Strauss, *CM*, 13.
[30] Strauss, *CM*, 6–11.

of Xenophon? The Straussian reply is not free of ambiguity. He says it is impossible to return to the unimpeded institution of classical political philosophy. On the other hand, the loss in confidence of the spokesmen for modernity, which is attributed to the self-professed inability to make value-judgments, makes it possible for us to employ historical de-sedimentation and thus to return to the natural or pretheoretical (and preideological) level of human nature: to a direct perception of the political phenomena.[31]

The problem here is that the reasoning begs the question. The return to the pretheoretical rank-ordering of natural political life depends upon the accessibility of historical de-sedimentation. In Strauss's own words:

Classical political philosophy is non-traditional, because it belongs to the fertile moment when all political traditions were shaken, and there was not yet in existence a tradition of political philosophy. In all later epochs, the philosophers' study of political things was mediated by a tradition of political philosophy which acted like a screen between the philosopher and political things, regardless of whether the individual philosopher cherished or rejected that tradition. From this it follows that the classical philosophers see the political things with a freshness and directness which have never been equalled. They look at political things in the perspective of the enlightened citizen or statesman.[32]

Strauss exaggerates here. If all political traditions were shaken, it does not follow that they collapsed. Nor does Strauss demonstrate that the political things viewed by Socrates and his immediate descendants were natural. What is the natural foundation from which we are enabled to choose between the political teachings of Plato and Thucydides? If it exists at all, why can it be found only in the collapse of ancient Greek political opinions? What of Strauss's own epoch, and the collapse of the Weimar Republic, not to forget the gradual descent of the epoch into nihilism, a process that apparently removed the screen of tradition from Strauss's eyes and enabled him to see the political things as they are by nature?

Unfortunately, we require a standard external to the historical process itself. Previous efforts in this direction, of which the most sophisticated is probably that of phenomenology, have not been encouraging to Strauss himself. I remind the reader that Husserl's de-sedimented paradigm of the life-world is already a neo-Kantian construction of the human intellect that is saturated with the reasoning of mathematical rationalism, just as Heidegger's *Dasein* analysis combines Aristotle with historicist ontology. It looks as if what we de-sedimenters find is a reincarnation of our sedimented self. While exercising great caution with

---

[31] Strauss, *CM*, 6–9.
[32] Strauss, "What is Political Philosophy," in *WPP*, 27.

respect to the possibility of uncovering the *Ur*-phenomena of nature, Strauss begins with a construction of the Platonic-Aristotelian interpretation of pretheoretical politics, the naturalness of which depends upon our adherence to the teaching of the Socratic school.

This teaching is not properly understood if we take it as an unqualified invocation to live in accord with nature. To say that something has a nature is not the same as to say that nature is philanthropic. The so-called conservatism of the classical Socratic philosophers is motivated to a considerable extent by the enmity or indifference of nature to human happiness. One can accept the Aristotelian maxim that man is by nature a political animal without saying much about the content or actualization of the best *polis*. The modern position on this point, typical of the French Enlightenment and thinkers like Condorcet and d'Alembert and, of course, of their great predecessor, Descartes, is that mankind suffers unnecessarily from the cruelty of nature. The discovery of nature is not enough to guarantee that we will achieve our freedom. Action is required; nature must be put to the torture. If the danger of a scientifically ordered civilization is self-annihilation, the ancient equivalent is stultification. This is why Plato's *Republic* conceives of the best city as a perpetual tyranny of Platonism.

One may summarize the Straussian discussion of the problem of modernity by seeing his approach as deeply influenced by Heidegger, whom Strauss regarded as the most profound thinker since Hegel. Let me allude once more to Strauss's introduction to Heidegger, where we find the following extreme judgment:

> There is no longer in existence a philosophic position, apart from neo-Thomism and Marxism crude or refined. All rational liberal philosophic positions have lost their significance and power. One may deplore this, but I for one cannot bring myself to cling to philosophic positions which have been shown to be inadequate. I am afraid that we shall have to make a very great effort in order to find a solid basis for rational liberalism. Only a great thinker could help us in our intellectual plight. But here is the great trouble: the only great thinker in our time is Heidegger.[33]

I emphasize this passage because it makes so clear Strauss's view that the road to the overcoming of nihilism passes through the reinterpretation of Heidegger's destruction of Platonism. However, it is insufficient merely to seek refuge in the bosom of Platonism. Strauss himself understands this; it remains for his successors to take up the gauntlet that he pointed out but did not manage to secure.

[33] Strauss, "An Introduction to Heideggerian Existentialism," in *RCPR*, 29.

BACK TO THE FUTURE

I am tempted to summarize my discussion of Strauss and modernity by means of a simple dilemma that seems to emerge from Platonic rationalism. According to Strauss, Plato and Aristotle make clear their belief that theory is detached from and higher than practice. In other words, we cannot deduce theoretical from practical knowledge. This being so, our study of political and ethical action may yield descriptive knowledge of practice but not of theory. There is for the Socratic school no such thing as the theory of practice, or of what is today sometimes called "action theory." As Strauss puts it, if we restrict ourselves to the mathematical paradigm of scientific reason or (what comes to the same thing in this context) to a Platonist dialectic of pure forms, then we can no longer preserve the notion of a rational knowledge of human existence. To allude to one of Strauss's most frequently developed arguments, modern science excludes the rationality of value judgments, and so too it excludes the possibility of achieving a good life. And this is, or leads to, nihilism.

The problem should now be evident. On the central point that concerns us, there seems to be little if any difference between the "ancients" and the "moderns." That was certainly Heidegger's view. Both strive for the replacement of opinion by knowledge, and both accept the paradigm of mathematical rationality. The upshot is the attempt to mathematize opinion; in both cases, it is granted (or insisted) that the very superiority of formalization to opinion is itself a matter of opinion. And this brings us back to Heidegger. As noted previously, Strauss wishes to inoculate us against Heidegger's ostensible destruction of Western European rationalism by turning to the Socratics and their purification of reason. However, in the relevant instance Heidegger's project is more radical than Strauss's because he attempts to demolish the rationalist conception of thinking or to clear the ground for the arrival of a new type of thinking, one that is free of the limitations placed upon our access to Being by ancients and moderns alike.

Heidegger is encouraged to see his own hope for "another way" as the attempt to bypass the nihilism endemic to Western philosophy. It is he rather than Strauss who is on this point more radical because Strauss is hindered by his allegiance to Platonism. He has not resolved the tension in Platonism between knowledge and opinion or theory and practice.

No doubt Strauss would reply that such a resolution is impossible, but this merely serves to confirm the Heideggerian thesis, which we may formulate as follows. Platonism (that is, Western philosophy from Parmenides to Nietzsche) is dominated by the equation of truth and formal structure. In Heideggerian jargon, the equation says that truth in the Western tradition is both presence and visibility. It follows from this that ethical judgments, or what Nietzsche calls the rank-ordering of values, are impossible – or rather, that ethical and political judgments can be true only in the sense that they express formal structures. But there is nothing in a formal structure that captures the act of attributing value to that structure. The correct approach to this problem is to turn away from presence to absence, that is, from the domination of Being by beings.

In these summary remarks, I have tried to show that Platonism expresses the same conception of terms like truth or Being as is defended by modern science. On this crucial point, there is no serious difference between Strauss and Heidegger. The difference lies, or is initially accessible, in the "value" that each places on this essentially correct interpretation of Western philosophy.

Parenthetically, I suggest that Strauss's rediscovery of the esotericism of the great philosophers was decisively motivated by the political necessity to conceal the nihilistic consequences of the separation of theory and practice. I note that one of the ambiguous problems bequeathed to us "post-moderns" is not whether Strauss is right about esotericism but whether we should continue to practice it in an age in which the cat, so speak, has been let out of the bag. Strauss is evidently aware of this problem. But he tends to shift from a statement of the problem to a critical analysis of the history of philosophy. This analysis is usually extremely interesting and often brilliant, but it tends to rest upon a presupposition that is hardly self-evident but remains to be proved, namely, the superiority of the Platonic teaching to that of modernity (or better, of various forms of modernity).

One can therefore praise Strauss highly for his extraordinary erudition and philosophical *eros*, as well as for his clarification of the crisis of modernity, while still doubting that he has come to grips with the very thinker whose work he both admires and by whom he has clearly been influenced, positively and negatively: Heidegger.

7 The Medieval Arabic Enlightenment

In memoriam Muhsin S. Mahdi[1]

THE PLATONIC POLITICAL TRADITION

Leo Strauss's turn to the Platonic political tradition transformed our understanding of the Islamic *falasifa* and their disciple Maimonides.[2] The decisive moment was the appearance of *Philosophie und Gesetz* in 1935, when Strauss was thirty-six, at the midpoint of his life.[3] I wish to focus on this decisive moment. I believe Strauss's fundamental approach to the *falasifa* and Maimonides was already apparent in *Philosophy and Law*. Like the medieval commentators on *The Guide of the Perplexed*, whom he read, Strauss was alert to Maimonides's heterodoxy and style of exoteric writing.

---

[1] Considered "the world's foremost scholar of medieval Arabic and Islamic political philosophy," Muhsin S. Mahdi, born in the Shi'ite holy city Karbala' in Iraq, came to the University of Chicago to study economics but was attracted by the teaching of Strauss. He dedicated his last book, *Alfarabi and the Foundations of Islamic Political Philosophy*, to his teacher: "For L.S. If we had to repay the debt of gratitude incurred by his kindness to us, not even the whole of time would suffice."

[2] The word *falasifa* is the plural of *faylasuf*, meaning "philosopher," derived from Greek *philosophos* and applied to "Aristotelian philosophers," such as Alfarabi (d. ca. 950), Avicenna (Ibn Sina, d. 1037), and Averroes (Ibn Rushd, d. 1198). For a detailed study of Strauss on the *falasifa*, see Georges Tamer, *Islamische Philosophie und die Krise der Moderne: Das Verhältnis von Leo Strauss zu Alfarabi, Avicenna and Averroes* (Leiden: Brill, 2001).

[3] *Philosophie und Gesetz: Beiträge zum Verständnis Maimunis und seiner Vorläufer* (Berlin: Schocken, 1935) was written from 1928 to 1932. Notice the poignancy of the place and date of publication. In 1935, Strauss was in Cambridge, England; reprinted in Strauss, *GS*, 2: 9–123; trans. Eve Adler, *Philosophy and Law: Essays Toward the Understanding of Maimonides* (Albany: State University of New York Press, 1995); all parenthetical references are to this edition. See also Strauss, *Maïmonide*, trans. Rémi Brague (Paris: Presses Universitaires de France, 1988), 11–142. Brague translated all of Strauss's important writings on Maimonides in chronological order.

There are many superb studies of Strauss's thought. Some I shall cite, but I prefer to encounter Strauss's writings directly. The problem is that each work is connected to the others and they are difficult to take in, let alone comprehend, like an intricate hall of mirrors, where we can never be sure of what we see. For instance, in *Philosophy and Law* he referred to Nietzsche's *Beyond Good and Evil* in an enigmatic note to the Introduction, and cited or alluded to Nietzsche elsewhere, the references to Nietzsche being all crucial for understanding Strauss's view of the *falasifa* and Maimonides.

As Strauss wrote in the esoteric style that he ascribed to philosophers, we need to distinguish his private doctrine from his public teaching. To this end, I make use of his conversations and correspondence with friends, where he conveyed his thoughts in plain, uncoded language, although Strauss was never forgetful of his particular addressee.

Strauss did not progress from a conventional view of Maimonides in 1935 to a radical understanding six or twenty-five years later when he had learned to appreciate the beauty and remarkable organization of the *Guide*. In fact, we do not fully grasp what he considered Maimonides's esoteric doctrines to be when he was writing in the early 1930s. Strauss considered Maimonides a rationalist, whose logic, physics, metaphysics, and ethics were Aristotelian and whose political science was Platonic. Maimonides was a philosopher, and being a philosopher, for Strauss, was incompatible with being a believing Jew.[4]

In the Introduction to *Philosophy and Law*, Strauss was unusually candid about his own philosophical orientation. He concurred with Epicurus, Spinoza, and Nietzsche that nature is beyond good and evil, indifferent and uncaring. There is no moral world order, and religion is a delusion. *Redlichkeit* ("probity"), a synonym for atheism, prevents escape from life's terrors into this soothing delusion.

SCHOLARLY PATH

First, I want to situate Strauss's writing on medieval Islamic and Jewish thought on the path of his intellectual itinerary, which followed an inner logic of growth. In his early period (the 1920s), Strauss studied Spinoza, who became a pillar of his intellectual universe.[5] His first publication (1924) was a critical review of an essay by Hermann Cohen's that portrayed Spinoza as a disloyal Jew whose excommunication was

---

[4] Cf., however, Kenneth Hart Green, *Jew and Philosopher: The Return to Maimonides in the Jewish Thought of Leo Strauss* (Albany: State University of New York Press, 1993).

[5] See Michael Zank, "Preface" to Strauss, *EW*, xii–xv.

well deserved.[6] Strauss's review was sharply critical of Cohen's attack on Spinoza. Strauss wrote that among other things, Cohen failed to understand Spinoza within his milieu.[7]

Later (1926), Strauss wrote that he owed the idea for his work on Spinoza to his critical study of Cohen's article, lauding it as paradigmatic and peerless among recent literature on Spinoza in its radicalness of questioning and its calling Spinoza to account.[8] Strauss added Cohen did not recognize that Spinoza's real intent was identical with that of the Enlightenment. Spinoza did not spurn Jewish monotheism or prophetic social ethics; he rejected organized religion as such.

Strauss's 1924 essay on Cohen impressed Julius Guttmann, then director of the Akademie für die Wissenschaft des Judentums, which offered Strauss a research fellowship to finish a monograph on Spinoza, to write a study of Gersonides, and to work on the Mendelssohn *Jubiläumsausgabe*.[9]

Strauss first wrote on "biblical science" in general, and then on Spinoza's biblical hermeneutics in particular.[10] Guttmann supported

---

[6] See Hermann Cohen, "Spinoza über Staat und Religion, Judentum und Christentum," *Jüdische Schriften* (Berlin: C. A. Schwetschke & Sohn), 3: 290–372; Strauss, "Cohens Analyse der Bibel-Wissenschaft Spinozas," *Der Jude* 8 (1924): 295–314; reprinted in Strauss, *GS*, 1: 363–387; trans. as "Cohen's Analysis of Spinoza's Bible Science" in *EW*, 140–172; cf. Strauss, "Preface to *SCR*" in *LAM*, 224–259. And see Franz Nauen, "Hermann Cohen's Perceptions of Spinoza: A Reappraisal, *AJS Review* 4 (1979): 111–124, on pp. 114–118. After Cohen's lecture in 1910, "Das Verhältnisse Spinozas zum Judentum," Nauen observes Cohen personally attacked Spinoza as an elitist who underestimated the potential of the many for enlightenment, neglected prophetic Messianism and the monotheistic idea, leading to defamation of Maimonides, hatred of Judaism, and antisemitism, making him a renegade and enemy of Judaism and the Jewish people. See also Steven B. Smith, *Reading Leo Strauss: Politics, Philosophy, Judaism* (Chicago: University of Chicago Press, 2006), 32–35 and "How to Commemorate the 350th Anniversary of Spinoza's Expulsion or Leo Strauss's Reply to Hermann Cohen" *Hebraic Political Studies* 3 (2008): 155–176.

[7] His criticism of Cohen's interpretation of Maimonides was equally negative. See Strauss, "How to Begin to Study Medieval Philosophy," in *RCPR*, 207–226, esp. 207–208, 210. Cohen had preceded Strauss in discerning a Platonic motif in Maimonides's philosophy mainly in ethics and stressing Plato's idea of the Good. Actually, Maimonides derived the idea of "the pure good" from an Arabic version of the *Elements of Theology* of the Neoplatonist Proclus.

[8] Strauss, "Zur Bibelwissenschaft Spinozas und seiner Vorläufer," in *GS*, 1: 389–414 on 389; trans. as "On the Bible Science of Spinoza and His Precursors," in *EW*, 173–200, on 173.

[9] See Steven B. Smith, "Leo Strauss: The Outlines of a Life," this volume.

[10] Strauss, "Biblische Geschichte und Wissenschaft," *Jüdische Runschau* 30 (1925): 744–745; reprinted in *GS*, 2: 357–361; trans., as "Bible History and Science" in *EW*, 130–137. And see "Zur Bibelwissenschaft Spinozas und

the Spinoza project as long as it was confined to biblical interpretation, but when he realized that Strauss was writing on Spinoza's critique of religion (which included biblical interpretation), he objected and delayed publication. The Spinoza book was completed in 1928 and published in 1930.[11] Spinoza, whom Strauss considered "the last of the medievals," remained a lifelong interest of Strauss, spanning more than thirty-five years.[12]

Die Religionskritik Spinozas had chapters on Maimonides and Hobbes, impelling Strauss to pursue independent studies of these two thinkers.[13] From here on, Strauss's scholarly itinerary took two divergent yet merging paths: Western political philosophy (e.g., Plato, Aristotle, Machiavelli, Hobbes) and medieval Islamic and Jewish thought (e.g., Alfarabi, Avicenna, Averroes, Maimonides). The two paths merged when Strauss traced Islamic and Jewish thought to Plato and Aristotle, or detected influences of Islamic and Jewish thought (Averroes or Maimonides) on Machiavelli, Hobbes, and Spinoza.

In his middle period from 1931 to 1937, Strauss turned to the Platonic political tradition.[14] The Spinoza book was based on the idea that a return to premodern philosophy was impossible.[15] A reorientation took place, which was first articulated, "not entirely by accident," in a review of Carl Schmitt's *Der Begriff des Politischen.*[16] He was thereafter

seiner Vorläufer," *Korrespondenzblatt (des Vereins zur Gründung und Erhaltung einer Akademie für die Wissenschaft des Judentums)* 7 (1926): 1–22. Reprinted in *Wissenschaft des Judentums im deutschen Sprachbereich. Ein Querschnitt,* ed. Kurt Wilhelm (Tübingen: J. C. B. Mohr, 1967), 1: 115–137; Strauss, *GS,* 1: 389–414; *EW,* 173–200.

[11] *Die Religionskritik Spinozas als Grundlage seiner Bibelwissenschaft: Untersuchungen zu Spinozas Theologisch-politischem Traktat* (Berlin: Akademie-Verlag, 1930); reprinted in Strauss, *GS,* 1: 1–361. On the circumstances of the Spinoza book and Spinoza's importance for German Jews, see Steven Smith, "Leo Strauss: The Outlines of a Life," this volume.

[12] Strauss, *PAW,* 5.

[13] Strauss, *Hobbes' politische Wissenschaft* was written in London and Cambridge in 1934–1935, at the time when *Philosophy and Law* appeared. It was published in English as *The Political Philosophy of Hobbes* (Oxford: Clarendon Press, 1936).

[14] Heinrich Meier, "How Strauss Became Strauss," in *Enlightening Revolutions: Essays in Honor of Ralph Lerner,* ed. Svetozar Minkov with the assistance of Stéphane Douard (Lanham, MD: Lexington Books, 2006), 363–382; Meier gives a detailed catalogue of Strauss's writings at this time on pp. 366 and 376, n. 11. This is a revised and expanded English version of the introduction to Strauss, *GS,* II, which includes the text of *Philosophie und Gesetz.* The introduction includes the circumstances of its writing.

[15] Strauss, "Preface to *SCR,*" in *LAM,* 257.

[16] Strauss, "Comments on *Der Begriff des Politischen* by Carl Schmitt," reprinted at the end of *SCR,* 331–351. For the original review, see

"compelled," as he said, to engage in studies that made him aware of how past heterodox thinkers wrote their books. He obviously considered the *falasifa* and Maimonides to be among these heterodox thinkers.

Strauss immersed himself in the study of Maimonides in the early 1930s. In 1931, as coeditor of Moses Mendelssohn's *Gesammelte Schriften*, he edited parts of Mendelssohn's commentary on Maimonides's *Treatise on the Art of Logic*.[17] In the same year, he wrote "Cohen und Maimuni,"[18] and in the summer he wrote on Maimonides's teaching of prophecy and its sources.[19] He returned to Spinoza in 1932 with an article on "Spinoza's Testament."[20]

During Strauss's late period from his immigration to America in 1937 until his death in 1973, he wrote on Maimonides and Alfarabi and on Hobbes and Spinoza. In the last decade of his life, he wrote his most important interpretations of Maimonides and published his book on Spinoza in English translation with a significant new autobiographical Preface. There were further reflections on the Jewish question, studies on ancient writers (Aristophanes, Aristotle, Plato, Xenophon, Thucydides) and premodern and modern political thought (Machiavelli, *Natural Right and History*).[21]

Strauss's career has been described as "a journey from Jerusalem to Athens."[22] Accordingly, Strauss first considered ancient Greek

"Anmerkungen zu Carl Schmitt, *Der Begriff des Politischen*," *Archiv für Sozialwissenschaft und Sozialpolitik*, 67:6 (1932): 732–749; reprinted in Strauss, *GS*, 3: 217–238; see Carl Schmitt, *The Concept of the Political* (Chicago: University of Chicago Press, expanded edition 2007).

[17] Moses Mendelssohn, *Jubiläumsausgabe* (Berlin: Akademie Verlag, 1931), vol. 2; reprinted (Stuttgart: Friedrich Frommann Verlag, 1972), 199–228. See *Kommentar zu den 'Termini der Logik'* (1931) in Strauss, *GS*, 2: 476.

[18] Strauss, "Cohen und Maimuni (1931)" in *GS*, 2: 393–436.

[19] Strauss, "Maimunis Lehre von der Prophetie und ihre Quellen." *Le Monde Oriental* (Uppsala) 28 (1934), 99–139. The article had been completed in July 1931; see Heinrich Meier, "How Strauss Became Strauss," 365; reprinted in *GS*, 2: 87–123; see also *PL*, 101–133. See the notes in *GS* 2: 87, n. 1; *PL*, 145, n. 1.

[20] Spinoza "Das Testament Spinozas." *Bayerische Israelitische Gemeindezeitung* (Munich) 8, no. 21 (November 1): 322–326; reprinted in *GS*, 1: 415–422; trans. as "The Testament of Spinoza," in *EW*, 216–223.

[21] See also *Jewish Philosophy and the Crisis of Modernity: Essays and Lectures in Modern Jewish Thought*, ed. Kenneth Hart Green (Albany: State Univesity of New York Press, 1997).

[22] See Rémi Brague, "Athens, Jerusalem, Mecca: Leo Strauss's 'Muslim' Understanding of Greek Philosophy," *Poetics Today* 19:2 (Summer 1998): 235–259, on 238–240. Brague notes that Strauss's first publications were concerned with Jewish thinkers (Maimonides, Spinoza, Mendelssohn, Hermann Cohen) and the last ones were mainly commentaries on Greek philosophers and authors, such as Aristophanes, Aristotle, Plato, Thucydides, and Xenophon.

philosophy as a source of medieval thought and read the Greeks from an Islamic point of view. In particular, Alfarabi was the source of Strauss's hermeneutics and his interpretation of Plato.[23] Later, he read Greek authors on their own without the intermediary of Alfarabi and other Islamic philosophers.

MEDIEVAL RATIONALISM AND MODERN ENLIGHTENMENT

Strauss began *Philosophy and Law* by quoting Cohen's observation that Maimonides is the "classic of rationalism" in Judaism.[24] The Introduction to *Philosophy and Law* presents itself as a trial. Strauss played the role of advocate, using legal language to defend the medieval rationalism of Maimonides from the attacks of modern rationalism. Strauss's declared aim was to arouse a prejudice in favor of Maimonides's rationalism – as the "true natural model, the standard to be carefully protected from any distortion, and thus the stumbling-block on which modern rationalism falls" – and to awaken a suspicion against "the powerful opposing prejudice" – the modern rationalism of the Enlightenment (*PL*, 21). By careful protection from distortion, Strauss apparently alluded to Guttmann's modernizing deformation, which he targeted in the first chapter.

   Strauss defined the modern Enlightenment as "the movement of the seventeenth and eighteenth centuries initiated by Descartes' *Meditations* and Hobbes' *Leviathan*" (*PL*, 22). The radical Enlightenment (e.g., Spinoza) undermined the foundations of the Jewish tradition – its

---

[23] See in this connection Strauss's letter to Gerhard Krüger of December 25, 1935, from Cambridge, in Strauss, *GS*, 3: 449–450, where he praised Alfarabi for opening up Platonism for him and observed that the main fault of traditional and contemporary Plato interpretation was that it belonged to a Christian tradition, and that Islam afforded a better starting point.

[24] However, *Philosophy and Law* was a break with the neo-Kantianism of the Marburg School, founded by Hermann Cohen; see *PL*, 21. See also Strauss, "Cohen und Maimuni," *GS*, 2: 395 and 403. In this essay, Strauss emphasized the centrality of ethics in Cohen's philosophy, his affinity with Plato, his relating Maimonides's ethics to Plato's teachings, and his presentation of Maimonides as "an enlightened Jew." Strauss mentioned Hermann Cohen on 10% of the pages of *PL*, far more than any other modern philosopher. Likewise, in the "Preface to *SCR*" he cited Hermann Cohen at least thirteen times, or on 35% of the pages of the essay; see "Preface," 240, for Strauss's assessment of Cohen as "a Jew of rare dedication, the faithful guide, defender, and warner of German Jewry, and at the same time, to say the least, the one who by far surpassed in spiritual power all the other German professors of philosophy in his generation." "It became *necessary*," Strauss continued, "to examine Cohen's attack on Spinoza [emphasis added]."

belief in creation, miracles, and the Law (*PL*, 23).[25] The moderate
Enlightenment (of Moses Mendelssohn) failed to compromise between
orthodoxy and radical Enlightenment, between belief in revelation
and belief in independent reason. Strauss observed that later thinkers
(Hermann Cohen and Franz Rosenzweig), realizing that any compromise
between the Enlightenment and orthodoxy is impossible, harmonized
them by allegorizing creation, miracles, and revelation, thereby depriv-
ing these beliefs of their true meaning. If God did not create the world
in a real sense, and if creation cannot be accepted as simply true, Strauss
argued, then one must in all probity (*Redlichkeit*) disavow creation or
steer clear of talking about it (*PL*, 24).

Strauss reinforced orthodoxy by asserting that its premises are
irrefutable, and that the most radical Enlighteners were reduced to disproving it by mockery. He may have thought of Spinoza or of Voltaire,
who ridiculed the Jews and the Hebrew Bible.[26] Yet the idea that the
Enlighteners were reduced to mockery when they realized that orthodoxy's premises are irrefutable is not historically accurate, and there is
reason to suspect that it was not meant to be.

Strauss maintained orthodoxy might be refuted if it could be proved
that life and the world "are perfectly intelligible without the assumption
of an unfathomable God" (*PL*, 32).[27] Strauss changed the playing field
here, moving from orthodoxy to natural theology. What is more, one
may object that even if life and the world are perfectly intelligible if
there exists an unfathomable God (a statement paradoxical in itself),
this does not have any bearing upon orthodoxy. Revelation cannot be
refuted because it must be admitted as logically possible. However, the
same may be said of astrology and divination.

Strauss's use of the term "orthodox" for the opponent attacked by the
Enlightenment is problematic. Orthodoxy was actually a reaction to the

[25] The "Law" capitalized means herein "the revealed law."
[26] See Adam Sutcliffe, *Judaism and Enlightenment* (Cambridge, UK: Cambridge
University Press, 2003), 19, 234–239. Strauss expressed great loathing for
Voltaire, using the traditional "May his name be blotted out," in a letter
to Gershom Scholem, May 10, 1950, *GS*, 3: 722.
[27] He referred to God as the unfathomable or the ultimate mystery in "Why We
Remain Jews," in *JPCM*, 328: "And an enigmatic vision in the emphatic sense
is the perception of the ultimate mystery, of the truth of the ultimate mystery.
The truth of the ultimate mystery – the truth that there is an ultimate mystery,
that being is radically mysterious – cannot be denied even by the unbelieving
Jew of our age." "Ultimate mystery" appears four times in two sentences and
"radically mysterious" once. Elsewhere, Strauss said: "The certainty that no
God exists would presuppose that there is no possible place for God in the
whole; in other words, there is no mystery." See also Strauss, "Freud on Moses
and Monotheism," in *JPCM*, 304.

Enlightenment, and emerged from the debate between Jewish reformers and traditionalists, who were called "Orthodox" in late nineteenth-century Germany.[28] From the Enlightenment viewpoint, the religious opponent was specifically Christianity, or the Church, and generally all religions. Strauss presented himself as a Jew litigating the claims of the Enlightenment and Jewish orthodoxy. In fact, some readers of *Philosophy and Law* thought that the author was an Orthodox Jew (e.g., Karl Löwith). Others were convinced that he was an atheist (e.g., Gershom Scholem).

As used by Strauss, the term "Enlightenment" is puzzling as well because there were many Enlightenment thinkers in various countries with different views on religion. There was a Scottish, French, and German Enlightenment, and the ideas of Hume, Diderot, and Kant were not the same, as Strauss certainly knew. Many Enlightenment thinkers held that although religion had limited cognitive value, faith in God was required for human morality. Others believed that religion was harmful and a catalyst for hatred and warfare.[29]

For the purposes of a trial, it appears Strauss was being schematic, not historically precise. He judged between two equal litigants and tried to instill in the reader a bias in favor of one. He was convinced that the Enlightenment's absolute rejection of religious belief was philosophically untenable, and that a quest for the truth had to acknowledge the possibility that the claims of faith may be real. Strauss reiterated the view that philosophy is forced to acknowledge that revelation is possible in *Natural Right and History*.[30] Man yearns to solve the riddle of being yet human knowledge is limited, and the requirement for divine illumination cannot be denied, so that the possibility of revelation cannot be rejected. He concluded that as neither of the two antagonists, philosophy and revelation, has succeeded in refuting the other, this in itself comprises revelation's refutation of philosophy.

EPICUREANISM

In the second part of the Introduction, Strauss expressed his own views more candidly than usual. Strauss observed that the basis of the

---

[28] The minimal beliefs of orthodoxy are the divine origin of the Law, the acceptance of the Oral Law (Talmud, Midrashim, responsa and codes) as the interpretation of the Written Law, the Law's immutability and eternity, the eternal bond of God with Israel, and expectation of salvation at the end of historical time.

[29] See Jonathan Israel, *Enlightenment Contested* (Oxford: Oxford University Press, 2006), ch. 26, "Is Religion Needed for a Well-Ordered Society?"

[30] Strauss "Natural Right and the Distinction between Facts and Values" in *NRH*, 35–80; see Nasser Behnegar, "Strauss and Social Science," this volume.

Enlightenment and the classic critique of religion is epicureanism, which liberates mankind from the religious delusion. Whereas classical epicureanism freed humans from fear of the gods, Enlightenment epicureanism released them from the delusion of religion. "One may therefore say that philosophy is productive of the deepest pain. Man has to choose between peace of mind deriving from a pleasing delusion and peace of mind deriving from the unpleasing truth."[31] It is "the unpleasing truth" that Strauss favored in *Philosophy and Law*.

Liberated from the religious delusion, awakened to sober awareness of his real situation, taught by bad experiences that he is threatened by a stingy, hostile nature, man recognizes as his sole salvation and duty not so much "to cultivate his garden" as, in the first place, to plant himself a "garden" by making himself the master and owner of nature.[32] Fortitude, equated with probity, prevents escape to the religious delusion:

A new kind of fortitude, which forbids itself every flight from the horror of life into comforting delusion, which accepts the eloquent descriptions of the misery of man without God as a proof of the goodness of its cause, reveals itself eventually as the ultimate and purest ground for the rebellion against the tradition of the revelation. This new fortitude, being the willingness to look man's forsakenness in its face, being the courage to welcome the terrible truth, being toughness (*Härte*) against the inclination of man to deceive himself about his situation, is probity.[33]

---

[31] Strauss, "Notes on Lucretius," in *LAM*, 85.

[32] Strauss, *GS*, 2: 24; *PL*, 36. The garden alludes to epicureanism and perhaps to Candide's "let us cultivate our garden." Here Strauss does not object to the modern idea of mastery over nature.

[33] Strauss, *GS*, 2: 25; *PL*, 37. See also "Preface to *SCR*," in *LAM*, 256. Scholem wrote to Strauss on November 28, 1962, questioning the wisdom of publishing the Preface to the English version of the Spinoza book because it was so candid and revealing, and Strauss replied on December 6, 1962; see Strauss, *GS*, 3: 747–748. Strauss said that he omitted all that comes after 1928 – the year he finished the Spinoza book – yet his review of Carl Schmitt's *Der Begriff des Politischen*, mentioned in the penultimate sentence of the Preface, appeared in 1932. In a letter (March 29, 1935) to Walter Benjamin, Gershom Scholem described *Philosophy and Law* as beginning with an "affirmation of atheism." Scholem admired Strauss's ethical position but regretted that it would undermine any chance of being appointed to a teaching position at the Hebrew University in philosophy of religion. Benjamin expressed interest in the book and spoke of the pleasant image of Strauss he always had. See *The Correspondence of Walter Benjamin and Gershom Scholem 1932–1940*, ed. G. Scholem, trans. Gary Smith and Andre Lefevere (Cambridge, MA: Harvard University Press, 1992), 155–161. Scholem was not shocked by what Strauss said; he was surprised by his willingness to say it. See also Steven Smith, "Leo Strauss: The Outlines of a Life," this volume.

Here Strauss spoke positively about "the rebellion against the tradition of the revelation." Probity rejects attempts to reconcile the
Enlightenment and orthodoxy in compromises or syntheses (PL, 37–
38). This atheism is the offspring of a tradition founded in the Bible. It
is "the heir and judge of the belief in revelation," of "the millennia-old
struggle (Streit) between belief and unbelief." In the wake of Nietzsche,
Strauss traced probity to the uncompromising iconoclasm of the Bible.
The final justification of the Enlightenment is "the atheism stemming
from probity, which overcomes Orthodoxy radically by understanding
it radically."

Nevertheless, Strauss moderated the force of probity by distinguishing between "the new probity" and "the old love of truth" (Wahrheit-
sliebe). If atheism, which is not demonstrable, becomes a dogmatic
premise, then its probity is unlike the love of truth, which rejects dogmatic solutions (PL, 37, n. 13). In brief, given Strauss's understanding of
philosophy as zetetic, a quest for rather than possession of the truth, he
could be an agnostic but not an atheist.[34]

"Probity" appears three times in the body of the Introduction and
once in a long footnote (PL, 137–38),[35] all without ascribing it to Nietzsche, who had made it a hallmark of the philosopher (PL, 136 n. 2;
141, n. 25). Nietzsche is said to be "the massive unnamed presence of
the Introduction."[36] When Strauss returned to probity in the Preface to
Spinoza's Critique of Religion, he ascribed it to Nietzsche explicitly.[37]
The end of the Preface reiterates the epicurean and Nietzschean sections of Philosophy and Law literally and forthrightly. It would not be
inappropriate to regard the Preface's end as Strauss's Final Testament.

---

[34] Daniel Tanguay, Leo Strauss: An Intellectual Biography, trans. Christopher
Nadon (New Haven, CT: Yale University Press, 2007), makes an excellent case
for Strauss being a zetetic philosopher.

[35] On Redlichkeit in Nietzsche, see Morgenröthe, no. 456, 536; Jenseits von
Gut und Böse, no. 227; Nietzsche Handbuch, ed. Henning Ottomann
(Stuttgart/Weimar: Metzler, 2000), s.v. Redlichkeit, intellektuelle, 308–309.
References are to the G. Colli/M. Montinari, ed. Sämtliche Werke (München/
New York, 1980). And see Karl Jaspers, Nietzsche: Einführung in das Verständnis seines Philosophierens, Vierte unveränderte Auflage (Berlin: Walter
de Gruyter, 1981), 202–205; Jaspers, Nietzsche: An Introduction to the Understanding of his Philosophical Activity, trans. Charles F. Wallraff and Frederick J. Schmitz (Baltimore, MD: Johns Hopkins University Press, 1997),
201–204.

[36] Laurence Lampert, Leo Strauss and Nietzsche (Chicago: University of Chicago
Press, 1996), 5–6; see also Pierre Manent, "Strauss et Nietzsche," Revue de
Métaphysique et de Morale 94, 3 (1989): 337–345.

[37] See Strauss, "Preface to SCR," in LAM, 256.

Nietzsche was the formative influence on Strauss in his youth. When he was in Gymnasium (1912–1917, age eleven to sixteen), he read Nietzsche and Schopenhauer furtively in his Orthodox household.[38] Philosophy was something undercover for him at an early age. He later studied Nietzsche at the university. He wrote to a friend that "Nietzsche so dominated and charmed me between my 22nd and 30th years that I literally believed everything I understood of him."[39]

THE MEDIEVAL ENLIGHTENMENT AND THE IDEA OF LAW

We need to understand the differences between modern rationalism and its medieval predecessor, and why Strauss said that he preferred the medieval Enlightenment to its modern counterpart.[40]

Law

Strauss wrote that an enlightened Judaism is imperative, and when we seek an alternative to modern Enlightenment, we find "that only new, unheard-of, ultra-modern thoughts can resolve our perplexity." We therefore turn to the medieval Enlightenment of Maimonides, whose main idea is the idea of the Law (*PL*, 39). How the medieval Enlightenment contains "new, unheard-of, ultra-modern thoughts" is left dangling, unexplained. Strauss may be reflecting Heidegger, who achieved new and unheard-of ideas by returning to the pre-Socratics and Aristotle. Strauss sought all his life to recover the authentic wisdom of Maimonides to serve as the basis of a new enlightened Judaism, and he believed that there was no other way to revive genuine Jewish thought.

Strauss was convinced that we can only study medieval rationalists in their own terms as demanding belief in revelation and living in "loving obedience" or "childlike obedience" to the religious law, according

---

[38] Strauss, "A Giving of Accounts," in *JPCM*, 460. The dialogue took place at St. John's College, Annapolis, Maryland, on January 30, 1970. It first appeared in *The St. John's Review* from *The College* 22, no. 1 (April, 1970): 1–5.

[39] See his letter to Karl Löwith of June 23, 1935, in Strauss, *GS*, 3: 648. Several commentators have claimed that Strauss was a Nietzschean but in different senses. See Lampert, *Leo Strauss and Nietzsche* and Shadia Drury *The Political Ideas of Leo Strauss* (New York: Saint Martin's 1988).

[40] Strauss, *GS*, 2: xvi–xxv; 3: xxii–xxiii. His comparison of medieval and modern rationalism and his critique of modernity takes up more than half of the Introduction (*PL*, 28–39). See also Strauss, *NRH*, passim; and *TWM*, 81–98. Nietzsche is the third wave. See also Strauss's *CM*, 1–12.

to which we are not meant to live as theoretical, knowing, and contemplating individuals.[41] Nothing is more fundamental than the alternative between "human guidance and divine guidance" or "a life of obedient love versus a life of free insight."[42] The one thing required by the Bible is "the life of obedient love," and the one thing required by Greek philosophy is "the life of autonomous understanding."[43] The Bible denies the norm of autonomous knowledge. The mysterious God is the last and highest of its themes.[44]

The reference to "obedience" is reminiscent of Spinoza, who presented obedience as the simple piety of someone who hearkens to the voice of God. Spinoza's obedience is the response to the revealed will of God, confirmed by miracles, not to the God we know by nature and reason. Speaking in a human way, not in the order of nature, one who loves God with his entire heart is obedient to God.[45] The alternative is a life in freedom in the spirit of the Greek philosophers. Strauss's own commitment was to a life in freedom as a philosopher. Nevertheless, he depicted the life of obedient love as a worthy option.

Nature

Strauss believed ancient and medieval rationalism contemplated nature as demonstrating a divine mind, expressed in its order, beauty, and mystery; whereas modern rationalism regards nature as alien and seeks to exploit it for human needs (PL, 32). Modern rationalism holds that natural science, as purpose-free and value-free, cannot teach human beings about ends and values, and hence the view that the right life is according to nature is meaningless (PL, 34).[46] Viewed by modern rationalism, nature is beyond good and evil, arbitrary and indifferent.

Strauss's discussion of nature is schematic. For instance, many medieval scientists in the world of Islam were interested in the practical study of nature (e.g., medicine, pharmacology, chemistry, geology,

---

[41] Strauss, "Progress or Return," in *RCPR*, 257.

[42] Strauss, *NRH*, 74.

[43] "Strauss, "Progress or Return," in *RCPR*, 246.

[44] Strauss, "On the Interpretation of Genesis," in *JPCM*, 374.

[45] Spinoza, *Political Treatise*, ii, 22, in *Complete Works*, trans. Samuel Shirley, ed. Michael L. Morgan (Indianapolis, IN: Hackett, 2002), 689; *Theological-Political Treatise*, xvi, 19, ed. Jonathan Israel, trans. Michael Silverthorne and Jonathan Israel (Cambridge, UK: Cambridge University Press, 2007), 205 (Gebhardt pagination in margin).

[46] In the note (*PL*, 137, n. 12), Strauss referred to Nietzsche, *Beyond Good and Evil*, Aphorism 9, where the philosopher criticized the Stoics for teaching that we should live according to nature. Nietzsche's point was that nature cannot serve as a model for human conduct.

mechanics, optics). Conversely, the great physicists in the modern world (e.g., Bohr, Born, Dyson, Fermi, Feynman, Hawking, Heisenberg) were driven by curiosity, love of theory, and the desire to understand and explain. Many modern physicists detect a universal reason manifested in nature, and do not view nature as alien and an object for exploitation. For instance, Einstein spoke of "the mystery of the eternity of life" and "the Reason that manifests itself in nature." He described religious feeling as "a rapturous amazement at the harmony of natural law, which reveals an intelligence of such superiority that, compared with it, all the systematic thinking and acting of human beings is an utterly insignificant reflection."[47]

Nature has been forgotten in the modern world in Strauss's view, and with the modern forgetting of nature the medieval Enlightenment's idea of philosophy and law vanished. We need to rediscover nature to revive the idea of law, which leads to the recovery of philosophy. The rediscovery of nature requires a radical critique of the principles of the Greek and Hebrew traditions, which can occur only by studying the history of philosophy. Strauss used a favorite image here – "[O]nly the history of philosophy makes possible the ascent from the second, 'unnatural' cave, into which we have fallen . . . into that first, 'natural' cave which Plato's image depicts, to emerge from which into the light is the original meaning of philosophizing" (PL, 135–136). Strauss's reference to mankind's oblivion to nature is his version of Heidegger's oblivion to Being. In fact, Heidegger disregarded nature in Being and Time. Strauss intended nature in several senses, including human nature and its supreme fulfillment in the life of a philosopher.

Disenchantment

The enchanted universe and the mystery of being of medieval rationalism were dispelled by the modern Enlightenment. Descartes and Spinoza believed that philosophy is wisdom itself rather than the love of wisdom, abandoning both Socratic skepticism and biblical faith. In Strauss's view, modern rationalism leads to the self-destruction of reason, culminating in nihilism. He advocated the supremacy of Socratic skepticism, biblical faith, and medieval rationalism over modern efforts to supplant them. Strauss's intention here and in later writings was to prevail over nihilism and its companions, historicism and relativism, by recovering ancient and medieval Islamic and Jewish thought.

[47] Albert Einstein, *Ideas and Opinions*, ed. C. Seeling, trans. S. Bargmann (New York: Three Rivers Press, 1982), "The World as I See It" (1931), 8–11; "The Religious Spirit of Science," 40.

In *Philosophy and Law*, Strauss did not explain how reason culminates in nihilism or even what he meant by it, relying perhaps on
the reader's familiarity with Friedrich Heinrich Jacobi (who coined the
term).[48] Indeed, the philosophers who drew Strauss's attention, such as
Spinoza (singled out by Jacobi as the iconic rationalist whose philosophy
led to pantheism, atheism, fatalism, and nihilism), Nietzsche, Heidegger, and Schmitt, have all been inscribed as nihilists.[49] Strauss viewed
reason as leading to nihilism because of its awareness that its principles were subjective and no better than any others. Also, beginning
with Cartesian rationalism, the knowing subject became the source
and creator of the external world, and hence its destroyer. Like Nietzsche, Strauss related nihilism to the crisis and decline of the West.
There is a hairsbreadth of difference between a nihilist and one who
strives to overcome nihilism, as Nietzsche attests. Nihilism is more
than negating all knowledge, meaning and value; it is ultimately fear of
the unknown, of entropy and death. The heavens were once friendly –
now we live in a dark and alien universe. Strauss wanted to veil this universe from our sight, to overcome nihilism with the comfort of religious
delusion.

ELITIST AND ESOTERIC CHARACTER OF PHILOSOPHY

In contrast to the modern Enlightenment, the medieval rationalists took
for granted the elitist and esoteric nature of philosophy. According to the
medieval rationalists, the great divide between the elite and the many
was a permanent feature of human societies, and no amount of education
or human advancement could change it. Hence, all proper philosophical
writing had to be exoteric. In contrast, most Enlightenment thinkers
believed that human beings can progress through education and the
development of their rational facilities. Strauss favored the medieval
Enlightenment precisely because it regarded elitism and exotericism as
permanent features of the human condition.

[48] See Strauss, *GN*, 352–378; Leo Strauss, *Nihilisme et Politique*, trans. Olivier
Sedeyn (Paris: Bibliotheque Rivages, 2001); both cited by William H. F. Altman,
"Leo Strauss on 'German Nihilism': Learning the Art of Writing," *Journal of
the History of Ideas* (October 1, 2007), note 2. And see David Janssens, "The
Problem of the Enlightenment: Strauss, Jacobi, and the Pantheism Controversy," *Review of Metaphysics* 56 (2003): 93–104; see also Susan Shell "'To
Spare the Vanquished and Crush the Arrogant': Leo Strauss's Lecture on 'German Nihilism'," this volume.
[49] See Karl Löwith, *Martin Heidegger and European Nihilism*, ed. Richard Wolin,
trans. Gary Steiner (New York: Columbia University Press, 1995).

THE THEORETICAL LIFE

The esoteric rhetoric of the medieval Enlightenment assumes the supremacy of the theoretical life, whereas the exoteric style of the modern Enlightenment presupposes the predominance of practical reason (PL, 103). According to the Greek and medieval ideal, an individual attains perfection by living a life devoted to theoretical inquiry. Maimonides viewed the theoretical life as the ultimate aim, not only of philosophy but of revelation as well – to know God and His works. He taught that the divine law is concerned with the refinement of belief, teaches correct opinions about "God and the angels," and brings human beings to true knowledge of all that exists.[50] Strauss was drawn to the medieval rationalists because of their dedication to the theoretical life, the life of true happiness.

POLITICAL PHILOSOPHY AND THE LAW

Criticism of Guttmann

Having established a presumption in favor of medieval rationalism, Strauss went on to consider political philosophy and the Law, criticizing modern scholars of medieval Jewish thought, primarily Julius Guttmann, for overlooking the Law's centrality.[51] Strauss blamed Guttmann *inter alia* for treating medieval thought as the product of religious consciousness and for regarding philosophy of religion's task to be the analysis of this consciousness, giving up belief in revelation from the outset (PL, 45).[52] Guttmann replied to Strauss's panoply of criticisms, having read also Strauss's subsequent studies, such as "The Literary Character of the *Guide of the Perplexed*."[53] Guttmann held that Maimonides

---

[50] Strauss referred to *Guide of the Perplexed*, II, 40; III, 27–28. See also Strauss, *CM*, 1.

[51] Chapter 1 of *PL* is titled: "The Quarrel of the Ancients and Moderns in the Philosophy of Judaism: Notes on Julius Guttmann, *The Philosophy of Judaism*." Strauss's criticisms addressed Julius Guttmann, *Die Philosophie des Judentums* (Munich: E. Reinhardt, 1933) and "Religion und Wissenschaft im mittelalterlichen und im modernen Denken," *Festschrift zum 50 jährigen Bestehen der Hochschule für die Wissenschaft des Judentums in Berlin* (Berlin, 1922): 147–216.

[52] Strauss traced Guttmann's concept of philosophy of religion to Schleiermacher, through whom one could understand religion and belief as "the subjectivity of the religious consciousness" rather than belief in the Law as revealed by God and as encompassing all aspects of human life, an idea that is close to Plato's *Laws*; PL, 73.

[53] Julius Guttmann, "Philosophie der Religion oder Philosophie des Gesetzes?" *The Israel Academy of Sciences and Humanities, Proceedings*, Vol. V, No. 6

was forthright and genuinely believed in the creation of the world and in prophecy and revelation as miracles displaying God's sovereign will. Along with Cohen, he believed that Maimonides recognized the differences between religious faith and philosophy yet ingeniously forged a bond between them by viewing Judaism as consistent with universal reason.

The Religious Law Subsumed under Political Philosophy

As Islam and Judaism regarded religion as essentially Law, the *falasifa* were able to portray religion as a political phenomenon. Platonic-Alfarabian political science subsumed religion under politics. What is more, God gave the divine law to mankind by means of a lawgiver-prophet, who is a political figure (*PL*, 70–71).

The starting point of political philosophy is the assertion that man is by nature a political being and needs laws, and therefore a lawgiver. In Plato's *Republic*, the lawgiver is the founder of the state, the philosopher-king (*PL*, 74). The philosopher-king of the *falasifa* is different. He is not expected in the future; he is an actual prophet who came in the past. Plato's doctrine is transformed in the light of the revelation that has actually occurred (*PL*, 75).

Alfarabi subsumed religion, jurisprudence (*fiqh*), and theology (*kalam*) under political science.[54] Maimonides likewise treated prophecy under this rubric.[55] The *falasifa* regarded Plato's *Laws* as the authoritative philosophical teaching on prophecy and the revealed laws (*PL*, 76, 125, 152 n. 65).

Strauss's eyes were opened to the importance for the *falasifa* of Plato's *Laws* in a serendipitous moment at the Berlin National Library in 1929

(Jerusalem, 1974). The rejoinder was written between 1940 and 1945 and was found among Guttmann's papers after his death. It was given by his widow to Gershom Scholem, who turned it over to the Israel Academy. See also Eliezer Schweid, "Religion and Philosophy: The Scholarly-Theological Debate between Julius Guttmann and Leo Strauss," *Maimonidean Studies*, ed. A. Hyman, 1 (New York: Yeshiva University Press, 1990): 163–195.

54 See *Ihsa' al-'ulum*, ed. 'U. Amin (Cairo, 1948), 124–132; trans. Fawzi M. Najjar, *The Enumeration of the Sciences*, *Medieval Political Philosophy*, ed. Ralph Lerner and Muhsin Mahdi (Ithaca, NY: Cornell Paperbacks, 1993), 24–28; and see M. Mahdi, "Science, Philosophy, and Religion in Alfarabi's *Enumeration of the Sciences*" in *The Cultural Context of Medieval Learning*, ed. J. E. Murdoch and E. D. Sylla (Dordrecht, 1975), 113–147, esp. 140ff. See also Plato, *Laws*, 624a–b and Alfarabi, *Talkhis Nawamis Aflatun* (*Compendium Legum Platonis*), ed. Fr. Gabrieli (London: Warburg Institute, 1952), I, 1: 5.

55 See Maimonides, *Treatise on the Art of Logic*, trans. Joel L. Kraemer, *Perspectives on Maimonides*, (Oxford: The Littman Library, 2008), ch. 14, p. 97 and *Guide of the Perplexed*, II, 40, trans. Pines, 382.

or 1930.[56] Reading Avicenna's *On the Divisions of the Rational Sciences*, he came across the philosopher's definition of political science (*PL*, 122):[57] "What relates to prophecy (*nubuwwa*) and the religious law (*shari'a*) is contained in two books that are on the laws (*nawamis*)."[58] "Through this part of practical philosophy the existence[59] of prophecy is known, as is the human species' need for the religious law for the sake of its existence, survival and ultimate destiny."[60] Strauss commented that when he read Avicenna's treatise, he had his initial glimpse of light and first understood Maimonides's prophetology, and eventually the entire *Guide of the Perplexed*.[61]

Limitations of Human Knowledge

Although revelation emerges as essential for the *falasifa* in their endeavor to create societies based on divine laws, the need for revelation was also predicated on the claim that the human capacity for knowledge

[56] H. Meier, "How Strauss Became Strauss," 367, 377 n. 13.

[57] See *PAW*, 10; "A Giving of Accounts," in *JPCM*, 463. For the text, see Ibn Sina, *Aqsam al-'ulum*, in *Majmu'at al-Rasa'il* (Cairo, 1908), 107–108; trans. Mahdi, in *Medieval Political Philosophy*, 96–97, and trans. James W. Morris, "The Philosopher-Prophet in Avicenna's Political Philosophy," in The *Political Aspects of Islamic Philosophy: Essays in Honor of Muhsin S. Mahdi*, ed. C. E. Butterworth (Cambridge, MA, 1992), 152–198, on 168–170; G. C. Anawati, "Les divisions des sciences intellectuelles d'Avicenne," *Mélanges de l'Institut Dominicain d'Études Orientales* 13 (1977): 323–325, on 326.

[58] Mahdi (trans. 97, n. 2) identified the two books as the *Republic* and the *Laws*. Morris, "The Philosopher-Prophet," 169, n. 16, affirmed the view that Ibn Sina referred to Plato and Aristotle. Actually, Ibn Sina alluded to Plato's *Laws* and to a magic pseudograph ascribed to Plato and called *On the Laws* (*Fi 'l-nawamis*); see Paul Kraus, *Jābir Ibn Íayyán: Contribution à l'histoire des idées scientifiques dans l'islam* (Paris, 1986), 104; F. Sezgin, *Geschichte des arabischen Schrifttums* (Leiden: Brill, 1971), IV, 98–99. On this work, see also S. Pines, "Shi'ite Terms and Conceptions in the *Kuzari*," Apppendix V, in *The Collected Works of Shlomo Pines*, Vol. V, *Studies in the History of Jewish Thought*, ed. W. Z. Harvey and M. Idel (Jerusalem, 1997), 290–293.

[59] Reading *wujud*. Mahdi translated "necessity," reading *wujub*.

[60] In the *Shifa'*, Ibn Sina stated that practical philosophy, which includes political science, economics, and ethics, is "realized in its totality only by means of theoretical demonstration and the testimony of revelation. It is realized in detail and determinateness by means of the divine law." See Ibn Sina, *Kitab al-Shifa', al-Madkhal*, ed. G. Anawati, M. al-Khudairi, and F. al-Ahwani (Cairo, 1952), 14; trans. Morris, "Philosopher-Prophet," 167, n. 13 (with a slight change here).

[61] Strauss, "A Giving of Accounts," in *JPCM*, 457–470, on 462–463. The epigraph, "the treatment of prophecy and the Divine law is contained in . . . the Laws," heads *AAPL*, 1.

is limited. Maimonides made the limitation of knowledge a cornerstone of his teaching (*PL*, 64–67).[62] As the ultimate objects of knowledge are mysteries for human beings, whose intellect has an impassable limit set by human nature, they must accept as true the incomprehensible and undemonstratable suprarational doctrines of revelation. Maimonides taught that revelation is superior to reason, as revelation attains truths inaccessible to reason (*PL*, 90–91). The insufficiency of human intellect means that the question whether the world is created or eternal cannot be resolved (*PL*, 91).

However, Averroes believed in the sufficiency of human reason, and hence passages in the Qur'an that indicate superiority of revelation over reason are in need of "interpretation" (*ta'wil*) (*PL*, 92).[63] Yet for Averroes, as for Maimonides, the primacy of the Law is well founded in that it authorizes philosophy. As Strauss pronounced in a lapidary sentence, "The freedom of philosophy depends upon its bondage."

The Legal Foundation of Philosophy

In their endeavor to assimilate Greek philosophy to an Islamic milieu, the medieval rationalists established a legal foundation of philosophy and defended it before the bar of revelation (*PL*, 81).[64] As the Law's actuality is a prephilosophic given, the *falasifa* had to show that it justified the study of philosophy and the sciences, and that the Law even urged the pursuit of knowledge as an act of piety. The purpose of legitimizing philosophy and the sciences before the tribunal of the Law was to assimilate them, to present them as orthogenic instead of heterogenic, native rather than alien.

---

[62] See Shlomo Pines, "The Limitations of Human Knowledge According to Al-Farabi, Ibn Bájja, and Maimonides," *Studies in Medieval Jewish History and Literature*, ed. Isadore Twersky (Cambridge, MA: Harvard University Press, 1979): 82–109 and "Les limites de la Métaphysique selon Al-Farabi, Ibn Bájja, et Maïmonide," *Miscellanea Mediaevalia* 13 (1981): 211–225. Pines suggested that Maimonides used the limitations of knowledge to make room for faith in a proto-Kantian move. I rather believe that the concept of the limitations of knowledge was deeply embedded in his religious outlook.

[63] *Ta'wil* is interpretation of the Qur'an that seeks its inner meaning (*batin*), which is generally identical with the ideas of the interpreter. It is sometimes called "allegorical interpretation." Averroes's *ta'wil* is the deep philosophic meaning of the Qur'anic text.

[64] Gerhard Endress discusses Islamic thought and the legitimization of philosophy in "The Defense of Reason: the Plea for Philosophy in the Religious Community," *Zeitschrift für Geschichte der Arabisch-Islamischen Wissenschaften*, ed. F. Sezgin et al., Band 6 (1990): 1–49.

Written in the form of a legal opinion, *The Decisive Treatise* by Averroes aimed to "determine the connection that exists between the religious law and philosophy" (*PL*, 82–83).[65] Averroes's stated intention was to harmonize philosophy with the Law, whereas his true intention was to distinguish between them and to rank philosophy above the Law. He cited Qur'anic verses that make philosophy obligatory, thereby securing the freedom to philosophize (*PL*, 83).[66]

Averroes portrayed philosophy's aim as identical with the aim of Law. The Law's purpose is to summon men to happiness, which is knowledge of God (*PL*, 84).[67] But we know God only from existent beings, which point to God as their maker. Contemplating beings in this way is to philosophize. Therefore, philosophy and the Law meet on the highest level, as they both seek to know God by contemplating the beings in this world. Averroes's intention was to persuade religionists that philosophy and religion are compatable. For Strauss, Averroes's rhetorical strategy filled a vital need – to assure freedom to philosophize without destabilizing the Law and society.

According to Averroes, the philosophers are the authoritative interpreters of the Law, and they must interpret it figuratively in case of a conflict between its literal sense and philosophy. They must conceal their interpretation from all who are unqualified to philosophize (*PL*, 85). Philosophy's right of interpretation means that it is free with respect to the Law. Religion authorizes philosophy; yet as the philosopher is the true interpreter of scripture, he achieves a status above the Law.

Strauss noted that we do not find in *The Guide of the Perplexed* the systematic treatment that we find in Averroes's *Decisive Treatise*. The legal foundation of philosophy is not its theme (*PL*, 89). Hence, we need to collect Maimonides's relevant statements from various parts of his treatise, understanding him to be teaching what Averroes taught.

Like Averroes, Maimonides embraced privately the doctrine that reason and revelation are distinct, even as publicly he taught that they are in harmony and have the same goal. The Law summons to belief in the most important truths (God's existence, unity, and incorporeality). Divine Law differs from human laws in that it serves the highest end, the specific perfection of human beings, which is knowledge, especially knowledge of the beings and of God. Hence, as Averroes taught, the end of the Law is identical with the end of philosophy (*PL*, 90).

[65] Averroes, *The Book of the Decisive Treatise*, trans. C. E. Butterworth (Provo, UT: Brigham Young University Press, 2001), 1.

[66] Averroes, *Decisive Treatise*, 2.

[67] Averroes, *Decisive Treatise*, 6–8.

The Philosophic Foundation of the Religious Law

In Averroes's view, as religion authorizes the freedom to philosophize, philosophy lays the foundation for prophecy, and prophecy creates societies based on revelation and the Law.

The *falasifa* and Maimonides held, along with Aristotle, that man is by nature a political being and in need of association. Aiming at the specific perfection of human beings, the Law is a divine Law, and its proclaimer is a prophet (*PL*, 121). But the Law aims at making it possible to live together. Hence, the prophet is the founder of a community intended for human perfection. If the founder of the perfect community must be a prophet and the prophet is more than a philosopher, then founding the ideal community is impossible for someone who is merely a philosopher.

For Alfarabi, the ruler of the ideal state, the "excellent state" (*al-madina al-fadila*), which only a prophet can be, must possess by nature the qualities that Plato's philosopher-kings must have by nature (*PL*, 126). Plato's *Republic* was the basic text for theorizing about politics. The Islamic philosophers understood political science to be examination of the best polity, ideal rule, types of regimes, justice, and human happiness. The *Republic* is the model for Alfarabi's *Opinions of the Inhabitants of the Virtuous City* and is decisive for all his political writings. He wrote a commentary on the *Republic*, now lost or unrecovered, and known from Averroes's citations in his own commentary.[68]

Averroes appealed to the *Republic* for thinking about politics because, as he said, he could not find an Arabic version of Aristotle's *Politics*, which he heard was available in the Muslim East.[69] He envisioned an ideal state ruled by philosophers and modeled after Plato's *Republic*.[70] He did not anticipate that political revolution would create this state in the near future, although he admitted the possibility that a long succession of enlightened rulers might bring it about. If individuals would

---

[68] *Averroes's Commentary on Plato's Republic*, ed. and trans. E. I. J. Rosenthal (Cambridge, UK: Cambridge University Press, 1969); *Averroes on Plato's "Republic,"* translated, with an introduction and notes by Ralph Lerner (Ithaca, NY: Cornell University Press, 1974).

[69] See Shlomo Pines, "Aristotle's *Politics* in Arabic Philosophy," *Israel Oriental Studies* 5 (1975): 150–160. See also Rémi Brague, "Notes sur la traduction arabe de la Politique, derechef, qu'elle n'existe pas," in *Aristote politique: Études sur la Politique de Aristote*, ed. Pierre Aubenque (Paris: Presses Universitaires de France, 1993), 423–433.

[70] See Shlomo Pines, "Translator's Preface," in *Guide of the Perplexed*, cxviii, citing his "Notes on Averroes' Political Philosophy" [Hebrew], *'Iyyun* (1957), 68ff. and 76. See also *Averroes on Plato's "Republic,"* 74–75.

arise with the required natural qualities, their particular religious law being close to universal human laws, then wisdom would be realized in their time. If it happens that their type comes to rule for a long time, then the virtuous city may come into being.[71] Averroes taught that the philosopher should live within the state as a full participant, seeking its welfare, while pursuing his studies on his own or with people of like mind, without teaching philosophy publicly.

STRAUSS'S PHILOSOPHIC ORIENTATION IN THE 1930S

Before we leave *Philosophy and Law*, I wish to take note of Straus's intellectual universe at the time and summarize his main ideas. By the early 1930s, Strauss had already read the authors who decisively shaped his philosophical outlook. These included Machiavelli, Hobbes, Spinoza, Nietzsche, Heidegger, and Schmitt. Heidegger's *Sein und Zeit* had been published in 1927, and the decade culminated in 1929 with the famous debate between Cassirer and Heidegger at Davos, and Strauss's enchantment with Heidegger and abandonment of the academic philosophy of the Marburg neo-Kantian school. Strauss studied Spinoza not only as the subject of historical research but as a truth-seeker. In fact, throughout the 1920s Nietzsche and Spinoza had been the philosophers who most dominated his mind.[72]

I suggest the following as the core ideas of Strauss's philosophic outlook in *Philosophy and Law*:

1. A life of reason in quest of the truth.
2. Freedom to philosophize, the highest human activity.
3. Incompatability of philosophy and religious faith.
4. Accommodation to religious custom and tradition.

[71] Averroes says that if the likes of these rulers come to rule for an infinite time (*zeman she-en takhlit lo*), or time without limit, but he must mean something like undetermined or indefinite time; see ed. and trans. E. I. J. Rosenthal, *Averroes' Commentary on Plato's Republic*, 180, n. 2 with the citation of Mantinus' Latin translation. See also his statement at the end of *Tahafut al-Tahafut* (*The Incoherence of the Incoherence*), trans. S. van den Bergh (London: Oxford, 1954), 1: 359–363, where he asserted that a philosopher is obligated to choose the best religion of his time, and if they are all true in his eyes, he must believe that the best will be abrogated by one that is better.

[72] A link between Spinoza and Nietzsche was perceived by Nietzsche himself. In a postcard to his friend Franz Overbeck (from Sils Maria, July 30, 1881), Nietzsche expressed his feeling of kinship with Spinoza: "I am utterly amazed, utterly enchanted. I have a *precursor*, and what a precursor! I hardly knew Spinoza: that I should have turned to him just *now*, was inspired by 'instinct.'" See *The Portable Nietzsche*, ed. and trans. Walter Kaufmann (New York: Viking Penguin, 1982), 92.

5. Nature as beyond good and evil without a moral world order.
6. Intellectual probity.
7. The division between the elite and the many as a permanent feature of human societies.
8. The exoteric-esoteric binarity as a key to understanding and as mode of communication.
9. Religion under the rubric of political philosophy.
10. Medieval rationalism preferred over the rationalism of the Enlightenment.

ALFARABI'S PLATO

From 1935 to 1941, Strauss continued to publish studies on Alfarabi and Maimonides.[73] He emphasized that Maimonides must be understood as a disciple of Alfarabi, suggesting that whatever can be said of Alfarabi can be said equally of Maimonides. The most important of his writings on Alfarabi was "Farabi's Plato," based upon Alfarabi's summary of Plato's philosophy, the centerpiece of a trilogy beginning with *The Attainment of Happiness* and ending with Alfarabi's summary of Aristotle's philosophy.[74]

In *The Attainment of Happiness*, Alfarabi gave his views on philosophy and religion. Philosophy is prior to religion in time, and religion is an imitation of philosophy.[75] Where philosophy gives an account based

[73] In this period, Strauss wrote: "Quelques remarques sur la science politique de Maïmonide et de Fârâbî," *Revue des Etudes Juives* 100 (1936): 1–37; Strauss, *GS*, 2: 125–165; trans. Robert Bartlett as "Some Remarks on the Political Science of Maimonides and Farabi," in *Interpretation* 18, no. 1 (Fall 1990): 3–30. "Eine vermisste Schrift Farabis," *Monatsschrift für Geschichte und Wissenschaft des Judentums* 80 (1936): 96–106; *GS*, 2: 167–177. "Der Ort der Vorsehungslehre nach der Ansicht Maimunis." *Monatsschrift für Geschichte und Wissenschaft des Judentums* 81 (1937): 93–105; *GS*, 2: 179–194. Strauss also reviewed Moses Hyamson's edition of Maimonides, *The Mishneh Torah*, book 1, in *Review of Religion* 3, no. 4 (1938): 448–456.

[74] *Kitab falsafat Aflatun*, ed. F. Rosenthal and R. Walzer (London: Warburg Institute, 1943); *Kitab falsafat Aristutalis*, ed. M. Mahdi (Beirut: Dar Majallat Shi'r, 1961). See *On The Philosophy of Plato and Aristotle*, trans. M. Mahdi (Ithaca, NY: Cornell University Press, 1969; London, 1972).

[75] See *Attainment of Happiness*, in *On The Philosophy of Plato and Aristotle*, trans. Mahdi, 44. Alfarabi ascribed to the ancients the idea that religion is an imitation of philosophy. The idea appears in all of Alfarabi's major works and is adopted by later Islamic philosophers and Maimonides. See R. Walzer, "Al-Farabi's Theory of Prophecy and Divination," *The Journal of Hellenic Studies* 77 (1957): 142–148; in *Greek into Arabic: Essays on Islamic Philosophy* (Cambridge, MA: Harvard University Press, 1962), 206–219. One is

on intellectual apprehension, religion bases its account on imagination. Philosophy uses demonstration and religion uses persuasion. Like the supreme ruler, the perfect philosopher teaches the general public and forms their character so they may reach the happiness they are capable of attaining.

As prophecy is an emanation from God, through the Agent Intellect to the prophet's rational faculty and then to his imaginative faculty, actuating it, it generates a symbolic representation of the truth. The prophet communicates symbols to the public by way of myth and ritual. Religion is an imitation of philosophy, and whereas philosophy is appropriate for the few, religion serves the many.

Hence, the founders of religions portray the truths of philosophy in parabolic form. In the perfect religion, it is the truth of philosophy that is portrayed symbolically and not primitive rhetoric, poetry, sophistry, or dialectics. Insofar as proponents of jurisprudence and theology reason from religious premises that imitate philosophical verities, they are twice removed from the truth. As in the case of Islam, if a religion comes to a community, like the Arab nation, before the appearance of philosophy, it may occur that the religion, though a parabolic version of philosophy, will discard the philosophy from which it evolves.

Strauss began "Farabi's Plato" by citing a letter of Maimonides to Samuel Ibn Tibbon, the translator of *The Guide of the Perplexed* into Hebrew, in which he said that the greatest authority in philosophy after Aristotle was Alfarabi. Maimonides recommended specifically *The Principles of Beings*, also known as *The Political Governments*.[76] One needs to start then from an analysis of *The Political Governments*. Alas, Strauss commented, this would be unwise for two reasons. First, there is no satisfactory edition.[77] Second, understanding the book requires

naturally reminded of Hegel's understanding of religion as having as its object the representation (*Vorstellung*) of scientific conceptual knowledge, to which he added emotion, festivities, cult practices, and so on.

[76] Strauss, "Farabi's Plato," 357–358. See Steven Lenzner, *Leo Strauss and the Problem of Freedom of Thought: The Rediscovery of the Philosophic Arts of Reading and Writing* (Harvard University Ph.D., 2003), 28–29.

[77] There was only a poor Hyderabad, Deccan (India), 1928 edition by the Osmania Press and Ibn Tibbon's Hebrew translation, as well as a German translation by Fr. Dieterici, *Die Staatsleitung von Alfarabi* (Leiden: Brill, 1904). See now *Al-Farabi's The Political Regime (Al-Siyasa al-Madaniyya also Known as The Treatise on the Principles of Beings)*, ed. Fawzi M. Najjar (Beirut: Imprimerie Catholique, 1964), and see "Alfarabi: The Political Regime," trans. F. M. Najjar, in *Medieval Political Philosophy: A Sourcebook*, 31–57. Najjar was a pupil of Strauss, who encouraged him in the work and helped him acquire manuscripts. Strauss's pupil Muhsin Mahdi found the most valuable

studying two corresponding works of Alfarabi – *The Principles of the Opinions of the People of the Virtuous City* and *The Virtuous Religious Community*.[78] Strauss described *The Political Governments* as showing the main trait of Alfarabi's philosophy, the treatment of philosophy within a political framework. Strauss proposed that the teaching of *The Political Governments* silently rejects certain beliefs that Alfarabi accepted in the two other works.

Alfarabi's summary of Plato's philosophy presented the dialogues in thematic sequence, stressing their political aspect and excluding neo-Platonic doctrines. Strauss viewed *The Philosophy of Plato* as the key for unlocking Alfarabi's thought on the assumption that he taught his own most personal views chiefly under the camouflage of an interpreter. Strauss argued that by omitting distinctive Platonic themes (theory of ideas, God, soul, immortality) in a summary of Plato's entire philosophy, these concepts are exoteric. The editors of *The Philosophy of Plato*, Franz Rosenthal and Richard Walzer, traced this politically oriented portrait of Plato to a mid-Platonic source and did not ascribe any original ideas to Alfarabi, as they could not compare the (unidentified) source with Alfarabi's version.[79]

Strauss presented Alfarabi as an innovator who studied Plato politically. He wrote as though Alfarabi had the dialogues before him without considering the millennium and a third that had elapsed between Plato and Alfarabi. He took Alfarabi's Plato to be the original Plato, but Alfarabi's Plato had been filtered through a long interpretive tradition.

---

manuscripts for the edition in Istanbul. Strauss was the fountainhead of scholarly editions and studies of Alfarabi, especially through Muhsin Mahdi and Mahdi's students Charles E. Butterworth and Miriam Galston.

[78] *The Principles of the Opinions of the People of the Virtuous City* was available to Strauss in a decent edition by Fr. Dieterici, *Der Musterstaat* (Leiden: Brill, 1895). A modern scholarly edition is found in *Al-Farabi on the Perfect State: Abu Nasr Al-Farabi's Mabadi' ara' ahl al-madina al-fadila*, ed. and trans. Richard Walzer (Oxford: Oxford University Press, 1985). *The Virtuous Religious Community* was published by M. Mahdi, *Alfarabi's Book of Religion and Related Texts* (Beirut: Imprimerie Catholique, 1968) and translated by Charles E. Butterworth, in *Alfarabi: The Political Writings: Selected Aphorisms and Other Texts* (Ithaca, NY: Cornell University Press, 2001), 87–113.

[79] Strauss, "Farabi's Plato," *Louis Ginzberg Jubilee Volume* (New York: American Academy for Jewish Research, 1945), 357–393. Similarly, in the philosophy of Aristotle, Alfarabi avoided discussing metaphysics save for brief, cryptic remarks such as: "We do not possess a metaphysical science." See T.-A. Druart, "Al-Farabi, Emanation and Metaphysics," in *Neoplatonism and Islamic Thought*, ed. P. Morewedge (Albany, NY: State University of New York Press, 1992), 127–148, at 131. See *Kitab falsafat Aflatun*, ed. F. Rosenthal and R. Walzer, Praefatio, ix–x, xii–xvi.

Alfarabi tells us about his intellectual forebears: his Christian teachers in Aleppo and Harran and the ultimate starting point in Alexandria.

For instance, Strauss put great stock in Alfarabi's omission of the Platonic "Ideas." Yet by the time of Middle Platonism, the Ideas were either immanent in existent beings or thoughts in the mind of God. The dramatic form of the dialogues was dropped in favor of summaries of Plato's philosophy as we find in Alfarabi's *Philosophy of Plato.*

Rosenthal and Walzer conjectured that Alfarabi's political interpretation of Plato did not appear in a vacuum, nor in the environment of the mystical, theurgic Athenian neo-Platonism of Proclus and Iamblichus. They suggested rather Middle Platonism as the probable context under the Romans with men such as Cicero, Plutarch of Chaeronea, Numenius of Apamea, and Albinus as conduits. Rosenthal and Walzer tentatively identified Theon of Smyrna (2nd century C.E.), who wrote a similar treatise as a possible intermediary between Plato and Alfarabi, and they found references to Theon in Arabic works.[80] We are familiar with the form in which Plato came down to the Arabs from Galen's *Summary of the Timaeus.* The editors demonstrated the existence of the Syriac *Vorlage* to Alfarabi's summary, for it was only on this basis that Rosenthal was able to decipher the names and titles of the dialogues that were beyond recognition in the single Arabic manuscript that they had, whereas the Syriac version, done by Christians who knew Greek, was more reliable.

Strauss was convinced that Rosenthal and Walzer, as strict philologists, could not admit that Alfarabi was in any way original. However, this was not their issue, and they had no problem assigning originality to an Arab philosopher when they deemed it justified.[81] In fact, the concepts that Alfarabi omits in *The Philosophy of Plato* (God, soul, immortality, the ideas) appear prominently in his main writings: *The Political Regimes, The Virtuous City,* and *The Virtuous Religious Community.* In his (nonextant) *Commentary on the Nicomachean Ethics,* Alfarabi wrote openly that the only happiness is of this life, and that all other statements are based upon "ravings and old women's tales."[82]

---

[80] See Paul Kristeller, review in *The Journal of Philosophy* 41, 6 (March 16, 1944), 164–165, who cites other Middle Platonist summaries.

[81] When I asked Rosenthal, my teacher of Arabic 1962–1967, about Strauss's criticism of Walzer and him, he replied in a pithy remark: "I can only read what I see."

[82] Strauss, "Farabi's Plato," 372. The quotation from his *Commentary on the Ethics* is taken from Ibn Tufayl, *Hayv ibn Yaqzān,* ed. L. Gautier (Beirut: Imprimérie Catholique, 1936), 14, and from an account of Averroes. Ibn Tufayl noted correctly that Alfarabi mentioned the afterlife of the soul in other writings, naming *The Virtuous Religious Community* and *The Political Regimes,* to which we may add *The Virtuous City.* Shlomo Pines discussed the passage

THE *SUMMARY OF PLATO'S LAWS*

In the *Summary of Plato's Laws*, Alfarabi showed how the notion of Greek divine laws helps us understand divine laws in general.[83] In a prelude to the *Summary of Plato's Laws*, Alfarabi portrayed Plato's style of writing.[84] He wrote that whereas the wise men know that men's natural disposition is to make a universal judgment on the basis of a few instances, and seeing that an individual had done something in a certain way many times, they suppose that he does it that way all the time.[85] For instance, when someone has spoken the truth on a number of occasions, men naturally assume that he is simply truthful, and similarly when someone lies. Afterward, when they act differently, men suppose that they are acting as they did formerly. He illustrated this with a marvelous anecdote.

An ascetic, famous for his probity, abstemiousness, and religious devotion, feared the tyrannical sovereign of his city and decided to escape. The sovereign ordered that he be arrested wherever he was found. He could not leave from any of the city's gates. So he dressed himself as a vagabond and came to the gate of the city early at night and pretended to be drunk, singing to the accompaniment of a cymbal. The gatekeeper asked him who he was, to which he replied jokingly, "I am so and so, the ascetic." The gatekeeper thought he was poking fun at him and did not detain him. The ascetic saved himself "without having lied in what he said."

Alfarabi explained that Plato did not wish to reveal the sciences to everyone. He therefore used "symbols, riddles, obscurity, and abstruseness" to exclude the undeserving or those who devalue science or misuse

from the *Commentary on the Ethics* in "The Limitations of Human Knowledge," 82–86, inferring Alfarabi's intention to be that the only happiness is political happiness in this world.

[83] Strauss, "How Farabi Read Plato's *Laws*," *Mélanges Louis Massignon* (Damascus: Institut Français de Damas, 1957), 3: 19–44; reprinted in *WPP*, 134–54. See Joshua Parens, *Metaphysics as Rhetoric: Alfarabi's Summary of Plato's "Laws"* (Albany, NY: State University of New York Press, 1995).

[84] The idea of affixing a prelude to a work is found in Plato: "For all speeches, and whatever pertains to the voice, are preceded by preludes – almost like warming-up exercises – which artfully promote what is to come." These exercises, Plato insists, are "composed with amazing seriousness." *The Laws of Plato*, trans. Thomas Pangle (New York: Basic Books, 1980), 722d–e.

[85] Alfarabi, *Plato's Laws*, trans. M. Mahdi, *Medieval Political Philosophy*, ed. Ralph Lerner and Muhsin Mahdi, 83–84, from *Alfarabius Compendium Legum Platonis*, ed. and trans. into Latin Fr. Gabrieli (London: Warburg Institute, 1952), 3–4.

it. Once Plato knew that he had become known for this practice, he discussed scientific subjects openly and literally. Whoever reads or hears his discourse assumes that it is symbolic and means something other than what was stated openly. This is one of the secrets of his books, and Plato wrote about laws in this manner.[86]

Strauss pointed out that in the *Summary of Plato's Laws*, Alfarabi was concerned with legislating for a city on the basis of the religious law. In *The Philosophy of Plato*, Alfarabi had stressed that philosophy is the ultimate happiness and perfection of a human being. However, the *Summary of Plato's Laws* is silent about philosophy. The *Laws* provides for the second best regime, not the best governed by philosophy and wisdom but by the laws, which were for Alfarabi the laws of Islam. Strauss suggested that Alfarabi may have rewritten the version of the *Laws* that came into his hands in consideration of the situation created by the rise of Islam or of revealed religion in general.[87] According to the *Summary*, happiness is brought about by obedience to the divine law or to the gods. It speaks often of God, gods, the after life, the revealed law (*shari'a*) and divine laws, whereas *The Philosophy of Plato* is completely silent about these subjects.

PERSECUTION AND THE ART OF WRITING

Persecution and the Art of Writing is a compilation of articles that made their first appearance between 1941 and 1948. It was meant to be a successor to *Philosophy and Law*, according to a 1946 plan of the book.[88] Strauss explained in the plan that as Alfarabi's philosophy was crucial for understanding Maimonides's thought, four essays were required for the book. He thought to include "The Literary Character of *The Guide of the Perplexed*" (1941) and "Farabi's Treatise on Plato's Philosophy" (1945). He also decided to reprint "The Law of Reason in the *Kuzari*" (1943) to show that the Alfarabian interpretation is valuable for understanding this "second classic of medieval Jewish philosophy." And he incorporated "Persecution and the Art of Writing" (1941) to show that contemporary totalitarian societies, whose policy is suppression of freedom of speech, help us grasp the conditions under which many free

---

[86] Alfarabi, *Compendium Legum Platonis*, 4; Strauss, "How Farabi Read Plato's *Laws*," in *WPP*, 136–137.

[87] Strauss, "How Farabi Read Plato's *Laws*," in *WPP*, 144.

[88] Strauss, "Plan of a Book Tentatively Entitled *Philosophy and the Law: Historical Essays*." See *JPCM*, 467–470. It was found by Kenneth Green in the Leo Strauss Archive in the Regenstein Library, University of Chicago, box 11, folder 11.

individuals in the past thought and expressed themselves in speech and in writing.

Persecution and the Art of Writing was published in 1952, three years after Strauss took up an appointment in Political Philosophy at the University of Chicago.[89] The essays had been written when he was teaching at the New School for Social Research. Therefore, it was a summing up of his scholarly activity during his years in New York.[90]

The essays in *Persecution and the Art of Writing* were written in an allusive style. What Strauss thought about Maimonides around this time we discover in two letters written in 1938 to Jacob Klein. Strauss wrote to Klein (January 20) that Maimonides is always thrilling, that he was "a really free spirit."[91] He added Maimonides naturally did not believe in the Jewish origin of philosophy, a widespread Hellenistic idea that he espoused publicly.[92] Strauss wrote what is more, it is difficult to say what the biblical Moses really meant for him.[93] The crucial question was not creation or eternity but whether the ideal lawgiver must be a prophet, which Maimonides denied along with Alfarabi and Averroes.

In a second letter (February 16, 1938), Strauss informed Klein that he was making progress understanding *The Guide* but had not written a line.[94] He wrote facetiously that the book *De tribus impostoribus*, which was supposedly written by Friedrich II von Hohenstaufen and others but is nonextant, is now found in all hands: "it is the *Moreh* or the work of Averroes, Alfarabi and others." He then noted the infinite subtlety and irony of Maimonides's treatment of religion. Maimonides talked about

---

[89] In 1952, Strauss wrote the Introduction to a book by Isaac Husik – "On Husik's Work in Medieval Jewish Philosophy," *Isaac Husik's Philosophical Essays: Ancient, Medieval, and Modern*, ed. Milton Nahm and Leo Strauss (Oxford: Basil Blackwell, 1952), vii–xli. There is a Hebrew translation with an English summary of Strauss's Introduction in *Iyyun: Hebrew Philosophical Quarterly* 2 (1951): 215–223, 259–260. Strauss did an amazing amount of historical research to write this tribute to a superb scholar of medieval Islamic and Jewish thought.

[90] On Strauss's New York Years, see Steven Smith, "Leo Strauss: The Outlines of a Life," this volume.

[91] Strauss, *GS*, 3: 544–546, written from John Jay Hall at Columbia University. "Free spirit" is evidently from Nietzsche's *Freigeist*, as in *Human All Too Human: A Book of Free Spirits*, trans. R. J. Hollingdale (Cambridge, UK: Cambridge University Press, 1986), Preface.

[92] See *Guide*, I, 71. Ibn Rushd credited Solomon and the ancient Israelites with having scientific books at the end of his *Tahafut al-tahafut* (*The Incoherence of the Incoherence*), trans. Simon van den Bergh (London: Luzac, 1954) [E. J. W. Gibb Memorial Series. New series, 19], II, end.

[93] See *Guide*, II, 35.

[94] Strauss, *GS*, 3: 548–550.

the stench in the Jerusalem Temple from the many sacrificial animals there "and 1000 other things."[95] Strauss claimed that readers failed to understand Maimonides because they did not consider that he was an Averroist.

Strauss's view that Maimonides was an Averroist was in line with the best of his medieval Jewish commentators, beginning with Samuel Ibn Tibbon and his school, including his son Moses and son-in-law Jacob Anatoli, and continuing with Moses of Narbonne, Shem Tov Falaquera, and others. The main Averroist doctrines were: separation of philosophy from theology, eternity of the universe, and denial of individual providence or individual survival of the soul.

Strauss added to his letter this ominous sentence: "When I let go of this bomb in a few years (if I am still living), a great war will break out." He mentioned that Nahum Glatzer, who was then in New York, told him that for Judaism Maimonides was more important than the Bible. "If one deprived Judaism of Maimonides, then one deprived it of its foundation." Strauss then observed that in his belief (*Glauben*) Maimonides was by no means a Jew (*schlechterdings kein Jude war*), citing the incompatibility (*Unvereinbarkeit*) of philosophy and Judaism.

The chapter titled "Persecution and the Art of Writing" argues for the permanence of natural differences among men, between the philosophic few and the nonphilosophic many.[96] Strauss wrote that modern authors masked their views to protect themselves from persecution, whereas premodern authors believed "that public communication of the philosophic or scientific truth was impossible or undesirable, not only for the time being but for all times."[97] It was this permanent distinction between the elite and the vulgar that the modern Enlightenment denied was necessary.[98] Strauss thought that it was necessary, and hence preferred the medieval Enlightenment to its modern counterpart, as he had worked out in *Philosophy and Law*.

---

[95] Maimonides discussed the stench of the sacrifices and the smell of the clothes of those who served in the sanctuary in *Guide*, III, 45 (trans. Pines, 579–580). Maimonides considered sacrifices to be an outmoded type of worship; see *Guide*, III, 32; Pines, "Translator's Introduction," lxxii–lxxiv. Yet in the messianic age sacrifices would be restored; *Mishneh Torah*, Hilkhot Melakhim, xi, 1. I do not believe that Maimonides was being disrespectful by mentioning the stench from sacrifices in the tabernacle. He wanted to explain why incense was used and gave the most plausible natural explanation. The addition of "and 1000 other things" is atypical Straussian hyperbole.

[96] Strauss, "Persecution and the Art of Writing," in *PAW*, 34; Michael Kochin, "Morality, Nature, and Esotericism in Leo Strauss's 'Persecution and the Art of Writing'," *The Review of Politics*, vol. 64, no. 2 (2002): 261–283, on 269–270.

[97] Strauss quoted Cicero and Plato without referring to the *falasifa*.

[98] Strauss, *PAW*, 33–34; Kochin, "Morality, Nature, and Esotericism," 271.

"The Literary Character of *The Guide for the Perplexed*" evoked a reaction of doubt and disbelief more than shock. Expecting "a war" to break out, Strauss evidently softened the blow, perhaps under the influence of Glatzer's astute warning. He decided to write an esoteric interpretation of *The Guide of the Perplexed*, which "seems to be not only advisable, but even necessary."[99] Although the essay had a mixed reception at the time, by now the general principle of exoteric writing and use of Strauss's hermeneutic methods have taken root among scholars dealing with these questions. The main criticism of Strauss's interpretation was that it was uncertain, even arbitrary.[100] Strauss argued that all interpretations are uncertain, but it is better to follow the author's instructions about how he wanted to be read rather than to disregard them.[101]

In the section "Secrets and Contradictions," Strauss gave hints as to how one might decode the secrets of *The Guide of the Perplexed*. Look for intentional lack of order and irregularities, as well as repetitions of the same subject with slight variations. For example, Maimonides gave three opinions on creation in *Guide* (II, 13) and referred to that enumeration when he gave three opinions on prophecy in *Guide* (II, 32). He gave five opinions on providence in *Guide* (III, 17) and then five again in (III, 23). Maimonides wanted us to compare the chapters because different ordering of the enumerations introduced concealed points of view. For instance, matching the three opinions on creation with the three on prophecy in (II, 13) and (II, 32) intimates Maimonides's acceptance of the Platonic theory of creation.[102] Other means of conveying esoteric messages are enigmas, obscurity of plan, contradiction, inexact repetitions, odd expressions, misquotations, allusions, pregnant silences, and so on.

Furtive messages are conveyed by what Strauss calls "ambiguous words" or, we may say, "equivocal terms." Observing that Maimonides

---

[99] See Strauss, "The Literary Character of the *Guide for the Perplexed*," (Section IV, "A Moral Dilemma") in *PAW*, 55–60, especially 56.

[100] See the critical review by George H. Sabine, "*Persecution and the Art of Writing* by Leo Strauss," *Ethics*, Vol. 63, No. 3, Part 1 (1953): 220–222. Speaking of exotericism, Sabine commented: "Whether this provides a workable rule for historical interpretation or an invitation to perverse ingenuity is to my mind questionable."

[101] See Strauss's response to Sabine's review of *PAW* in "On a Forgotten Kind of Writing," in *WPP*, 221–232, on 223–228.

[102] There is good reason for suspecting on other grounds that Maimonides suggested as the model for creation the bringing order out of chaos as in the *Timaeus*; see *Guide*, II, 26 and his comments on rabbinic sages such as Rabbi Abahu in *Guide*, II, 30 (trans. Pines, 349).

was Spinoza's guide in addressing the multitude, Yirmiyahu Yovel counts as a key feature of philosophic rhetoric the use of "metaphoric-systematic equivalence."[103] Spinoza translated metaphors into philosophical language, transferring the semantic nucleus from the realm of the imagination to the realm of reason. A term has two meanings, a traditional meaning (e.g., "God's will") and a philosophical meaning into which it can be transferred, acquiring its new meaning. For instance, for Spinoza God's intellect/mind means the totality of adequate ideas in their interrelations. God's decrees/laws/precepts are the eternal laws of nature. God is nature. Maimonides used biblical "Rider of the Clouds ('aravot)" for the One who dominates the highest heaven, or heavenly sphere.[104] Metaphoric-systematic equivalence obtains between the God of Abraham and the First Mover or Necessary Being.[105] The divine actions are the natural actions.[106]

Strauss called attention to the importance of the addressee for understanding the message of *The Guide of the Perplexed*. Joseph ben Judah is the primary "you" addressed in the treatise. Maimonides wrote it for Joseph and for those like him. He tells us the type of person Joseph was, what he knows, what he does not yet know, what perplexes him, and how he should proceed in his studies. Maimonides said the main aim of *The Guide of the Perplexed* is to explain the Account of the Beginning and the Account of the Chariot with a view to him for whom it has been composed.[107]

Strauss's great contribution was to focus our attention on "the art of writing" and "the literary character" of premodern philosophical writings, written at times when free speech was denied. However, Strauss did not relate his hermeneutic method to literary analysis and to cryptological writing by authors who were not philosophers, such as Dante and Shakespeare.[108] Persecution was not the only reason for cautious writing. Another reason was to preserve society from the corrosive effect of philosophical questioning opinions necessary for order and survival.[109]

---

[103] Yirmiyahu Yovel, *Spinoza and Other Heretics*, 2 vols. (Princeton, NJ: Princeton University Press, 1989), 1: 143, 146–147.

[104] See Ps 68: 5; *The Guide of the Perplexed*, I, 70 (trans. Pines, 171).

[105] See *Mishneh Torah*, Foundations of the Law, i, 5; *Guide*, II, 1 (246–249).

[106] *Guide*, III, 32 (trans. Pines, 525).

[107] *Guide*, III, (Introduction), 415–416; Strauss, "How To Begin To Study," xvii.

[108] See, for instance, Frank Kermode, *The Genesis of Secrecy: On the Interpretation of Narrative* (Cambridge, MA: Harvard University Press, 1979) and especially Annabel Patterson, *Reading between the Lines* (London: Routledge, 1993), with her criticism of Strauss on 22–29.

[109] Strauss, *PAW*, 36–37. Michael S. Kochin, in his "Morality, Nature, and Esotericism in Leo Strauss's 'Persecution and the Art of Writing'," observes that,

A third reason was educational, leading potential philosophers from conventional opinions to the eternal questions of philosophy by the various tactics of exoteric writing. These irritants do not disturb the dogmatic slumber of the credulous, those who have eyes and cannot see, but arouse the vigilant.[110] Exotericism in nonliberal societies uses education to reconcile order that is not oppressive with freedom that is not chaotic. Strauss also mentioned social acceptance, which has not received attention yet it is a primary motive for exoteric writing. David Hume and contemporaries, who shared his atheism, wanted to secure the favored opinion of mankind and therefore masked their true doctrines.

"HOW TO BEGIN TO STUDY *THE GUIDE OF THE PERPLEXED*"

Strauss's final contribution to Maimonidean studies was "How to Begin to Study *The Guide of the Perplexed*," which is too long and complex to be discussed here.[111] After presenting the plan of *The Guide of the Perplexed* as it had become clear to him "in the course of about twenty-five years of frequently interrupted but never abandoned study," he observed that it consists of seven sections, each divided into seven subsections or, in one case, into seven chapters. He explained that Maimonides achieved secrecy in three ways: selecting every word with exceeding care, self-contradictions, and scattering the "chapter headings" of the secret teachings throughout the book.[112]

"Exoteric writing is a written imitation, as far as that is possible, of the oral Socratic method" (262). Kochin covers all five chapters of *Persecution* and has a superb analysis of Maimonides (275). Steven Jay Lenzner, in his dissertation, *Leo Strauss and the Problem of Freedom of Thought*, stresses the motivations of education and freedom of thought.
[110] Cf. Gospel of Mark 4: 11–12.
[111] In *Guide of the Perplexed*, trans. Shlomo Pines, xi–lvi; reprinted in *LAM*, 140–184. See also "On the Plan of *The Guide* of the Perplexed," in *Harry Austryn Wolfson Jubilee Volume*, ed. Saul Lieberman, Shalom Spiegel, et al. (Jerusalem: American Academy for Jewish Research, 1965). Cf. "How to Study Spinoza's Theological-Political Treatise" and "How to Begin to Study Medieval Philosophy."
[112] We find the method of dispersal (*tabdid*) in alchemical writings, which were esoteric and depended on this style along with alphanumeric symbolism; see *Guide*, Introduction, 6–7; Paul Kraus, *Jābir ibn Ḥayyān: Contribution à l'histoire des idées scientifiques dans l'Islam* (Paris: Les Belles Lettres, 1986), 32, 42–43, 49, and 336. The work called *Picatrix* (*Ghayat al-hakim*, or *The Aim of the Sage*), on astrology, magic and the talismanic art, is a disorderly book, with an irregular sequence of chapters, containing a large amount of

In "How to Begin to Study," Strauss made ample use of numerical symbolism, which alienated the essay for many readers.[113] Maimonides used numerical symbolism to serve as a mnemonic device for memorizing large amounts of material, as an authorial signature and an aid for scribes, and as a way of conveying hidden meanings. Numerical symbolism goes back to the Pythagoreans, is found in Plato, was continued by the Neopythagoreans and by Augustine, Dante, Machiavelli, Shakespeare (especially the *Sonnets*), and others.

CONCLUSION

Strauss praised modern man's liberation from "the religious delusion" and awareness of his existential situation, threatened by an uncaring, hostile nature and needing to make himself its master.[114] A new fortitude and intellectual honesty forbids flight from life's terrors into comforting delusion, and is willing to acknowledge honestly man's forsakenness and to accept the dreadful truth without self-deception. Yet Strauss avoided dogmatic assertion and set love of truth over probity. Love of truth admitted the presence of the unfathomable or the ultimate mystery in the universe, the truth that there is an ultimate mystery, that being is radically mysterious. The ideas that mattered to Strauss, which he sought in Machiavelli, Hobbes, Spinoza, Averroes, and Maimonides, were the freedom to philosophize and the separation of philosophy from

---

irrelevant material. See *"Picatrix": das Ziel des Weisen von Pseudo-Magriti*, translated into German from the Arabic by Hellmut Ritter and Martin Plessner (Nendeln/Lichtenstein: Kraus Reprint, 1978), Introduction, lix–lxxv. Subjects that should be joined are separated. Lengthy definitions appear unexpectedly, breaking continuity. This form of presentation occurs also in one of its sources, the Encyclopedia of the Brethren of Sincerity (*Ikhwan al-Safa'*).

[113] See Strauss's earlier treatment of numerical symbolism in "Maimonides' Statement on Political Science," in WPP, 165–168. He observed that "Considerations of this kind are necessarily somewhat playful. But they are not so playful as to be incompatible with the seriousness of scholarship" (165). Strauss's own writing combines seriousness with playfulness.

[114] Strauss later called Judaism "a heroic delusion" in "Why We Remain Jews," in JPCM, 327–328. There Strauss observed that a delusion may be said to be a dream and that "No nobler dream was ever dreamt." He commented that dream is like aspiration, which is a form of "divination of an enigmatic vision," which is "the perception of the ultimate mystery ... the truth that there is an ultimate mystery, that being is radically mysterious." He also spoke of averting the danger to life by restoring "the Platonic notion of the noble delusion" in NRH, 26.

religion or theology. He was a philosopher and wanted to die a philosopher's death, as he wrote to Gershom Scholem on September 30, 1973,
about two weeks before he died, citing Averroes – *moriatur anima mea
mortem philosophorum.*[115]

[115] Strauss, *GS*, 3: 771. See also letter to Scholem (Stanford, November 22, 1960),
Strauss, *GS*, 3: 742, where he cites the aphorism "in the beautiful Arabic Latin
created by some of our ancestors" Averroes is supposed to have uttered these
words (in Arabic), during the period of his disgrace and accusations of heresy
against him, in the face of a surging mob.

8 "To Spare the Vanquished and Crush the Arrogant":

Leo Strauss's Lecture on "German Nihilism"

Few political theorists are more controversial today than Leo Strauss. Strauss has been called an enemy of liberal democracy and its champion, a Nietzschean atheist and a believing Jew, a retiring scholar and the intellectual inspiration behind current efforts to democratize the Middle East by force.[1] There is no denying that Strauss began his scholarly career as a staunch critic of Weimar liberalism. A student of Edmund Husserl and Martin Heidegger and associate of Karl Löwith, Gershom Scholem, and others, Strauss came of age at a time of radical challenge to liberal political and intellectual positions generally. Strauss later observed that in that German postwar atmosphere, Oswald Spengler and Karl Jünger were widely admired and Nietzsche's influence deeply felt.[2] (As Strauss later told Löwith, Nietzsche so "bewitched" him between his twenty-second and his thirtieth year that he literally believed everything that he could understand.)[3] Strauss's youthful aversion to the assimilationist path that had been followed by an earlier generation of liberal German

---

[1] For a sampling of the range of critical responses, see for example, Shadia B. Drury, *The Political Ideas of Leo Strauss* (New York: St. Martin's Press, 1988); Kenneth Hart Green, *Jew and Philosopher: The Return to Maimonides in the Jewish Thought of Leo Strauss* (Albany, NY: State University of New York Press, 1993); Laurence Lampert, *Leo Strauss and Nietzsche* (Chicago: University of Chicago Press, 1996); Catherine and Michael Zuckert, *The Truth About Leo Strauss: Political Philosophy and American Democracy* (Chicago: University of Chicago Press, 2006); Heinrich Meier, *Leo Strauss and the Theologico-Political Problem*, trans. Marcus Brainard (Cambridge, UK: Cambridge University Press, 2006); Leora Batnitzky, *Leo Strauss and Emmanuel Levinas: Philosophy and the Politics of Revelation* (Cambridge, UK: Cambridge University Press, 2006); Steven B. Smith, *Reading Leo Strauss: Politics, Philosophy, Judaism* (Chicago: University of Chicago Press, 2006; Thomas L. Pangle, *An Introduction to his Thought and Intellectual Legacy* (Baltimore, MD: Johns Hopkins, 2006); Daniel Tanguay, *Leo Strauss: An Intellectual Biography* (New Haven, CT: Yale University Press, 2007).

[2] Strauss, "Living Issues of German Postwar Philosophy," in Meier, *Leo Strauss and the Theologico-Political Problem*, 115–139.

[3] Letter to Löwith, June 23, 1935, in *GS*, 3: 648; see also CCM, 183.

171

Jews (an aversion he shared with figures such as Walter Benjamin and Gershom Scholem), combined with his early exchanges with Carl Schmitt,[4] whom he accused of remaining too beholden to liberal thinking, have cemented Strauss's reputation among some as a lifelong opponent of liberal ideas.

But Strauss's "liberal" critics do not rely only upon his youthful writings. What especially arouses them is his later claim to have rediscovered a tradition of "exoteric" writing, formerly common among philosophers forced by the threat of persecution to hide their deepest thoughts. According to Strauss, that tradition reflected the natural and ineradicable tension that obtains between philosophy as an unimpeded search for knowledge and the needs of the political community. A concomitant distinction between the "many" and the "few," and a related allowance for "noble myths," has further fueled the suspicion in some quarters that Strauss's thought – despite his many statements to the contrary – is deeply hostile to liberal democratic principles. In the view of some, his overt expression of patriotic loyalty to the principles of his adopted country was merely the mask under which he hid a powerful antipathy to all things democratically liberal.[5]

A lecture on "German Nihilism" that Strauss delivered in late February 1941 sheds instructive light upon Strauss's final political views as they relate to liberal democracy. As Strauss's first extended public statement as a U.S. citizen on contemporary politics, that lecture is of exceptional biographic interest. Its venue was the General Seminar of the New School for Social Research (formerly the "University in Exile"), an institution that had been set up to shelter political refugees unable to secure other academic employment in the United States. Strauss, who had become a U.S. citizen two years earlier (one year after his arrival), had recently been joined by his wife and stepson. However, several close family members, including his father and stepmother, remained in Germany. In sum, Strauss delivered "German Nihilism" in his earliest (and still financially precarious) years as an American citizen, and before the outcome of the current global conflict and the extent of his own personal losses were known.[6]

---

[4] For a thorough study of Strauss's relations with Schmitt, see Heinrich Meier, *Carl Schmitt and Leo Strauss: The Hidden Dialogue*, trans. J. Harvey Lomax (Chicago: University of Chicago Press, 1995).

[5] See Stephen Holmes, *The Anatomy of Anti-Liberalism* (Cambridge, MA: Harvard University Press, 1993), 61–87; for a withering response, see Peter Berkowitz, "Liberal Zealotry," *Yale Law Journal* 103 (1994); 1363–1382.

[6] On Strauss's personal circumstances at the time, see Eugene R. Sheppard, *Leo Strauss and the Politics of Exile: The Making of a Political Philosopher* (Waltham, MA: Brandeis University Press, 2006), 81–100.

Strauss's audience consisted of fellow members of the General Seminar, a group of distinguished scholars, most of them refugees, whose common topic that year was "Experiences of the Second World War." Members of the Seminar included Eduard Heineman, Erich Hula (a follower of Hans Kelsen), Karl Mayer, Albert Salomon, Kurt Reizler (later Strauss's friend and colleague at the University of Chicago), Horace Kallen (a former student of George Santayana), and Felix Kaufmann (who had been associated with the Vienna Circle). The assigned reading that week was Hermann Rauschning's *The Revolution of Nihilism*, which had recently been translated into English.[7] Rauschning was a former Nazi who criticized the movement from the standpoint of a disillusioned conservative nationalist.

The larger political and military context is also worth noting. In February of 1941, Roosevelt was on the verge of signing the Lend-Lease Act. France had fallen the previous June. The United States would not enter the war until December of that year. And Britain, under heavy German bombardment, was preparing to face Rommel in North Africa. As Winston Churchill's speeches of the previous months had made ringingly clear, the outcome of what Strauss could still refer to as the "Anglo-German" war was anything but certain.

At the time of the lecture, Strauss was immersed in his own studies of exoteric writing and the hidden Platonism of such thinkers as Alfarabi and Maimonides. He had already been liberated (thanks to his earlier medieval Jewish studies) from the "prejudice" that a return to premodern philosophy is impossible.[8] And he had already completed a seminal work urging the specifically moral, rather than strictly philosophical or scientific, foundation of Hobbes's thought.[9] A number of contemporaneous reviews appearing in *Social Research* throw further light on Strauss's wide-ranging interest during this period in larger questions of political philosophy. Those sketches, subsequently republished in *What is Political Philosophy?* include reviews of Karl Löwith's *Von Hegel bis Nietzsche* [*From Hegel to Nietzsche*], Charles Howard McIlwain's *Constitutionalism, Ancient and Modern*, and Elmer Ellsworth Powell's *Spinoza and Religion*.[10]

Still, in 1941 most of Strauss's major publications lay in the future. *On Tyranny*, his exchange with Alexandre Kojève, appeared in 1948, and most of the works for which he is best known were completed in

---

[7] Hermann Rauschning, *The Revolution of Nihilism: Warning to the West*, trans. E. W. Dickes (New York: Longmans, Green & Co., 1939).

[8] Strauss, "Preface to *SCR*," in *LAM*, 257.

[9] Strauss, *PPH*.

[10] Strauss, *WPP*, 268–275.

the 1950s and 1960s. That certain important discoveries or deepened perspectives indeed lay ahead is strongly suggested by a 1946 letter to Löwith, in which Strauss speaks of suffering a "ship wreck" that has forced him to "begin once again from the very beginning."' The context of those remarks – a renewed interest in Kierkegaard along with his own earlier religious doubts – makes clear what is again at stake for him: namely the "right and necessity" of philosophy as the ancient philosophers understood it, given the *factum brutum* of revelation.[11] The lecture on German nihilism may then make assumptions, especially pertaining to the justification of philosophy, that Strauss later corrected or rescinded. Whether such qualifications have any bearing on the political meaning of the lecture of 1941 remains to be seen.

WHAT IS NIHILISM?

Strauss's lecture opens with a Socratically inflected question followed by another: What is nihilism, and how far can it be said to be a specifically German phenomenon?[12] The second part of the question is not without immediate political bite. Strauss will later insist (both against the Nazis and, implicitly, thinkers like Spengler) that science, or the search for knowledge as such, knows no national or racial boundaries: to the extent that nihilism is essentially German, it removes itself from any undiluted claim to truth.

Strauss does not here attempt an immediate or thorough answer to either question. He says the phenomenon is too complex to permit more than a "scratching of the surface." Instead, he begins with an assertion: National Socialism – the most famous and most vulgar form of German nihilism – is not the deepest nor necessarily the most powerful. The defeat of National Socialism, should it come, will not necessarily resolve the problem that has helped give rise to it.[13] To explain German nihilism, he will attempt first to explain its ultimate, non-nihilistic motive, then to describe the situation that has given rise to its nihilistic aspirations, and finally to offer a definition that is acceptable from the standpoint of that motive (357). In other words, Strauss seeks

[11] Letter to Löwith, August 15, 1946 in *GS*, 3: 663.
[12] Strauss, "German Nihilism," *Interpretation* (Spring 1999), vol. 26, no. 3, 352–378; with corrections by Wiebke Meier, *Interpretation* (Fall 2000), vol. 28, no.2, 33–34; subsequent references appear in parentheses in the text.
[13] Strauss would later come closer to Klein's view, as expressed in a letter written in the early 1930s, stating that the sole Nazi principle was "negation of the Jews" (Letter to Strauss, June 19–20, 1934 in *GS*, 3: 512). Cf. Strauss, "Why We Remain Jews," in *JPCM*, 320.

such a definition as might have appealed to, and potentially guided, the pre-nihilistic German youth whom he will later describe with a certain sympathy.

Nihilism might mean to will the nothing; that such a definition is inadequate is clear from the goal that German nihilism manifests by word and deed – not suicide, but the destruction of modern civilization. The ultimate motive of German nihilism is not the sheer will to destruction, whether of oneself or others, but a peculiar focus. This will to something specific and hence limited becomes "almost absolute" only because the "No" directed against modern civilization is unaccompanied by any clear conception of a positive alternative (357). In what follows, Strauss will proceed to sketch his own positive alternative to modern civilization as the German nihilists understand it, a conception that might have supplied rational guidance when it was needed.

But German nihilism's antipathy to modern civilization has an even more specific focus: modern civilization is opposed not for its technical achievements but for its "moral meaning" (358). Strauss here raises the specter of two moralities: one (as with the new morality he had earlier traced to Hobbes) is known by such slogans as the "rights of man" and the "greatest happiness of the greatest number." Its ultimate aim is the open society, or a unified humanity living in peace and comfort. The other abides in the conviction that this goal cannot be reconciled with the demands of moral life, which involve seriousness and sacrifice. By the lights of this conviction, the "root of all moral life is essentially and therefore eternally the *closed* society," lacking which human life is without responsibility or seriousness (358). In bringing attention to the moral meaning of modern civilization, Strauss calls to mind the "slave morality" decried by Nietzsche; however, unlike Nietzsche Strauss links the morality in question not to Christianity (or the slave revolt against noble values) but to the modern Anglo-Saxon West. By way of contrast, the reactive role of moral protest is assigned by Strauss to those who see themselves in the mold of Nietzsche's "masters."

In expressing the self-understanding of that rebellion, Strauss appropriates the language of Carl Schmitt, much as he had done in his 1932 review of Schmitt's *Concept of the Political*.[14] On Schmitt's account, the root of moral life is the closed society because without war and its immanent threat, life lacks the sublime intensity that makes us truly human. Whatever moral value the West retains depends entirely upon

[14] Strauss, "Anmerkennung zu Carl Schmitt, *Der Begriff des Politischen*," *Archiv für Sozialwissenschaft und Sozialpolitik* 67, no. 6 (August–September, 1932): 732–749; republished in Meier, *The Hidden Dialogue*, 91–119.

their being closed societies (i.e., ready for war). But the closed society that aims at openness is morally inferior not only in its reduced readiness for war but also in its hypocrisy or lack of honesty.

Strauss concludes that the conviction in question has basically nothing to do either with nationalism or with love of war as such but a "sense of responsibility for endangered morality." That conviction, or passion, is not unique to modern times but long familiar to readers of Plato and Rousseau as well as Nietzsche (not to speak of the Hebrew Bible). It seems as long as there have been cities, there have been passionate moral protests against the city's easygoing ways.[15] Cities breed a certain openness or cosmopolitanism that conflicts with the morality of duty and self-sacrifice. Yet in our time, that protest has assumed a "more passionate and infinitely less intelligent form" as born out by its alleged enemies: "cultural bolshevism" and "the subhuman beings of the big cities" (359). Why has this happened? It is not only due to Nietzsche's own remarkably irresponsible language. Certainly neither Plato nor Rousseau ever spoke of *Untermenschen*. Nor is it merely Nietzsche's overestimation, as Strauss will later suggest, of modern man's "tameness." Perhaps it is partly the peculiar rottenness that has inspired that protest (as with the refusal of Oxford students to defend their king and country, to which he alludes).

A survey of what is superficially manifest yields a tentative definition of nihilism as "a desire to destroy the present world and its potentialities" unaccompanied by the clear conception of any positive alternative (359). What circumstances have led to it? In answering this question, Strauss avoids those factors that have already, in his view, been sufficiently emphasized (whether economic or psychological); instead, he attempts to help his listeners grasp from the inside the motives or ideal that has inspired it. In other words, his account of the relevant circumstances is not genetically reductive; nor does it allow his audience to remain in the position of disinterested or value-free observers. To understand German nihilism adequately, one must acknowledge and oneself respond to the ideals that have at least partially inspired it.

To be sure, Strauss lacks the "lyrical" gifts of reportage that would facilitate this rhetorical task (359). (One is tempted to say Strauss is no Churchill.) He nevertheless begins to try to elicit such a nonreductive understanding by inviting the listener to admit that postwar Weimar could satisfy "no one." That justified dissatisfaction led to an unacceptable and unreasonable outcome, owing to the peculiar political

---

[15] Cf. Strauss, "Jerusalem and Athens: Some Preliminary Reflections," in *SPPP*, 158: by biblical lights, "civilization and piety are two very different things."

circumstances of Germany. The apparent inability of German liberal democracy to deal with the country's difficulties confirmed a profound German prejudice against liberal democracy as such. One source of that prejudice has already been hinted at: the association of liberal democracy with its Anglo-Saxon place of origin. As Strauss will elsewhere stress, German liberalism suffered the unhappy fate of being imposed twice by conquest rather than emerging freely, as in the Anglo-Saxon West.

Of the two "articulate" alternatives to liberal democracy that were present, one – the conservative reaction of men like Rauschning – seemed to lead nowhere (359). The other pointed in two directions: both to communism, or a world without "blood, sweat and tears," and to the powerful and complex moral response that it provoked. That response arose out of the revulsion felt by certain thoughtful youth when confronted with the prospect of a future when sacrifice would no longer be possible. The motivations of such youth were neither economic nor explicitly religious; indeed, most considered themselves atheists. It was rather a case of one moral vision, ostensibly supported by reason, confronted by morality of a different sort. To some "very intelligent, and very decent, if very young, Germans," the prospect of "eternal peace" seemed the fulfillment not of some Kantian dream but instead of a Nietzschean nightmare (360). Understandably, these youth could not articulate a clear positive alternative – an alternative that Nietzsche had failed irresponsibly to offer. Presented with the choice on which the communists insisted between communism or the destruction of civilization, such youth chose the latter. To be sure, they were wrong in assuming that the communists had reason on their side. However, they were supported in that unreasonable presumption by the then-reigning intellectual fashions, which tended to equate rational argument with argument from history and social science with rational prediction, that is, by historicism and positivism (360).

However shocking it may initially appear, Strauss's claim as to the moral basis of German nihilism reaches to the heart of his understanding of the peculiar weakness of modernity. In their effort to conquer chance, the founders of modernity set forth what he elsewhere calls a new, fundamentally mercenary moral "Decalogue" whose actualization could be counted on.[16] On Strauss's account, young German nihilists are primarily motivated by moral revulsion against the communist ideal in which that new morality appeared to reach its fruition.

In part due to those reigning fashions, the intellectual defense of the liberal status quo proved inordinately weak. The "progressive"

---

[16] See Strauss, "What is Political Philosophy?" in *WPP*, 44.

educators whom those youths encountered shared their own impatience with the old.[17] What was needed were old-fashioned teachers, who could furnish intellectual discipline while being sufficiently "undogmatic" to understand their students' "aspirations." Such teachers might have arisen from the "old and noble educational system" that had been founded by "great liberals" of the early nineteenth century. Unfortunately, that system had been drastically weakened by both the "inroads" of William II and the "enlarge[ments]" of republican Weimar. The system that might have served could not survive the political and hence institutional weakness of the liberal cause in Germany (361).

But the decline in reverence for old age was even more striking on the right. In turn, this phenomenon was linked to the emergence for the first time, at the end of the world war, of right-wing atheism as a potent intellectual movement. Atheism had previously been associated with philosophic materialism, as distinguished from the deistic and pantheistic idealism that characterized Germany's reigning philosophic schools of the nineteenth century. By way of contrast, Nietzsche challenged communism by way of atheism, that is, through a rejection of the belief in providence to which the materialist left continued covertly to subscribe. Modern civilization, which had previously triumphed on the basis of what Strauss elsewhere calls its "Napoleonic strategy," faltered when it found itself on the defensive.[18]

The teachers to whom the youth in question in fact turned shared an extreme aversion for "liberalism."[19] Moreover, unlike traditional conservatives they lay special stress not upon reverence for the past but upon the future, and on the potentially salvational role of Germany's youth. (Hitler's rude reference to the age of von Hindenberg, Germany's then leader, is thus for Strauss especially telling.) In other words, the thinkers in question attacked liberalism by radicalizing liberalism's own open-ended progressivism and related veneration of history. Faced with an enemy that claims to be history's new wave, liberals of a less thoughtful stripe than the "great liberals" of the previous century were

---

[17] See Strauss's review of John Dewey, *German Philosophy and Politics* in *Social Research* 10 (1943): 505–507; reprinted in *WPP*, 268–270.

[18] Strauss, "Introduction," in *PL*, 32, originally published as *Philosophie und Gesetz: Beiträge zum Verständnis Maimunis und seiner Verläufer* (Berlin: Schocken, 1935); see also "Preface to *SCR*," in *LAM*, 255–256.

[19] Strauss refers explicitly to Oswald Spengler, Moeller van den Bruck, Carl Schmitt, Ernst Jüenger, and Martin Heidegger. An additional name mentioned in the original manuscript remains illegible.

left in the uncomfortable, and ultimately self-contradictory, position of appealing in the name of progress to what had evidently become merely the conventional wisdom (361). In other words, the principles of the liberal enlightenment had degenerated into mere "prejudice" (362). The defenders of that wisdom were burdened with a dogmatism that could not resist the skepticism of an intellectual proletariat. To a historically attuned audience, the situation of modern civilization and its "back-bone" – modern science in both its natural and, especially, civil form – seemed comparable to that of an earlier scholasticism (i.e., ripe for revolution). Hegel, the last great modern rationalist, claimed to be able to shed light only on the past. And Hegel's peculiar sort of rationalism, in its conceptually based perfection, was followed by a technical proliferation that only obscured the "basic problems" (363).

In a single tense paragraph, Strauss sketches the fatal course on which later works (such as *Natural Right and History*) will elaborate: the self-destruction of reason on the basis of a flawed initiating modern premise. "Not humanism as such" but "only a specific humanism ultimately led to nihilism." That this flawed philosophic premise relates especially to matters "civic" calls to mind his later focus on the peculiarly "political" direction in which Hobbes and others took a hedonism and corpuscularism that had ancient roots.[20] What distinguishes Hobbes from his ancient Epicurean and Democritean counterparts is less his natural science as such than the practical "conquest of nature" in which he enlists it. The paragraph in question also calls to mind Strauss's later treatment of a modern "method" meant to end the ongoing and, as it seems, "fruitless" philosophical conflict between "dogmatism" and "skepticism." The modern declaration of philosophical peace involves adoption of a technical "method" that makes possible a progressive accretion of predictive knowledge into the indefinite future.[21] However, the price of such progress is a closing off the most fundamental questions – questions that had given rise to that very conflict – and with them of the most direct or natural path to philosophic inquiry. The recent turn to "history" is itself a symptom of that forgetting of the basic questions in the name of scientific progress. History becomes ever more the fundamental subject of study (rather than merely referring, as in the past, to a type of inquiry) as nature, the original and proper subject of philosophical inquiry, grows ever more obscure. But history so conceived cannot finally present itself as other than a net both inescapable and impervious to reason, especially as concerns action and the future.

---

[20] Strauss, *NRH*, 169–170, 188–190, 279; see also "Notes on Lucretius," in *LAM*, 76–139.
[21] Strauss, *NRH*, 172–174.

However, a way out was possible. In contrast with the modern view of history as rational process or fated dispensation, Strauss draws attention to the power of chance, both for the youth in question and for his own understanding, in determining the outcome of events.[22] The one answer to the young German nihilists that was "adequate" and "that would have impressed them had they heard it" was given only in 1940 (i.e., too late) and by an Englishman. "Those young men who refused to believe that the period... following the communist revolution would be the finest hour of mankind in general and Germany in particular would have been impressed as much as we were by what Winston Churchill said after the defeat in Flanders about Britain's finest hour" (363).

In this reference to Churchill (to whom he will return), Strauss also calls attention to the capacity to learn from strangers that marks civilization as he will subsequently define it; he also suggests that the intellectual movement he describes, though understandable under the circumstances, was not in fact inevitable. The young men in question were ripe for a lesson that they might have but did not receive. Churchill's statement was prepared "in a way" by Spengler. For Spengler, for all his historicism, could not help admiring Rome more for its grit when defeated at Cannae than for its successful imperial expansion.[23]

If only because one cannot refute what one does not understand, from the standpoint of the young German nihilists, who remained trapped by their "historical consciousness," Hitler and the Nazis are just the insubstantial "tool of history," and the ensuing destruction of the present

---

[22] Cf. Letter to Löwith, August 15, 1946 in GS, 3: 662: "Today we need historical reflection – only I assert that it is neither a progress nor a fate to submit to with resignation, but...an unavoidable means for overcoming modernity...The conception I sketch has nothing *at all* to do with Heidegger...for with Heidegger, 'historicity' has made nature disappear *completely*, which however has the merit of consistency and compels one to reflect." See also "The Living Issues of German Post-War Philosophy," in *Leo Strauss and the Theologico-Political Problem*, 133: liberation from nihilism requires more than "refutation"; historical consciousness must itself come to be recognized as "the product of a *blind* process. "By bringing that process to light" – e.g., by showing it to be the result at least in part of motives that cannot be fully justified – "we free ourselves from the power of its result. We become again, what we cannot be before, *natural* philosophers, i.e., philosophers who approach the natural, the basic and original question of philosophy in a natural, an adequate way." Strauss's remark casts instructive light on the overall purpose of his counter-historicist history of modern thought.

[23] Oswald Spengler, *The Decline of the West* vol. 1, trans. Charles Francis Atkinson (New York: Knopf, 1926), 36; originally published as *Der Untergang des Abendlandes, Gestalt und Wirklichkeit* (Munich: C.H. Beck'sche Verlagsbuchhandlung, 1918). See also Strauss, *PL*, 28.

era, which began with the destruction of scholasticism (i.e., in 1517 or so) is a hopeful and creative sign of future greatness (363).[24] Against that emotional appeal to such a consciousness, all appeals to "history" without stable and unchanging standards can give no resistance. From such a perspective, even fascism's extraordinary baseness and vulgarity (to which a much younger Strauss may himself have been insufficiently attentive)[25] can seem unimportant. Strauss concludes the ultimate cause of the success of nihilism is the depreciation and contempt for reason as a source of stable and unchanging standards. Absent such standards, reason becomes only a servant of the emotions, and nonarbitrary distinctions between noble and base grow shaky (364).

Strauss characterizes the previous remarks as a condensed set of recollections meant to convey a needed "impression" – in this case, of an irrational movement and the often irrational responses to it. In other words, the theoretical argument that Strauss wishes to impart must be prepared, as it was for Strauss himself, by something that "impresses" outside of or despite one's prior theoretical framework (cf. 363).

Having thus laid the groundwork for an historical attack upon historicism itself, Strauss can at last venture a "definition of nihilism" – he does not here speak of nihilism that is specifically "German" – in the wake of Rauschning's (telling) failure to provide one. Nihilism is a conscious rejection of the principles of civilization as such. Strauss's earlier description of German nihilism as a desire for the destruction of modern civilization thus proves to need correction. The German nihilist may take specific aim against modernity; in fact, he is enemy of civilization proper (364). But he is not merely a barbarian, civilization's time-worn enemy. He is distinguished not only by his arrogance and cruelty (which he shares with Ariovistus, the savage Teutonic chieftain defeated by the Romans) but in part by a peculiar (and peculiarly modern) educational formation. His attraction to war, and disdain for peace, often goes together with a professed love of "culture" (e.g., art and music).[26] He is less an alien to civilization than its ill-gotten child.

By "civilization," Strauss means "the conscious culture of humanity," hence of reason, active in two ways: as theory and as practice. The "pillars of civilization" are "morals and science, and both united." Science without morals becomes cynicism, which eliminates the very

---

[24] In 1517, Machiavelli completed the *Discourses on Livy* and Luther posted his famous ninety-five theses.

[25] Letter to Löwith, May 19, 1933, in *GS*, 3: 624–625.

[26] See Spengler's invidious comparison of civilization to a more genuinely alive "culture." For Spengler, the "two basic ideas" of every civilization (which he treats in the plural) are "world-city" and "province" – the former deracinated and overly intellectualized, the latter the decayed residue of "culture-cities" that grew organically from local soil (*Decline of the West*, 3: 32).

possibility of science. Morals without science "degenerates into superstition," and is "thus apt to become fanatic cruelty." Civilization then
is the bond that unites science and morals without destroying their dis-
tinctiveness. Science grows from and can never altogether abandon the
moral attitudes that constitute its natural base; morals need science not
for its base but to secure its perfection (365). In a few short sentences,
Strauss outlines the classical understanding of civilized decency – an
understanding that he here describes, in the manner of Aristotle, as
equally distant from a taking pleasure in inflicting pain and an inability
to inflict pain at all. Like the classical understanding of "humanity,"
civilized decency then is to be distinguished from mere "compassion" –
a typically modern error. One could say it is also to be distinguished
from both the humanitarian "immorality" characteristic of modernity's founders (e.g., Machiavelli and Descartes) and the violent moral
reaction that motivated the young German nihilists.

For its part, science is the attempt to understand the universe and
man, and is hence the same thing as philosophy. Modern science is
something else: an indication that the dependence of genuine science,
as Strauss here presents it, upon morals is not merely external. A science that loses sight of what makes man human may well irrevocably
compromise its knowledge of the world of which man is a part. In degen-
erating into "cynicism," Strauss suggests science ceases to be scientific.

Whatever the precise relation between science and morals, art is not
to be counted among those twin pillars. Modern civilization is characterized not only by the aforementioned parting of the ways between
science and philosophy but also by a peculiar elevation of "art" (or the
"aesthetic") as an autonomous conceptual category. Science, morals,
and art all suffer when poetry ceases to be understood as imitative (in
the classical manner) rather than autonomous, as Kant puts it, or otherwise "creative." The crucial relation between science and morals is
obscured when their joint superiority to the imitative and productive
arts ceases to be manifest. *Pace* Nietzsche, and in a way that Strauss
will soon elaborate, science and morals have more in common at the
highest level than either has with either imitation or production (366).
Philosophy and statemanship have more in common than either has
with the merely imitative arts (like poetry) nor does their high standing
depend on their being fundamentally "creative."

To be a radical critic of modern civilization then (as Strauss surely
was) one need not be a nihilist – a point that his newly proffered definition of nihilism makes explicit. According to an older understanding,
civilization assumes the accessibility of natural or unchanging standards and limits. The "natural" character of civilization does not imply
(as in the view of nature that is assumed by modern natural science)

that it is everywhere present, or present in the same way. It does mean that civilization's naturally supported aspirations also confront certain necessary limits. However preferable in itself the state of peace is to that of war, all communities require armies to defend themselves against threats, the causes of which will never be abolished. As the need for armed force makes especially obvious, civilization "has a certain natural basis which it *finds* and cannot create" (366).

By way of contrast, modern civilization overlays the twin pillars of science and morals with natural and civic "sciences" that refuse to recognize such limits. In so doing, they not only exaggerate the extent of human power to "conquer chance"; they also obscure the difference between the productive arts, or *technai*, which are indeed progressive, and the type of knowledge that arises from the unity of science and morals proper. Strauss implies that the origin of the modern deformation lies in the elevation of such arts to the status of science in the true sense. Historicism is the ultimate result of an effort on the part of earlier modern thinkers to replace the zetetic search for wisdom (Platonic philosophizing as originally conceived) with a progressive science modeled on the productive arts.With the romantic backlash and related elevation over science of poetry, reason itself is threatened. Nihilism is peculiarly dominant in Germany then mainly because of the importance of romanticism to its modern political formation.[27] In its privileging culture over civilization, romanticism invites the notion of national sciences in the plural (as in the "Faustic" science spoken of by Spengler). But as Strauss here insists, whoever accepts the notion of a Faustic science "rejects the idea of science," which is singular or nothing. The openness to other cultures that Spengler had attributed to "German" or "Faustic" science cannot be essentially parochial if it is to be truly scientific. Civilization rightly understood implies a willingness to learn from any source, be it foreign or familiar. A barbarian, as distinguished from a civilized person, is one who believes that everything worthwhile is contained within his own tradition. The notion of an essentially German science – that is, of a "science" that rejects potential claims to knowledge solely on the basis of their accidental source – contradicts the idea of civilization as such (366).

The goal of nihilism is not then the destruction of all traditional spiritual standards; nor is it the sheer maintenance of power, and the world-empire needed to sustain it, at any cost and by any means, as Rauschning claims. German nihilism is moved by something like an aesthetic ideal in roughly the Kantian sense. The Nazis appear to desire

[27] See also Strauss, "The Living Issues of German Postwar Philosophy," in *Leo Strauss and the Theologico-Political Problem*, 115–116.

world dominion not only out of a selfish lust for power but also for the sake of a certain "disinterested pleasure." They find that pleasure in a prospect they find "glamorous" and in a related presentation of the "warlike virtues" (368). Uprooted from their natural foundation, such qualities, which are not altogether "ignoble," become highly distorted: preference for the warlike virtues above all is almost indistinguishable from a taking of disinterested pleasure in the subjugation and torture of the weak and helpless (369). One could say that preference lies at an extreme whose opposite is the inability to inflict pain when necessary.

Germany's affinity for the martial virtues partly arises from the accident of having reached its own literary and philosophical peak after the advent of modern civilization in France and England. In rightly resisting early modernity's own moral and spiritual deformations, German philosophers were tempted to exaggerate the importance of self-sacrifice; they also tended to loose sight of the goodness of happiness as it naturally comes to sight. The result was an unwarranted contempt for the aims of human life as envisioned by common sense. Objecting to "the unqualified identification of the morally good with the object of enlightened self-interest," German philosophers were "apt to forget" the "natural aim of man." The specific failure of the German idealists to unify the modern and premodern ideals led, in turn, to an appreciation of premodern ideals that was hampered by its polemical intention (371). In opposing modern civilization, German thinkers tended to treat civilization as such as something foreign, a prejudice that seems to have blinded even Nietzsche. What England might have taught German philosophers beguiled by war (and by their own parochial loyalties) were the civilized blessings of moderation and prudence.[28] "While the English originated the modern ideal – the premodern ideal, the classical ideal of humanity, was no where better preserved than in Oxford and Cambridge" (372).

In responding to the urgencies of the present, Strauss then brings to bear a philosophical approach whose disappearance helps explain the current debacle. Here *in nuce* is an outline of the teaching that might have given positive direction to youths who were misled by Nietzsche and others. To be sure, as Strauss argues in a lecture of the previous year before a more theoretically inclined audience, the direction in which some were thus led was not philosophically fruitless. In ways that the

---

[28] See also Strauss, "What is Political Philosophy?" in *WPP*, 27. As Strauss there notes, Heidegger's contempt for these enduring problems led him to welcome as a dispensation of fate "the least wise and least moderate part of his nation" when it was in "its least wise and least moderate mood." Strauss's specific criticism of Heidegger for his contempt for the "superficial" sheds light on Strauss's famously enigmatic reference elsewhere to the "surface" that alone reaches to the "heart of things."

earlier lecture lays out, the "radicalism" of German thought – a radicalism that proved disastrous for German politics – also opened a path toward the genuine recovery of ancient philosophy as undertaken or inspired by Socrates. Strauss owes German immoderation this much: that without it, that recovery would have been far more difficult. Historicism, especially in its radical Heideggerian form, exposed the roots of the philosophical tradition and, with it, the original problems that constitute philosophy's enduring theme.

Strauss's current lecture has as its more urgent practical purpose a defense of Britain and for what it stands. English "common sense" and a related willingness to "muddle through" fostered virtues that the Germans, with their exaggerated emphasis on "sacrifice" and contempt for "common sense," tended to neglect (372).[29] Both in its aesthetic idealization of cruelty and its fusion of science and parochial loyalty, German nihilism takes conscious and deliberate aim at civilization as such. As Strauss concludes, the present war between England and France is thus a struggle over fundamental principles. The "symbolic significance" of that struggle might well call to mind Thucydides's famous depiction of the Peloponnesian War. To be sure, unlike the ancient struggle between Athens and Sparta, the outcome of the present war is undecided. However, one conclusion is clear to Strauss: by choosing Hitler, Germany has shown "beyond any doubt" that it is unfit to rule the planet.[30] Rather than Germany, England is the Reich or empire that is and deserves to be compared to Rome. For it and not Germany understands, having learned it for "a very long time," how to "spare the vanquished and crush the arrogant: *parcer subjectis et debellare superbos.*"

A NEW ROME

The phrase "to spare the vanquished and crush the arrogant" epitomizes the virtuous mean that Strauss identifies in "German Nihilism" with "decent and noble conduct" (305). It is therefore especially disturbing to find the same phrase favorably linked, in an early letter to Löwith, with "fascist, authoritarian and imperial principles":

the fact that the new right-wing Germany does not tolerate us says nothing against the principles of the right. To the contrary: only from the principles of the right, that is from fascist, authoritarian and *imperial* principles, is it possible with decency, that is, without the laughable and despicable appeal to the

---

[29] The phrase "muddling through" is specifically associated with Churchill in Strauss's 1942 lecture "What Can We Learn from Political Theory?" *Review of Politics* 69 (2007): 517–518; see also Smith, *Reading Leo Strauss*, 197.

[30] Cf. Strauss, "Philosophy as Rigorous Science and Political Philosophy," in *SPPP*, 33: Nietzsche "saw the twentieth century as an age of world wars leading up to planetary rule."

droits imprescriptibles de l'homme to protest against the shabby abomination [*meskine Unwesen*]. I am reading Caesar's *Commentaries* with deep understanding, and I think of Virgil's *Tu regere imperio...parcere subjectis et debellare superbos.* There is no reason to crawl to the cross, neither to the cross of liberalism, as long as somewhere in the world there is a glimmer of the spark of Roman thought. And even then: rather than any cross, I'll take the ghetto.[31]

Finding himself, like Virgil before him, in a state of precarious refuge from a tyrant, a much younger Strauss looks hopefully to the glory of the Roman Empire at its peak. The protest against Hitler can be decently leveled only on the basis of "Roman" thought, meaning that of the great imperial, pre-Christian Caesar who destroyed the Roman Republic. Liberalism for Strauss at this time is only a diluted Christianity, which no Jew – even one who is an atheist – can embrace without losing self-respect. Better remain in the ghetto (like Maimonides) than genuflect (like Heine) before an unworthy ideal. Strauss does not here say what he has come to understand better through Caesar's *Commentaries*, though his later criticism of "Caesarism," or the ascription to Roman imperial rule of a peculiar sort of political insight, strongly suggests that his early views on Rome and its empire were later superseded if not abandoned.[32]

In reply,Löwith took strong objection to Strauss's association of fascism with the true spirit of ancient Rome: he reminds Strauss that fascism is a thoroughly "*democratic* growth." And though Löwith, too, is very far from endorsing "spiritual freedom" in a "liberal sense," he wonders if Strauss's own distinction between left and right does not "abstract dogmatically from politics."

Read in the light of this earlier usage, Strauss's reprisal in "German Nihilism" of the phrase (minus the "*Tu regere imperio*") is thus especially striking. This usage, combined with repeated favorable allusions to ancient Rome, casts Britain as the new Rome and Hitler, implicitly, as a new Ariovistus. But Strauss refrains from comparing Churchill, for all his greatness, to Julius or Augustus.[33] Churchill's qualities as a statesman are more republican than Caesarian; and it is England, rather than

---

[31] Letter to Lowith, May 19, 1933, in *GS*, 3: 625. "Crawling to the cross," a term used in the traditional Lutheran Order of Baptism, is historically associated with Henry IV's appeal to Pope Gregory VII to reverse his ban of excommunication. The phrase also appears, derisively, in Heinrich Heine's famous poem "To an Apostate" written shortly after Heine's own official conversion. On the relevance of Henry IV, see Sheppard, *Leo Strauss and the Politics of Exile*, 62–63.

[32] In a letter to Klein of February 14, 1934, written from England, Strauss reveals his growing admiration for both Churchill and the British Parliament, which he specifically compares to the Roman Senate (*GS*, 3: 493).

[33] Comments to that effect are crossed out in Strauss's draft (377).

its current leader, however exemplary, that is singled out as deserving
of imperial rule. As he will write to Löwith five years later:

I *really* believe... that the perfect political order, as Plato and Aristotle have
sketched it, *is* the perfect political order. Or do you believe in the world-state?
If it is true that genuine unity is only possible through knowledge of the truth,
or through search for the truth, then there is a genuine unity of all men only
on the basis of the popularized final *teaching* of philosophy (and naturally this
does not exist) or if all men are philosophers (not Ph.D.s, etc.) – which likewise
is not the case. Therefore there can only be closed societies, that is, states. But
if that is so, then one can show from political considerations that the small
city-state is in principle superior to the large state or to the territorial-feudal
state. I know very well that *today* it cannot be restored... Whoever concedes
that Horace did not speak nonsense when he said 'one can expel nature with
a pitchfork but it always returns' concedes thereby precisely the legitimacy *in
principle* of Platonic-Aristotelian politics.[34]

As he adds five days later:

A man like Churchill proves that the possibility of *megalopsychia* [magnanim-
ity] exists today *exactly* as it did in the fifth century, B.C.[35]

Later, he will cite Churchill in answer to the seemingly insoluble problem posed by Weber: how to reconcile devotion to principle with political "responsibility."[36]

In his 1942 lecture "What Can We Learn From Political Theory?" and
later in *Natural Right and History*, Strauss expands upon that possibility. As Plato and Aristotle understand it, the best regime by nature is
the "object that the best men pray for," or "the wish of the gentleman
as interpreted by the philosopher." Although the existence of such a
regime is not impossible, its coming into being depends on chance and
is accordingly most rare. And the best practicable regime (a political
community small enough to be encompassed at a glance, and ruled by
an educated patrician elite)[37] is unjust wherever, as is most often the
case, it is not in fact feasible.[38] Finally, the best practicable regime – and
the most desirable regime for men like Plato and Aristotle, who chose
to live in more easy-going democracies – are not identical.[39]

Strauss's remarks shed helpful light not only on the specific human
possibility that Strauss sees realized in Churchill but also on the basis

---

[34] Letter to Löwith, August 15, 1946, in *GS*, 3: 662–663; see also, *CCM*, 107–108.
[35] Letter to Löwith, August 20, 1946, in *GS*, 3: 667; *CCM*, 111.
[36] Strauss, *NRH*, 70 fn. 29.
[37] Strauss, *NRH*, 130, 141–142, 157.
[38] Strauss, *TWM*, 85.
[39] See Letter to Löwith, August 20, 1946, in *GS*, 3: 667.

of Strauss's insistence upon the necessity of "closed" political communities. Only on the basis of knowledge of the truth, or the search for that knowledge, is genuine unity among men possible. Morals, the other "pillar" of civilization, always depends in part on authoritative opinions that by their nature vary, and on a natural affection for kin and kind that is necessarily limited in reach. According to the ancient view that he here endorses, "every political society that ever has been or ever will be rests on a particular fundamental opinion which cannot be replaced by knowledge and hence is of necessity a particular or particularist society."[40] It is true that morality as such has a universal aspect (as in the general rule against stealing, murder, and so on, which is honored in all societies); but morality must be "completed," either by philosophy and its gentlemanly political "imitation" or by belief in divine sanction.[41] Both the variety of such beliefs and a related attachment of communities to their own traditions makes war an ever-present possibility for which they must prepare and that necessarily leavens their concern for universal justice: the standards that apply at home cannot be fully extended to one's country's actual or potential enemies.[42]

Strauss's "closed society" is then not the pseudo-Platonic tyranny decried by Karl Popper. Even the most tolerant and civilized societies are closed in the decisive sense of resting on foundations that are not fully rational. What renders them civilized nonetheless (taking that term in the sense conveyed in Strauss's lecture on "German Nihilism") is their openness to learning from any source that "has something worthwhile to teach." However, on Strauss's account such openness is always at best partial.[43] The unity of every society depends finally on some "authoritative" element. As both open and closed to the whole, the city may well be the one "partial" whole, on his account, that can be known definitively.[44] If this is so, it furnishes another reason why philosophy, in his view, is necessarily "political."

MAGNANIMITY, STATECRAFT, AND LIBERAL DEMOCRACY

In *What is Political Philosophy?* Strauss uses "to spare the vanquished and crush the arrogant" once again, and with a particularly emphatic eloquence:

[40] Strauss, "Preface," in *LAM*, viii.
[41] Strauss, "Liberal Education and Responsibility," in *LAM*, 13–14; *NRH*, 151–153.
[42] Strauss, *NRH*, 149.
[43] Strauss, *CM*, 28–29.
[44] Strauss, "What is Political Philosophy?" in *WPP*, 24; see also *CM*, 138: Because its limits can be known "the city is the only whole within the whole or the only part within the whole whose essence can be wholly known."

Classical political philosophy is non-traditional, because it belongs to the fertile moment when all political traditions were shaken, and there was not yet in existence a tradition of political philosophy... From this it follows that the classical philosophers see the political things with a freshness and directness which have never been equaled. They look at political things in the perspective of the enlightened citizen or statesman.[45] They see things clearly which the enlightened citizens or statesmen do not see clearly, or do not see at all. But this has no other reason but the fact that they look further afield in the same direction as the enlightened citizen or statesmen.[46] They do not look at political things from outside, as spectators of political life... Hence their political philosophy is comprehensive; it is both political theory and political skill; it is as open-minded to the legal and institutional aspects of political life as it is to that which transcends the legal and institutional; it is equally free from the narrowness of the lawyer, the brutality of the technical, the vagaries of the visionary, and the baseness of the opportunist. It reproduces, and raises to perfection, the magnanimous flexibility of the true statesman, who crushes the insolent and spares the vanquished.[47]

"Raised to perfection," the magnanimous flexibility of the statesman epitomizes the peculiar "unity" of science and morals of which the lecture on "German Nihilism" had earlier spoken.[48] The outlook of the

[45] See also Strauss's 1945 essay "On Classical Philosophy": "The political philosopher first comes to sight as a good citizen... In order to perform [this] function he has to raise ulterior questions... but in so doing he does not abandon... [the] fundamental orientation inherent in political life" (*WPP*, 81). The greatest statesmen possess "political science" in "the original meaning of term."

[46] Strauss, *CM*, 28, 140; *NRH*, 142–143. According to Strauss, at least for Aristotle the philosopher "articulates the unwritten *nomos*" that is the "limit of the perfect gentleman's vision" while himself standing "above that limit." The "enlightened statesman" is the "highest case" of the gentleman thus affected by philosophy. By way of contrast, Thucydides looks "not only in the same direction as the citizen or statesman but also within the same horizon." One of the "noblest duties" of the historian is to make retrospectively manifest to all what the statesman must decide "on the spot," without relying on any general rule: namely, the objective difference between "extreme actions that were just" and those that were unjust (*NRH*, 161). On Strauss's account, Churchill would seem to have been one of those rare individuals who could perform at the highest level the tasks of both the statesman and the historian (see *NRH*, 308).

[47] Cf. Strauss, "Jerusalem and Athens," in *SPPP*, 164.

[48] In "What is Political Philosophy?" Strauss writes apropos of Plato's *Laws*: "The vicarious enjoyment of wine through a conversation about wine, which enlarges the horizon of the law-abiding old citizens, limits the horizon of the philosopher. This... achievement of harmony between the excellence of man and the excellence of the citizen is, it seems, the most noble exercise of the virtue of moderation." As Strauss adds, moderation "is not a virtue of thought" but of "speech" (*WPP*, 32).

"true statesman" that the political philosopher takes as his own starting point is no longer specifically identified with empire though it remains linked to magnanimity.

The implications of that outlook for American liberal democracy are taken up in a contemporary essay on the proper task of social science. Social science in the best sense "must indeed look farther afield than the civic art, but it must look in the same direction as the civic art. Its relevances must become identical, at least at the outset, with those of the citizen or statesman." Accordingly, "the guiding theme of social science" in this age and country will be "liberal democracy, especially in its American form." At the same time, "the dangers inherent in liberal democracy" must be "set forth squarely," along with its peculiar "self-contradictions and half-heartednesses," for "the friend of liberal democracy is not its flatterer."[49]

Political philosophy in the present age takes the form of "social science" whose outlook is identical, at least initially, with that of the liberal-democratic citizen and statesman. The social scientist "in the best sense" seeks to guide liberal democracy as its friend while also alerting it (as only the political philosopher, who sees further, can) to the particular dangers of the present. Nihilism now threatens liberal democracy as an invitation not to immoderation, as in Weimar Germany, but to irresponsible half-heartedness. On America's thinner classical soil, the "taking things easy" that permitted England to keep classical ideals alive becomes an invitation to thoughtlessness.[50] Rather than disturbing, as it did in Weimar, the conviction that knowledge of the truth is unavailable lulls men into a complacent affirmation of "tolerance." For example, in insisting that the "Jewish Question" cannot be definitively solved even in America, Strauss means to disturb that complacency by alerting his liberal audience to the contradiction harbored in the fact that liberal democracy imposes, against its own explicit self-understanding, an authoritative conception of the right way of life.[51] If that conception is rationally defensible, it is so on the basis of principles other than modern ones.[52] He thus seeks to elicit not only a healthy respect for religious traditions that continue to flourish in America especially but also that passionate interest in ancient thought for which his students have become justly famous.

[49] Strauss, "Liberal Education and Responsibility," in *LAM*, 24; see also Timothy Fuller, "The Complementarity of Political Philosophy and Liberal Education in the Thought of Leo Strauss," this volume.

[50] Cf. Strauss, GN, 372, with *NRH*, 5; "An Epilogue" in *LAM*, 222–223; "What is Political Philosophy," in *WPP*, 18–20, 23.

[51] See Strauss, "Why We Remain Jews," in *JPCM*, 317.

[52] Strauss, TWM, 98.

CONCLUSION

Strauss's "On German Nihilism" marks a key moment in his own political transformation from a harsh critic of liberal democracy to its "unhesitating" supporter.[53] At the same time, the pivotal role of Churchill for Strauss is particularly revealing of the reasons for that transformation. By his own account, the fact of Churchill not only helps Strauss correct a personal, historically conditioned prejudice[54]; it also makes manifest the ongoing possibility of magnanimity and, therewith, an outlook from which philosophy even in an historicizing age can find its bearings.

In postwar America, Strauss will adapt that awareness to the peculiarities of his adopted country and his own position, not altogether freely chosen, as a professional "social scientist."[55] The initiating outlook of the liberal democratic citizen and statesman will continue to inform his major writings of the 1950s and 1960s. At the same time, religion, and Judaism in particular (Jerusalem as well as Athens), receives new and newly respectful emphasis.[56] The twin roots of Western civilization are "Jerusalem and Athens," whose vital tension America at its best helps keep alive.[57] This new emphasis arises not only out of patriotic or human loyalty; the challenge of religion, as Strauss had subsequently come to see, cannot be answered in the "abstract" any more than the challenge posed by nihilism. The "shipwreck" of the mid-1940s seems to have precipitated a new and more searching investigation on his part of the claims of biblical faith.[58] The example of the magnanimous

---

[53] Strauss, "Liberal Education and Responsibility," in *LAM*, 24: wisdom "cannot be separated from moderation" and hence requires "unhesitating loyalty to a decent constitution and even to the cause of constitutionalism."

[54] See Letter to Löwith, August 20, 1946 in *GS*, 3: 666–667.

[55] Cf. Strauss, "What is Political Philosophy?" in *WPP*, 13–15.

[56] See his opening statement in "What is Political Philosophy?" in *WPP*, 9–10. By way of contrast, in his 1941 review of Löwith's *From Hegel to Nietzsche* Strauss can still speak confidently and almost casually of the "historical and soluble antinomy" between the "ideal of Christianity and that of classical antiquity" (*WPP*, 270).

[57] On the potentially "fruitful and ennobling tension" in America between (classically) liberal education and religious education, see Strauss, "Liberal Education and Responsibility," in *LAM*, 18, 22; cf. "Progress or Return," in *RCPR*, 270.

[58] See Letter to Löwith, August 15, 1946, in *GS*, 3: 660–663. As Daniel Tanguay notes, Strauss became deeply interested around this time in the work of a number of Jewish thinkers including Isaac Husik, whose own consideration of "Hebraism and Hellenism" prefigures in some ways Strauss's later thematic treatment of "Jerusalem and Athens." (See Strauss, "Preface to Isaac Husik,

statesman faces at least an equally impressive rival.[59] The power of providential thinking can be fully confronted only through a direct, personal encounter.[60] In this way too, "German Nihilism" offers an important clue to Strauss's final understanding of the relation between science and morals.

Philosophical Essays: Ancient, Medieval, and Modern," in *JPCM*, 235–266; and Tanguay, *Leo Strauss: An Intellectual Biography*, 144–147). In a 1948 Lecture at the Hartford Theological Seminary, Strauss offers an account of how what is called the "experience of revelation" might possibly have arisen through natural causes. See his "Reason and Revelation" in Meier, *Leo Strauss and the Theological-Political Problem*, 141–180. For Strauss's views on the justification of philosophy prior to the aforementioned "shipwreck," see "On Classical Political Philosophy," in *WPP*, 78–94.

[59] See Strauss, "Progress or Return," in *RCPR*, 249: "Biblical humility excludes magnanimity in the Greek sense."

[60] Cf. Letter to Löwith, June 23, 1935, in *GS*, 3: 649, and "Preface to *SCR*," in *LAM*, 232–233. For a lucid attempt to articulate what such an encounter might involve, see Thomas Pangle, *Philosophy and the God of Abraham* (Baltimore, MD: Johns Hopkins, 2003).

9   Leo Strauss's Qualified Embrace of Liberal Democracy

CLASSICAL POLITICAL PHILOSOPHY AND MODERN POLITICS

The topic of Leo Strauss's understanding of democracy and the American regime is fraught with controversy. Strauss's many detractors claim that he was hostile to democracy, and Strauss's students disagree about the implications of his views for the United States.[1] It may help orient the reader if at the outset I state the view for which I shall argue – namely, that in this matter there are compelling reasons to take Strauss at his word. "Wisdom," he declared, "requires unhesitating loyalty to a decent constitution, and even to the cause of constitutionalism."[2] The word "even" may appear curious but is easily explained: constitutionalism is a modern version of the rule of law, an approach to governance that, as Strauss often emphasized, leans inherently against arbitrary power, regardless of the specific content of a legal code. At any rate, there can be no doubt that Strauss regarded the U.S. Constitution as decent and as orienting the United States to the rule of law, so far as any polity can maintain that commitment. It is easy to believe that Strauss endorsed modern liberal democracy on essentially negative grounds, as a bulwark against tyrannies of the left and right. This is part of the story, but only part: he also favored it on positive grounds, as a decent form of government that embodied certain partial but nonetheless real goods and virtues.

My thesis is exposed to an obvious objection: everybody knows that Strauss sought to restore classical political philosophy as arguably the best account of politics, and classical political philosophy certainly did not endorse democracy as the best form, or even the best achievable form, of political order. Nonetheless, he insisted that even from the classical standpoint as he understood it, there is no serious alternative

---

[1] For the single most accessible account of these controversies, see Catherine and Michael Zuckert, *The Truth About Leo Strauss: Political Philosophy and America Democracy* (Chicago: University of Chicago Press, 2006), ch. 4–7.

[2] Strauss, "Liberal Education and Responsibility," in *LAM*, 24.

to liberal democracy today: "Liberal or constitutional democracy comes closer to what the classics demanded than any alternative that is viable in our age."[3]

The apparent paradox begins to dissolve when we observe Strauss's flat denial that classical political philosophy could be used straightforwardly to guide contemporary practice. His fullest statement to this effect is important enough to deserve extended quotation:

We cannot reasonably expect that a fresh understanding of classical political philosophy will supply us with recipes for today's use. For the relative success of modern political philosophy has brought into being a kind of society wholly unknown to the classics, a kind of society to which the classical principles as stated and elaborated by the classics are not immediately applicable. Only we today can possibly find a solution to the problems of today.[4]

This does not mean that classical philosophy is irrelevant to contemporary concerns, Strauss continued: "An adequate understanding of the principles as elaborated by the classics may be the indispensable starting point for an adequate analysis, to be achieved by us, of present-day society in its peculiar character, and for the wise application, to be achieved by us, of these principles to our tasks."[5] That represents Strauss's understanding of what he himself was doing. The question then becomes, what was the path that could lead Strauss, however circuitously, from classical principles to an endorsement, however qualified, of liberal democracy and American constitutionalism?

There is one thing we can say with certainty at the outset: Strauss's endorsement of liberal democracy could not have included an endorsement of its explicit philosophical underpinnings. For decades, Strauss argued that the philosophical impasse of the twentieth century – its descent into relativism and nihilism – was prefigured in the very origins of modern thought. He contended there was an inexorable dialectic leading from the early modern rejection of teleology and of contemplation as the highest form of human existence to the self-undermining of reason itself. Each step in this dialectic represented both an inference from and critique of the prior step. Thus, Strauss insisted that "The critique of modern rationalism or of the belief in reason by Nietzsche cannot be dismissed or forgotten. This is the deepest reason for the crisis of liberal democracy."[6] Specifically, "All rationalistic liberal philosophic positions have lost their significance and power. One may deplore this, but I for one cannot bring myself to [cling] to philosophic positions

[3] Strauss, "Restatement on Xenophon's *Hiero*," in *OT*, 194.
[4] Strauss, *CM*, 11
[5] Strauss, *CM*, 11.
[6] Strauss, TWM, 98.

which have been shown to be inadequate."[7] Even more specifically, Strauss could not have accepted and did not accept approaches to liberal democracy inspired by Locke, Spinoza, or Kant as philosophically viable. To the extent that contemporary understandings of individual rights rest on these foundations, he could not accept them either.[8]

Strauss observed that the theoretical crisis of liberal democratic philosophy had not led and would not necessarily lead to a practical crisis. He offered two different but not mutually exclusive explanations for this gap. In the first place, as he often argued, practical politics is the realm of opinion or belief rather than knowledge or philosophical understanding. To make a compelling argument against a mode of political thought and organization is not necessarily to undermine its practical effectiveness. So even as Strauss worried that German historicism would weaken a regime taking its bearings from the Declaration of Independence, he offered reasons why it might not. Choosing his words carefully, he asked whether the United States in its maturity still cherished "the *faith* in which it was conceived and raised..."[9] We may hold certain propositions to be self-evidently true even when they are not. What is most important politically is the sustainability of these beliefs, not their epistemological status. (This is not to say that sustainability and substance are unrelated; manifestly absurd or counterfactual premises are more difficult to maintain.) Therefore, it was uncertain whether historicism would in fact weaken Americans' historic embrace of individual rights as the core of their creed.

There was a second reason why the theoretical crises had not led to a practical crisis: wise political judgments do not necessarily rest on theoretical foundations. Strauss distinguished between Socrates and Plato, for whom true understanding of politics depends on cosmology and metaphysics, and Aristotle, who argued that practical wisdom enjoyed autonomy from theory. As Strauss summarized Aristotle's stance, "The sphere ruled by prudence is closed since the principles of prudence – the ends in light of which prudence guides man – are known independently of theoretical science."[10] Although Strauss offered a lucid summary of the Socratic-Platonic stance as well, he made it tolerably though not unambiguously clear that he inclined toward the Aristotelian, which not only made it possible to found political science as an "independent discipline" but also to remain rooted in the perspective of citizens

---

[7] Strauss, "An Introduction to Heideggerian Existentialism," in *RCPR*, 29.

[8] For an argument along similar lines, see Christopher Bruell, "A Return to Classical Political Philosophy and the Understanding of the American Founding," *Review of Politics* 53 (1991): 173–176.

[9] Strauss, *NRH*, 1 (emphasis added).

[10] Strauss, *CM*, 25.

and political leaders – precisely the stance Strauss himself regularly urged. One needs no theory to see the superiority of liberal democracy to its twentieth-century competitors; Strauss contended it is "obvious enough" to ordinary common sense.[11] He made a similar point in his eulogy of Winston Churchill: "The tyrant [Hitler] stood at the pinnacle of his power. The contrast between the indomitable and magnanimous statesman and the insane tyrant – this spectacle in its clear simplicity was one of the greatest lessons which men can learn, at any time."[12] Although speech is the medium of politics, there are limits to its political effects. Misguided ideas may deform, but cannot altogether expunge, the permanent features of human nature and facts of political life, and the capacity for moral awareness will not disappear as long as we remain human.

In the context of autonomous moral perception and prudential judgment, Aristotelian political philosophy serves not as the basis of morality and prudence but rather as their guardian against theoretical error. As Strauss explained, "Prudence is always endangered by false doctrines about the whole of which man is a part, by false theoretical opinions; prudence is therefore always in need of defense against such opinions, and that defense is necessarily theoretical."[13]

For Strauss, the basis for this atheoretical capacity of moral perception is found in human nature: "By virtue of his rationality, man has a latitude of alternatives such as no other earthly being has ... Man's freedom is accompanied by a sacred awe, by a kind of divination that not everything is permitted. We may call this awe-inspired fear 'man's natural conscience.'"[14] It was to drive home this point that Strauss began his most famous book with the story of the rich man and the poor man from 2 Samuel: the natural conscience tells us, always and everywhere, that it is wrong for the rich man to seize what little the poor man possesses. And it is by virtue of this claim that Strauss could reject the "untrue assumption that man as man is thinkable as a being that lacks

---

[11] Strauss, TWM, 98.

[12] Quoted and discussed in Harry V. Jaffa, "Strauss at One Hundred," in Kenneth L. Deutsch and John A. Murley, eds. *Leo Strauss, The Straussians, and the American Regime* (Lanham, MD: Rowman & Littlefield, 1999), 44.

[13] Strauss, "An Epilogue," in *LAM*, 206. Kant makes a very similar point toward the beginning of the *Critique of Pure Reason*. This is no accidental resemblance. Once one posits a sphere of moral knowledge that does not depend on prior theoretical knowledge of natural law, metaphysics, or God, then valid theory is bound to assume an essentially negative role of defending morality against false theory. Strauss tersely remarks that "Aristotle is the founder of political science because he is the discoverer of moral virtue" (*CM*, 27).

[14] Strauss, NRH, 130.

awareness of sacred restraints or as a being that is guided by nothing but a desire for recognition"[15] – the assumption that he saw at the heart of the utopian-tyrannical excesses of the twentieth century.

It was in part the complexity of the relation between theory and practice that allowed Strauss to move from classical political philosophy to a qualified endorsement of liberal democracy. There was a second consideration that pointed in the same direction: Strauss discerned some important resemblances between the orientation of contemporary liberal democracy and that of the classics. One is psychological realism – the recognition that human beings combine admirable and undesirable traits and that even the most successful political reforms will not alter this basic fact. Not only did the authors of the *Federalist Papers* understand that men are not angels, they did not expect them ever to become angels. Communists dreamed of the "New Soviet Man," but liberal democrats knew that although wise institutions could improve the human condition, they would never change human nature.

Psychological realism leads to politics conducted in an anti-utopian spirit. As Strauss put it, classical political philosophy is "free from all fanaticism because it knows that evil cannot be eradicated and therefore that one's expectations from politics must be moderate."[16] Conversely, the belief that the cessation of evils is possible is the source of the anger and indignation that drives utopian politics and creates new evils.[17] Liberal democrats have not always been able to resist utopian hopes – that rational persuasion might obviate the need for coercion, that war might ultimately be abolished, or that affluence might minister to the "deepest evils."[18] But liberals have been far less prone to such dreams than have their antagonists.

Finally, although the rule of law does not in itself guarantee justice, it tends toward justice and constitutes a necessary condition of justice. There is at least a family resemblance between Aristotle's account of law and modern liberal constitutionalism. To be sure, liberals sometimes go too far in attempting to eliminate the element of discretion from law and politics; there will always be a gap between the generality of the law and specific cases to which it must be applied. But far worse was the arbitrary, lawless rule that characterized modern tyrannies of the left and right. Although the rule of law was not in Aristotle's view the highest

---

[15] Strauss *OT*, 192.
[16] Strauss, "What is Political Philosophy," in *WPP*, 28; quoted and discussed in Nathan Tarcov, "Leo Strauss and American Conservative Thought and Politics," paper delivered at the American Society for Legal and Political Philosophy, Washington DC, January 5, 2005, p. 5.
[17] Strauss, *CM*, 129.
[18] Strauss, *CM*, 6.

manifestation of political life, it was the foundation of the decency and moderation that Strauss saw as often the best that circumstances would permit, and far more likely to characterize liberal democracy than any of its more ambitious antagonists.

A third consideration enabled Strauss to narrow the gap between classical philosophy and modern democracy. In his view, the classics' stance toward democracy was itself more nuanced than most modern interpreters have understood. Plato noted the duality of Athenian freedom: although it allowed a riotous anarchy of ways of life, many unrestrained and degraded, it also permitted Socrates to go about his business for seven decades, an outcome that would have been impossible in Sparta. And Aristotle's depiction of popular decision-making was in important respects affirmative. Those who must wear the shoes are competent judges of their fit, even if they lack the skill to make them, and the pooled judgment of average individuals may well be wiser than the judgment of a single individual.

More than that, Strauss's thesis that modern philosophy has helped bring into being a new type of society suggests the corollary that modern democracy has features that sharply distinguish it from the type of democracy known to Plato and Aristotle. Strauss explicitly affirms this: "The democracy with which [Aristotle] takes issue is the democracy of the city, not modern democracy or the kind of democracy which presupposes the distinction between state and society."[19] What are the key differences, and what difference do they make?

First, given economic conditions in ancient Greece, the rule of the majority was almost certain to be the rule of the poor. This generated many difficulties. Not only did the poor lack education and leisure, they were very likely to be locked in combat with the wealthy few, whose property they would seek to appropriate. By contrast, in modern democracies the core of the ruling majority is likely to be the middle class, a source of moderation and stability. In this respect, modern democracy resembles what Aristotle called "polity" and praised as a desirable arrangement when a favorable class structure permitted it. Although this might appear to be a clear win for modernity, Strauss argued it could be achieved only by substantially liberating economic growth – and its key driver, technological innovation – from moral and political control. Whether Strauss regarded this great transformation to have conferred benefits greater than its costs is an exceedingly complex question, discussed at length below.

According to Strauss, Aristotle believed that the poor were inherently opposed to the life of the mind, especially when philosophical inquiry

[19] Strauss, *CM*, 35.

raised doubts about dominant moral and religious beliefs.[20] This points to a second important difference between classical and modern democracy: coupled with modern constitutionalism, the dominance of the middle class tends to relax the tension between philosophy and politics. Relax, but not eliminate; today scholars who advocate unpopular views are often excoriated and ostracized, and from time to time an aroused public tries to rein in what it regards as the dangerous irresponsibility of faculty members at public universities. Still, dissenting thinkers tend not to be deprived of liberty, let alone life, in modern democracies – a clear gain from the classical standpoint.

Third, in a decisive respect Greek democracy was more egalitarian than modern democracy; most magistrates and leaders were selected by lot. To the extent that considerations of merit and fitness for office figure in elections, "voting for candidates is aristocratic rather than democratic." In this respect, Strauss concluded the intention of modern democracy would have to be described from Aristotle's point of view as a "mixture of democracy and aristocracy."[21]

Finally and decisively, classical democracy was as "comprehensively political" as any other regime-type, whereas modern democracy is limited in its scope – that is, "liberal."[22] Liberal democracy distinguishes between state and society; classical democracy did not. As Strauss observed, Aristotle was aware of a view of politics as limited to the promotion of commerce and the prevention of fraud and illicit force. Aristotle regarded these goods as necessary but not sufficient; if political community is for the sake of living well, not just comfortably surviving, then there must be some agreement concerning justice and nobility, and that agreement must be operative in the laws as well as ethos of the community.[23] Aristotle was not wholly at odds with the fundamental principle of modern liberalism; he too believed that politics is not coextensive with the totality of human life, and that some aspects of life transcend rightful political authority. Substantively, his view is very different: as Strauss observed, Aristotle differed from modern liberalism "by limiting this transcendence only to the highest in man."[24] He rejected what many liberals regarded as their crowning achievement – a capacious and protected sphere of individual and civil liberties.

The classics' judgment of "comprehensive" democracy cannot then be directly applied to liberal democracy. Whether restricting the

---

[20] Strauss, *CM*, 37.
[21] Strauss, *CM*, 35.
[22] Strauss, *CM*, 36.
[23] Strauss, *CM*, 32; Aristotle, *Politics* 1280a25–b35.
[24] Strauss, *CM*, 49.

scope of democratic governance represents a change for better or worse is a question that deserves, and will now receive, a more extended treatment.

THE PUBLIC-PRIVATE DISTINCTION

Strauss saw a clear difference of principle between classical and modern democracy. The Greeks did not limit the scope of democratic public authority, either in theory or in practice; as in every other regime, authority potentially extended to every aspect of life. Although democracy typically offered more scope for freedom and human diversity than any other regime, the people were free to change their mind about what the law should permit. Socrates plied his philosophical trade at the sufferance of the people, not as a matter of right.[25] By contrast, modern democracy is limited, "liberal" democracy. As Strauss states, "Liberalism stands and falls by the distinction between state and society or by the recognition of a private sphere, protected by the law but impervious to the law."[26] But wherever the line may be drawn, a politics organized in accordance with this principle opens up the possibility that societies in liberal democracies will not wholly reflect the public principles of liberal democracy – to freedom, equality, and nondiscrimination, among others. A tension exists between the fundamental principles governing liberal democratic public life and its equally fundamental commitment to a protected sphere of private life. As Strauss observed, "Given this – the necessary existence of such a private sphere – the liberal society necessarily makes possible, permits, and fosters what is called by many people 'discrimination.'"[27]

The immediate practical question is what, if anything, to do about this tension. Moderate reformers have responded by rethinking the definition of what is public. If a motel or restaurant is best understood as a "public accommodation," then the arbitrary exclusion of customers based on race ceases to be a purely private matter and comes within the scope of the law, and similarly for buses and other forms of transportation as "public conveyances." In the same spirit, fair housing laws have drawn a distinction between homeowners renting rooms as they see fit and apartment owners offering multiple units; in this context at least, the home is plausibly regarded as private, the apartment as public. And the line is not only a matter of physical location. Under scrutiny, it was difficult to defend the proposition that marriage established a zone

[25] Strauss, "The Liberalism of Classical Political Philosophy," in *LAM*, 61.
[26] Strauss, "Preface to *SCR*," in *LAM*, 230.
[27] Strauss, "Why We Remain Jews," in *JPCM*, 314.

wholly impervious to the law. Assault is assault, rape is rape, regardless of where they occur and what the legal relationships between the parties happens to be.

Although Strauss never commented publicly on such measures, there is no reason to believe that he regarded them as inconsistent with the principle of liberal democracy. Not so for the more extreme critiques of the public-private distinction as inherently invidious, as sheltering hierarchy and abuse from public remedies guided by democratic principles. The remedy for these ills – effacing the line and totalizing democratic public authority – would be worse than the disease: "The prohibition against every 'discrimination' would mean the abolition of the private sphere, the denial of the difference between state and society, in a word, the destruction of liberal society; and therefore, it is not a sensible objective or policy."[28] The experience of twentieth-century totalitarianism showed that modern technology had dangerously expanded the capacity of governments to do evil on a massive scale and to deny human freedom more completely than ever before. The choice is between the demonstrated risks of unlimited public power and the ills that limits on such power may perpetuate. In practice, Strauss judged that "There is nothing better than the uneasy solution offered by liberal society, which means legal equality plus private 'discrimination,'"[29] all the more so if, as Strauss believed, many of these ills are aspects of the human condition beyond the power of politics to remedy.

Liberalism understood as limited government means that substantial portions of social life – religion, art, music, the humanities, and science – stand substantially outside the sphere of sovereign authority. But what transpires in the civil sphere – the "extended regime" – is consequential for official politics, for the regime in the narrow sense. This fact creates a number of possibilities. The optimistic view is that liberal democracy's official principles create a climate of opinion that influences the civil sphere without resort to law or coercion, such that the civil society spontaneously supports and even improves political institutions. The pessimistic view is that at some point, the self-limitation of liberal democracy in effect undermines the integrity of the regime, as autonomous developments within civil society undermine allegiance to basic political institutions. The liberal democratic regime would then have to choose between its defining principle and its self-preservation.

To the extent that the classics (and Strauss) are correct in arguing that the regime's aims and principles suffuse the entire society, the optimists would seem to have the stronger case. But note that optimism

[28] Strauss, "Why We Remain Jews," in *JPCM*, 315.
[29] Strauss, "Why We Remain Jews," in *JPCM*, 317.

can quickly turn to another type of pessimism: if the perpetuation of liberal democracies requires the influence of forces other than liberal democratic principles, then the regime-induced liberalization and democratization of these forces will weaken their efficacy over time. So the deeper issue is whether liberal democratic principles are stably self-perpetuating. Strauss doubted that they were, which is why he stressed the importance of "premodern" elements of America's society for maintaining its political institutions.

But a single case hardly suffices to establish the general proposition. Consider Strauss's reflections on the Weimar Republic. Weimar Germany was a liberal democracy but it was "weak." The question was why? Strauss considered but rejected as inadequate the standard explanations – that the republic was resented as imposed from outside, or that inflation weakened and depression destroyed the middle class. What needed explanation was why liberal democracy had triumphed in other nations but had always been weak in Germany. Strauss's explanation began with the observation that according to a core principle of liberal democracy, the bond of society is universal morality rather than any particular religion. The difficulty was that the vast majority of Germans, including non-Christian cosmopolitans such as Goethe, never accepted this principle. For the majority, it was Christianity that defined German culture and identity. Although German Jews placed their hope in a republic whose political institutions were neutral regarding differences between Jews and Christians, most non-Jewish Germans rejected this neutrality outright. The Weimar Republic was weak then because key features of German life stood outside the scope of public law and contradicted the principles of the public realm. In the end, German society proved stronger than the liberal democratic state.[30]

Although Strauss never explicitly compared the United States and Weimar Germany, his assessment of Weimar provides the basis for doing so. In the United States, what lay outside the formal institutions of liberal democracy helped strengthen those institutions; in Weimar Germany, what lay outside its institutions helped weaken and ultimately destroy them. Strauss often emphasized that the "Jewish Question" is not amenable to a purely human solution. But to the extent that a narrower problem – the ability of Jews to live on terms of civic equality and social acceptance in a nation without a Jewish majority – is responsive to human contrivance, it has been solved in the country where liberal democracy is strongest; in the beginning, through protective public institutions and supportive leaders such as George Washington; later and more fully through gradual changes in public sentiment and

[30] Strauss, "Preface to *SCR*," in *LAM*, 224–228.

belief – changes that reflect the progressively deepening influence of liberal democratic public principles in U.S. civil and even private life.

The United States then enjoyed enviable good fortune that might appear paradoxical: its civil society both provided a counterweight to liberal democratic principles and was open to their influence, in both instances to the advantage of liberal democracy. By contrast, Germany's failure to solve the problem of Jewish civic equality and social acceptance reflected not an inherent incapacity of liberal democracy but rather the weakness of liberal democracy in Germany in the face of civil and cultural forces that were closed to, and stronger than, the formative influence of the regime's public principles. It is impossible to say whether Strauss would have been surprised by the sharp decline in American anti-Jewish sentiment since his death; it is possible that he underestimated the gravitational force of entrenched liberal political principles on the evolution of liberal society.

THE CHALLENGE OF TECHNOLOGY

In a surprising passage, Strauss went so far as to say, without overt qualification, that "the essential difference between our view [that is, the modern democratic view] and the classical view consists ... not in a difference regarding moral principle, not in a different understanding of justice: we, too ... think that it is just to give equal things to equal people and unequal things to people of unequal merit. The difference between the classics and us with regard to democracy consists exclusively in a different estimate of the virtues of technology."[31]

The surprise dissipates when we consider an obvious fact: if democracy – rule by the many – is not to be rule by the uneducated poor, then it requires a robust middle class and widely available education. Creating and sustaining these conditions requires an economy of abundance, which we have learned cannot exist without ceaseless technological innovation that meets and creates public desires in an endless cycle. In turn, this requires the emancipation of technology from the type of moral and political control the classics recommended. And it implies the end of public efforts to rein in desire and consumption; John Adams was among the last American statesmen to embrace sumptuary laws.

Strauss often expressed grave reservations about the modern stance toward technology, which he linked to a narrowed and lowered understanding of virtue as enlightened self-interest.[32] And he often noted that for the first time in human history, modern technology has made

---

[31] Strauss, "What is Political Philosophy?" in *WPP*, 37.
[32] Strauss, "Liberal Education and Responsibility," *LAM*, 21.

possible the destruction of the human race through its own acts, not just through natural cataclysm.

Nor was this all: by expanding human powers, modern technology opens grave moral questions that it is incompetent to answer. To be sure, some of what technology makes possible can be understood as completing nature, understood in a classical or common-sense manner: laser-guided surgery operates by the standard of undistorted vision, antipsychotic drugs by the standard of undistorted consciousness, and so forth. But many emerging applications of technology cannot be understood in this manner; witness rising public concern about the genetic modification and cloning of human beings. Although the need for public regulation of these processes is more widely recognized than it was a generation ago, the principled grounds for public restraints are disputed, and efforts to move in this direction are often thwarted by powerful economic interests. Technology thus joins hands with morally dubious desires.

The technology-based economy of abundance not only reflects but also exacerbates the liberation of acquisitiveness from moral limits. Although it is possible for individuals living in prosperous societies to observe such limits, and to teach their children to do so as well, it is not easy. A technologically dynamic society sends a tacit moral message to its citizens: there are no enduring limits. And because technology produces abundance through economic markets, its moral thrust is toward freedom rather than virtue, however understood. Strauss's judgment on the theoretical underpinnings and practical consequences of technology-based prosperity was often severe. "Economism," he asserted, is "Machiavellianism come of age."[33] And it could not contribute to one of the Declaration's fundamental aims, the pursuit of happiness; Strauss famously declared the quest for satisfaction through ever-increasing prosperity was the "joyless quest for joy."[34]

Finally, Strauss observed technology-based abundance tends both to lower the standards of popular culture and to promote an understanding of education as instrumental to individual prosperity and economic growth. Working in tandem, these tendencies make it more difficult to sustain genuine liberal education and to hear the small still voices of human excellence.

But that was only one side of the story, and Strauss urged his readers "not for one moment [to] forget the other side." In the first place, justice requires a "reasonable correspondence" between social hierarchy and natural hierarchy. In economies of scarcity, it is impossible to achieve that correspondence: education and leisure for some means ignorance

---

[33] Strauss, "What is Political Philosophy?" in *WPP*, 49.
[34] Strauss, *NRH*, 251.

and drudgery for others, and many who are condemned to live out their lives in poverty would have been capable of genuine distinction under the correct conditions. (Witness the explosion of achievement when previously impoverished immigrants enter societies that offer opportunities for advancement.) In economies of scarcity, the choice is then between equality at a low level and inequality that produces an able ruling class at the expense of injustice to the many whom chance has excluded.

This injustice was difficult to bear even when the wealthy ruled the community with an eye to the common good; it was indefensible and insupportable when (as was more often the case) the wealthy ruled in their own interest. "With... increasing abundance," Strauss argued, "it became increasingly possible to see and admit the element of hypocrisy which had entered into the traditional notion of aristocracy; the existing aristocracies proved to be oligarchies rather than aristocracies."[35] Abundance helps clear the way for a more genuine meritocracy in which everyone has the same right to equal opportunity. Although conventional inequality rests on the morally arbitrary distribution of opportunity, natural inequality manifests itself in the use or neglect of opportunities available to all. In this manner, Strauss concluded "it became possible to abolish many injustices or at least many things which had become injustices."[36] Not only could individuals with great natural gifts rise but also nearly everyone could achieve a basic level of literacy, mental development, and liberation from the grossest forms of ignorance.

Technology-based abundance has another positive political consequence as well. Whenever economies of abundance have been allowed to develop more or less freely over time, the middle class has tended to grow, first in size, then in political influence. As Aristotle observed, political communities with large middle classes enjoy important advantages. The middle class tends to be moderate, not only in its economic ambitions but also in the pursuit of honor and public eminence. And a society no longer divided between the few rich and the many poor is less likely to be riven by strife and violence. Whereas for the classics, politically healthy class structures were a matter of chance, something to be wished for, modern technology enables wise governments to plan and encourage the expansion of the middle class. The result is enhanced prospects for regimes that are decent and stable if not particularly elevated and inspiring.

It is difficult to believe that the global expansion of constitutional democracy since World War II is unrelated to the astonishing economic growth of this epoch. More broadly, the promise held out at the dawn of

---

[35] Strauss, "Liberal Education and Responsibility," in *LAM*, 21.
[36] Strauss, "Liberal Education and Responsibility," in *LAM*, 21.

modernity to "relieve man's estate" – to make human life longer, healthier, and more abundant – is being substantially redeemed. Few either in prosperous modern societies or in those that hope to become so would willingly give up the opportunity to enjoy these fruits of technology.

If Strauss offered a fair summary of the technological balance sheet, it is by no means clear in which direction morally serious judgment should incline. At various points, Strauss expressed grave reservations about the modern stance toward technology, and it is difficult to avoid the conclusion that, all things considered, he preferred the classical stance. But in this regard as elsewhere, classical standards offer no clear guidance to practice here and now. As Strauss emphasized against Hegel, morally speaking, what happens bears no reliable connection with what should happen. But if we must not succumb to history, neither can we repeal it. As Strauss emphasized, rather than seeking to escape into seductive but unproductive dreams, it is our duty to act as wisely and virtuously as possible within the context created by modern technology.[37]

LIBERAL DEMOCRACY IN AMERICA

To move from liberal democracy *simpliciter* to liberal democracy in America is to enter contested terrain. As many commentators have noted, although Strauss may have inspired generations of students to reexamine the American founding and regime, he himself wrote relatively little about his adopted country.[38] And because his most talented students have disagreed so fundamentally about the meaning of Strauss's thought for America, we must be very cautious about reasoning backward from his students' writings, however meritorious they may be in their own right, to his own thoughts.[39]

One of the few things we know for sure about Strauss's understanding of America only deepens the perplexity. After opening the lectures that became *Natural Right and History* by quoting the most famous passage from the Declaration of Independence, he commented that "The nation dedicated to this proposition has now become, no doubt partly as a

---

[37] Strauss, "Review of Yves R. Simon, *Philosophy of Democratic Government*," in *WPP*, 311.

[38] On this point, see Steven B. Smith, *Reading Leo Strauss: Politics, Philosophy, Judaism* (Chicago: University of Chicago Press, 2006), 166.

[39] Strauss's invocation of the Declaration follows from his well-known methodological dictum that "It is safer to try to understand the low in the light of the high than the high in the light of the low. In doing the latter one necessarily distorts the high, whereas in doing the former one does not deprive the low of the freedom to reveal itself fully as what it is" ("Preface to *SCR*, in *LAM*, 225).

consequence of this dedication, the most powerful and prosperous of the nations of the earth."[40]

This comment raises a number of difficulties, one of which was mentioned earlier: if Locke's philosophy is the principal source for the Declaration, and if that philosophy is subject to Strauss's overall critique of liberal rationalism, then the Declaration's truth-claims are called into doubt. America's strength and prosperity might then rest on a misconception, or even a myth. To be sure, Strauss might have been mistaken in his meta-narrative – the inevitable self-destruction of modern reason – or in the link he discerned between Locke and the Declaration. But within the four corners of Strauss's own thought, there is a problem that cannot be evaded.

How big a problem this represents depends on other considerations. According to Steven Smith, "Strauss accepted the view, less popular today than it once was, that Lockean ideas formed the theoretical foundation of the new American republic. It is not an exaggeration to say that Strauss's judgment on Locke *is* his judgment on America."[41] And if his judgment on Locke is negative, as it certainly appears to be, then his judgment on America must be negative as well.

There are several ways of escaping this conclusion. First, one may argue that although Strauss may have been right about the centrality of Locke, he was wrong to equate the Founders' Locke with his own. That is, they may have taken from Locke not only the obvious innovations but also the ways in which he tried rhetorically to separate himself from "justly decried authors" such as Hobbes and Spinoza and to link himself to a safer and more respectable tradition ("The judicious Hooker").[42] Strauss himself opens the door to the possibility, noting at one juncture that his interpretation of Locke "stands in shocking contrast to what is generally thought to be his doctrine."[43] To my knowledge, there is no evidence that the founding generation understood Locke in anything other than the conventional way, and considerable evidence pointing in the opposite direction. Consider the words of the aged Thomas Jefferson, a reasonably authoritative source on the meaning of the Declaration: "It was intended to be an expression of the American mind...All its authority rests then on the harmonizing sentiments of the day, whether expressed in conversation, in letters, printed essays, or in the elementary books of public right, as Aristotle, Cicero, Locke, Sidney, etc."[44]

[40] Strauss, *NRH*, 1.
[41] Smith, *Reading Leo Strauss*, 168–169.
[42] For an argument along these lines, see Thomas G. West, "Leo Strauss and the American Founding," *Review of Politics*, 53 (1991): 158.
[43] Strauss, *NRH*, 220.
[44] Jefferson, Letter to Henry Lee, May 8, 1825.

To preserve Strauss's conclusion, one would have to argue that the conventional understanding amounted to a sugar-coated pill with a bitter core: the Founders may have thought they were getting from Locke a suitably updated version of traditional natural law, but in the long run the practical effect of what they took was Hobbes's version.

There is a second escape route from a simply negative judgment of America, and the evidence suggests that Strauss seriously entertained it. Put simply, Strauss seemed to reject Smith's stark reduction of America to Locke, at least to the Hobbesian Locke of *Natural Right and History*. After all, he observed Locke recommended liberal education for a gentlemanly ruling class and took his models from the "ancient Greeks and Romans." In America, the authors of the *Federalist* "reveal their connection with the classics simply enough by presenting themselves at the work of one Publius" and contended that the Constitution they defended had a fair chance of elevating representatives and executives "who possess most wisdom to discern, and most virtue to pursue, the common good of society."[45] And Strauss was well aware of the impact of Protestant Christianity during the founding period and thereafter.

It was on this basis that Strauss was able to contend that liberal democracy rests on more than modern rationalism: "liberal democracy, in contradistinction to communism and fascism, derives powerful support from a way of thinking which cannot be called modern at all: the premodern thought of our western tradition."[46] This raises the question whether Strauss regarded this amalgam of modern and premodern principles as sustainable. He surely feared that influence of premodernity was on the wane, not least in America. In assessing the moral condition of contemporary liberal democracy, he said "we must disregard ... the older traditions which fortunately still retain some of their former power; we must disregard them because their power is more and more corroded as time goes on."[47] Obviously, much depends on whether Strauss's pessimistic observation is correct, and if so, whether anything can be done about it. Anyway, it is not irrelevant that up to now, America (unlike Europe) has stubbornly resisted Max Weber's thesis that modernization and secularization go together, and also that the aspiration to meritocracy rather than the reproduction of oligarchy remains alive and well, however far our system of education and employment may diverge in practice from this ideal.

We may understand Strauss's gesture toward the influence, however attenuated, of religion and premodern philosophy in America as the

---

[45] Strauss, "Liberal Education and Responsibility," in *LAM*, 14.
[46] Strauss, TWM, 98.
[47] Strauss, "Liberal Education and Responsibility," in *LAM*, 23.

beginning of his answer to the question raised by his description, quoted earlier, of the Declaration's effect: if it is "partly" responsible for America's power and prosperity, what else has contributed to this historic success? At the beginning of the *Federalist*, Hamilton remarked that "it seems to have been reserved to the people of this country, by their conduct and example, to decide the important question, whether societies of men are really capable or not of establishing good government from reflection and choice, or whether they are forever destined to depend for their political constitutions on accident and force."[48] It was on the basis of sentiments such as these that, as Strauss put it, "The United States may be said to be the only country in the world which was founded in explicit opposition to Machiavellian principles... At least to the extent that the American reality is inseparable from the American aspiration, one cannot understand Americanism without understanding Machiavellianism which is its opposite..."[49] But to what extent did American reality in fact reflect American aspiration. However one might characterize the founding period, it would be difficult to defend the proposition that America's continental expansion was devoid of "accident and force." As Strauss went on to observe, "Machiavelli would not hesitate to suggest a mischievous interpretation of the Louisiana Purchase and of the fate of the Red Indians,"[50] and Smith is surely right to suggest that Strauss himself endorsed that interpretation.[51]

We may generalize this point. As a particular political community, Strauss contended America could not be and was not exempt from the wrenching demands of practical politics. From time to time, extreme situations arise in which the very existence or independence of a society is at risk. In such situations, there may be a conflict between the requirements of self-preservation and the requirements of justice or ordinary morality. Strauss declared a decent society "will not go to war except for a just cause. But what it will do during a war will depend to a certain extent on what the enemy – possibly an absolutely unscrupulous and savage enemy – forces it to do. There are no limits which can be defined in advance."[52] And there is no guarantee that these exigencies of war will be confined to the overseas theater, that they will not spill over into the practices of domestic security as well. Political morality contains two sets of principles, one for normal circumstances, the other for the extreme, and there is no bright-line principle that can say when it is

---

[48] James Madison, Alexander Hamilton, and John Jay, *The Federalist Papers*, ed. Clinton Rossiter (New York: New American Library, 1961), 33.

[49] Strauss, *TM*, 13–14.

[50] Strauss, *TM*, 14.

[51] Smith, *Reading Leo Strauss*, 177.

[52] Strauss, *NRH*, 160.

right to set aside ordinary moral maxims. Despite the dangers of abuse, we cannot avoid investing leaders with discretionary power. This is not to say that political morality implodes into Machiavellianism; although Machiavelli took his bearings from the extreme situation, decent statesmen in the Aristotelian sense will presume the applicability of normal morality and will deviate from it with the greatest reluctance. Still, the need for wisdom and virtue – sound prudential judgment – is perennial; although in Strauss's words there may be a "universally valid hierarchy of ends," there are no comparable "universally valid rules of action," a fact with which even the most legalistically inclined constitutional democracy must somehow come to grips.[53]

It is for this reason among others that Strauss offers sober counterpoints to the utopian dreams liberal democrats have sometimes entertained: "The lack of order which necessarily characterizes the 'society' of the cities or, in other words, the omnipresence of War puts a much lower ceiling on the highest aspiration of any city toward justice and virtue than classical political philosophy might seem to have admitted."[54] The wish for a war to end all wars is entirely understandable, not only to extirpate the brutal horrors of armed conflict that challenge the moral core of even the most decent human beings but also to improve the prospects of achieving domestic justice and tranquility. But unless the nature of the international order as a system of independent political communities without a sovereign is fundamentally transformed, war remains an ever-present possibility.

PERENNIAL PROBLEMS

The foregoing is an example of how Strauss used classical political philosophy – particularly Aristotle – to diagnose what he understood as the perennial problems of democracy. There are many others. For example, the partisans of democracy typically move from the premise that citizens are equal in citizenship to the conclusion that they are equal in all politically relevant respects. But this is to overlook the existence of and need for political excellence, even in democracies, and especially in times of domestic or foreign crisis. Thomas Jefferson could still speak of elections as institutions designed to identify the "natural *aristoi*" and elevate them to political power. Even though the need for political excellence has in no way diminished, today it is much more difficult to offer a public defense of aristocracy as a valid and essential element of constitutional democracy. Indeed, the principle of civic equality has

[53] Strauss, *NRH*, 162.
[54] Strauss, *CM*, 239.

broadened into a comprehensive egalitarianism that throws meritocracy as such on the defensive. In some circles, equality of opportunity
is questioned whenever it fails to yield equality of result, and the idea
of unequal merit as such is often regarded as a covert defense of unjust
privilege.

Strauss feared that modern liberal democracies were in danger of
forgetting the need for civic excellence; and more broadly, that liberal
democratic "mass culture" pulls against even individual excellence.
He denounced the "perverted liberalism" that contends that "'just to
live, securely and happily, and protected but otherwise unregulated, is
man's simple but supreme goal' and which forgets quality, excellence, or
virtue."[55] And he defended liberal education as the best antidote to this
truncated and debased view. "Liberal education," he declared, "is the
ladder by which we try to ascend from mass democracy to democracy as
originally meant . . . Liberal education reminds those members of a mass
democracy who have ears to hear, of human greatness."[56]

Another example: Democrats, especially modern liberal democrats,
are tempted by a type of psychological reductionism that blinds them
to key human motivations and political phenomena. Characteristic of
liberal theory is an emphasis on the interplay between reason and interest. From a classical perspective, this leaves out something of crucial
importance for politics – the third part of the soul, *thumos* or spiritedness, which can be the source of dignified self-assertion and noble deeds
but also of anger, foolish pride, and destructiveness. Protoliberals such
as Hobbes focused on the negative aspects of spiritedness and used coun-
tervailing passions such as fear of death to minimize its effects. Enlightenment thinkers believed that an interest-based politics, in particular
one oriented toward economic gain, would soften hard, spirited men.
Modern liberal thinkers have all but forgotten the problem. For Rawls,
the challenge is simply to ensure that a "reasonable" moral orientation limits the pursuit of "rational" self-interest and fairly coordinates
acquisitive activities.

The difficulty with all this is obvious. If Strauss is correct that human
nature does not change, then spiritedness will not disappear and will
always seek to express itself. Many young men greeted the outbreak of
World War I with enthusiasm, even joy, because it offered a venue for
spirited deeds that found no outlet in the bourgeois societies of early
twentieth-century Europe. Nationalism may be regarded as spiritedness
collectivized. Nearly half a century ago, Strauss penned a sentence that
may serve as the epitaph for America's misadventure in Iraq: "Generally

---

55 Strauss, "The Liberalism of Classical Political Philosophy," in *LAM*, 64.
56 Strauss, "What is Liberal Education?" in *LAM*, 4–5.

speaking, even the lowliest men prefer being subjects to men of their own people rather than to any aliens."[57]

If the liberal effort to replace spiritedness with interest governed by reason is bound to fail, then we may expect to find characteristic expressions of this passion within liberal democratic society. And we do. As Joseph Cropsey puts it, "The institutionalization of acquisitiveness does seem to have fostered a self-assertiveness, aggressiveness, or simple egotism that comports particularly well with egalitarianism, and that might be called the variety of spiritedness peculiar to a liberal society."[58] If liberal self-assertion begins with acquisition, it does not end there. Americans instinctively assert their rights and equal standing, as citizens and human beings. "I'm just as good as you are" is not always an irritable gesture of populist envy; it may be, and often is, the proud expression of reasonable self-regard, a sense of self-worth that undergirds the possibility of dignity in everyday life.

Another example is that the partisans of democracy typically move from the premise that citizens should be able to live freely to the conclusion that they should be able to lead their lives just as they choose, without self-restraint. But to live without self-restraint is to live without virtue because virtue is a type of self-restraint. In the Aristotelian understanding, which Strauss endorsed, every type of political community requires its own form of civic virtue. The modern acceptance, or endorsement, of living without self-restraint gives rise to the liberal democratic emphasis on the artful arrangement of institutions as a substitute for virtue. Strauss doubted the adequacy of this substitution.

Yet the framers of the U.S. Constitution were neither unaware of nor indifferent to the older understanding. The same James Madison who famously advocated in *Federalist* #51 "a policy of supplying, by opposite and rival interests, the defect of better motives"[59] also insisted in *Federalist* #55 that human beings are capable of virtue as well as vice, and that republican government presupposes these better qualities more than does any other form of government.[60] But the new constitution made little if any provision for the virtue its perpetuation admittedly required. This vacuum was to be filled by a strategy Strauss, following Locke, summarized (controversially) as "religious education of the people . . . and liberal education of the representatives of the people,"[61] a

---

[57] Strauss, *CM*, 239.

[58] Quoted and discussed by Christopher A. Colmo, "Joseph Cropsey: Modernity and the American Regime," in *The Straussians and the American Regime*, 229.

[59] Madison, *Federalist Papers*, 322.

[60] Madison, *Federalist Papers*, 346.

[61] Strauss, "Liberal Education and Responsibility," in *LAM*, 18.

strategy given authoritative political expression in George Washington's Farewell Address.

It would be a mistake to suggest that Strauss was a solitary voice; it suffices to mention today's widespread public concern about the moral condition of American life, and the renewed attention to family, religion, voluntary association, and civic and character education in public schools. Still, the prevailing understanding of liberty as living in accordance with desire and exercising unfettered individual choice constantly tugs against awareness of the need for self-restraint. That both the market and mass entertainment so powerfully reinforce this understanding is anything but encouraging.

Nonetheless, Martin Diamond, perhaps the soberest analyst of the American polity to have been inspired by Strauss, observed that "in order to defuse the dangerous factional forces of opinion, passion, and classic interest, Madison's policy deliberately risks magnifying and multiplying in American life the selfish, the interested, the narrow, the vulgar, and the crassly economic."[62] But this was not the whole story, Diamond contended: "While the American founders turned away from the classic enterprise regarding virtue, they did not thereby abandon the pursuit of virtue or excellence in all other possible ways. In fact, the American political order rises respectably high enough above the vulgar level of mere self-interest in the direction of virtue."[63] He argued there were four strata of liberal virtues and excellences that American democracy permitted and to some extent encouraged: first, the bourgeois virtues generated by and required for daily commercial and social life; second, the civic virtues generated by the Tocquevillian progression from narrow self-interest through self-interest rightly understood to broader civic virtues; third, the capacity of American society occasionally to produce, and of the American people to recognize and admire, great leaders who rise to great challenges; and finally, the willingness of the people not only to tolerate but even to finance enclaves of excellence within an egalitarian society.[64] Strauss explicitly noted the existence of the last two strata, and by implication granted the presence of the first two as well.

These hopeful facts are anything but an argument to forget Strauss's warnings. One need not read Plato's *Republic* to know that democracy

---

[62] Martin Diamond, "Ethics and Politics: The American Way," in William A. Schambra, ed., *As Far as Republican Principles Will Admit* (Washington, DC: AEI Press, 1992), 355.

[63] Diamond, "Ethics and Politics," 359.

[64] For a lucid exposition, see William A. Schambra, "Martin Diamond's Doctrine of the American Regime," *Publius*, 8, 3 (Summer 1978): 213–218.

is endangered, not only from without but also from within. Strauss regarded the reservations of the classics concerning democracy as useful warnings against democratic complacency. They serve as a reminder that like all other forms of government, democracy contains inherent weaknesses and dangerous tendencies that require constant vigilance and correction. Ignored too long, they can undermine even the most established democratic regime. It is in this spirit that Strauss penned one of his most quoted and least understood lines: "We are not permitted to be flatters of democracy precisely because we are friends and allies of democracy."[65]

---

[65] Strauss, "Liberal Education and Responsibility," in *LAM*, 24.

10 Strauss and Social Science

As early as 1932, long before he joined any department of political science, Strauss wrote of the necessity of a radical criticism of the work of Max Weber;[1] three years later, he wrote to his friend, Jacob Klein, that he has been reading a lot of Weber.[2] His famous criticism of Weber in *Natural Right and History* was then the result of a twenty-year-long reflection on that thinker.[3] Indeed, he incorporated a criticism of present-day social science in a number of essays, and in small ways in every book he wrote in the United States other than his later Socratic books. He even organized a reading group with some of his students on the works of the leading scholars (Harold Lasswell, Arthur Bentley, Herbert Simon, and so on) around what he called the new science of politics, or what others have called the behavioral revolution in political science. This effort culminates in the publication of the *Essays on the Scientific Study of Politics*, the epilogue to which is written by Strauss himself.[4] Why did this single-minded student of political philosophy devote so much of his time and energy to a critique of contemporary social science?

This question assumes that political philosophy and social science are fundamentally different activities. However, Strauss questioned this assumption because he denied its underlying premise, namely, that modern natural science is the model for all scientific work. Accordingly, he can distinguish "present day social science" (social science positivism in its final form) from "classical social science" (the political science of Plato, Aristotle, and Xenophon) and "modern social science" (the political science of Machiavelli, Hobbes, Locke, Montesquieu), categories that do not exist for adherents of present-day social science. Consider

[1] Strauss, "Die geistige Lage der Gegenwart," in *GS*, 2: 447.
[2] Letter to Jacob Klein, January 8, 1935, in *GS*, 3: 536.
[3] Strauss, *NRH*, 35–80.
[4] Strauss's "An Epilogue" was originally published in Herbert J. Storing, ed. *Essays on the Scientific Study of Politics* (New York: Holt, Rinehart, and Wington, 1962), 307–27; reprinted in *LAM*, 203–223.

the following criticism of positivist social science with which Strauss began his "Restatement on Xenophon's *Hiero*":

A social science that cannot speak of tyranny with the same confidence with which medicine speaks, for example, of cancer, cannot understand social phenomena as what they are. It is therefore not scientific. Present day social science finds itself in this condition. If it is true that present day social science is the inevitable result of modern social science and modern philosophy, one is forced to think of the restoration of classical social science.[5]

Strauss criticized present-day social science because it is not scientific, that is, because it denies what is known to common sense – namely, that tyranny is bad for political life. According to Strauss, the task of social science should be the clarification of common-sense awareness, a clarification in which common sense remains the standard for judging scientific results. In this sense, his work is closest to the efforts of Edmund Husserl, the founder of phenomenology, who attempted to defend rationalism by criticizing the outlook of modern science, which neglects to examine its own presupposition – that is, our natural awareness of our world. Strauss concluded that the political science of Plato and Aristotle met that standard to a higher degree than either phenomenology or Heidegger's analysis of man, the demand of phenomenology that science must begin with an adequate analysis of the prescientific world. Accordingly, in a letter to Karl Löwith Strauss described his primary task as the restoration of classical political science: "The possibility of a non-positivistic science of human society and in particular of political society (i.e., of a science which does not use 'constructive concepts' but the concepts inherent in political society, its institutions, 'movements' etc.), i.e., of fundamentally Platonic-Aristotelian political science is so buried by centuries of a radically different approach that I regard it as *my primary task* to recover the classical approach."[6]

Because it denies access to the real essence of things, modern positivistic science understands all concepts as mental constructs. We do not see things as things but only as perceptible qualities that are related to each other. Scientific concepts are regarded as superior to prescientific concepts because they are constructed consciously and therefore follow the dictum that we know only what we make (*verum = factum*).[7] Now

---

[5] Strauss, *OT*, 177.
[6] Letter to Karl Löwith, July 11, 1964, in *GS*, 3: 693.
[7] The principle that we know only what we make ("The criterion and rule of the true is to have made it") is originally associated with Vico's *La Scienza Nuova*. Strauss refers to this work only once in the Preface to the seventh impression of *NRH*, vii. He attributes a view very much like this to Hobbes; see *NRH*, 172–175.

Husserl questioned the superiority of the concepts of modern science. First, whatever immediate clarity modern scientific concepts may possess, they cannot be said to be a clarification of prescientific concepts. Instead of showing the errors of prescientific concepts, they simply make a break with them.[8]

Second, prescientific concepts are at the bottom of our interest in science, for we turn to science because we want to understand the world in which we live. Accordingly, instead of leaving behind prescientific concepts we must make the understanding of these concepts the first task of science. On this much Strauss agrees with Husserl, but unlike Husserl Strauss does not focus his attention on the origin of prescientific concepts, that is, on how we make these concepts. (This fact explains the apparently undertheorized character of his appeal to common sense.) Instead, he provisionally accepts them and attempts to clarify them by ferreting out the contradictions that are inherent in some but not all such concepts. This approach has the advantage of addressing the objection that prescientific concepts vary from society to society: "Plato, as it were says: Take any opinion about right, however fantastic or 'primitive,' that you please; you can be certain prior to having investigated it that it points beyond itself, that the people who cherish the opinion in question contradict that very opinion somehow and thus are forced to go beyond it in the direction of the one true view of justice, provided that a philosopher arises among them."[9]

The classical social science to which Strauss sought to return is twofold – Aristotelian and Platonic-Xenophontic; the present-day social science is also twofold – Weberian and behavioralist. This twofold diversity informs Strauss's two major statements on social science. The major concern of Plato's political science is the defense of the philosophical life through the clarification of the political understanding of human

---

[8] For instance, there are no steps that lead one from prescientific concepts that combine Is and Ought to scientific concepts that eschew such a combination. Or to turn from social science to modern physics, it has been observed that every attempt to explain modern science in the language of nonscientists necessarily involves a distortion of the scientific theory. Jacob Klein, a student of Husserl, had argued in a work that won Strauss's highest admiration that this is so not because of the mathematical nature of modern science but because of the particular character of its mathematics, which makes a break with common-sense understanding of the world (Jacob Klein, *Greek Mathematical Thought and the Origin of Algebra*, trans. Eva Brann (Cambridge, MA: Massachusetts Institute of Technology, 1968). For a work that carries on Klein's argument, see David Lachterman, *The Ethics of Geometry: A Genealogy of Modernity* (London: Routledge, 1989).

[9] Strauss, *NRH*, 125. For the role of the "pretheoretical" or "natural consciousness," see also "Political Philosophy and History" in *WPP*, 75.

ends.[10] Strauss's critique of Weber, which focuses on Weber's objections to the possibility of political philosophy, provides a bridge to Platonic political science. The major concern of Aristotelian political science is the protection and improvement of decent political communities, which naturally include nonphilosophers. Although Aristotle's acceptance of Platonic conclusions affects his political science, the defense of the philosophical life is not its central focus. In this respect, Aristotle's political science is more political than Plato's. Strauss's "Epilogue" to the *Scientific Study of Politics* is a bridge to Aristotle's political science. In this essay, Strauss supported traditional political science, which is more interested in politics than in methodology, by freeing the study of politics from its subservience to the methods of modern science and by providing it with a framework in light of which it can understand its own activity. Although Strauss did not change and probably never expected to change the political science profession's bias toward the modern scientific approach, it is often unnoticed how successful he has been in influencing the scholarship of a great number of political scientists.[11]

STRAUSS AND THE "NEW POLITICAL SCIENCE"

In "An Epilogue," Strauss focused his attention on what he calls "the new political science." His choice of this confusing term is justified because in the final analysis, there is a close kinship between modern political science, which also conceived itself to be a new political science, and the new political science that emerged in the beginning of the twentieth century. However, to avoid confusing the two sciences we note that they rebelled against different authorities. Whereas modern political science (Machiavelli and Hobbes) rebelled against classical political science, it preserved to some extent the humanistic orientation. On the other hand, the new political science rebelled against the humanistic orientation that was common to both classical and modern political science.

Unlike both of its predecessors, the new political science is a mass phenomenon, and this makes it difficult to characterize. Strauss defined it by observing five governing premises that have come to prevail among scientific students of politics – the distinction between philosophy and science, the depreciation of common sense, the neutral perspective, the

[10] See Christopher Bruell, *On The Socratic Education: An Introduction to the Shorter Platonic Dialogues* (Lanham, MD: Rowman & Littlefield, 1999).

[11] See Thomas Pangle, *Leo Strauss: An Introduction to his Thought and Legacy* (Baltimore, MD: Johns Hopkins Press, 2007), 89–128. This is a uniquely comprehensive summary of Strauss's influence on political scientists who are not students of political philosophy.

distinction between facts and values, and the rejection of the existence of the common good – and he shows that each is a necessary consequence of the revolution against Aristotelian political science by modern political science. This does not mean that every adherent of the new political science consistently maintains these views; indeed, Strauss argued that they cannot be consistently maintained. But it does mean that they are the consequences of modern natural science's view of science and reality. Accordingly, as long as one recognizes the authority of modern natural science, these views necessarily make their presence felt.

First, the new political science rests on the distinction between philosophy and science, which is the result of the crisis of modern philosophy or science. According to both Aristotle and modern philosophers, philosophy is identical with science. We can understand this thought by first identifying philosophy and science as different activities: science is knowledge of classes of beings, and philosophy is the quest for wisdom or knowledge of the whole. If one cannot understand a part without referring to the whole to which it belongs, each of the sciences has philosophizing as its core. The identification of philosophy and science has important implications for the study of human affairs. It implies that economics (household management) must be guided by an understanding of politics, and both economics and politics must be guided by an understanding of human virtue and happiness (ethics), for a political community becomes a whole in light of the end it seeks. As Strauss once put it, ethics is "the legitimate queen of the social sciences."[12]

However, this rank order was undermined by the ambiguous result of the revolution against the Aristotelian tradition. Whereas early modern political philosophy faced formidable objections starting with Rousseau, modern physics succeeded in replacing every form of premodern physics. Now the new physics has peculiar features. Platonic-Aristotelian physics has natural theology as its highest theme, but the modern philosophers removed the burden of proving God's existence from physics. To be sure, they provided the new physics with an independent theological foundation, but the success of the new physics made many wonder whether it needed these theological trappings. Accordingly, the new physics came to be seen as metaphysically neutral. Now if the only truly successful science is metaphysically neutral, it becomes reasonable to separate philosophy and science in principle. This separation led to the disintegration of political science as "the all-embracing study of human affairs"[13]: "It paved the way for an economic science which is independent of ethics, for sociology as the study of nonpolitical

---

[12] Strauss, "Social Science and Humanism," in *RCPR*, 6.
[13] Strauss, "What is Political Philosophy?" in *WPP*, 17.

associations as not inferior in dignity to political association, and, last but not least, for the separation of political science from political philosophy as well as the separation of economics and sociology from political science."[14]

Second, the new political science is animated by a distrust of common sense. This distrust is inherent in modern natural science, which received its foundation in Descartes's radical doubt of all opinions. Because the new political science is governed by a logic that takes modern natural science as its standard, it too preserves "Descartes' universal doubt of pre-scientific knowledge and his radical break with it."[15] In doing so, the new political science completes a tendency that was already present in modern political science beginning with Hobbes.[16]

The other three distinctive features of the new political science follow from this break with common sense, which underlies modern natural science. Because the latter looks at nature from a detached point of view, the new political science also looks at human affairs from the perspective of a neutral observer or an engineer. Accordingly, it employs a language that is different from the language of nonscientists. Because the new understanding of nature, which conceives of nature as matter and motion or more sophisticated versions of this conception, knows nothing of natural ends, the facts as discerned by such a science cannot be the basis of any value judgment.[17] Finally, because our access to things as things is through common sense, the scientific distrust of common sense amounts to distrust of our perception of things as wholes as opposed to our perception of their elements, which are more clear and distinct. Because the new science rejects any understanding of the wholes that is more than knowledge of their elements, it tends to understand wholes by reducing them to their parts. For instance, it tends to understand politics in terms of economics, sociology, or psychology. Strauss brings out the troubling political implication of this methodological decision: "The reduction of the political to the subpolitical is the reduction of primarily given wholes to elements which are

---

[14] Strauss, "An Epilogue," in *LAM*, 205. All parenthetical references in this section are to this text.

[15] Strauss, "What is Political Philosophy?" in *WPP*, 23.

[16] Strauss suggests that Hobbes's polarity of fear and pride is "the consequence of modern natural science's view of the whole for man's 'common sense' understanding of himself. To the extent to which Hobbes attempts to replace the 'common sense' understanding by a scientific understanding of man, he endangers his political science as a normative science and prepares the 'value-free' political science of our time" ("On the Basis of Hobbes's Political Philosophy," in *WPP*, 181).

[17] Strauss, *PL*, 34.

relatively simple, that is, sufficiently simple for the research purpose at hand, yet necessarily susceptible of being analyzed into still simpler elements *in infinitum*. It implies that there cannot be genuine wholes. Hence, it implies that there cannot be a common good" (219).

Because the prestige of the new political science is chiefly due to the authority of the modern notion of science, we will focus on Strauss's exposition of the problem of knowledge, an exposition that is based on Platonic and Aristotelian reflections. All knowledge of things involves a grasp of the thing as a whole and an understanding of its parts. We cannot grasp a thing as a thing without some awareness of its parts, but the knowledge of its parts can never exhaust that knowledge that is available in our perception of a thing: although a thing is not more than its parts, it is also not reducible to its parts. To use one of Aristotle's examples, a syllable (say, "ba") is not more than its parts ("b" and "a") but it is something in addition to "b" and "a" (*Metaphysics*, 1041b12–14). Accordingly, all statements about things in terms of their parts depend on this primary grasp of a thing that is both reliable and mysterious. Strauss identifies this difficulty as "the riddle of being." He illustrates this difficulty by considering the man from Missouri, "who has to be shown." He discusses this man to show that the demand to be empirical does not require one to deny the validity of common-sense knowledge. The man from Missouri is "the incarnation of the empirical spirit" who accepts many political facts that are known to common sense. However, he does reject "speculations based on extrasensory perception." But it can be shown that the man from Missouri is naïve: "he does not see things with his eyes: what he sees with his eyes is only colors, shapes, and the like; he would perceive 'things' in contradistinction to 'sense data,' only if he possessed 'extrasensory perception'; his claim – the claim of common sense – implies that there is 'extrasensory perception'" (212). The attempt to meet the demand to be empirical while accepting the legitimacy of common-sense awareness leads to a contradiction, to the simultaneous acceptance and rejection of the legitimacy of common sense. This puzzle points to a difficulty of common-sense understanding, namely, that it is susceptible of certain excesses. It claims to perceive not only men and political parties but also witches. Although this difficulty makes understandable the rejection of common sense by scientists, Strauss denies that it justifies it, for common sense also provides the evidence by which one can correct the errors of common sense.

The consequences of the scientific break with common sense justify Strauss's preference for correcting the errors inherent in common-sense awareness by means of common sense. Because the wholes "are not available in such a way that we could make them the premises of our reasoning,"[18] modern science turns its attention away from wholes to their elements. It denies the riddle of being by denying that our grasp of things as things is a real perception of them: "what is perceived or given is only sense data, the 'thing' emerges by virtue of unconscious or conscious construction: the 'things' which to common sense present themselves as 'given' are in truth constructs" (212). The demand for objectivity leads to the rejection of the common sense understanding of things:

Common-sense understanding is understanding by means of unconscious con-struction; scientific understanding is understanding by means of conscious con-struction. Somewhat more precisely, common-sense understanding is under-standing in terms of "things possessing qualities": scientific understanding is understanding in terms of "functional relations between different series of events." Unconscious constructs are ill made, for their making is affected by all sorts of purely "subjective" influences; only conscious constructs can be well made, perfectly lucid, in every respect the same for everyone, or "objective." (212)

This approach suffers from the following general difficulty: although it rejects the evidence of common sense, it cannot carry conviction if it does not explain the wholes that are known to common sense: "if a logical positivist tries to give an account of 'a thing' or a formula for 'a thing' in terms of mere sense data and their composition, he is looking, and bids us to look, at the previously grasped 'thing'; the previously grasped 'thing' is the standard by which we judge of his formula" (211). In other words, the modern scientific approach contradicts itself by both accepting and denying the evidence of common sense. Strauss shows the fundamental character of this difficulty by noting that "empiricism cannot be established empiricistically: it is not known through sense data that the only possible objects of perception are sense data" (212).

In addition to this general difficulty, there is another that particu-larly affects social science. The attempt to reconstruct political things or patterns on the basis of sense data leads to the disregard of the ele-ments that constitute political life, "for the soul's actions, passions, or states can never become sense data" (212). It is not surprising then that scientific social scientists are compelled to borrow from common-sense knowledge but such borrowing does not solve the problem, for the unconscious character of such borrowing prevents them from themati-cally examining the borrowed knowledge: "If the primary grasp [of the whole] lacks definiteness and breadth, both the analysis and synthesis will be guided by a distorted view of the whole, by a figment of a poor

---

[18] Strauss, "Social Science and Humanism," in *RCPR*, 3.

imagination rather than by the thing in its fullness. And the elements at which analysis arrives will at best be only some of the elements."[19]

The difficulties that social science faces on account of its distrust of common sense knowledge can be seen more clearly if one considers the procedure of the humanistic political science that Strauss preferred. Aristotelian political science is guided by criteria of relevance that "are inherent in the prescientific understanding of political things" (214). To a contemporary social scientist, these criteria appear hopelessly subjective: what one man considers important, another considers unimportant. But it is precisely the awareness of this disagreement that leads intelligent and informed citizens to "distinguish soundly between important and unimportant political matters." Every man is a member of a society, and what makes that society a whole is what it looks up to. There is a variety of societies (societies that look up to different things) and it is the disputes between these societies that constitute what is most important politically: "To illustrate this by the present-day example, for the old-fashioned political scientists today, the most important concern is the Cold War, or the qualitative difference which amounts to a conflict, between liberal democracy and Communism" (214). The universals that this science seeks are not laws of human behavior that apply everywhere but rather the various regimes and their purposes, universals that set in motion great political struggles and the quest for the knowledge of the ultimate universal: the true purpose of political community.

Because the logic underlying the new political science does not offer it any criteria of relevance, it is forced to borrow its orientation surreptitiously from common sense. But because this borrowing is made by a science that is "anxious to comply with the demands of logical positivism," it will follow predetermined general paths. Strauss identifies two tendencies of the new political science: formalism and vulgarianism. The new science's denial of irreducible differences among things inclines the new political science to understand heterogeneous things in light of their common homogeneous elements. This tendency gives the new political science its formalism. For instance, one may be led to explain politics by a theory of behavior of groups in general:

The result of this reduction of the political to the sociological – of a reduction for which it is claimed that it will make our understanding of political things more "realistic" – is in fact a formalism unrivaled in any scholasticism of the past. All peculiarities of political societies, and still more of the political societies with which we are concerned as citizens, become unrecognizable if restated in terms of the vague generalities which hold of every conceivable group. (215)

[19] Strauss "Social Science and Humanism," in *RCPR*, 4.

The other tendency of the new political science comes from its rejection of value judgments. Being forced to borrow concepts from common-sense understanding and anxious to avoid any value judgments, the new political science uses in a value-free manner "terms that originally were meant only for indicating things of a noble character – terms like 'culture,' 'personality,' 'values,' 'charismatic,' and 'civilization'" (218). This debasing of terms is what Strauss calls the vulgarianism of the new political science. According to Strauss, there is "a tension" between the formalism and the vulgarianism of the new political science[20]: the former seems to foster a high-minded contempt for the claims of political life, and the latter devalues the claims of every pretension to high-mindedness.

The tension between the formalism and the vulgarianism of the new political science is evident in the tension between its nonpolitical character and its democratism. We will begin by describing its nonpolitical tendency. First, a political man looks at the affairs of his political community not with the detachment that is characteristic of scientists or philosophers but with the loving and spirited attachment that is characteristic of citizens and statesmen. A citizen is necessarily interested in knowledge of politics but the knowledge that he seeks is not of regularities in political behavior, or more generally of the causes of political behavior, but of the actions that will lead to the preservation and improvement of the political order to which he belongs. Unless he lives on an isolated island, a citizen as citizen is apt to be interested in the foreign affairs of his country and hence in the laws that govern the affairs between nations ("international law") but not in relations among nations or states in general ("international relations"). A citizen as citizen is apt to be interested in the formulation of the laws that place citizens and government in a good and just order ("public law") but not in how in general parties representing the interests or passions of various sections of society struggle for control of governments ("politics and parties"). As we can see from the previous examples, whole subfields of political science that today we take for granted presuppose a break with the perspective of citizens and statesmen.[21]

Second, a political man necessarily believes in the existence of a common good in his political community, but the new political science rejects the existence of a common good. It sometimes does so explicitly,

---

[20] Strauss, "Reply to Schaar and Wolin," *American Political Science Review*, 57 (1963): 153.

[21] The prior discussion is a gloss on Strauss's description of the state of political science in *LAM*, 204. Our discussion may exaggerate somewhat the legalistic spirit of political men (consider also 208).

as in the case of political scientists like Arthur Bentley, who denied the common good because there can be no laws that are good for everyone, and it sometimes does so implicitly, as in theories of political behavior that assume that individuals or groups involved in political action are always animated by purely selfish considerations. Third, a political man is concerned with the welfare of his community but he understands by his community not only the human beings who are parts of it but the regime that constitutes it. For instance, it might be possible to save the lives of Americans by destroying the Constitution and adopting communism or a government based on Islamic law, but no one who recommends such measures can be described as a good American. However, the adoption of the scientific outlook leads political scientists to "express the political phenomena par excellence, the essential differences or heterogeneity of regimes, in terms of the homogeneous elements which pervade all regimes [say, coercion and freedom]" (215). Fourth, a political man knows that societies that are constituted by different regimes have different images of the future and therefore cannot "live together, in contradistinction to uneasily co-existing," and therefore each society must take measures to preserve itself and its regime. The new political science's denial of the essential difference between regimes leads to neglect of this knowledge: "everyone knows what follows from the demonstration, which presupposes the begging of all important questions, that there is only a difference of degree between liberal democracy and Communism in regard to coercion and freedom" (215).

Fifth and finally, a political man knows that the future of his society is unpredictable and that governments must "determine the future of their societies with the help partly of knowledge, partly of guesses, the recourse to guesses still being partly necessitated by the secrecy in which their most important opponents shroud their most important plans or projects" (209). However, the new political science seeks to make politics into a predictive science. For example, Shulsky and Schmitt have captured the de-politicization of intelligence gathering as this field became influenced by present-day social science. According to them, the attempt to make intelligence into a predictive social science has led to an emphasis on social scientific analysis of nonsecret information with "a tendency to depreciate the importance of counterintelligence in general, and deception and counterdeception in particular." They point out that William Colby, former Director of Central Intelligence, even foresaw "an era of free trade in intelligence."[22] Accordingly,

---

[22] Abram Shulsky and Gary Schmitt, *Silent Warfare: Understanding the World of Intelligence* (Dulles, NC: Potomac Books, 2002), 164–165.

we arrive at the strange situation in which many political scientists are less political than the average citizen.

However, this political science cannot consistently maintain its apolitical character. On the most general level, the new political science is unpolitical because it denies the common good. In human terms, this means that man is fundamentally a selfish being. As Herbert Storing and Robert Horwitz show in their criticism of the work of Herbert Simon and Harold Lasswell, a social scientist who accepts this view should choose tyranny as his goal, a choice that Simon and Lasswell did not make.[23] This is not surprising, for it is difficult as members of society to deny the fundamental assumption of society. Strauss suggests that the distinction between facts and values helps obscure the conflict between man's political nature and the denial of common good. Whereas in truth the denial of the common good is based on the denial of the existence of genuine political wholes or the admission of the fundamentally selfish character of man, "the denial of the common good *presents itself today* as a direct consequence of the distinction between facts and values according to which only factual judgments, not value judgments, can be true or objective" (220, emphasis added). Because according to this distinction one can posit "death as his value" no less than "self-preservation," it is up to the free choice of individuals to choose or reject tyranny. Thus, the distinction between facts and values allows the social scientist to reject tyranny without examining the soundness of the premise that supports tyranny, a premise which he himself accepts. This rejection of tyranny is only the first but necessary step toward the politicization of political science.

The distinction between facts and values also leads to a particular politicization of the new political science. Strauss had observed in the beginning of his essay that the new political scientists are "liberals almost to a man." The distinction between facts and values both justifies a particular understanding of liberal democracy and silences all doubts about that interpretation. This contention of Strauss is counterintuitive. Because a political scientist cannot justify value judgments, he as a political scientist "is neutral in the conflict between liberal democracy and its enemies." But Strauss observes that the general denial of the possibility of deriving values from facts leads to the discrediting of all traditional value systems that were based on "superior or perfect beings which as such unite in themselves fact and value" (220). On the other hand, it is possible for men to posit certain values without justifying them. The values that lend themselves to this approach are the "objects

[23] Storing, ed., *Essays on the Scientific Study of Politics* 108–109, 296–300.

of desire." Religious practices or fighting for one's country require reasons but gratifying one's basic appetites does not. Because according to
the new political science "values are nothing but objects of desire," and
because "before the tribunal of reason all values are equal," the new
political science's interpretation of the distinction between facts and
values results in the affirmation of the nonideological society as the
rational society. This society is characterized by permissive egalitarianism: "if a man is of the opinion that as a matter of fact all desires
are of equal dignity, since we know of no factual consideration which
would entitle us to assign different dignities to different desires, he cannot but be of the opinion, unless he is prepared to become guilty of gross
arbitrariness, that all desires ought to be treated as equal within the
limits of the possible, and this opinion is what is meant by permissive
egalitarianism" (222).

The new political science not only supports a particular interpretation of liberal democracy but prevents the discussion of that interpretation "with full consideration of all relevant pros and cons" (222). First, its
techniques promote the identification of human behavior with behavior in democratic societies. Because the new political science seeks to
discover general laws of human behavior, it "puts a premium on the
study of things which occur frequently now in democratic societies:
neither those in their grave nor those behind the Curtains can respond
to questionnaires or interviews" (222). It makes democracy "the tacit
presupposition of the data," for human beings are shaped by the political
order in which they live. Accordingly, the new political scientists have
a difficult time understanding the character of democracy. This character can only be seen by comparing democracy to its alternatives, but
when the new political scientists seek to make such comparisons – for
instance, by distinguishing between democracy and authoritarianism –
they merely absolutize democracy by remaining within the horizon,
which is defined by democracy.[24]

Second, the distinction between facts and values allows the new political scientists to disregard the importance of facts that are inconvenient
for democracy. Strauss observes that "the new political science came
into being through the revolt against what one may call the democratic
orthodoxy of the immediate past. It had learned certain lessons which
were hard for that orthodoxy to swallow regarding the irrationality of
the masses and the necessity of elites" (222–223). But it "succeeded
in reconciling these doubts with the unfaltering commitment to liberal democracy by the simple device of declaring no value judgments,
including those supporting liberal democracy, are rational and hence

[24] Strauss, "What is Political Philosophy?" in WPP, 24.

that an ironclad argument in favor of liberal democracy ought in reason not even to be expected" (223).

Aside from obliterating "the very complex pros and cons of liberal democracy," this commitment to liberal democracy is not good for liberal democracy because it "has nothing to say against those who unhesitatingly prefer surrender, that is, abandonment of liberal democracy, to war" (223). The protection of liberal democracy requires sacrifices, and these sacrifices require reasons to support them, reasons that the new political scientists cannot give. What is more, it encourages the worst proclivities of liberal democracy, proclivities that inspire a rebellion against liberal democracy by high-minded young men and women: "By teaching in effect the equality of literally all desires, it teaches in effect that there is nothing of which a man ought to be ashamed; by destroying the possibility of self-contempt, it destroys with the best of intentions the possibility of self-respect. By teaching the equality of all values, by denying that there are things which are intrinsically high and others which are intrinsically low as well as by denying that there is an essential difference between men and brutes, it unwittingly contributes to the victory of the gutter" (222).

Strauss's "Epilogue" is his most political and polemical work: it is an attempt to direct "the best men of the coming generation" away from a political science that is harmful to liberal democracy toward another type of political science. In this essay, he says nothing about the superiority of the theoretical life to political life but he has much to say about the new political science's failure to oppose communism and its debasement of liberal democracy. This essay would be unintelligible if Strauss did not believe himself to be a friend of liberal democracy, but this does not mean that in the final analysis he was a liberal democrat. Strauss's alternative to the new political science is a political science that begins with the political perspective, and its goal is best captured by his account of the difference between his understanding of "nobility of spirit" and that of the new political science:

Does "nobility of spirit" or "generosity of the spirit" call in the first place for the improvement (which presupposes the preservation in freedom from barbarian domination) of *the political community to which one belongs*, for its pursuit of excellence, for one's adorning the Sparta which fate has allotted to one; or does it call in the first place, as the critics seem to believe, for "compassion which cannot but sorrow for the common lot of *all mankind*"?[25]

[25] Strauss, "Reply to Schaar and Wolin," 155; emphasis added. This passage is taken from Strauss's response to a very hostile review of *Essays on the Scientific Study of Politics*. Strauss suggests that the authors of this review, who were themselves humanistic critics of the new political science, share

The goal of Straussian political science is the preservation of American liberal democracy and its adornment. As to Strauss himself, the very fact that he could describe the modern West as a Sparta is sufficient indication that one can be a friend and defender of liberal democracy without being a liberal democrat.

MAX WEBER AND THE FACT-VALUE PROBLEM

Both Max Weber and the new political science belong to a larger whole that Strauss called "social science positivism." But according to Strauss, Weber is not a new political scientist. Whereas the new political science accepts the methods of modern natural science, Weber is concerned "with preserving the integrity of the historical or cultural sciences against ... the attempt to shape these sciences on the pattern of natural sciences" (77).[26] Weber denied that the goal of social science is the discovery of the laws of human behavior, which allows him to focus on singular but highly important events such as the emergence of capitalism. Strauss contrasted Weber's conceptual scheme (three principles of legitimacy: traditional, rational, charismatic), which can be traced to the French Revolution, to the new political science, which has "no reason to be more interested in a world-shaking revolution which affects directly or indirectly all men than in the most trifling 'social changes.'"[27] When Strauss criticized the new political science for debasing terms like "culture," "personality," "values," "charismatic," and "civilization," he is implicitly praising Weber, for these are the terms Weber used to signify "things of a noble character." Strauss compared the new political science's understanding of values according to which "values are nothing but objects of desires" to a more adequate view of values according to which they are radically different from mere desires, but he lets his readers figure out that this more adequate view is one that is espoused by Weber.[28]

Nonetheless, Weber's political science has something in common with the new political science: they both espouse the distinction between facts and values. This distinction was such a defining feature of social science positivism in the 1950s that Weber's vehement insistence that social science must avoid value judgments (together with his

the latter's implicit notion of "nobility of spirit." For a recent discussion of the debate, see Benjamin Barber, "The Politics of Political Science: 'Value-Free' Theory and the Wolin-Strauss Dust-Up of 1963," *American Political Science Review* 100 (2006): 539–545.

[26] All parenthetical references in this section are from *NRH*.

[27] Strauss, "Epilogue," in *LAM*, 216.

[28] Strauss, "Epilogue," in *LAM*, 221.

impressive substantive studies that attempted to follow this rule) made him one of the leading lights of the scientific study of politics.[29] Moreover, despite his attempts to protect the integrity of historical or cultural sciences from the influence of natural science, Weber also accepted, if not consistently, the authoritative character of modern science. For instance, he accepted the neo-Kantian notion of reality, according to which "reality is an infinite and meaningless sequence."[30]

According to Strauss, the ultimate difference between the new political science and Weber's social science is that Weber is conscious of the metaphysical implications of the modern notion of science. The new political science follows an understanding of science that conceives of itself as metaphysically and morally neutral. But according to Strauss, "one's opinion regarding the character of the Is settles one's opinion regarding the character of the Ought."[31] If one understands facts in such a way that they are to be fundamentally distinguished from values, one will deny the existence of God, a being who unites in Himself fact and value. If one believes that there are no radical differences between beings, one will reject traditional moral teachings. It is thus that we can understand Strauss's strange suggestion that dogmatic atheism is "the hidden basis" of the new political science.[32] To Weber, this basis was not hidden: "That science today is irreligious no one will doubt in his innermost being, even if he will not admit it to himself."[33] Because Weber is aware of the atheism of modern science, and because he is aware of the hypothetical character of this science, he takes seriously the possibility of revelation. As Strauss put it: "Max Weber...took the possibility of Revelation seriously; hence his writings, even and especially those dealing with science as such, possess a depth and a claim to respect which, I believe, I have properly recognized; I venture to say

---

[29] Although Strauss's deep interest in Weber predated his arrival in America, the general acceptance of Weber's work offered an opportunity for Strauss to address students of modern social science. More than half a century after Strauss wrote his criticism, today Weber has lost much of his luster among contemporary social scientists, and perhaps this is partly because of lack of interest in the foundation of social science. After the attack on behavioral social science in the name of "values" or "relevance" that occurred in the late sixties and seventies, social scientists have become less inclined to insist on the distinction between facts and values even though that distinction continues to determine the character of social science.

[30] For the role of Kantianism in Weber's thought, see NRH, 43, 60, n. 22, 77.

[31] Strauss, "Epilogue," in LAM, 221–222.

[32] Strauss, "Epilogue," in LAM, 218.

[33] Max Weber, "Science as a Vocation," in From Max Weber, ed. H. H. Gerth and C. Wright Mills (New York: Oxford University Press, 1946), 142.

that this particular open-mindedness was ultimately the reason why he was not a new political scientist."[34]

Although both the new political science and Weber espoused the distinction between facts and values, their understandings of that distinction are fundamentally different. For the new political science, the distinction is a consequence of the modern understanding of the Is from which no Ought can be derived. For Weber, in the final analysis the distinction is the consequence of a conflict between ultimate values that reason cannot resolve (40–42). Given this difference, the two doctrines have different practical implications. Strauss described the effect of the non-Weberian understanding of the distinction between facts and values as follows:

I have never met any scientific social scientist who apart from being dedicated to truth and integrity was not also wholeheartedly devoted to democracy. When he says that democracy is a value which is not evidently superior to the opposite value, he does not mean that he is impressed by the alternative which he rejects, or that his heart or his mind is torn between alternatives which in themselves are equally attractive. His "ethical neutrality" is so far from being nihilism or a road to nihilism that it is not more than an alibi for thoughtlessness and vulgarity: by saying that democracy and truth are values, he says in effect that one does not have to think about reasons why these things are good, and that he may bow as well as anyone else to the values that are adopted and respected by his society. Social science positivism fosters not so much nihilism as conformism and philistinism.[35]

On the other hand, Strauss showed that nihilism is the consequence of Weber's distinction between facts and values. Although Weber is not consistently aware of this result, he does see it, for Strauss arrives at this consequence by following Weber's own footsteps (see especially 42).

Strauss's approach to Weber's doctrine is also different from his approach to that of social science positivism in general. Strauss treated Weber's doctrine as a serious challenge to the possibility of political philosophy or of genuine knowledge of right or justice. According to Strauss, "the whole galaxy of political philosophers from Plato to Hegel" believed that the fundamental political problem (What type of man should rule the community or set its tone?) is susceptible of a rational solution because they believed philosophy is the best life. This belief casts its shadow on all other ways of life, for the disputes of various nonphilosophical ways of life are settled by the standard set by philosophy. The belief that the life of the philosopher is the correct way

---

[34] Strauss, "Reply to Schaar and Wolin," 153.
[35] Strauss, "What is Political Philosophy?" in *WPP*, 20.

of life is established by the questioning to which Socrates devoted his life, questioning that shows that the authorities in one's community are ignorant of the most important things: "By realizing that we are ignorant of the most important things, we realize at the same time that the most important thing for us, or the one thing needful, is quest for knowledge of the most important things or quest for wisdom" (36). Because wisdom or nonhypothetical knowledge of the whole or the universe is not currently available, it is possible that the Socratic quest or philosophizing could lead to the view that the best thing is not philosophizing but the "life of obedient love" of God (36, 74). Strauss expressed doubts as to whether this possibility undermines the Socratic answer, for the conclusion itself is a result of philosophizing, but he observed that the possibility of this answer together with the persistence of the alternative to the Socratic answer gives "the impression that the Socratic answer is as arbitrary as its opposite." Accordingly, Weber denied the possibility of knowledge of the correct life because he denied that "human reason is capable of solving the conflict between these [fundamental and unchanging] alternatives" (36).

Although Weber wrote of a number of irresolvable fundamental conflicts, Strauss observed that he tries to prove the irresolvability of the conflict in only "three or four" cases (67n). Strauss suggested that "two or three" of these cases are indeed proofs of a kind (67). The conflict between the view of justice according to which "one owes much to him who achieves or contributes much" and the view of justice according to which "one should demand much from him who can achieve or contribute much" becomes irresolvable if the second view is supported by what Weber calls "the ethics of intention," an ethics that questions the importance of the consideration of expediency that decides the superiority of the first view of justice (69). The conflict between "the ethics of responsibility" and "the ethics of intention" in turn becomes irresolvable if "the ethics of intention" is a manifestation of Christian ethics, for "the ethics of intention, which Weber imputed to syndicalism is, in reality, an ethics alien to all this-worldly social or political movements," which as such are concerned with the consequences of their actions in this world (69–70). Strauss tactfully avoided discussing Weber's example of the conflict between Christian ethics and this-worldly ethics, but admitted that Weber does prove that a certain interpretation of Christian ethics, the interpretation that is strictly otherworldly, is "incompatible with those standards of human excellence or human dignity which the unassisted human mind discerns" (70–71).

According to Strauss, the incompatibility of these two ethics would have no bearing on social science, which does not pretend to be anything more than "human knowledge of human life," so long as the legitimacy of social science, or this-worldly understanding, is not questioned. But that legitimacy becomes questionable to Weber for both moral and theoretical reasons. Strauss's difficult explanation of this remarkable fact can be divided into three parts that correspond to three different notions of science held by Weber. Each notion is more adequate than the previous one, and as we make this ascent we arrive at a different understanding of the implications of the crisis of science for human life. Whereas earlier Strauss had shown that Weber's thesis about values leads to nihilism (42–49), in his discussion of the problem of science (which is the problem that gave birth to the thesis about values) nihilism is only the first stopping point.

The first notion is science as a technique for limited "mastery" of the world, a science that can help man find the means to the ends he wishes. The goodness of this science is questionable because it cannot help us determine which ends we should pursue: "The goodness of science or philosophy was no problem as long as one could think that it is 'the way to true being' or to 'true nature' or to 'true happiness.' But these expectations have proved to be illusory" (72). But the new science could still be of some value because it can "ascertain that very limited truth which is accessible to man," and thus be of some practical use. However, Weber refused to understand the value of science in these terms. Why? Strauss suggests an answer by omitting in the passage quoted previously Weber's additional contention that science could no longer be thought to be "the way to God." It seems that Weber only halfheartedly believed that science could no longer be "the way to God"; he continued to be attached to a semireligious understanding of science – "science as a vocation." Hence, he continued to regard science as valuable in itself even though it could no longer honestly understand itself as the "'the way to 'true being' or to 'true nature' or to 'true happiness'" (72). This insistence on the intrinsic value of even this limited science leads to the acknowledgment of the irrationality of all values: "By regarding the quest for truth as valuable in itself, one admits that one is making a preference which no longer has a good or sufficient reason. One recognizes therewith the principle that preferences do not need good or sufficient reasons" (72). Instead of elevating the value of science, Weber's insistence on the intrinsic value of science under the new circumstances leads to nihilism, or to the conclusion that every pursuit is as defensible or legitimate as any other.

Strauss observed that Weber sometimes resisted this conclusion by appealing to a stern and more philosophic notion of science in which science discovers harsh truths, in which discovery is a means to something very high: freedom. According to this understanding, the goal of "science or philosophy" is "clarity about the great issues, and this means ultimately clarity *not indeed about the whole*, but about the situation of man as man" (72, emphasis added). It is valuable because it is the way "toward freedom from delusion" (72). Strauss suggested that for Weber, science frees us from more than one delusion. In the first place, Weber believed that science shows that the human situation is essentially that of war, that peace is derivative (64–65). But in clarifying man's social situation in this manner, science by implication rejects the theological foundation of Christianity. We live in a disenchanted world, a world without a god (73). This is the second delusion that science destroys.

Yet Weber could not hold on to his belief that science liberates us from delusions because he also accepted the contention of historicism that the whole is fundamentally mysterious (30–31, 73). Indeed, he believed that the infinitely progressive character of science supports this contention. If the whole is fundamentally mysterious, one cannot be certain that what presents itself as the situation of man at this time in history is really the true situation simply. Accordingly, Weber denied that the disenchantment caused by modern science is the discovery of man's true situation: "What claims to be freedom from delusions is as much and as little delusion as the faiths which prevailed in the past and which may prevail in the future" (73). Moreover, he had an almost overwhelming moral reason for hoping for a revival of religion: "he was certain that all devotion to causes or ideals has its roots in religious faith and, therefore, that the decline of religious faith will ultimately lead to the extinction of all causes or ideals" (73–74).[36] Yet he also believed that modern man cannot accept this faith without being dishonest. Weber's thesis that the conflict between values cannot be resolved by human reason is then the result of his inability to solve one pregnant conflict: on the one hand, the modern this-worldly experiment is tied to a science which he was "fated to believe;" on the other hand, he believed this experiment tends to bring about the extinction of "every human possibility but that of 'specialists without spirit or vision and voluptuaries without heart'" (42). He could neither reject modern science nor accept its corrosive effect on human life. The result here is no longer nihilism but an acceptance of the tragic situation of the modern man, who must live an atheistic life while accepting the guilt imposed by theism.

Strauss takes the reader to the third stage of Weber's doubts about the idea of science by observing that "the crisis of modern life and modern

---

[36] This certainty seems to be due to Weber's acceptance of modern political philosophy's thesis about the nature of man (man's natural selfishness which makes his natural condition a state of war) as the expression of the truth of this-worldly understanding (64–65).

science does not necessarily make doubtful the idea of science" (74). In this part of the argument, he presents a different and fuller understanding of philosophy or science. This philosophy or science is not the foundation of free life but it itself is the life of free insight. And unlike the modern philosophy or science that looks reality sternly in the face, this philosophy or science is not so clearly at odds with our natural inclinations: "man is so built that that he can find his satisfaction, his bliss, in free investigation, in articulating the riddle of being" (75). However, philosophy or science faces a challenge from revelation, which maintains that the best life is that of obedient love and which in addition promises a solution to the riddle of being, a solution for which man naturally yearns. Accordingly, Strauss presented Weber's conflict in broad terms as the conflict between philosophy or science and the Bible. He observed that "a bird's eye view of the secular struggle between philosophy and theology" leads to the conclusion that "neither of the two antagonists has ever succeeded in really refuting the other" (75). Yet this state of affairs does not lead to a stalemate, for it forces philosophy "to grant that revelation is possible" and therefore that "philosophy is perhaps something infinitely unimportant." As a man who is on the quest for evident knowledge, the philosopher or the scientist must be open to, and even welcome, any objections to his views. Yet precisely because he recognizes as knowledge only what is evident to our natural powers, he cannot be open to the claim that one should accept the teachings of the prophets on faith, a claim which as the prior stalemate shows may be valid. The philosopher's claim to openness is bogus; his call for rationality rests on a fundamental irrationality (75).

Only at this point does Strauss suggest that Weber could not preserve his attachment to the idea of philosophy or science: "Weber *tried to* remain faithful to the cause of autonomous insight" (75, emphasis added). Weber's thesis that the conflict between values cannot be resolved by reason was an attempt to preserve the value of science, but this very attempt led to a break with the spirit of science, for reason shows (at least on the basis of the evidence known to Weber) that the position of revelation is superior to that of philosophy or science.[37] It

---

[37] Strauss suggests that Weber ultimately made this break with the spirit of science on moral grounds: "The greatest representative of social science positivism, Max Weber, has postulated the insolubility of all value conflicts, because his soul craved a universe in which failure, that bastard of forceful sinning accompanied by still more forceful faith, instead of felicity and serenity, was to be the mark of human nobility" (*WPP*, 23). He suggests that this craving was the result of Weber's attempt to justify his moral revulsion against modern political philosophy's thesis about the natural selfishness of man while refusing to deny the truth of that thesis (65–66).

would have been more philosophical of Weber to look more deeply into the conflict between philosophy or science and revelation and to consider the possibility of a return to faith, that is, to see whether upon a fuller examination intellectual probity would allow for such a return.[38] Strauss's sympathy for the return to faith is at least partly due to his greater clarity about the demands of philosophy or science.[39]

It is fair to say that Strauss did not give up on the cause of autonomous insight, and this means that he believed, rightly or wrongly, that he had found a way out of the difficulty that crippled Weber. His approach is not primarily to refute revelation but rather to show that revelation could use the assistance of reason. In an autobiographical statement that traces a path that led to the same conflict that troubled Weber, Strauss writes: "The victory of orthodoxy through the self-destruction of rational philosophy was not an unmitigated blessing, for it was a victory not of Jewish orthodoxy, but of any orthodoxy, and Jewish orthodoxy based its claim to superiority to other religions from the beginning on its superior rationality (Deut. 4:6)."[40] More specifically, Strauss called for "a comprehensive analysis of social reality as we know it in actual life," a social reality that is known both to believers and unbelievers. This focus on moral-political investigations is not an attempt to disregard Weber's problem but rather an attempt to meet that problem more adequately, for one's attitude toward philosophy and revelation is not unconnected to one's attitude toward morality. Scholars of Strauss already argue and will continue to argue about Strauss's conclusions on this matter, but it is wise to distrust any judgment that is not based on an exact understanding of Strauss's very difficult Socratic writings, for Strauss has made it clear that his approach is actually a rediscovery of Socrates's approach to this matter.[41]

Although the conflict between philosophy or science and the Bible is not absent in Strauss's discussion of the new political science, it does

---

[38] Strauss, "Epilogue," in *LAM*, 218–219, 231, 239.

[39] Compare Nietzsche's discussion of the apostate of the free spirit (*Day-Break*, 56), which is an impressive characterization of the philosophic spirit, to Strauss's criticism of Nietzsche's position ("Preface to *SCR*," in *LAM*, 256).

[40] Strauss, "Preface to *SCR*," in *LAM*, 256.

[41] Strauss, *PL*, 21–39; "Preface to *SCR*," in *LAM*, 257. See Christopher Bruell, "Strauss on Xenophon's Socrates," *Political Science Reviewer*, 14 (1984): 263–318. Bruell shows that "the theological-political problem" that Strauss identifies as the theme of his thought is indeed the theme of his late Socratic writings.

not there receive the thematic treatment that it gets in his criticism of Weber.[42] This is not surprising because in the former essay Strauss champions Aristotelian political science, which maintains that "the sphere governed by prudence is in principle self-sufficient or closed."[43] This political science is akin to the "self-enclosed" humanistic social science championed by Husserl, but according to Strauss humanism is not ultimately sufficient:

Yet, even if all were said that could be said, and that cannot be said, humanism is not enough. Man, while being at least potentially a whole, is only a part of a larger whole. While forming a kind of world, and even being a kind of world, man is only a little world, a microcosm. The macrocosm, the whole to which man belongs, is not human. The whole, or its origin, is either subhuman or superhuman. Man cannot be understood in his own light but only in the light of either the subhuman or the superhuman.[44]

Although Strauss did not accept the soundness of the break with common sense that was inaugurated by the founders of modern philosophy or science, he suggests that they made that break because they were more aware of the previous difficulty than Husserl.[45] He himself suggests the following path. Because man cannot be understood in light of the subhuman, we must understand him in the light of superhuman. This approach does not preclude the possibility that a proper analysis of man may support the subhuman character of the origin of the whole: "It is safer to try to understand the low in the light of the high than the high in the light of the low. In doing the latter one necessarily distorts the high, whereas in doing the former one does not deprive the low of the freedom to reveal itself fully as what it is."[46]

CONCLUSION

Both Strauss and Husserl present their criticisms of modern science and present-day social science in the context of the crisis of the Western world or of liberal democracy, which is the most successful Western movement. Because to many social scientists this talk about crisis

[42] This theme is discussed at length by Leora Batnitzky, "Leo Strauss and the Theologico-Political Predicament," this volume.

[43] Strauss, "Epilogue," in *LAM*, 206.

[44] Strauss "Social Science and Humanism," in *RCPR*, 7; see also "What is Political Philosophy?" in *WPP*, 38.

[45] Compare Strauss, "Epilogue," in *LAM*, 206, to "On the Basis of Hobbes's Political Philosophy," in *WPP*, 180–181.

[46] Strauss, "Preface to *SCR*," in *CAM*, 225, in *LAM*, 225.

smacks of hot air, it might be useful to state the view held by Strauss and Husserl. According to them, the Western world is a unique community of nations because it is a community that is shaped by philosophy. The universalism of the European world and its universal appeal is due to this fact. Comparing the European culture to other cultures, Husserl writes:

There is something unique here [Europe] that is recognized in us by all other human groups, too, something that, quite apart from all considerations of utility, becomes a motive for them to Europeanize themselves even in their unbroken will to spiritual self-preservation; whereas we, if we understand ourselves properly, would never Indianize ourselves, for example.[47]

If a society has received its decisive orientation from philosophy or science, doubts about philosophy or science are apt to breed a lack of self-confidence in that society, and may even lead to upheavals as can be seen from the connection between irrationalism and various twentieth-century mass movements hostile to liberal society. The crisis is serious because there are valid reasons for doubting the goodness of philosophy or science. These doubts cannot be resolved by an act of will, by a willful commitment to science, or by denying that science needs an adequate justification. Such attempts only deepen the crisis by revealing what has happened to men whose predecessors followed reason wherever it took them. As Strauss put it: "the almost willful blindness to the crisis of liberal democracy is part of that crisis."[48]

According to Strauss, the crisis can only be met by an adequate political science, and it is this fact that is the immediate justification of Strauss's interest in social science. As we have indicated, Strauss's political science is partly a development of Husserl's phenomenology. According to Husserl, there is a "natural" perspective prior to the theoretical perspective, an outlook that has features that are essentially the same everywhere. The theoretical outlook emerges out of this more primary outlook, which is fundamentally practical in nature. Because the practical outlook (which can never be completely destroyed) is the presupposition of the theoretical outlook, science can have clarity about

---

[47] Edmund Husserl, "The Vienna Lecture," in *The Crisis of European Sciences and Transcendental Phenomenology*, trans. David Carr (Evanston, IL: Northwestern University Press, 1970), 275. Although Strauss gives equal weight to the biblical heritage in his characterization of the West, he shares Husserl's view that it is the influence of philosophy that distinguishes the West from the rest of the world, for he traces the crisis of the West to the crisis of political philosophy.

[48] Strauss, "Epilogue," in *LAM*, 223.

itself only by an analysis of this natural world or what Strauss calls the world of common sense. Of course, this requires nothing less than a revolution in modern scientific thinking:

> Husserl had realized more profoundly than anybody else that the scientific understanding of the world, far from being the perfection of natural understanding, is derivative from the latter in such a way as to make us oblivious of the very foundations of the scientific understanding: all philosophizing must start from our common understanding of the world, from our understanding of the world as sensibly perceived prior to all theorizing.[49]

However, Strauss argued that Husserl, who was insufficiently attentive to religion, and Heidegger, who was insufficiently attentive to politics, failed to recover this natural world:

> As long as we identify the natural or prescientific world with the world in which we live, we are dealing with an abstraction. The world in which we live is already a product of science, or at any rate is profoundly affected by the existence of science. To say nothing of technology, the world in which we live is free from ghosts, witches, and so on, with which, but for the existence of science, it would abound. To grasp the natural world as a world that is radically prescientific or prephilosophic, one has to go back behind the emergence of science or philosophy.[50]

Our political world too is a product of science, and Nietzsche, more than Husserl and Heidegger, recovered the natural moral-political outlook by undoing the philosophical demotion of courage and sense of shame.[51] According to Strauss, the natural outlook is a political outlook, and politics proper can never do without religion and morality. In Strauss's remarkable exposition of the classical approach to the study of political affairs, the beginning of political science and its end stand in a jarring contrast to each other. It begins by looking at politics from the perspective of citizens or statesmen and it ends with the realization that "the ultimate aim of political life cannot be reached by political life, but only by a life devoted to contemplation, to philosophy."[52] But more importantly, this change of orientation is accomplished by

---

[49] Strauss, "Philosophy as Rigorous Science," in *SPPP*, 31.

[50] Strauss, *NRH*, 79.

[51] Strauss, *PL*, 135–136. Strauss pays tribute to Nietzsche by using a formulation of his to characterize a premise of Aristotelian political science: Man is "the beast with red cheeks" (*LAM*, 207). He does not use Aristotle because Aristotle's own devaluation of shame obscures the natural outlook that is indeed the premise of his political science.

[52] Strauss, "On Classical Political Philosophy," in *WPP*, 90.

climbing a ladder made out of the problems that are inherent in political life: classical political science claims to show that the theoretical life is the perfection of man's natural understanding of human excellence.

I am grateful to Alice Behnegar, David Bolotin, Christopher Bruell, Robert Faulkner, Susan Shell, Steven B. Smith, and Richard Zinman for their critical comments on earlier drafts of this essay.

11 The Complementarity of Political Philosophy and Liberal Education in the Thought of Leo Strauss

POLITICAL PHILOSOPHY AS POLITICAL EDUCATION

Leo Strauss established himself among the leading students of Western political thought in the second half of the twentieth century and a renowned teacher of future teachers of that subject. He taught but also thought carefully about teaching.[1] In his maturity, he was a professor in a number of American universities (New School, University of Chicago, with which he is most famously identified, Claremont Men's College and St. John's College in Annapolis) and one who reflected on liberal education in a liberal democracy. At the same time, Strauss was an inheritor of classical German education as it existed in the early twentieth century. In this capacity, he contributed two important essays explicitly devoted to the problem of liberal education, although his work as a whole can be seen as an ongoing and open-ended set of reflections on the broader problem of education and democracy.[2]

---

[1] For some recollections of Strauss as a teacher, see Werner Danhauser, "Becoming Naïve Again," *American Scholar*, 44 (1975): 636–642; see also Diskin Clay, "On a Forgotten Kind of Reading," *Leo Strauss's Thought: Toward a Critical Engagement*, ed. Alan Udoff (Boulder, CO: Lynne Rienner, 1991), 253–266, esp. 253–254.

[2] Strauss's two major statements on liberal education are "What is Liberal Education?" and "Liberal Education and Responsibility" in *LAM*, 1–8 and 9–25. The problem of education to which Strauss devoted himself is perhaps best summed up in an early essay on Rousseau: "Modern democracy might seem to stand or fall by the claim that 'the method of democracy' and 'the method of intelligence' are the same." See Strauss, "On the Intention of Rousseau," *Social Research*, 14 (1947): 455–487, on 455; reprinted in *Hobbes and Rousseau: A Collection of Critical Essays*, ed. Maurice Cranston and Richard S. Peters (Garden City, NY: Anchor, 1972), 254–290, on 254. The phrases in quotations could likely refer to John Dewey's Page-Barbour Lectues *Liberalism and Social Action* in *The Later Works, 1925–1953*, vol. 11 (1935–1937), ed. Jo Ann Boydon, intro. John J. McDermott (Carbondale, IL: Southern Illinois University Press, 1987), 35, 37–38, 46, 55–56, 64–65. Strauss's only published work on Dewey was a review of Dewey's *German Philosophy and*

In America, debates over the relation between traditional liberal learning and democratic culture were established long before Strauss entered the American university scene, but he was already a student of the issues and crises of modernity that appeared in the wake of the democratizing movements in Europe and North America constituting the transformations of culture in the modern age. As a student of classical political philosophy, Strauss was fully conversant with the question of the relation between politics and education, and he knew that the American Founders had insisted that to secure republican virtue required an educated citizenry.[3] To state Strauss's understanding of liberal education clearly, it will be necessary to set forth Strauss's idea of political philosophy.

In the tradition stemming from the Platonic Socrates, we have perennially thought about and debated the tension between the philosophical pursuit of wisdom and the requirements of stability and security in the polity. Liberal learning is not propaganda or merely patriotic rhetoric, and yet it also cannot simply be abstracted from the circumstances of time and place in which we must operate. We live in the intersection between our ideals and hopes on the one hand, and our contingent conditions of time and place on the other, in the tension between the eternal things and the things that change and can be otherwise. At the heart of liberal learning is the task to make sense of ourselves situated as we are and must be as human beings.

In this respect, Strauss defined himself as a friend to liberal democracy. In doing so, he expresses the tension that results from the fact that no matter how admirable any existing political regime may be, it cannot be beyond question or criticism. Strauss could distinguish between the philosophical quest for insight into the best polity and the careful analysis of the existing regimes with respect to their advantages and disadvantages. To be a friend to liberal democracy is not to be uncritical of

---

Politics in *Social Research* 10 (November, 1943): 505–507; reprinted in *WPP*, 179–181.

[3] The theme of civic education has been an explicit topic of a range of Strauss-inspired work; for some of the better studies, see Nathan Tarcov, *Locke's Education for Liberty* (Chicago: University of Chicago Press, 1984); Thomas Pangle and Lorraine Smith Pangle, *The Learning of Liberty: The Educational Ideas of the American Founders* (Lawrence, KS: University of Kansas Press, 1993); Christopher Bruell, *On the Socratic Education: An Introduction to the Shorter Dialogues* (Lanham, MD: Rowman & Littlefield, 1999). The best-known work of this genre was certainly Allan Bloom's best-selling *The Closing of the American Mind: How Higher Education has Failed Democracy and Impoverished the Souls of Today's Students* (New York: Simon & Schuster, 1987).

liberal democracy. But this does not imply that the political philosopher has a program of action to achieve an alternative, putatively superior, regime. Strauss admired Winston Churchill and respected his observation that democracy is the worst regime except for the others that have been tried from time to time. Plato's Socrates argues in the *Republic* that one who has seen, through the intellect, the best city (the "heavenly city") can conform his soul to it and live in accordance with it even though it does not exist anywhere on earth.

This is to speak transpolitically; to see beyond the current state of affairs, not as an activist intellectual aiming to perpetrate drastic change but as one who seeks to understand what there is to be understood so far as possible within the limits of human reason. Strauss saw that human beings can initiate changes but they cannot altogether control what unfolds through time as a result of their efforts. Human beings can be creative but they do not control history. If they seek to live by history, they can also die by history. In short, Strauss thought of himself as a seeker of wisdom through the philosophical examination of politics. One can be vitally interested in politics as revealing of the truth of existence without believing that politics is a means to salvation or perfection. On the contrary, Strauss also accepted with Aristotle that man is by nature political. If we are by nature political, then we would cease to be human without politics. If we in our utopian dreams seek to end politics by superseding politics, we are seeking in effect to supersede our humanity even though we speak of perfecting humanity. Politics is interminable, not a temporary feature of existence progressing toward a suppositious end of history.

Political philosophy at its heart begins with careful thinking and reflection on what we observe going on in politics around us. In this respect, political philosophy is political science classically understood. Like other philosophical students of politics, Strauss accepts the need to begin with the facts on the ground, with interest in historical developments, and with care for concepts and vocabulary. The answer to the question, "What is political philosophy?" is at one level quite simple: It is careful thinking about politics. Of course, thinking carefully about politics leads eventually into matters that are difficult to resolve and fraught with mystery. But the point is to start from something straightforward, which gives a reference point to keep control over speculation. Insofar as Strauss was a Platonist, he understood that the great conflicts and debates in political life give rise eventually to the desire for wisdom about these awful, life-threatening, life-delimiting matters. Opinion reigns in the marketplace but the conflict of opinions excites, at least in some, a desire to have knowledge, to gain a perspective that is more than assertion, and the success of which is not dependent on coercion or clever speeches. The trial and death of Socrates suggests that even if the clash of opinions implies the need for knowledge for genuine insight, to take the quest for knowledge seriously is to court disaster as the world understands disaster. Politics may be said to point beyond itself but yet also to resist what the beyond reveals. Politicians may talk of solving problems and getting to permanent peace, prosperity, and stability, but in a certain way they do not really mean to bring to an end their stock in trade. Moreover, they cannot bring it to an end in any case. It may seem to some peculiar to think that wanting this end is to want to cease to be human, but that is the implication.

One can also say that political philosophy is thinking about politics philosophically, that is, thinking about politics at some remove from political engagement, rejecting the view that all important human undertakings are only forms of politics "by other means," and affirming that philosophy is not ideology. To distinguish philosophy from ideology requires thinking through what philosophy is. In our time, this includes the requirement to examine modern philosophy in relation to classical or ancient philosophy. We are aware of this distinction and regularly employ it in intellectual exchanges. The old philosophy is not "idealistic," as modern philosophy became. To take our bearings from what we observe around us constrains the imagination in the sense that thinking up and advocating alternative political universes denies or ignores the constraints of things that impose upon us, and as our study of the past tells us such constraints have always been.

Given the trial and death of Socrates, one cannot ignore the possibility of another connotation of political philosophy: that it is the pursuit of philosophy with an eye to the danger to philosophy and the philosopher inherent in philosophy's allegiance to that which transcends political allegiance. The philosopher must be aware of the uses to which philosophy may be put, and also of the imputation to philosophy of disloyalty. Thus, the philosopher must also consider how to preserve philosophy from the corruption that follows from the intermingling of political and philosophical pursuits. The philosopher must be wise to the ways of politics even if skeptical of politics, or disinterested with respect to policy alternatives.

On the other hand, there is no reason to think that philosophers must inevitably be detached or disinterested with respect to policies. But if they are interested and do entertain inclinations in one policy direction or another, their commitment to philosophy will not relieve them from the contingencies and conflicts attending all entry into political expressions and actions. Ascending from the cave, so to speak, does not ward off the unavoidable descent back into the cave and, furthermore, what becomes clear in the ascent is clouded in the return. Philosophical insight does not control politics but rather shows why the suggestion of such control will always be resisted. The philosopher sees what others see but does not see as they see. Unification of philosophy and politics – of wisdom and power – is imaginable but unlikely, to say the least. The search for truth does not promote success in the struggle for power. Speculations about the best polity naturally arise, but the distance between visions of political fulfillment and actual human conduct is, if not categorical, nevertheless immense. Machiavelli rubs our noses in it in *The Prince*. But already in Plato's *Republic*, the consolation offered is to order one's soul toward the best city in speech even if everything around us is in decline toward chaos, and no earthly regime is the best regime.

Political philosophy is then the examination of what is to be learned about human beings and the human condition as revealed in the practice of politics. Because politics is a most dramatic form of human endeavor – the enactment of orders and arrangements and, ultimately, a matter of life and death – one might expect to learn as much or more about humanity by looking carefully at politics as by observing any other activity. To make these observations is to acknowledge, more or less openly, that the vocation of the philosopher is a peculiar one, not immediately attractive or understandable, especially insofar as the "usefulness" of philosophy is, to say the least, unclear. And yet philosophy, and the examination of politics philosophically, persist. Why should this be?

Upon emerging from domination by sheer necessity, there appears in us an awareness of the distinction between duty and desire, between necessity and freedom. Everything need not be as it is; all peoples do not live in the same manner; there is more than one way to survive and prosper; what ought to be is not identical with what is; what ought to be is itself a matter of argument within societies and between them; there is distance between things as they are and as we imagine they might become. This is the release from sheer economic necessity into a situation evoking the faculty of imagination and a sense of self, transition from mere economic relations to incipient politics, the experience of divided allegiance between duties and interests, between self and others, one's own and that of others.

A set of people undergoing this experience must attend to their arrangements with each other where disagreement has become unavoidable even if unsought and regretted – they are cast into the realm of freedom. There is argument about how they ought to live, infused as they are with a sense of the deficiency in and incoherency of how they already live. Some welcome the arguments; others seek to escape them. As rational animals endowed with the gift of speech, we are able both to understand and misunderstand each other, even as we incompletely understand, or even misunderstand, ourselves. The dissatisfying sense of "not yet" or "not quite" imposes itself. Politics incites a mixture of observations as to "what is the case" with opinions both about the adequacy of competing descriptions of what is the case and opinions about how to respond to what is the case: there is affirmation and critique, collaboration and discord, the desire to preserve and the desire to change things.

Because this is now a situation in which everything might be otherwise than it is, the issue of authority, of determining the authoritative or best opinions, intrudes on practical decision making amid uncertainty. Even if we are deliberating among alternative goods, we cannot pursue all things worthy of pursuit equally and simultaneously – someone must render decisions, someone who is not simply issuing decrees and commands or using force against us. Aristotle calls this the rule of free men over free men, exalting participation in deliberation and debate. The distinction between "power" and "authority," between command and agreement, is a great achievement intellectually and in practice, and is a hallmark of Western civilization. The collapse of that distinction bespeaks the darkening and coarsening of insight into the human predicament.

In this respect, politics is hoped for as the adequate response to departure from conditions that seemed once to be unarguable and unavoidable but seem so no longer. But because politics perpetuates arguments in the very effort to resolve them, it eventually occurs to some that one must go beyond politics, that politics points to something beyond itself. If we are to resolve the issues politics confronts us with, we shall want definitive answers to the questions of what we are and how we ought to live. We say politics is natural to humans but, precisely because natural to us, thereby also interminable. To complete politics or bring politics to a close would be the end of humanity. The effort to do this has had its laboratory experiment in the twentieth century, as Strauss well understood.

Every proposal to resolve matters once and for all incites further arguments and the temptation to suppress further arguments. The economic city is limited and we cannot go back to it. The political city dramatizes our predicament, sometimes in a deadly way, rather than resolving and transcending it. The thought arises that perhaps there is a philosophical city, the "best city in speech," the "beautiful city," the "heavenly city." The desire for this best city seems to be spawned by the experience of the political city. This is not to say that everyone is interested in or consciously seeks the best or heavenly city; indeed, some reject the idea. But it seems that the full unfolding of the human condition implicates this possibility whether embraced or rejected. We are by nature economic and political beings, but we are also something more.

If we cannot retreat from polity into economy, it seems we cannot retreat from philosophical awareness either. As Plato's Socrates asserts in the *Apology*, we can kill Socrates but we cannot kill philosophy. It is a mistake to think that Socrates is the source of philosophy. He is a peculiarly vivid instantiation of something present in all humanity. Many will come after him who may be more difficult to deal with than he has been. The relation between politics and philosophy will always be tension-ridden. The trial and death of Socrates symbolizes both acknowledgment of, and resistance to, the philosophical implications of politics. It may be true that philosophy emerged first in wonder, not in politics, and thus might have been indifferent to politics. But philosophy did not remain aloof from politics. Philosophy's vocation is to examine what there is to be examined. There is no natural limit to what philosophy might inquire into. To cut off such investigation is to truncate or obscure the full depth of human experience, and implicitly to admit that some fundamental human experience is inaccessible to philosophical understanding.

Human beings encounter reality's structure through historical experience. History as such (whatever that might be) is not an object open to investigation and, although there are many speculations preoccupied with progress or decline, this also is not the object of investigation. There is always a constricting social field out of which our accounts emerge. The order of things is both that which elicits our attention and also the medium within which we seek understanding. The tension between the constraints of time and place, of locality, and the movement of thought pressures the quest for truth, imposing uncertainty as to how to proceed. The tension itself is the reality to be explored wherein we know that we do not know, which means that we know something but seek to know better what in a way we already know but insufficiently. Ignorance is a form of awareness. Philosophical dialogue is the means to opening ourselves to the full weight of this tension as we seek wisdom about our situation. This tension is present in all humanity, albeit more attended to in some individuals and under some circumstances than others. Ideology, as opposed to philosophy, seeks to end the tension by replacing the quest for knowledge with a claim to knowledge that ends the quest. The modern age is an age seduced by the idea of completing the quest. Strauss saw, experienced, what this meant in actuality.

THE POLITICIZATION OF EDUCATION

Strauss's formation was in the situation of Europe's self-destruction in the first half of the twentieth century.[4] He shared with other thinkers of his generation the haunting task of trying to understand what had happened and how it could have happened. He felt compelled to make

---

[4] For Strauss's account of this world, see "Preface to *SCR*," in *LAM*, 224–259.

sense out of what had happened to destroy the claims of enlightenment and progress that were supposed to come to fruition in the very
moment when they were brutally undermined in the heart of Western
civilization. Kant had answered positively the "old question" whether
the human race is advancing, at least insofar as he considered any answer
not oriented to the prospects of an enlightened future to imperil human
dignity. But then in the second half of the twentieth century, the old
question had to be raised again under dire circumstances as the quest
for human dignity produced most undignified results.

Was totalitarianism a new and unprecedented phenomenon requiring
entirely new modes of analysis to make sense of it? Many thought so.[5]
Strauss was cautious in this regard. He argued famously in his debate
with Alexandre Kojève over the interpretation of Xenophon's Hiero – his
dialogue on tyranny – that the beginning of understanding the modern
phenomenon of tyranny lay in recovering a clear understanding of the
ancient understanding of tyranny.[6]

Strauss did not deny that modern technology had changed many features of modern life, vastly increasing the power at our disposal for
destruction and control. But he also felt compelled to deny the historicist argument, inherited from Hegel and Marx and espoused by Kojève,
that tyranny is a catalyst for positive historical progress. He could see
that the use of force to end the use of force is a doubtful proposition, to
say the least. Ancient tyranny is transformed into modern tyranny by
its association with modern technology. But also tyranny is transformed
by the dismantling of tradition and of common-sense constraints on the
justification of the use of political power. But Strauss went still more
deeply into this. The expansion of the power of control at human disposal through technology, together with the project of perfecting humanity, reinforces arguments for centralizing and concentrating power in

[5] Perhaps the best-known defender of the claim that totalitarianism represents a
radically new kind of regime unknown to previous history is Hannah Arendt,
The Origins of Totalitarianism (New York: Harcourt, Brace, 1951); see also
Karl R. Popper, The Open Society and its Enemies (New York: Harper, 1962).

[6] See OT which includes Strauss's original commentary on Xenophon, Kojève's
review "Tyranny and Wisdom," and Strauss's "Restatement on Xenophon's
Hiero" along with their correspondence. The Strauss-Kojève debate has given
rise to a range of interpretations; for some of the most noteworthy see, Victor
Gourevitch, "Philosophy and Politics I-II," Review of Metaphysics 22 (1968):
58–84, 281–328; Michael Roth, "Natural Right and the End of History: Leo
Strauss and Alexandre Kojève," Revue du Metaphysique et du Morale 3
(1991): 407–422; Robert Pippin, "Being, Time, and Politics: The Strauss-Kojève
Debate," History and Theory, 2 (1993): 138–161; Steven B. Smith "Tyranny
Ancient and Modern" Reading Leo Strauss: Politics, Philosophy, Judaism
(Chicago: University of Chicago Press, 2006), 131–155.

governments, seeming to lend plausibility to the belief that we can take our destiny into our own hands and reshape the world as we deem fit.

Strauss saw that an adequate political science would need to pay attention to our historical situation but also to the sources of wisdom about political life. Attention must be paid to technology, to the dismantling of tradition, and to the displacement of philosophy, classically understood as the seeking of the eternal things, by programs of reform or revolution with a view no longer merely to understand the world but to change it. Marx's eleventh thesis on Feuerbach proclaims the abandonment of the Socratic insight, an abandonment that had already been underway a long time. The result in Nietzsche is succinctly described by Strauss:

The difficulty inherent in the philosophy of the will to power led after Nietzsche to the explicit renunciation of the very notion of eternity. Modern thought reaches its culmination, its highest self-consciousness, in the most radical historicism, i.e., in explicitly condemning to oblivion the notion of eternity. For oblivion of eternity, or, in other words, estrangement from man's deepest desire and therewith from the primary issues, is the price which modern man had to pay, from the very beginning, for attempting to be absolutely sovereign, to become the master and owner of nature, to conquer chance.[7]

The estrangement from our deepest desires – the program of modern thinkers to demythologize that desire as superstition and self-delusion – is for Strauss the modern corruption of philosophy. Classically, philosophy did not deny the desire for eternity but sought to make sense of it so far as that may be possible through reason. Strauss thought to reject this desire's centrality is to abandon the philosophical commitment to consider the full range of human experience. This must have an impact on modern politics, where power has been regularly employed to suppress man's deepest desire, supported by the intellectual effort to rationalize a claim to have fulfilled or completed philosophy by transposing it into a program for an earthly regime. The purpose of much modern thought and politics is to root out man's "deepest desire," which is recognized as a barrier to an imagined fulfillment through rule by a "right-thinking" elite, the vanguard of a universal, homogeneous state.

Thus, it is modern thought that is "idealistic" and classical thought that is "realistic." Idealism in this respect is ideology. The argument that an ideal is coming to be in history – or that we must conduct ourselves as if it were coming to be – is an ideological argument, a form of political action justified by the claim, implicit or explicit, that the tragic conflict between the search for wisdom and the exercise of power is an opposition that is in the process of being overcome. Strauss says this

---

[7] Strauss, "What is Political Philosophy?" in *WPP*, 55.

in his argument with Kojève over how best to comprehend the phenomenon of tyranny:

Philosophy on the strict and classical sense is quest for the eternal order or for
the eternal cause or causes of all things. It presupposes then that there is an eternal and unchangeable order within which History takes place and which is not
affected by History. It presupposes in other words that any "realm of freedom"
is no more than a dependent province within the "realm of necessity" ... Kojève
rejects it in favor of the view that "Being creates itself in the course of History,"
or that the highest being is Society and History, or that eternity is nothing but the
totality of historical, i.e., finite time. On the basis of the classical presupposition,
a radical distinction must be made between the conditions of understanding and
the sources of understanding, between the conditions of the existence and perpetuation of philosophy (societies of a certain kind, and so on) and the sources
of philosophic insight ... On the basis of Kojève's presuppositions, unqualified
attachment to human concerns becomes the source of philosophic understanding: man must be absolutely at home on earth, he must be absolutely a citizen
of the earth, if not a citizen of a part of the inhabitable earth. On the basis of the
classical presupposition, philosophy requires a radical detachment from human
concerns: man must not be absolutely at home on earth, he must be a citizen of
the whole.[8]

As Strauss specifies it, philosophy does not cease to be what it is
when it turns its attention to politics. The insight into what philosophy
is does not derive from politics, although politics could be a gateway
to philosophy for a reflective and acute mind. Politics in its limitations may intimate the need for philosophy but will try to control both
what it learns from philosophy and also the manner in which philosophy is allowed to speak. Politics wants philosophy to know as politics
"knows." Political philosophy has a starting place in political experience. As such, we may begin with something we think we know. Yet
because we do not know, because there is uncertainty and doubt, knowing what we know we come to suspect that we are still ignorant.

LIBERAL EDUCATION AND LIBERAL DEMOCRACY

It is in this framework that we can understand Strauss's view on liberal
education. One notices Strauss's sharp distinction between ancient and
modern thought. This is central to his analysis of each of the important
topics he addressed in his work. We have referred to modern technology
and the technological society, to modern tyranny or totalitarianism, to
ideology or revolutionary politics, and so on. One central feature in common to these is what Strauss might call abstraction from concreteness,

---

[8] Strauss, "Restatement on Xenophon," in *OT*, 212.

wherein we guide ourselves by abstract ideas of how we would like the world to be and experience resentment at the resistance of the world to our aspirations and plans.

At the same time, in twentieth-century university education the idea of the "multiversity" emerged fully to sight.[9] The idea of "pluriform" truth or truths appears. From Strauss's point of view, this explained a loss of confidence in agreeing on the purpose of the university. In the modern situation, there is a passion to make everything a matter of choice that obscures or relativizes the standard of choice-making. Insofar as it is still spoken of, the quest for wisdom seems to be a passion for self-defined self-fulfillment. This is the age of "modern Liberty," as Benjamin Constant famously described it, promoting individualism. This must affect the way in which thinking about education and its purpose is to proceed, creating painful tensions. Strauss put it as follows:

There is a tension between the respect for diversity or individuality and the recognition of natural right. When liberals became impatient of the absolute limits to diversity or individuality that are imposed even by the most liberal version of natural right, they had to make a choice between natural right and the uninhibited cultivation of individuality. They chose the latter.[10]

The most liberal version of natural right is that derived from Locke's individualism, which proclaims that man is by nature free, equal, and independent, and has a right of revolution (even if Lockean humanity does not often exercise the right of revolution) against whatever appears repressive to self-fulfillment. Nevertheless, Locke also believed in the rule of law and asserted that God had made man in such a way as to move him to a social life in cooperation with others. In short, there is a tension in the Lockean inheritance between self-assertion and a self-control inspired by the law of reason that respects or even positively cares for the well-being of others.

To put it in Straussian terms, the tension is between the understanding that there is correct conduct for human beings that restrains and shapes how they understand the happiness they have a right to pursue, and the view that there is no shaping foundation or natural limit to guide their choice of pursuits. Modern liberalism heightens this tension, or even in the extreme case, tries to override it. This will affect thinking about education, and especially liberal education or education for liberty

---

[9] The term "multiversity" was coined by Clark Kerr, former President of University of California at Berkeley; see his *The Uses of the University* (Cambridge, MA: Harvard University Press, 1972); see also Nicholas von Hoffman, *The Multiversity: A Personal Report on What Happens to Today's Students at American Universities* (New York: Holt, Rinehart, & Winston, 1966).

[10] Strauss, *NRH*, 5.

and self-dependence. The virtues of civility and moderation can come to seem repressive rather than essential requirements of responsible conduct in the company of others. Liberal learning may come to be seen merely as facilitating self-assertion governed by careful calculations of the opportunities available for success, as it equips us to aggregate necessary resources. This is the university as industrial machine, a process to manufacture a "product" that embodies certain skills that contribute to "productivity."

One of the implications of Strauss's understanding of classical philosophy is this: To pursue wisdom is to transcend the self without losing one's identity. Dialectical engagement differs from the persuasive speech of politics in that its intent is to examine proffered opinions independently of the individual or individuals who are expressing the opinions. Dialogue is to open the soul to the ascent from opinion to knowledge, and this demands a dying of the self in the effort to encounter the eternal things. Opinions are manifestations of the temporal, and hence temporary. In the realm of opinion, what is thought true today may well be thought false tomorrow, and maybe thought true again the day after. This is not to say that individuality is not real but, as we saw previously, it is embedded in a structure of reality that confines it. In this understanding to be free is to conform the order of one's soul to the order of reality that is characterized, so far as possible, through expressions of what is right by nature for us. Individuality is thus not an end in itself, and self-fulfillment has a larger context.

Strauss had seen the upheavals in the universities of Europe and North America that strained if they did not altogether deny collegiality and conversation.[11] These upheavals threatened the very mission of the university, which is education of the individual:

Liberal education is concerned with the souls of men and therefore has little or no use for machines. If it becomes a machine or an industry, it becomes indistinguishable from the entertainment industry unless in respect to income and publicity, tinsel and glamour.[12]

As previously noted, a recurring debate about Strauss is over the question of his attitude to democracy or liberal democracy.[13] This is

---

[11] Strauss did not comment, at least publicly, on the campus upheavals of the 1960s but the dangers of the politicization of the German universities during the 1930s were never far from his mind; see Strauss, "An Introduction to Heideggerian Existentialism," in RCPR, 30–31; see also "A Giving of Accounts," in JPCM, 461. The connection between Germany and the politicization of the American university during the 1960s was drawn explicitly by Bloom, Closing of the American Mind, 313–335.

[12] Strauss, "Liberal Education and Responsibility," in LAM, 25.

[13] See William A. Galston, "Leo Strauss's Qualified Embrace of Liberal Democracy," this volume.

significant beacuse our primary focus is on the relation of liberal democracy to liberal education. Strauss saw that liberal education and the modern liberal tradition are not identical. Liberal education existed long before the modern liberal tradition. It could persist (of course, there are no guarantees) in some postliberal era. It is common today to take the two as inseparable, but it is not so. It is true that the liberal tradition is most accommodating to liberal education, and this is all the more reason why, for Strauss, a friendly critique of liberal democracy is part and parcel of the reflections appropriate in liberal learning. We recall that for Strauss, there is no permanent dwelling place on earth for man. No historical period is a permanent dwelling place for man – the moments of history are ever slipping away. Liberal learning cannot simply identify itself with any time and place, even if one's time and place are fascinating and exciting (or devastating and depressing).

For Strauss, liberal learning calls us beyond ourselves and away from our locality. We have seen already that for Strauss the search for wisdom cannot be totally satisfied even through the most thorough examination of our earthly surroundings. Those who think that Strauss, insofar as he was not wholly attached to the liberal democratic tradition, must therefore have been attached to some earthly alternative that he, secretly or otherwise, advocated, have misunderstood him. It is possible to be attached in friendship and admiration to liberal democracy while thinking beyond it, not with a project for an alternative regime in mind but in response to the drawing of the soul toward the love of wisdom. To be "liberal" is not necessarily to be "modern," especially if to be modern means to radicalize the exploration of individuality. He says:

We are not permitted to be flatterers of democracy precisely because we are friends and allies of democracy. While we are not permitted to remain silent on the dangers to which democracy exposes itself as well as human excellence, we cannot forget the obvious fact that by giving freedom to all, democracy also gives freedom to those who care for human excellence. No one prevents us from cultivating our garden or from setting up outposts which may come to be regarded by many citizens as salutary to the republic and as deserving of giving to it its tone . . . We are indeed compelled to be specialists, but we can try to specialize in the most weighty matters or, to speak more simply and more nobly, in the one thing needful.[14]

Strauss did not seek therefore to politicize liberal education but to combat its politicization. To set up "outposts salutary to the republic" is a way of restating a basic characteristic of institutions of liberal learning, as companions, not propagandists.

But insofar as there is a widespread conviction that all human endeavor is political, it might look as if to depoliticize education is to

---

[14] Strauss, "Liberal Education and Responsibility," *LAM,* 24.

engage in a clever (or not so clever) form of politicization. At the same time, in a free society this eccentric philosophical vocation may be tolerated as the peculiar "specialty" of some individuals in a world of proliferating specialties in the division of labor. For Strauss, the peculiar specialty here is the pursuit of greatness through the study of great works as gateways to greatness.

Political greatness is one form of greatness but it is not, according to Strauss, the form of greatness sought by the philosopher. Indeed, the philosophical pursuit suggests the possibility of unknown or unrecognized greatness, or greatness in obscurity. Strauss rejected the thesis (derived from Hegel) that the fundamental and universal motive of human action is "recognition," which entails the proposition that philosophers must disguise their desire for power (or risk deceiving themselves), using philosophy for the sake of power, or their desire to influence those who have power, while talking as if they care more for the eternal things; or that the eternal things are not real and thus a great self-deception is at work, which is being overcome in modernity. Strauss rejects this modern historicization and politicization of philosophy – for him, political philosophy is not politicized philosophy:

It would not be difficult to show that the classical argument cannot be disposed of as easily as is now generally thought, and that liberal or constitutional democracy comes closer to what the classics demanded than any alternative that is viable in our age. In the last analysis, however, the classical argument derives its strength from the assumption that the wise do not desire to rule.[15]

Strauss was quite clear on the transpolitical character of the philosophic pursuit. Consider the following:

The classics identified satisfaction with happiness. The difference between the philosopher and the political man will then be a difference with respect to happiness. The philosopher's dominating passion is the desire for truth, i.e., for knowledge of the eternal order, or the eternal cause or causes of the whole. As he looks up in search for the eternal order, all human things and all human concerns reveal themselves to him in all clarity as paltry and ephemeral, and no one can find solid happiness in what he knows to be paltry and ephemeral.[16]

We do not have to pry into the heart of any one in order to know that, insofar as the philosopher, owing to the weakness of the flesh, becomes concerned with being recognized by others, he ceases to be a philosopher . . . being recognized by others has no necessary connection with the quest for the eternal order . . . The self-admiration of the philosopher is in this respect akin to "the good conscience" which as such does not require confirmation by others.[17]

[15] Strauss, "Restatement on Xenophon," in *OT*, 194.
[16] Strauss, "Restatement on Xenophon," in *OT*, 197–198.
[17] Strauss, "Restatement on Xenophon," in *OT*, 203–204.

For Strauss, the pursuit of greatness through the study of the great works can be combined with – perhaps even will encourage – the moderation of expectations in the world, that is, will moderate both excessive individualism and also abstract utopianism. The primary motive for such study is not the hope of political success. However, there is another side to this because the Socratic example shows us philosophy entering the public arena. In a liberal democratic society, there is a threat to greatness insofar as there is a prejudice in favor of strong egalitarianism. Such a society is both liberal, emphasizing freedom, independence, and self-development, but also democratic, emphasizing the equality of all persons and concern for the welfare of others, even to the point of sacrificing the self. Under the influence of classical philosophy, Strauss could conclude that the search for wisdom is the highest way for human beings to take, that there is a ranking of the ways of life possible for us. But in deference to the liberal democratic dispensation, one must seek reconciliation of the tension between lifting one's sights to the quest for the eternal things with the requirements of democratic citizenship.

Education to perfect gentlemanship, to human excellence, liberal education consists in reminding oneself of human excellence, of human greatness.[18]

How does Strauss make sense of this? Education to "perfect gentlemanship" has an aristocratic ring that may seem at first incompatible with education for democratic citizenship. All educators speak of excellence, but there is chronic debate over what we mean by it. Philosophical reflection on the meaning of excellence cannot be confined in advance to a limited range of thoughts. In liberal education, there is the matter of both encouraging the examined life, which may carry one beyond any earthly regime – even the least imperfect – and accepting the character of the democratic regime, which is actually open to friendly criticism to a degree not found everywhere on earth. We recall that the American Founders accepted the idea of a "natural aristocracy," one not based on status or inheritance, and they thought the presence of such naturally excellent individuals would improve the chances of sensible decisions in the continual task of maintaining equilibrium in the pursuit of both liberty and equality.[19]

At the same time, the Founders knew that to insure the success of the liberal democratic regime requires an educated citizenry beyond natural aristocracy. They saw that education is essential to the future well-being of the country. Strauss argues that democracy, understood in its ideal

[18] Strauss, "What is Liberal Education?" in *LAM*, 6.
[19] See William A. Galston, "Leo Strauss's Qualified Embrace of Liberal Democracy," this volume.

form, requires adult citizens who are virtuous. To be virtuous means
to understand the character of the polity such that there can be active,
intelligent, thoughtful participation. As Strauss puts it, "Democracy,
in a word, is meant to be an aristocracy which has broadened into a
universal aristocracy."[20] But in actuality, he points out we have failed
to universalize political virtue in this sense. We have instead elites and
a "mass culture" in which it is possible to indulge with little or no
liberal education, under the influence of those who have clever ideas
and schemes.

Strauss is saying that there is "good democracy" and "bad democracy." Good democracy promotes political education for all citizens.
Bad democracy encourages vulgar pleasure-seeking. Lest we lose sight
of good democracy altogether, we need liberal education:

Liberal education is the counterpoison to mass culture, to the corroding effects
of mass culture, to its inherent tendency to produce nothing but "specialists
without spirit or vision and voluptuaries without heart" [Max Weber]. Liberal
education is the ladder by which we try to ascend from mass democracy to
democracy as originally meant. Liberal education is the necessary endeavor to
found an aristocracy within democratic mass society. Liberal education reminds
those members of a mass democracy who have ears to hear, of human greatness.[21]

To encounter human greatness, if not directly at least through the
great works, will help us to recognize the "least unwise" among us.
Strauss thought that in a world of imperfect regimes what we should
hope for is the rule of the "least unwise." In rejecting the idea of a universal, homogeneous state that could only be pursued through tyrannical means involving the aggregation of enormous power, and which he
thought in any case to be impossible, not to say repugnant, he tried to
show that the "politics of recognition" encourages a tyrannical aspiration perhaps only restrained by pragmatic calculations. The education
of citizens, which is one central task of liberal education, will guide the
perfectly legitimate aspiration to greatness toward what, for Strauss, is
an even higher aspiration that transcends greatness understood as holding power. Those who seek to rule the world must assume knowledge
and insight which, on the Socratic principle, they cannot have. Such
rule will always come by imposition.

Strauss wrote:

Hence, what pretends to be absolute rule of the wise will in fact be absolute
rule of unwise men. But if this is the case, the universal state would seem to
be impossible. For the universal state requires universal agreement regarding

[20] Strauss, "What is Liberal Education?" in *LAM*, 4.
[21] Strauss, "What is Liberal Education?" in *LAM*, 5.

the fundamentals, and such agreement is possible only on the basis of genuine knowledge or wisdom. Agreement based on opinion can never become universal agreement. Every faith that lays claim to universality, i.e., to be universally accepted, of necessity provokes a counter-faith which raises the same claim. The diffusion among the unwise of genuine knowledge that was acquired by the wise would be of no help, for through its diffusion or dilution, knowledge inevitably transforms itself into opinion, prejudice, or mere belief. The utmost in the direction of universality that one could expect is, then, an absolute rule of unwise men who control about half of the globe, the other half being ruled by other unwise men. It is not obvious that the extinction of all independent states but two will be a blessing. But it is obvious that absolute rule of the unwise is less desirable than their limited rule; the unwise ought to rule under law.[22]

When Strauss said this in the 1950s, he was of course thinking of the Cold War and the politics of bipolarity. He expressed a reservation about a bipolar world without saying in so many words that smaller is better, but he is clear on the need for limited government as achieved in a rule of law regime. He adds: "There will always be men (*andres*) who will revolt against a state which is destructive of humanity or in which there is no longer a possibility of noble action and of great deeds."[23]

It seems therefore that universal empire is not conducive to nobility and great deeds, as Strauss understood them. This is his "classical restraint" preferring the small republic, seeking to articulate an outlook that he saw is definitely not in favor in the modern situation. Those who revolt against, or are revolted by, mediocrity are natural prospects for liberal education and maybe the philosophical life. What course of action should follow?

It would be easy enough for the philosopher to stand aside and seek comfort within a circle of like-minded friends, but this can become itself a type of cave in which friends cultivate and reinforce inadequately examined prejudices.[24] Thus, the philosopher must go out into the marketplace and mingle with the politicians in the multiplicity of the realm of opinions. Strauss insisted that he must do this actually to remain a philosopher, but not because he wishes to achieve political recognition or success in the Hegelian/Marxist manner. Dialogue with others, including those who are not immediately congenial or are hostile, is essential to maintaining the vitality of the philosophical life,

[22] Strauss, "Restatement on Xenophon," in *OT*, 193.
[23] Strauss, "Restatement on Xenophon," in *OT*, 209.
[24] For the suggestion that Strauss himself anticipated the dangers of a self-reinforcing sect, see Nathan Tarcov, "On a Certain Critique of 'Straussianism,'" *Review of Politics*, 53 (1991): 3–18.

and to keeping alive the reference to life's circumstances, and avoiding abstraction. Moreover, dialogue is not intended to be a competition for victory in debate, or to produce material rewards. When Socrates asserts that the philosopher must learn to make a friend of death, he means to show that the ordinary motives of life include efforts – ultimately vain, of course – to fend off mortality. The courage to philosophize will thus be tested. Conflict will arise from this venture into the public realm because such ventures inevitably look to many to be political – entry into the political sphere makes one unavoidably subject to political and economic interpretations of motive – even if they are not. All human beings seek happiness, to be sure, but the varying meanings of happiness make a crucial difference.

These reflections on philosophy and the philosopher are essential to Strauss's formulation of the nature of liberal education. This is his Socratic questioning of conventional wisdom. He is also saying that not to question in this way is not to meet the requirements of liberal education. It is likely that liberal education as Strauss understands it will encourage a way of life that passes between dogmatism and radical skepticism, a way of life that avoids either claiming absolute knowledge or rejecting the quest for knowledge as illusory. Liberal education moderates the passions in one way while exciting them in another, thus encouraging a response to the call of greatness in a way that neither seeks political power nor demands ruthlessness, nor encourages disruptive disobedience. It is said that liberal learning involves the commitment to learning "for its own sake." It is also said that liberal learning must be "relevant" to the current needs and desires of society. In seeking to explain or justify itself, liberal learning is always caught between these considerations. In a way, the insistence on learning for its own sake is what makes liberal learning relevant because it tries to safeguard the openness of the soul to the higher things in an atmosphere conducive to blocking that openness.

Strauss's antagonist Kojève identified clearly what is at stake in asserting his historicist opposition to Strauss's neoclassicism. Kojève wrote:

Indeed, in order to justify the philosopher's absolute *isolation*, one has to grant that Being is essentially immutable in itself and eternally identical with itself...If such is indeed the case, then the philosopher can and must isolate himself from the changing and tumultuous world...But if one does not accept this *theistic* conception of Truth (and of Being), if one accepts the radical Hegelian atheism according to which Being itself is essentially temporal (Being = Becoming) and creates itself insofar as it is discursively revealed in the course of history...and if one does not want to sink into the skeptical relativism which ruins the very idea of Truth and thus the quest for it or philosophy, then one has to flee the absolute solitude... [and] "participate" in history.[25]

Strauss's response to this is to insist on the distinction between Being and Becoming, but also to qualify the philosopher's felt need of isolation (or distance from distraction) in respect to the necessity of the marketplace. The philosophical task is to keep openness to the question of Being alive, especially in pursuers of wisdom themselves but also among those who are inclined to avoid it or deny its significance. Conducted according to a principle of moderation, this is a service to humanity compatible with the character of a liberal democracy. It is the friendly criticism of which we have previously spoken.

Liberal education thus requires fostering this openness, not by opposing a dogmatic version of "Natural Right" or the "eternal things" to a dogmatic version of historicism and the endlessness of becoming but by insisting on addressing the question forthrightly and rigorously. One may not assume that these alternatives will be adjudicated by the movements of world history: that would be to presuppose the modern answer. The choice to think unhistorically will be seen to be a choice that must be argued for. But equally, the choice to think historically must be seen as a choice that must be argued for. For Strauss, the philosophical quest involves the assessment of the alternatives and, because they are fundamental alternatives, educational programs that do not address the fundamental alternatives are insecurely founded and are likely to lose their way in proliferating disciplinary investigations that obscure what is at stake but that have great appeal for their relevance to the moment and the opportunities for employment they may afford.

To really encounter the fundamental alternatives is to participate in the drama of human existence. Liberal education thus understood directs us away from distractions of the here and now to the quest for wisdom. Yet even if most human affairs are "paltry and ephemeral," they still affect the prospects of liberal learning. The value of liberal education does not disclose itself automatically; figuring out how to defend and expound it in our time and place is a task we cannot avoid. Liberal education has been kept alive and handed down to us, and we must keep it alive and hand it on to our successors. To experience such education is to know this obligation and to embrace it. If there is doubt about our duty, then we have not yet attained a sufficient grasp of liberal education. The encounter discloses a greatness that far exceeds human greatness, revealing both the teacher and the learner to be oriented to

[25] Kojéve, "Tyranny and Wisdom," in *OT*, 151–152.

each other in the intersection of the eternal and the temporal, destined to live most humanly when most immersed in the tension.

As a practical matter, Strauss also reflects on a basic curricular issue: What should students be doing? He answers that they should read great books.[26] Liberal education may encourage modesty about politics while also encouraging philosophical boldness:

The responsible and clear distinction between ends which are decent and ends which are not is in a way presupposed by politics. It surely transcends politics. For everything which comes into being through human action and is therefore perishable or corruptible presupposes incorruptible and unchangeable things – for instance, the natural order of the human soul – with a view to which we can distinguish between right and wrong actions.[27]

But how to initiate the encounter with greatness? In answering this question, Strauss elaborated on the distinction between "liberal education" and "responsibility." He found the term "responsible" to be morally ambiguous, as it has replaced words such as "just" or "conscientious." We can be responsible in widely varying ways for better or worse. We can be responsible job holders without being particularly admirable, let alone noble or courageous. To Strauss, this meant a lowering of expectations stimulated by the momentum toward equalizing life situations in a democratic environment. This fits also with the resort to "behavioral objectives" or "outcomes" as the means to measure, in a quantitative way, "success" in education. "Success" in terms that are difficult to measure, or impossible to measure in quantitative terms, become invisible. How shall we resist this?

We cannot speak only of "responsible" teaching or "responsible classroom performance" given the moral ambiguity of the term "responsible." The distinction of greater and lesser works – the distinctions between high and low culture – and the ways in which students naturally distinguish themselves from each other in their performances are all called into question as if to raise them is to act "irresponsibly," which in this context may well mean to act "insensitively" in an "elitist" or "politically incorrect" fashion. The great works encourage distinctions and analyses that challenge the contemporary environment in which we nowadays encounter them. Strauss here again conjoins modesty with boldness:

[26] Strauss, "What is Liberal Education?" in *LAM*, 6: "We are compelled to live with books. But life is too short to live with any but the greatest books." For a qualified critique of the great books curriculum, see *mirabile dictu*, Bloom, *Closing of the American Mind*, 344.

[27] Strauss, "Liberal Education and Responsibility," in *LAM*, 13.

Liberal education, which consists in the constant intercourse with the greatest minds, is a training in the highest forms of modesty, not to say of humility. It is at the same time a training in boldness: it demands from us a complete break with the noise, the rush, the thoughtlessness, the cheapness of the Vanity Fair of the intellectuals as well as their enemies. It demands from us the boldness implied in the resolve to regard the accepted views as mere opinions, or to regard the average opinions as extreme opinions which are at least as likely to be wrong as the most strange or least popular opinions. Liberal education is liberation from vulgarity. The Greeks had a beautiful word for "vulgarity"; they called it *apeirokalia*, lack of experience in things beautiful. Liberal education supplies us with experience in things beautiful.[28]

We are thus led to the distinction between "current wisdom" or "prevailing wisdom" and "wisdom as such." This begins with a respect for ancient thinkers and a willingness to reflect on their teachings:

The facile delusions which conceal from us our true situation all amount to this: that we are, or can be, wiser than the wisest men of the past. We are thus induced to play the part, not of attentive and docile listeners, but of impresarios or lion tamers. Yet we must face our awesome situation, created by the necessity that we try to be more than attentive and docile listeners, namely, judges, and yet we are not competent to be judges. As it seems to me, the cause of this situation is that we have lost all simply authoritative traditions in which we could trust, the *nomos* which gave us authoritative guidance, because our immediate teachers and teachers' teachers believed in the possibility of a simply rational society. Each of us here is compelled to find his bearings by his own powers, however defective they may be.[29]

To think seriously about these matters requires thinking philosophically; to think seriously about education is to think seriously about the situation of society, and hence to think through the question of education means to think through the political situation of our time. We cannot do this without coming up against the differences between modern and ancient ways of thinking through:

According to classical philosophy the end of the philosophers is radically different from the end or ends actually pursued by the nonphilosophers. Modern philosophy comes into being when the end of philosophy is identified with the end which is capable of being actually pursued by all men. More precisely, philosophy is now asserted to be essentially subservient to the end which is capable of being actually pursued by all men ... the modern conception of philosophy is fundamentally democratic. The end of philosophy is now no longer what one may call disinterested contemplation of the eternal, but the relief of man's estate.[30]

[28] Strauss, "What is Liberal Education?" in *LAM*, 8.
[29] Strauss, "What is Liberal Education?" in *LAM*, 8.
[30] Strauss, "Liberal Education and Responsibility," in *LAM*, 19–20.

Strauss thus distinguished – without denying a necessary connection – between educating for democracy and elucidating the problem of liberal education in a democracy. In this respect, we distinguish between Strauss's substantial doubts about unqualified democracy and his regard for liberal democracy, or the regime in which the rule of law prevails and government is in the hands of the "least unwise." Nonetheless, the risk is there that the liberal education Strauss proposes will be accused of lacking compassion, constituting barriers to the fulfillment of the democratic/egalitarian project. Strauss will make "weaker arguments" stronger and "stronger arguments" weaker. Moreover, Strauss is fully aware that there is a further risk that some who are exposed to this education will take it as a license to satisfy their *libido dominandi*:

For we cannot expect that liberal education will lead all who benefit from it to understand their civic responsibility in the same way or to agree politically. Karl Marx, the father of communism, and Friedrich Nietzsche, the stepgrandfather of fascism, were liberally educated on a level to which we cannot even hope to aspire. But perhaps one can say that their grandiose failures make it easier for us who have experienced those failures to understand again the old saying that wisdom cannot be separated from moderation and hence to understand that wisdom requires unhesitating loyalty to a decent constitution and even to the cause of constitutionalism. Moderation will protect us against the twin dangers of visionary expectations from politics and unmanly contempt for politics. Thus it may again become true that all liberally educated men will be politically moderate men. It is in this way that the liberally educated may again receive a hearing in the market place.[31]

Strauss's analysis of politics and education led him to the defense of virtue manifested in a combination of boldness and moderation, in a willingness to defend constitutional government, and in the insight that tyranny is tyranny whatever grandeur may be attached to its defense. The safeguard of the modern achievement will be found in ancient philosophy and traditional liberal education, and the essential experience of liberal learning will be conveyed through the great books, which are great because they instantiate the essential experience.

[31] Strauss, "Liberal Education and Responsibility," in *LAM*, 24.

12   Straussians

More than most thinkers of the twentieth century, Leo Strauss polarized his audience. One was either for him or against him, influenced by him, or repelled by him. Thus has arisen the phenomenon, nearly unique among the century's academic thinkers, of a recognized group of followers, called "Straussians." Where and when the label arose, and what exactly it means, are uncertain. It seems originally to have been a label invented by the opponents of Strauss and applied to individuals who had studied with or were manifestly influenced by him. Over time, and somewhat reluctantly, the label appears to have been accepted by many, if not all, of those to whom it has been applied.

The label originally applied to a loosely defined group of academics, but in the early twenty-first century, especially in the moment near the beginning of the Iraq War of 2003, it leaped across the fire line separating the academic world and the world of politics and became attached to a group of political figures identified with the neoconservative movement and the Bush administration. Strauss was said to be the "guru" or the intellectual father of the neoconservatives and somehow, thirty years after his death, the inspiration for the Iraq War.[1] Most striking about the wildfire of accusation and denunciation of the political Straussians was how ill-informed and irresponsible this outburst of "Straussian-hunting" was. Some but nowhere near as many as those called Straussians had had some contact with Strauss or students of Strauss. But even with regard to them, no real connection between their political action and the thought of Strauss was ever established. These Straussians have about as much to do with Strauss as owners of Levi's, or admirers of the soundtrack of the film *2001: A Space Odyssey*. They will henceforward be ignored in this essay.

As originally applied, the label "Straussian" referred to a set of academics. It was meant to designate them as a group uncommonly

---

[1] See Shadia Drury, *The Political Ideas of Leo Strauss*, 2nd ed. (New York: Palgrave Macmillon, 2005); Nichols Xenos, *Cloaked in Virtue* (London: Routledge, 2007).

dedicated to following the doctrines of one individual. It was originally a label proposed in a spirit of enmity because it was intended to suggest, at the extreme, something like a cult or, more moderately, a group with a unified set of views, which views were decidedly not those of mainstream academics in the fields of political science or philosophy. In other words, it was meant to designate an "unorthodox orthodoxy."

That original attribution of unity of outlook has since given way to wide recognition, both by those within and without the Straussian world, that no such unity exists. The so-called Straussians have broken into different, sometimes warring, camps and to a discerning eye embody much less unity of viewpoint than, say, rational choice theorists or international relations realists in political science.

Indeed, it is now a question (as it always was) whether there is any real content to the label "Straussian." At first, it could plausibly be applied to the students of Strauss, a direct biographical criterion of belonging. Now over thirty years after his death and with the entry of many of Strauss's ideas into the mainstream, and with the attenuated chains of filiation that arise from the existence of students of students, and even of students of students of students of Strauss, the number of those who might be identified in some way or another with Strauss has increased greatly, although the content of what they share has dropped dramatically. Given the variety of alleged "Straussians" it is a serious question whether the label has any real content or meaning. As one recent survey of the Straussians concluded:

Contrary to what is often said, those who have followed [Strauss] are far from single-minded in what they take from him, except perhaps for some threshold or methodological commitments. That philosophy is important, that political philosophy is a viable enterprise, that philosophic texts must be read in a particularly attentive manner, that the distinction between ancients and moderns means something (although just what remains contested in Straussian circles) – these propositions are what individuals known as Straussians mostly agree about.[2]

To this list of common characteristics must be added a self-conscious admiration and orientation toward but by no means comprehensive agreement with Strauss himself. A "Straussian" is then one who works to a degree that cannot be entirely specified within a framework of Strauss's question and chief concepts and, if the scholar in question is concerned with textual studies, deploys Strauss's methods of close reading.

---

[2] Catherine and Michael Zuckert, *The Truth About Leo Strauss* (Chicago: University of Chicago Press, 2006), 267.

According to these very loose criteria, the number of Straussians is quite large, and the studies they pursue extremely diverse and varied in character.[3] The large number and the diversity of subject matter make it quite impossible to canvass or catalogue the universe of Straussians. The principle of selection to be followed here will focus on the major lines of cleavage discernable among the Straussians. Those are often spoken of in terms of East Coast and West Coast, and even Midwest Straussians.[4] This classification serves some rough and ready purposes, but it is probably more revealing to identify some of the actual substantive disagreements among the Straussians. Of course, there are disagreements on how to read Plato's *Phaedrus*, or how to understand Locke; disagreements over whether the Supreme Court is a good or bad political institution – a myriad of disagreements of that sort. However, I propose to focus on a series of disagreements that cut closer to the core of Strauss's own thinking. The disagreements in question center on certain puzzles in Strauss's thinking. We might identity two such puzzles: what is the status of religion, or the problem of Athens and Jerusalem, and what is the status of morality, or the problem of Plato and Aristotle.

PUZZLE I: ON RELIGION

Strauss is well-known for having promoted interpretations of some philosophers, particularly early modern philosophers, as essentially antireligious, or at best tolerant of religion as civil religion – that is, as a social institution useful for procuring good order in society. Thus, he controversially reads Hobbes and Locke as atheists or near atheists who merely use religion for this-worldly purposes. This position is then often attributed to him as well.

There is much evidence to suggest that this is a misattribution, however. In his early book on *Spinoza's Critique of Religion*, Strauss does bring out the antireligious character of Spinoza's thinking, in particular his claim or assumption that he can supply a successful rationalist critique of biblical revelation. However, the chief point of Strauss's book is to deny that Spinoza had or could succeed at that critique. Indeed, there as in many places in his later writings Strauss explicitly asserts that reason cannot refute the possibility of revelation, and thus the possible

---

[3] See John Murley, ed., *Leo Strauss and His Legacy* (Lanham, MD: Lexington Books, 2005); Thomas Pangle, *Leo Strauss: An Introduction to His Thought and Intellectual Legacy* (Baltimore, MD: John Hopkins University Press, 2006), 89–120.

[4] See Zuckert and Zuckert, *Truth About Leo Strauss*, 197–260.

inherent validity of religion. He does not agree with the early moderns about religion.

Moreover, in a much later statement Strauss described his early work as devoted to the "theological-political problem" or the question of "how far the critique of orthodox theology – Jewish and Christian – deserved to be victorious."[5] In raising the question in this way, he clearly is not taking for granted that the critique deserved to be victorious. Significantly, he concluded the thought by affirming that "the theological-political problem has since remained *the* theme of my investigations."[6]

How Strauss himself meant to answer questions about religion has proved to be puzzling. Perhaps most striking is his insistence, contrary to the explicit doctrine of much of the tradition, that philosophy and revelation are altogether different and irreconcilable, to such a degree that no synthesis of the sort championed by, for example, Thomas Aquinas is possible. Strauss insists it is reason or revelation, not both.

Posing the philosophy-revelation issue as an either/or raises a whole further set of problems. Strauss also insisted that philosophy, properly understood – Socratically understood – was knowledge that one did not know, that is, that one did not know the whole. Philosophy is the quest for knowledge of the whole, but this knowledge is not attainable. Strauss argued that lacking knowledge of the whole, philosophy cannot refute the possibility of revelation. It cannot establish comprehensive knowledge of the whole such that it could demonstrate that there is no room for a mysterious revealing God as the source of that whole. The case is quite symmetrical for revelation considering philosophy: it can no more refute the possibility or even rightfulness of philosophy than philosophy can refute it. The one can "refute" the other only by question-begging, by assuming in advance the favored answer.

Therefore, it is not evident that one should opt for revelation, but it is also not evident that one should opt for philosophy. However, this state of things is particularly problematic for philosophy, for philosophy is the effort to take one's bearings by what is evident on the principle of sufficient reason. Strauss appears to say to rest on the inevident is fatal to the enterprise and life of philosophy. The failure of revelation to rest on evident foundations is not fatal for it because revelation has no such demand to fulfill. Given this line of reasoning, it seems especially difficult to affirm the philosophical life, but this is nonetheless precisely what Strauss does.[7]

---

[5] Strauss, "Preface to '*Hobbes Politische Wissenschaft'*," in *JPCM*, 453.

[6] Strauss, "Preface to '*Hobbes Politische Wissenschaft*,'" in *JPCM*, 453.

[7] See Catherine Zuckert, "Srauss's Return to Pre-Modern Thought" this volume.

Strauss's apparent position can be stated in a yet more concise way in the form of three propositions, or even a syllogism of sorts.

Proposition 1: To be a rationally defensible pursuit, philosophy must be able to refute revelation in a non-question-begging way.

Proposition 2: Philosophy cannot refute revelation.

Proposition 3: Philosophy is a rationally defensible pursuit.

Now it does not require mastery of the science of logic to appreciate that there is a problem of some sort in holding those three propositions together. In the case of the Athens-Jerusalem problem, the split among Straussians revolves around the attempt to figure out how Strauss himself resolved this problem.[8] Although they differ greatly among themselves, those Straussians who pursue this question follow a common strategy in attempting to resolve Strauss's puzzle. All in effect claim that Strauss denied one of the three propositions. But they disagree over which proposition to reject, producing four large alternatives, with some variants, among Straussians on the status of religion in Strauss's thinking: *rationalists*, who believe that philosophy can indeed refute the claims of revelation; *decisionists*, who deny that philosophy, as Strauss saw it, can refute revelation, and thus claim that Strauss arbitrarily or only exoterically decided for philosophy; *zetetics*, who argue that Strauss persisted in his view that the possibility of revelation could not be refuted by philosophy but who also maintain that Strauss had worked out a way to rationally justify the choice of the philosophical life without that refutation; and finally, *faith-based Straussians*, who believe that Strauss's position on the relation between faith and reason opens the way for faith or even compels it.

The most outspoken of the Straussian rationalists is Heinrich Meier, whose book *Leo Strauss and the Theological-Political Problem* purports to present Strauss's resolution to the problem, a resolution that according to Meier disposes of the claims of revealed religion of all types. Meier takes particularly seriously Strauss's claim that the theological-political problem was the abiding theme of his life work. He took that to mean that Strauss had recovered a notion of philosophy not as a set of doctrines but as a way of life devoted to rational inquiry and rational understanding. Philosophy is thus obliged to bring itself before the bar of reason and ask whether the philosophical life is itself defensible. The justification of philosophy must occur in dialogue with or against the chief alternative, or "the most powerful objection to

[8] See Leora Batnitzky, "Leo Strauss and the Theolologico-Political Predicament," this volume.

philosophy."[9] He quotes Strauss as affirming that "the Bible... offers the only challenge to the claims of philosophy which can reasonably be made..."[10] The two claims – the claim of philosophy that the true human good or happiness "consists in free investigation or insight" and the claim of the Bible that man's good or happiness "consists in obedience to God" – stand as the two most serious claims facing a human being. "No alternative," says Strauss, "is more fundamental that the alternative: human guidance or divine guidance. *Tertium non datum.*"[11]

Meier emphasizes the tension within Strauss's thinking between the first two propositions previous. He realizes that Strauss cannot draw the conclusion contained in Proposition 3 unless Strauss can achieve what Proposition 2 says cannot be achieved. Meier thus disregards Strauss's many affirmations of Proposition 2:

In order to counteract the avoidance of the most important question [the either/or of philosophy or obedience to God], the question of the right or the best life, Strauss not only makes the challenge posed by faith in revelation as strong as he possibly can. He also occasionally makes it stronger than it actually is, or... he allows the position of philosophy to appear weaker than it proves to be on closer examination.[12]

Meier in effect dismisses Proposition 2 as a type of rhetoric. He feels confident that he can do that, for he believes he has found the refutation of revelation that Strauss left in one page of unpublished notes for a lecture he delivered at a theological seminary in 1948. Meier devotes a chapter of his book to expanding these notes; that chapter presents the core of rationalist Straussianism.

The notes present a "genealogy" of the idea of the revealing God, and of what He reveals. As explicated by Meier, it is a dazzling explanation, which does indeed give us a theory of revelation. Starting from the fact of the need for human social or political existence and therefore of law, Strauss (as read by Meier) generates the biblical God and the main tenets of His revelation. That is, it reveals religion and the God of religion to be serving the needs of political society.

Although the substance of Strauss's genealogy certainly differs from that of, say, Freud or Hobbes, or any number of others who have developed genealogies of the religious phenomena, yet the type of explanation is just the same. Given this fact, one wonders whether Strauss himself would endorse Meier's form of rationalism. He surely was aware of

---

[9] Heinrich Meier, *Leo Strauss and the Theologico-Poliical Problem* (Cambridge, UK: Cambridge University Press, 2005), xiii.

[10] Meier, *Leo Strauss and the Theologico-Political Problem*, 6.

[11] Leo Strauss, "Reason and Revelation," in Meier, *Leo Strauss*, 149.

[12] Meier, *Leo Strauss and the Theologico-Political Problem*, 16.

genealogical accounts, and his general response to accounts of this sort would seem to apply to this one as well. A genealogy is an attempt to account by natural causes for what appears or claims to be the result of supernatural causes, of a miracle. However, Strauss asserts quite vehemently "there is... only one way of disposing of the possibility of revelation or miracles: one must prove that God is in no way mysterious, or that we have adequate knowledge of the essence of God."[13] Strauss's genealogy does not even presume to supply such knowledge of the divine essence nor, as he elsewhere demands, knowledge of the whole such that there could be no room in it for the mysterious creating revealing God whose ways are not man's ways.

Thus, many Straussians do not accept Meier's resolution of the Athens-Jerusalem issue. Meier quotes but does not seem to attend closely enough to an important programmatic statement by Strauss in his notes for his lecture on "Reason and Revelation": "The starting point of philosophic explanation of *revelation* would therefore be the fact that the foundation of belief in revelation is the belief in the central importance of morality."[14] Indeed, Strauss's genealogy takes the central importance of morality as its central thought, but note that Strauss speaks of the "philosophic explanation of *revelation*," not the philosophic refutation of revelation. Philosophy as the enterprise of explaining phenomena rationally must attempt to explain revelation, or purported revelation, along with many other phenomena of the natural and the human world. So long as philosophy cannot disprove that revelation is a superhuman or miraculous event, every explanation it supplies of revelation as a natural event is hypothetical or question-begging. Thinkers who begin from the premise of revelation can equally give an "explanation" of philosophy as a way of life: "philosophy is self-deification: philosophy has its root in *pride*."[15] This too is a question-begging or hypothetical explanation, but it has as much power in principle as Strauss's genealogy. Philosophy as philosophy must attempt such an explanation, and must be able on its own terms to mount a successful explanation, but Strauss points out that such explanations, in particular genealogies of all types, are incapable of supplying a refutation.

All the other sorts of Straussians but the rationalists thus affirm (at least on Strauss's behalf) Proposition 2. The decisionist Straussians like Stanley Rosen and Lawrence Lampert conclude from the conjunction

---

[13] Strauss, "Reason and Revelation," in Meier, *Leo Strauss and the Theologico-Political Problem*, 154.

[14] Strauss, "Reason and Revelation," in Meier, *Leo Strauss and the Theologico-Political Problem*, 165.

[15] Strauss, "Reason and Revelation," in Meier, *Leo Strauss and the Theologico-Political Problem*, 163.

of Propositions 1 and 2 that Proposition 3 cannot be true. Thus, they say Strauss is ultimately a skeptic about philosophy. The choice for philosophy is itself arbitrary or the product of a mere ungrounded act of will. On this account, Strauss is a decisionist. Lampert takes this thought in the direction of maintaining that Strauss is at bottom a Nietzschean – human life is an act of will performed on a tightrope over an abyss. Strauss endorses philosophy, thinks Lampert, but in the Nietzschean sense of philosophy as legislation of values.[16]

However, Lampert's Strauss is a timid Nietzschean. Lampert's Strauss differs greatly from the Strauss most readers meet on the pages of his books. The Strauss we normally see is one who objects to the very term "values"; he certainly does not admit to "legislating values." Lampert's Strauss is too timid to legislate values in the open as Nietzsche did, but he reverts in public to the view of philosophers as discoverers rather than creators of truth. But Lampert surmises Strauss knows better, but is afraid to shed his Clark Kent-everydayness to step forth as the Superman he could be.[17]

Rosen endorses a variant of this view but, if anything, he is even more radical than Lampert. Like Lampert, Rosen accepts the impossibility of Strauss's accepting Proposition 3. Strauss arbitrarily decides for philosophy. But Rosen does not dismiss Proposition 1 as Lampert does. His Strauss is therefore a decisionist with a bad conscience, or a decisionist who cannot believe in his own decision. Thus, at the end of the day his Strauss does not, cannot, believe in philosophy. Rosen concludes the Straussian teaching of the possibility and goodness of philosophy is an exoteric doctrine, persisted in by Strauss to keep other human beings from despairing of their situation out of despair for the truth. Strauss's "noble lie" is philosophy.[18]

In some respects, Rosen's Strauss is truer to the surface of Strauss than Lampert's because he takes seriously Strauss's Proposition 1 whereas Lampert merely ignores it or attributes it to Strauss's timidity. But in other respects, it is much further from the Strauss of the Strauss corpus, for no theme is more prominent in Strauss than philosophy itself and

---

[16] Lawrence Lampert, *Leo Strauss and Nietzsche* (Chicago: University of Chicago Press, 1996).

[17] Strauss himself always denied that he was a "philosopher," preferring the more humble term "scholar." See Strauss, "An Introduction to Heideggerian Existentialism," in *RCPR*, 29; see also "What is Liberal Education?" in *LAM*, 7: "We cannot be philosophers, but we can love philosophy, we can *try* to philosophize" (emphasis added). Whether Strauss's professions of modesty were sincere or an exoteric guise remains debatable.

[18] Stanley Rosen, *The Elusiveness of the Ordinary* (New Haven, CT: Yale University Press, 2002): 135–158.

Lampert, far better than Rosen, gives an account of Strauss that keeps the commitment to philosophy at the center.

Like the decisionists, faith-based Straussians also take very seriously Strauss's insistence on the limits of philosophy, that is, on philosophy as an incompletable quest for wisdom rather than wisdom itself. They take especially seriously his insistence that philosophy shows its limits in its inability to refute the possibility of revelation. There are at least two subgroups of faithful Straussians, one associated with so-called West Coast Straussians (as the rationalist position is loosely associated with East Coast Straussians) and one a rather separate grouping.

Like almost everything associated with West Coast Straussians, this branch of the faith-based group owes its main inspiration to Harry V. Jaffa who, in his earliest scholarly work, a book called *Thomism and Aristotelianism*, wrote like an orthodox Straussian in insisting on the wide distance that separated Aquinas's and Aristotle's moral philosophies.[19] Later on, Jaffa moved toward reconciliation of philosophy and the Bible, a reconciliation made possible, he thought, by the very limitation of philosophy that Strauss always emphasized. "Does not philosophy – confidence in the ultimate significance of reason – depend on an act of faith as much as belief in the God of the Bible?"[20] Jaffa is looking at the same aspect of Strauss's thinking that the decisionists do, the inability to fully establish Proposition 3, yet he sees that as an opening toward the reconciliation of reason and faith.

One of the most interesting of the adumbrations of the West Coast faith-based option is Susan Orr's *Jerusalem and Athens*, a book-length commentary on Strauss's essay "Jerusalem and Athens."[21] Like many of the close students of Strauss, she finds him to be practicing a special and surprising type of rhetoric in this essay and elsewhere. Strauss's rhetoric makes him "appear more impious on the surface than he is upon deeper examination."[22] It is the reverse of the rhetoric Strauss usually uncovered in philosophers of the past, who had a far more pious veneer than the depth of their thought supported. Why would Strauss

---

[19] Harry V. Jaffa, *Thomism and Aristotelianism: A Study of the Commentary by Thomas Aquinas of Aristotle's 'Nicomachean Ethics'* (Chicago: University of Chicago Press, 1952); reprinted, Westport, CT: Greenwood Press, 1979. For Strauss's critique of Thomas, see *NRH*, 163–164; see also James V. Schall, "A Latitude for Statesmanship? Strauss on St. Thomas," in *Leo Strauss: Political Philosopher and Jewish Thinker*, ed. Kenneth Deutsch and Walater Nicgorski (Lanham MD: Rowman & Littlefield, 1994), 211–230.

[20] Harry Jaffa, "The Bible and Political Philosophy," in *Leo Strauss: Political Philosopher and Jewish Thinker*, 199–200.

[21] Susan Orr, *Jerusalem and Athens* (Lanham, MD: Rowman & Littlefield, 1995).

[22] Orr, *Jerusalem and Athens*, 149.

practice this reverse rhetoric? Because according to Orr, the "orthodoxies" of the day are different: "atheism *had* become the reigning academic fashion."[23] Orr thinks that Strauss wants to "draw the reader
into discovering the Bible only after he has sufficiently disarmed him
by allowing him to hold on to his prejudices, at least temporarily." Having hooked his reader with his secular rhetoric, Strauss can then show
how Genesis "provides a comprehensive account of the whole." More
than that, he shows that Genesis "can even be understood as a rebuke
to philosophy."[24] She wavers between arguing that Strauss is essentially
neutral or even-handed in his presentation of Jerusalem and Athens, and
that "he tips the scales...towards Jerusalem."[25] Her last word indeed
is this: "Strauss's exegetical defense [comes] to the aid of the God of
Abraham, Isaac, and Jacob. Such an endeavor is undertaken with pious
intention and pious results."[26] In the last analysis, she gently aligns
Strauss with Jerusalem. Like the decisionists, she rejects Proposition 3
but unlike them, takes very seriously the alternative that Strauss always
holds up, that is, biblical revelation.

Not even all the faith-based Straussians, much less all the other sorts,
are satisfied with this solution, however. The other wing of the faith-
based camp has more filiation with the East Coast Straussians but has
decisively broken with them as well. It has taken a more oppositionist
stance toward Strauss himself, for it does not accept Orr's conclusion
that Strauss sides with Jerusalem over Athens, or Jaffa's various attempts
at making Strauss into a synthesizer almost of the Thomist type.

This second group of faith-based Straussians are serious critics. As
Ralph Hancock concludes one of his essays: "And so, without for a
moment forgetting our immense debt to Leo Strauss's unsurpassed elucidation of the political-philosophical problem, we must forsake once and
for all his 'final solution' and rediscover or find other ways to bring the
good of thinking together with the good of humanity."[27] Hancock's declaration of independence from Strauss confirms the point that Strauss
made about the centrality of morality for the faithful. Hancock and the
others in his camp "actually find human beings and their concerns (as
expressed in politics, religion, art) interesting, perhaps even lovable."[28]
They suspect that Strauss does not. Most importantly, they say Strauss
does not give sufficient weight to the connection between the moral and

[23] Orr, *Jerusalem and Athens*, 150.
[24] Orr, *Jerusalem and Athens*, 151.
[25] Orr, *Jerusalem and Athens*, 158.
[26] Orr, *Jerusalem and Athens*, 158.
[27] Ralph Hancock, "What Was Political Philosophy? Or The Straussian Philosopher and His Other," *Political Science Reviewer*, 36 (2007): 39.
[28] Hancock, "What Was Political Philosophy?" 39.

the sacred or the holy. All forms of human life including, or perhaps especially, philosophy, must recognize "the authority of something above oneself, even if one cannot fully – perhaps can hardly begin – to articulate the nature of this authority." However, the Straussian philosopher recognizes no such authority but aims and claims to achieve autonomy or full self-sufficiency.[29]

The faith-based Straussians thus break with Strauss, but do so in dialogue with him and in part via the path he has set forth. They rely heavily on his demonstration both of the nature of modernity (as, they say, inherently atheistic) and on his demonstration of its failures, moral, political, and philosophic. They accept Strauss's explanation of the self-unraveling dialectic of modernity, whereby the movement from Machiavelli's innovation of a new type of philosophy to Heidegger's declaration of the end of philosophy is a necessary or inevitable development.

The faith-based Straussians take seriously Strauss's three propositions, and unlike Rosen do not suspect him of insincerity or exotericism in affirming Proposition 3. They even more strongly reject the rationalist position. They rely on Strauss's case against philosophy's ability to refute revelation: Strauss has shown that revelation cannot be dismissed. They also emphasize Strauss's invocation of the erotic, that is, of the recognition of incompleteness and the striving for completeness and for eternity in the souls of human beings, a striving to which modern philosophy is blind.

Where they most emphatically take issue with Strauss is on the adequacy of the philosophical life as the fulfillment of that erotic striving. In this, they remind more than a little of Augustine but they find their way back to Augustine via Strauss's own depiction of the philosophical life. Strauss's rendition of the philosophical life, as opposed to, say, the neo-Platonic vein with which Augustine was most familiar, brings out all on its own the severe limitations of the philosophic life. It is a quest for knowledge of the whole but the chief discovery of Straussian Socratic philosophy is that such knowledge is in principle unattainable. Moreover, the Socratic philosopher is tied to society and other human beings, to the normal ways and concerns of ordinary persons, because the Socratic "way of opinion" requires the philosopher to begin from and remain ever in contact with "the city." As Peter Lawler well summarizes the faith-based Straussian position: they dissent "from both Strauss and Straussians by doubting that philosophy can truthfully liberate a human being, even the greatest thinkers, from their natural orientation toward morality and God."[30] Thus, although the faithful

---

[29] Hancock, "What Was Political Philosophy?" 38.

[30] Peter Lawler, "Introduction: Strauss, Straussians, and Faith-Based Students of Strauss," *Political Science Reviewer*, 36 (2007): 12.

Straussians are open to and, one presumes, committed to revelation, they claim to rest their case on an "anthropology" that points toward, if it does not fully get them to, the morality and divinity affirmed in revelation.[31]

In the final analysis, the faith-based position is surprisingly similar to the theological position Strauss described in his 1948 lecture on "Reason and Revelation." They charge Strauss with the same pridefulness, self-deification, and illusory self-sufficiency that Strauss identified as the standard theological case against philosophy.[32] Strauss demonstrates that the orthodox objections do not amount to a refutation of philosophy, for they are question-begging. In 1948, Strauss developed responses to all these criticisms. Perhaps most pertinent is this:

Take Pascal's famous argument of the misery of man without the God of Abraham, Isaac, and Jacob, an argument which is meant to be conclusive "*par nature*." This argument does not in any way refute Plato's thesis that the philosopher, as exemplified by Socrates in particular, lives on the islands of the blessed.[33]

That is to say, the admitted limitations of the philosopher's achievement do not destroy the fullness and satisfactoriness of the philosophical life, as witnessed by the testimony of those who have lived and observed that life.

The zetetic or Socratic Straussians deny Proposition 1. They notice that Strauss posits Proposition 1 only when he is presenting the modern philosophical position or "present day argument," as in his oft-quoted statement of the position in "Progress or Return," or the "social science position," as in his chapter on Max Weber in *Natural Right and History*.[34] The demand that philosophy refute revelation to secure its own enterprise is said by the Socratic Straussians not to be a demand of classical or Socratic philosophy but of modern philosophy. They maintain that the rationalists and decisionists, in particular, fail to take account of the recurring distinction Strauss draws between Socratic and modern philosophy vis-à-vis the problem of revelation. The moderns do indeed come to decisionism but, according to Strauss, the Socratics do not because the case for philosophy does not depend on a refutation of revelation. This is one of the important reasons for Strauss's call for a "return to the ancients."

[31] Hancock, "What Was Political Philosophy?" 26.
[32] See Marc Guerra, "Leo Strauss and the Recovery of the Theologico-Political Problem," *Political Science Reviewer*, 36 (2007): 75, 81.
[33] Strauss, "Reason and Revelation," in Meier, *Leo Strauss*, 101–102.
[34] Strauss, "Progress or Return," in *RCPR*, 260; Strauss, *NRH*, 35–80; Zuckert and Zuckert, *Truth*, 149–154; Guerra, "Leo Strauss and the Recovery of the Theologico-Political Problem," 67.

Strauss's clearest and fullest statement of the case is worth quoting. In a paragraph starting out as an explication of the thinker Yehuda Halevi, a great defender of orthodoxy, Strauss speaks of "the philosopher who refuses assent to revelation." Such refusal amounts to rejection of revelation, which is "unwarranted if revelation is not disproved." That is to say, "the philosopher, when confronted with revelation, *seems* to be compelled to contradict the very idea of philosophy by rejecting without sufficient grounds."[35]

But Strauss shows that there is a "philosophic reply" to this argument of the sophisticated orthodox like Halevi:

> The question of utmost urgency, the question which does not permit suspense [of judgment], is the question of how one should live. Now this question is settled for Socrates by the fact that he is a philosopher. As a philosopher he knows that we are ignorant of the most important things. The ignorance, the evident fact of this ignorance, evidently proves that quest for knowledge of the most important things is the most important thing for us.[36]

Strauss's conclusion is significantly framed in language that directly responds to the orthodox position to which he is replying. "Philosophy is then *evidently* the right way of life." As he emphasizes in this context, it is most definitely a "way of life" and not a set of doctrines, for what is "evident" is the rightfulness of the quest, not any given conclusions. The substance of any refutation must remain hypothetical, but the case for the philosopher's life rests not on the "evidentness" of the refutation but on the Socratic or zetetic case for the philosophical life. Philosophy is the "right way of life," Socrates and the Socratics conclude, despite the fact that Socratic ignorance is unable to refute the possibility of revelation.

PUZZLE 2: ON MORALITY

Strauss's first puzzle implicates one of his most well-known polarities – Jerusalem and Athens. The second puzzle implicates another much less recognized polarity in his thinking, that of Plato versus Aristotle. Normally, Strauss treats the classical thinkers as more or less agreeing in their understanding of natural right and philosophy. But implicitly, and at least in one place very explicitly, he insists on a distinction between Plato (or Socrates) and Aristotle. Socrates invented or discovered political philosophy, but Aristotle is said to have invented political science,

---

[35] Strauss, "Progress or Return," in *RCPR*, 259; emphasis added.
[36] Strauss, "Progress or Return," in *RCPR*, 259.

that is, a discipline supplying knowledge of political matters, which is "one discipline among a number of disciplines."[37] Aristotle's political science articulated the political as a closed and autonomous sphere, with prudence as its governing principle; Socrates and Plato see no such sphere. The "discovery" that allows Aristotle to treat the political in this way is, according to Strauss, the Aristotelian affirmation of "moral virtue," that is, the claim that "just and noble deeds" are "choice worthy for their own sake."[38]

Despite this large and important difference between the Socratic and the Aristotelian, Strauss commends both founders to his readers. Thus, in his "Epilogue" to a book critical of "the new science of politics," Strauss urges political scientists to adopt or take their bearings by Aristotelian political science.[39] But he is even better known for his championing of Socrates.

The group often known as East Coast Straussians gravitate most strongly to Strauss's Platonic pole and the so-called West Coast Straussians to the Aristotelian pole, although many Straussians adhere to the Aristotelian alternative without any particular connection to West Coast Straussianism. However, the issue between Platonic Straussians and Aristotelian Straussians is not over whether they have particular allegiance to one or the other of the Greek thinkers but rather how they understand the status of morality and politics, especially in relation to philosophy. And of course, to be a Platonist or an Aristotelian Straussian does not require that one focus one's attention or write on either of these two philosophers at all.

Aristotelian Straussians

This set of Straussians is in many ways much closer in their political philosophy to standard readings of the classical philosophers than are other Straussians. An early and outstanding version of the Aristotelian Straussian position was presented by one of Strauss's first students, Jaffa, who studied with Strauss at the New School for Social Research not long after Strauss arrived there. Jaffa has been a major figure in Straussian circles from the beginning, being the founder of what has come to be called West Coast Straussianism and one of the first to develop a Straussian approach to the study of American politics. He is probably best known for his two books on Abraham Lincoln, *Crisis*

---

[37] Strauss, *CM*, 25.
[38] Strauss, *CM*, 27.
[39] Strauss, "An Epilogue," in *LAM*, 203–223; see Nasser Behnegar, "Strauss and Social Science," this volume.

of the House Divided and *A New Birth of Freedom*, both devoted to developing an Aristotelian Straussian understanding of Lincoln and the American regime.[40]

Jaffa's two books on Lincoln both contain an underlying Aristotelian Straussianism as their central point. In his earlier *Crisis of the House Divided*, Jaffa argued that Lincoln came on the scene of American politics not merely to counter the pernicious doctrine of popular sovereignty sponsored by his debate opponent Stephen Douglas but to counter, reform, and elevate the principles of the American regime as bequeathed by the American Founders. The Founders had adopted the modern principles of Locke (and behind him of Hobbes) in constructing their regime, and that flaw at the outset threatened the integrity, success, and very existence of the American experiment by the 1850s. The crisis of the house divided was a crisis over the American principle, the principle of equality. The regime based on this principle proved remarkably vulnerable to the beguilements of the institution of slavery, either directly, as in the "slavery as positive good" ideology, or indirectly, as in Douglas's idea that one group of people had a right to vote on whether another group of people could be enslaved. Jaffa's Lincoln saw the American regime was in danger of becoming attached to the "might makes right" doctrines of Plato's Thrasymachus or Callicles. Jaffa thought this danger was not merely adventitious. Following Strauss, he saw the problem to reside in the deficient modern principle embodied in the American political order. According to those principles, the standard of right, natural rights, was nothing but the Hobbesean doctrine of right as based on the strongest passion, the fear of death. Such a doctrine lacks all nobility, and does not even secure the equality and right it aims to secure, for it says that if one group can get away with enslaving another, then this Hobbesean doctrine has very little to say against it.

The solution to which Jaffa appealed was an Aristotelianization of the regime. Lincoln's greatness resided not merely in his reaffirmation of the principle of equality in such a form as to stand unequivocally against slavery and in favor of government by consent, or government of, by, and for the people. More than that, Lincoln reconceived the good of equality in Aristotelian terms. Those terms involved affirming the deeper truth of human inequality: some human beings belong to "the tribe of the eagle" and are indeed "better" and deserve to rule. In effect, such was Aristotle's argument in Book III of his *Politics*. But the greatness of

---

[40] Harry V. Jaffa, *Crisis of the House Divided: An Interpretation of the Issues of the Lincoln-Douglas Debates* (Garden City, NY: Doubleday, 1959); *A New Birth of Freedom: Abraham Lincoln and the Coming of the Civil War* (Lanham, MD: Rowman & Littlefield, 2000).

MICHAEL ZUCKERT

a man is a moral greatness, superiority in virtue. As Jaffa presents the Aristotelian-Lincolnian position, the peak of moral virtue is magnanimity – the great-souled man who, in his greatness and virtue, is beyond concern for honor and power. The great-souled man is truly superior but has no interest in asserting his superiority.[41] The theoretical truth is then inequality because of the differential achievement of virtue or excellence but the practical or political truth is equality, for the truly excellent man will not raise claims to honor and rule, and those who do raise such claims are not truly excellent.[42]

Forty years later in *New Birth*, Jaffa has transformed many elements of his story but the Aristotelianism of his position remains constant. However, here he carries his Aristotelianism deeper into the founding: the Founders themselves were Aristotelians, as perhaps was Locke. Lincoln did not improve on the Founders, but he instead reaffirmed their position. Lincoln, Jefferson, and Locke all emphasized doctrines that seem the opposite of, or at least very different from, Aristotle's but Jaffa expends considerable energy establishing how, on Aristotelian grounds, they might arrive at such doctrines as are affirmed in the Declaration of Independence. The aim of this account is very similar to the earlier account in *Crisis*: to show that on Aristotelian grounds the American regime was aimed at the rationally noble and just (i.e., at virtue as understood by Aristotle). In other words, Jaffa's political science is a version of the Aristotelian political science Strauss recommended; it takes its bearings by the Aristotelian Straussian orientation around moral virtue. Jaffa has devoted his considerable polemic skills to defending this doctrine against liberals, other conservatives and, most vehemently, against other Straussians.

Another extremely thoughtful version of Aristotelian Straussianism, which focuses more directly on Aristotle himself, is Mary Nichols's *Citizens and Statesmen*.[43] Nichols is no West Coast Straussian but instead was a student of Joseph Cropsey, a man very close to Strauss personally and his literary executor. Her work almost exclusively concerns the Greek philosophers, with two books on Plato in addition to her book

---

[41] For Jaffa's views on magnanimity, see *Thomism and Aristotelianism*, 116–141. The theme of magnanimity or greatness of soul has been widely discussed in a number of recent Strauss-inspired works; see in particular Harvey C. Mansfield, *Manliness* (New Haven: Yale University Press, 2006) and Robert Faulkner, *The Case for Greatness: Honorable Ambition and Its Critics* (New Haven: Yale University Press, 2007).

[42] Jaffa, *Crisis of the House Divided*, 183–235.

[43] Mary P. Nichols, *Citizens and Statesmen* (Lanham, MD: Rowman & Littlefield, 1992).

on Aristotle, and a book on the films of Woody Allen, only an apparent exception.[44] Her book on Aristotle is explicitly addressed against the Platonic Straussian reading of Aristotle and political life. Her study shares the spirit of Aristide Tessitore's comment about Aristotle:

Unlike Plato, Aristotle gives greater scope to the kind of moral and political excellence constrained by the vicissitudes of political life. Indeed he maintains that ethical virtue possesses a certain kind of self sufficiency, qualified to be sure, and is characterized by the high and admirable standard of reflectiveness found in the individual who embodies practical wisdom. Aristotle invests the non-philosophic way of life with unplatonic seriousness ... [45]

Like Jaffa, Nichols sees Aristotle as supplying a way to reconcile democracy and aristocracy, the claims of freedom (and equality) and the claims of virtue (excellence). However, more explicitly than Jaffa she probes the issue that tends to divide the Platonic from the Aristotelian Straussians, that is to say, the issue of philosophy. If philosophy is the highest human possibility, as Strauss and the Straussians tend to hold, and if philosophy is in inexorable tension with the city (i.e., with polit-ical life), as Strauss and the Straussians tend to aver, then political life cannot be the locus of the good life in any simple or straightforward way. If philosophy is the highest or best human life, what is then the status of morality and justice? And what is the status of political life itself?

As opposed to the Platonic Straussians who, as we shall see, tend to emphasize the differences and tensions among these three things, Nichols sees in Aristotle a comprehensive and successful reconcilia-tion of the three that Plato himself admittedly could not effect. Nichols locates her study between two alternative positions: the democratic view, which finds grounds for "participatory democracy" in Aristotle's theory, and the aristocratic view, which sees Aristotle's politics as sat-isfying (or suited only) to the "well-bred gentlemen" or the "few" who "are capable of such fulfillment."[46] At the extreme end of the aristo-crats, she locates the Platonic Straussian position that "views the value

[44] Mary P. Nichols, *Socrates and the Political Community: An Ancient Debate* (Albany, NY: State University New York Press, 1987); *Socrates on Friendship and Community: Reflections on Plato's 'Symposium,' 'Phaedrus' and 'Lysis'* (Cambridge, UK: Cambridge University Press, 2008); *Reconstructing Woody: Art, Love, and Life in the Films of Woody Allen* (Lanham, MD: Rowman & Littlefield, 1998).

[45] Aristide Tessitore, *Reading Aristotle's Ethics* (Albany, NY: State University New York Press, 1996), 69.

[46] Mary P. Nichols, *Citizens and Statesmen*, 2–3.

of politics, finally, less as a fulfillment of human nature than as a means of fostering the conditions in which the philosophic – and hence apolitical – virtue of the few [philosophers] can flourish."[47] She believes that both the democratic and aristocratic views have something to be said for them, even the extreme Platonic Straussian view, but she finds all three partial and incomplete. The truth about Aristotle and human nature is that "human beings realize their freedom – and fulfill their highest natural capacities – through the activities of citizens and statesmen." Aristotle brings out "the connection between the freedom the democrats seek through political participation and the virtue that aristocrats seek through elite rule."[48] His model of "polity," a combination or variety of combinations of the many and the few, is the basis for the existence in theory and practice of that "connection" or comprehensive presentation of the human political good.[49] She clearly affirms moral virtue, as Strauss identified that as the basis of Aristotle's "discovery" of political science.

Philosophy thus finds its place in Nichols's version of Aristotelian Straussianism. The philosopher is paradigmatically the political philosopher, not the apolitical contemplative. Aristotle's activity as a political philosopher is the model; it is at once a participation in ruling and being ruled, and a form of the type of "rational" life that is the political life. There is a continuity not a diremption between the democratic concerns with freedom, the aristocratic concern with virtue, and the philosophical concern with thinking and understanding. "*Politikē* [political science] is both the means to self-knowledge and the activity that best expresses it."[50]

Platonic Straussians

Many Straussians belong in this category but perhaps the one who has carried this line of thought furthest is Seth Benardete and the circle around him. Of course, there are many others including most of those known as East Coast Straussians.[51] The Platonic Straussians are far from affirming the comprehensive harmony that Nichols identifies as the one of true political philosophy. Benardete is perhaps the most radical spokesman for Platonic Straussianism. Unlike many of Strauss's

[47] Nichols, *Citizens and Statesmen*, 4.
[48] Nichols, *Citizens and Statesmen*, 4
[49] Nichols, *Citizens and Statesmen*, 85–125.
[50] Nichols, *Citizens and Statesmen*, 167.
[51] Just as the West Coast Straussians were created by Harry Jaffa, the East Coasters were the product of Allan Bloom; see Zuckert, *Truth About Leo Strauss*, 231–239.

other students, who were political scientists or members of philosophy departments, Benardete was a classicist, renowned in classical circles for his extraordinary expertise in the Greek language. He was also the author of a very large number of books and articles on topics in Greek poetry and philosophy.[52]

Benardete clearly saw his own work on Plato as rooted in Strauss's "rediscovery" of Plato, a rediscovery Benardete thought was as fundamental as Alfarabi's rediscovery of philosophy in the tenth century.[53] However, Benardete finds the original "rediscoverer" of philosophy to have been Socrates, as presented by Plato.[54] That first rediscovery, which was at the same time the discovery of political philosophy or the overcoming of the "false start of philosophy," was called by Socrates in the *Phaedo* his "second sailing." That type of Socratic philosophy is what Benardete saw Strauss to be practicing; it is also how he identified his own works, as his interpretation of Plato's *Republic*, titled *Socrates' Second Sailing*, illustrates.[55]

The idea of the "second sailing" is central to Benardete's understanding of Plato's philosophy and forms the basis for his often brilliant and always difficult interpretive studies of the dialogues. Every dialogue, when read Benardete-like – that is, when read in the full appreciation of the interaction of argument and action – induces in the reader the Socratic experience of the second sailing, that is, the emergence of "an entirely new argument . . . that could never have been expected from the argument on the written page."[56] That emergence comes with "revolutionary unexpectedness" and involves a "turnaround" in what the reader sees in the dialogue. It is not too much to say that Benardete sets the dialogues on their heads in that he discovers meanings in them almost

---

[52] Among some of Benardete's prodigious works, see "Sophocles' *Oedipus Tyrannus*" in *Ancients and Moderns*, ed. Joseph Cropsey (New York: Basic Books, 1964), 1–15; *Herodotean Inquiries* (The Hague: Martinus Nijhoff, 1969); *The Rhetoric of Philosophy and Morality: Plato's 'Gorgias' and 'Phaedrus'* (Chicago: University of Chicago Press, 1991); *Plato's 'Laws': The Discovery of Being* (Chicago: University of Chicago Press, 2000). For a selected bibliography of Benardete's work, see *Achilles and Hector: The Homeric Hero*, ed. Ronna Burger and Michael Davis (South Bend, IN: St. Augustine's Press, 2005), 136–140.

[53] Seth Benardete, *The Argument of the Action: Essays on Greek Poetry and Philosophy*, ed. Ronna Burger and Michael Davis (Chicago: University of Chicago Press, 2000), 407.

[54] Benardete, *The Argument of the Action*, 408.

[55] Seth Benardete, *Socrates' Second Sailing: On Plato's 'Republic'* (Chicago: University of Chicago Press, 1992).

[56] Ronna Berger and Michael Davis, "Introduction," in Benardete, *The Argument and the Action*, xi.

opposite to what the surface of the dialogue would appear to be presenting. He argues the surface argument always fails and metamorphoses
into something quite different. His "revolutionary" readings of Plato
are clearly descendents of Strauss's own remarkable and controversial
readings. Strauss famously argued the *Republic* is not an advocacy of the
rule of philosopher-kings but a demonstration that such rule is highly
unlikely if not impossible, and perhaps not even desirable.[57] Benardete
takes what we might call Strauss's tendency to perverse readings (as
measured against the standard scholarly literature) of classical texts and
radicalizes it. Benardete is the master of paradox and reversal.

A particularly revealing case in point, which is also highly revealing of
Benardete's treatment of the puzzle about morality, is his interpretation
of Plato's *Gorgias*. That dialogue is an especially difficult test case for
the general line that Strauss takes on Plato. Rather than depreciating
or even dismissing moral virtue as mere "vulgar" or "political" virtue,
Socrates argues in *Gorgias* that "it is better to suffer injustice than to
do it." Socrates's interlocutors, worldly men one and all, have a difficult
time believing Socrates is serious about this thesis. So does Benardete.

In the "Introduction" to his study of *Gorgias*, Benardete boldly announces that "Socrates . . . is not out to defend morality but to understand 'so-called rhetoric.'"[58] The radicalism of Benardete's interpretation stands out when we place it in the context of the more standard
reading of the dialogue: In *Gorgias*, Socrates has conversations with
three men – the famous rhetorician Gorgias; Polus, a student of Gorgias,
now a professor of the subject himself; and Callicles, a young Athenian
aspiring politician who has also studied rhetoric with Gorgias. In appearance, the discussion finds Socrates pitted against three men who are at
best indifferent to justice (Gorgias) or, at worst, a friend to tyranny
(Polus) or a defender of injustice (Callicles). In that context, Socrates
rises to the defense of justice and promotes the very strong thesis about
morality quoted previously. That is how the dialogue is usually read.

Benardete turns all this almost on its head. The rhetoricians are not
champions of injustice; Socrates is not a champion of justice. (It is not
that Socrates is a champion of injustice – not at all – but he is a champion of philosophy, i.e., of his knowledge of ignorance.) The morality
that the rhetoricians champion (somewhat contrary to their own self-
understanding) is the position that Socrates brings to explicitness in his

---

[57] The *locus classicus* of Strauss's famous thesis about the undesirability of the
philosopher-kings is his "On Plato's *Republic*" in *CM*, 50–138; see also, Allan
Bloom, "Interpretive Essay," *The Republic of Plato* (New York: Basic Books,
1968), 307–436.
[58] Benardete, *The Rhetoric of Morality and Philosophy*, 1.

moral formula "it is better to suffer injustice than to do it." Benardete argues the rhetoricians are moralists, and rhetoric as such is a type of moralism. Socrates does not defend this moralism in *Gorgias* but supplies a critique of it. The critique is needed because moralism is the form of dogmatism that stands in the way of philosophy as genuinely open-minded inquiry into the truth of being. Socrates's critique does not have a practical aim (e.g., to overturn public morality) but is solely oriented toward opening up the philosophical life for those capable of it. The common misreading of the dialogue as a Socratic defense rather than critique of moralism is an indication of the degree to which Plato/Socrates do not aim to overturn ordinary morality.

The deeper ground for the claims Benardete raises in his interpretation of *Gorgias* are contained in the *Republic* as he reads it. The *Republic* is the attempt to "postulate ... utopia's reality," an attempt necessary to ground "morality" as "based on the absoluteness of the will," that is, the attempt to show how morality can be an end "in itself."[59] It is a positing meant to reveal the nature of justice, not to effectuate justice. Therefore, the *Republic* is not merely, as Strauss always said, a critique of political idealism and the utopian desire for perfect justice but a critique of justice or moral virtue as such.[60] As Benardete says, "the 'idea' of justice ... is the delusion of thumos," that is, of the spirited part of the soul.[61] The centerpiece of Benardete's interpretation of the *Republic*, perhaps of all of his own thinking, is his analysis of the "thumoeidetic," the term Socrates uses in the *Republic* to refer to the spirited part of the soul. Benardete points out it is an odd term, for it combines the word *thumos* ("spirit, heart") with the root for the word *eidos*, one of the terms Plato uses in developing his famous doctrine of the ideas. In a subtle analysis of the brief discussion of the thumoeidetic in Book IV of the *Republic*, Benardete attributes to Plato (and apparently accepts as his own) the views that the thumoeidetic (i.e., a nonrational part of the soul) is the source of both the stable intellectual (eidetic) structures human beings, particularly philosophers, posit in their quest to understand, and at the same time the source of the understanding of human soul as capable of morality and thus under moral injunctions. In effect, the structures developed by the thumoeidetic are the results of the "first sailing." The "second sailing," which perforce begins with the opinions and moral-intellectual structures of the "first sailing," necessarily but subtly has the character of a deconstruction of those "given" structures. Indeed,

---

[59] Seth Benardete, "Leo Strauss's *The City and Man*," *Political Science Reviewer*, 8 (1978): 1–20.

[60] Strauss, *CM*, 65, 138.

[61] Benardete, *Second Sailing*, 91–102.

genuine philosophy is deeply and thoroughly in tension with the city, which is constituted precisely through the moral idealism produced by the thumoeidetic. According to this version of Platonic Straussianism, philosophy is thus very far from affirming moral virtue, the discovery or affirmation of which formed, according to Strauss, the basis for Aristotle's political science.

This version of Platonic Straussianism is also very far from affirming the type of harmony among morality (the just and the noble), politics, and philosophy that Nichols defends, as is visible in Michael Davis's very different book on Aristotle's *Politics*. Davis never studied with Strauss; the largest influence on him has been his friendship with Benardete, who is for him "the full embodiment ... of the philosophic life."[62] One needs look no farther than the introduction to his *The Politics of Philosophy* to see how different his grasp of the political in relation to both morality and philosophy is from that of Nichols. Where she treats the moral virtues as largely unproblematic, Davis begins with a very different picture:

The *Nicomachean Ethics* as a whole is the working out of the problematic nature of human virtue and so of human nature itself first within the particular virtues themselves and then in relations among the particular virtues that culminate in this tension between the godlike self-sufficiency of pride and the acknowledged mutual dependence of justice. The problem is then worked through in terms of the tension between the whole of moral virtue, understood as the correct disposition of our appetites, and intellectual virtue itself in the tension between *sophia* [wisdom] and *phronesis* [prudence].[63]

The multiple tensions or dualisms reproduced at every level of Aristotle's presentation can find no "third" in which they are reconciled.[64] Davis's Aristotle is not a thinker of harmonies as is Nichols's.

The particular character of Davis's interpretative method comes out in his analysis of nearly every book of the *Politics*. Where Nichols attempts to supply an overall and coherent account of the argument following for the most part Aristotle's own presentation, Davis instead begins with puzzles, anomalies, and oddities in the Aristotelian text. Although he does not use the language of Benardete, Davis treats the surface of the text, what most readers focus on, as elements of the "first sailing," and the oddities that pop up every now and again as the clues to get to the "second sailing" thought. Thus, Book V of the *Politics*,

---

[62] Michael Davis, *Wonderlust: Ruminations on Liberal Education* (South Bend, IN: Saint Augustine's Press, 2006), 131.

[63] Michael Davis, *The Politics of Philosophy* (Lanham, MD: Rowman & Littlefield, 1996), 5.

[64] Davis, *The Politics of Philosophy*, 5.

which appears to be about revolution, turns out to be about *eros*. The significant point of departure for understanding Book II of the *Politics* is not so much the substance of what Aristotle has to say in criticism of his predecessors but the fact that the book is obtrusively divided and subdivided into units of three, for doing which Aristotle criticized Hippodamus, his predecessors, in this very part of the *Politics*.

For Davis moral virtue, about the coherence of which he has his doubts, then does not provide the ground or orienting principle for understanding politics as an autonomous or self-enclosed sphere, but philosophy itself is the model, pattern, and core of political life and provides the "solution" to the political problem so far as there is one. However, this is not to say that Davis accepts the type of diminution of the tension between politics and philosophy that Nichols does. That tension is central, and if anything intensified, by Davis's attempt to demonstrate "that the connection between politics and philosophy is much deeper than is ordinarily understood."[65]

His treatment of Book I of the *Politics* is indicative of the Benardete-like reversals he effects. It seems to most readers Book I is meant by Aristotle to establish the thesis that the *polis* (the political association) and therewith political life is natural, and "that we who are by nature political can for that reason live naturally, and so, happily, within a political order." According to Davis, Aristotle no more is defending that thesis than Plato, according to Benardete, is arguing that "it is better to suffer injustice than to do it." What Aristotle does show in the *Politics* is "the problematic character of [the] claim that it is [natural]."[66] Davis shows that it is problematic in multiple senses. The *polis* is held to be the natural end for the lesser and prior human associations, which are themselves said to be natural. The basic unit of the *polis* is the household, which consists according to Aristotle of father-husband, wife-mother, children, and slaves. Given the natural sexual force that brings man and woman together and the natural process that brings children, it is not implausible to affirm these relations as natural.

But what about slavery? Davis maintains Aristotle is driven to his notions about natural slaves to salvage the surface thesis that the household is natural, a minimal prerequisite to the thesis that the *polis* is natural. The attempt to establish the naturalness of slavery in turn drives Aristotle to formulate what Davis calls a doctrine of "strong teleology," that is, the claim that natural entities not only have ends within their own class of being (e.g., for a man to be a good man) but across classes, or in relation to something like a "great chain of being." Lower beings

---

[65] Davis, *The Politics of Philosophy*, xii.
[66] Davis, *The Politics of Philosophy*, 1, 29.

are naturally ordered to the good of the higher beings. Thus, animals exist for the sake of human beings, some men are slaves for the sake of other (higher) men. But this notion of teleology threatens the integrity of all classes, and points toward a rigid hierarchy and subordination of all to the one best, which is incompatible with the nature of politics and the generic character of classes. Davis concludes that the point of the discussion of natural slaves is to show how problematic the notion of the naturalness of the *polis* is, and how problematic the conception of nature to which one would have to appeal to make good the claims about natural slaves. It is an argument meant to undercut or, better put, transform the thesis Aristotle is purportedly defending in Book I. To see the problem with the "first sailing" notion of naturalness is the point of the "second sailing" argument. Davis emerges at the end of the day then with a very Platonic reading of Aristotle and political life. It does not rest on the certainty of moral virtues; it does not abolish the tensions between the human good, philosophy, and the political life.

I have given the barest sketch here of Davis's argument, as I have of the others I have discussed. More than that, I have discussed only a few of the Straussians who can be located in terms of the two sets of puzzles that serve to distinguish many of the different groups of Straussians from each other, to say nothing of the fact that I have said nothing at all about the very large number of Straussians whose work cannot plausibly be related to these two puzzles. What is perhaps most striking at the end of this brief survey is how diverse the Straussians are. Strauss himself worried that schools were dangerous things for philosophy in that dogmas and other substitutes for thinking take root in philosophical schools. Although one could not fairly say that none of these vices ever appears in Straussian circles, still it would be yet fairer to say that intellectual vigor and disagreement are more apparent than hardening of the intellectual arteries. This result is largely the outcome of Strauss's way of presenting his thought. To the chagrin of the professionals, he left much unsaid, he left ambiguities and puzzles. His aim was not to transform the world but to understand it and to encourage the young, the ones he called "the puppies of the race," toward philosophy.[67] The existence of vibrant disagreements among the so-called Straussians are testimony to the degree to which he succeeded in not inspiring a set of dogmas and orthodoxies that straightjacket those who, loosely, follow him.

---

[67] Strauss, "Persecution and the Art of Writing," in *PAW*, 36. The reference is to Plato, *Republic*, 539b.

SELECT BIBLIOGRAPHY

BOOKS, ESSAYS, AND ANTHOLOGIES OF STRAUSS'S WRITINGS

The Argument and Action of Plato's Laws (Chicago: University of Chicago Press, 1975).

Correspondence Concerning Modernity, trans. George Elliott Tucker, *Independent Journal of Philosophy*, 4 (1983): 105–119 and 5/6 (1988): 177–192.

The City and Man (Chicago: University of Chicago Press, 1964).

The Early Writings (1921–32), ed. and trans. Michael Zank (Albany, NY: State University of New York Press, 2002).

Faith and Political Philosophy: The Correspondence Between Leo Strauss and Eric Voegelin, 1934–1964, ed. and trans. Peter Emberley and Barry Cooper (University Park, PA: Pennsylvania State University Press, 1993).

"Farabi's Plato," *Louis Ginzberg Jubilee Volume* (New York: American Academy for Jewish Research, 1945), 357–393.

Gesammlte Schriften, vols. 1–3, ed. Heinrich and Wiebke Meier (Stuttgart: J. B. Metzler, 1996–2001).

"German Nihilism," *Interpretation*, 26 (1999): 352–378.

Jewish Philosophy and the Crisis of Modernity, ed. Kenneth Hart Green (Albany, NY: State University of New York Press, 1997).

Liberalism Ancient and Modern (New York: Basic Books, 1968).

Natural Right and History (Chicago: University of Chicago Press, 1953).

"Notes on Carl Schmitt, *The Concept of the Political*," Heinrich Meier, *Carl Schmitt and Leo Strauss: The Hidden Dialogue*, trans. Harvey Lomax (Chicago: University of Chicago Press, 1995), 88–119.

"On Abravanel's Philosophical Tendency and Teaching," *Isaac Abravanel*, ed. J. B. Trend and H. Loewe (Cambridge, UK: Cambridge University Press, 1937), 93–129.

"On Collingwood's Philosophy of History," *Review of Metaphysics*, 5 (1952): 559–586.

"On the Intention of Rousseau," *Social Research*, 14 (1947): 455–487.

On Tyranny: Including the Strauss-Kojève Correspondence, ed. Victor Gourevitch and Michael S. Roth (Chicago: University of Chicago Press, 2000).

Persecution and the Art of Writing (Chicago: University of Chicago Press, 1952).

Philosophy and Law: Contributions to the Understanding of Maimonides and his Predecessors, trans. Eve Adler (Albany, NY: State University of New York Press, 1995).

The Political Philosophy of Hobbes: Its Basis and Its Genesis, trans. Elsa M. Sinclair (Oxford: Clarendon Press, 1936).

The Rebirth of Classical Political Rationalism, ed. Thomas Pangle (Chicago: University of Chicago Press, 1989).
"The Re-education of Axis Countries Concerning the Jews," *Review of Politics*, 69 (2007): 530–538.
Socrates and Aristophanes (New York: Basic Books, 1966).
"Some Remarks on the Political Science of Maimonides and Farabi," trans. Robert Bartlett *Interpretation*, 18 (1990): 3–30.
Spinoza's Critique of Religion, trans. Elsa M. Sinclair (New York: Schocken, 1965).
Studies in Platonic Political Philosophy, ed. Thomas Pangle (Chicago: University of Chicago Press, 1983).
Thoughts on Machiavelli (Chicago: University of Chicago Press, 1958).
"What Can We Learn From Political Theory?" *Review of Politics*, 69 (2007): 515–529.
What Is Political Philosophy and Other Studies (Glencoe, IL: The Free Press, 1959).
For a complete bibliography of Strauss's work see Heinrich Meier, *Die Denkbewegung von Leo Strauss* (Stuttgart: J. B. Metzler, 1996), 47–63. Readers can also consult the Leo Strauss Center Website at http://leostrausscenter@uchicago.edu/.

BOOKS ABOUT LEO STRAUSS

Batnitzky, Leora, *Leo Strauss and Emmanuel Levinas: Philosophy and the Politics of Revelation* (New York: Cambridge University Press, 2006).
Bluhm, Harald, *Ordnung der Ordnung: Das politische Philosophieren von Leo Strauss* (Berlin: Akademie Verlag, 2002).
Cohen, Jonathan, *Philosophers and Scholars: Wolfson, Guttmann, and Strauss on the History of Jewish Philosophy*, trans. Rachel Yarden (Lanham, MD: Rowman & Littlefield, 2007).
Devigne, Robert, *Recasting Conservatism: Oakeshott, Strauss, and the Response to Postmodernism* (New Haven, CT: Yale University Press, 1994).
Drury, Shadia, *The Political Ideas of Leo Strauss* (New York: Saint Martin's 1988).
Green, Kenneth Hart, *Jew and Philosopher: The Return to Maimonides in the Jewish Thought of Leo Strauss* (Albany, NY: State University of New York Press, 1993).
Janssens, David, *Between Jerusalem and Athens: Philosophy, Prophecy, and Politics in Leo Strauss's Early Thought* (Albany, NY: State University of New York Press, 2008).
Kartheininger, Markus, *Heterogenität: Politische Philosophie im Frühwerk von Leo Strauss* (Munich: Wilhelm Fink, 2006).
Kauffmann, Clemens, *Leo Strauss zur Einführung* (Hamburg: Junius, 1997).
Kauffmann, Clemens, *Strauss und Rawls: Das philosophische Dilemma der Politik* (Berlin: Duncker & Humblot, 2000).
Lampert, Laurence, *Leo Strauss and Nietzsche* (Chicago: University of Chicago Press, 1996).
Meier, Heinrich, *Carl Schmitt and Leo Strauss: The Hidden Dialogue*, trans. Harvey J. Lomax (Chicago: University of Chicago Press, 1995).
Meier, Heinrich, *Leo Strauss and the Theologico-Political Problem*, trans. Marcus Brainard (Cambridge, UK: Cambridge University Press, 2006).
Norton, Anne, *Leo Strauss and the Politics of American Empire* (New Haven, CT: Yale University Press, 2004).
Orr, Susan, *Jerusalem and Athens: Reason and Revelation in the Works of Leo Strauss* (Lanham, MD: Rowman & Littlefield, 1995).

Pangle, Thomas L., *Leo Strauss: An Introduction to his Thought and Intellectual Legacy* (Baltimore, MD: Johns Hopkins University Press, 2006).

Pelluchon, Corine, *Une autre raison, d'autres lumières. Essai sur la crise de la rationalité contemporaine* (Paris: Vrin, 2005).

Sfez, Gérald, *Leo Strauss, lecteur de Machiavel. La modernité du mal* (Paris: Ellipses, 2003).

Sfez, Gérald, *Leo Strauss, foi, et raison* (Paris: Beauchesne, 2007).

Sheppard, Eugene R., *Leo Strauss and the Politics of Exile: The Making of a Political Philosopher* (Waltham, MA: Brandeis University Press, 2006).

Smith, Steven B., *Reading Leo Strauss: Politics, Philosophy, Judaism* (Chicago: University of Chicago Press, 2006).

Sorenson, Kim A., *Discourses on Strauss: Revelation and Reason in Leo Strauss and His Critical Study of Machiavelli* (Notre Dame, IN: University of Notre Dame Press, 2006).

Taboni, Pier Franco, *La città tirannica: La prima educazione di Leo Strauss* (Urbino: Quattro Venti, 2005).

Tanguay, Daniel, *Leo Strauss: An Intellectual Biography*, trans. Christopher Nadon (New Haven, CT: Yale University Press, 2007).

Zuckert, Catherine and Michael, *The Truth About Leo Strauss: Political Philosophy and American Democracy* (Chicago: University of Chicago Press, 2006).

ARTICLES ON STRAUSS

Abbeele, Georges Van den, "The Persecution of Writing: Revisiting Strauss and Censorship," *Diacritics*, 27 (1997): 3–17.

Altmann, Alexander, "Leo Strauss (1899–1973)," *Proceedings of the American Academy for Jewish Research*, 41 (1973–1974): xxxiii–xxxvi.

Banfield, Edward C., "Leo Strauss," *Remembering the University of Chicago: Teachers, Scientists, and Scholars*, ed. Edward Shils (Chicago: University of Chicago Press, 1991), 490–501.

Behnegar, Nasser, "Leo Strauss's Confrontation with Max Weber: A Search for a Genuine Social Science," *Review of Politics*, 59 (1997): 97–125.

Benardete, Seth, "Leo Strauss's *The City and Man*," *Political Science Reviewer*, 8 (1978): 1–20.

Biale, David, "Leo Strauss: The Philosopher as Weimar Jew," *Leo Strauss's Thought: Toward a Critical Engagement*, ed. Alan Udoff (Boulder, CO: Lynne Rienner, 1991), 31–40.

Bloom, Allan, "Leo Strauss (September 20, 1899–October 18, 1973)," *Political Theory*, 4 (1974): 372–392.

Brague, Rémi, "Leo Strauss and Maimonides," *Leo Strauss's Thought: Toward a Critical Engagement*, ed. Alan Udoff (Boulder, CO: Lynne Rienner, 1991), 93–114.

Brague, Rémi, "Athens, Jerusalem, Mecca: Leo Strauss's 'Muslim' Understanding of Greek Philosophy," *Poetics Today*, 19 (1998): 235–259.

Burnyeat, Myles, "Sphinx Without a Secret," *New York Review of Books* (May, 1985), 30–36.

Cantor, Paul, "Leo Strauss and Contemporary Hermeneutics," *Leo Strauss's Thought: Toward a Critical Engagement*, ed. Alan Udoff (Boulder, CO: Lynne Rienner, 1991), 267–314.

Cavaillé, Jean-Pierre, "Leo Strauss et l'histoire des texts en régimes de persécution," *Revue Philosophique*, 130 (2005): 39–60.

Cropsey, Joseph, "Leo Strauss and the University of Chicago," *Leo Strauss, the Straussians, and the American Regime*, ed. Kenneth L. Deutsch and John A. Murley (Lanham, MD: Rowman & Littlefield, 1999), 39–40.

Dalmayr, Fred, "Leo Strauss Peregrinus," *Social Research*, 61 (1994): 877–906.

Dannhauser, Werner, "Leo Strauss: Becoming Naïve Again," *American Scholar*, 44 (1974–1975): 636–642.

Dannhauser, Werner, "Leo Strauss as Jew and Citizen," *Interpretation*, 17 (1990): 433–447.

Drury, Shadia, "Leo Strauss's Classic Natural Right Teaching," *Political Theory*, 15 (1987): 299–315.

Ferrari, G. R. F., "Strauss's Plato," *Arion*, 5.2 (1997): 36–65.

Fradkin, Hillel, "Philosophy and Law: Strauss as a Student of Medieval Jewish Thought," *Review of Politics*, 53 (1991): 40–52.

Fradkin, Hillel, "A Word Fitly Spoken: The Interpretation of Maimonides and the Legacy of Leo Strauss," *Leo Strauss and Judaism: Jerusalem and Athens Revisited* (Lanham, MD: Rowman & Littlefield, 1996), 55–85.

Frazer, Michael, "Esotericism Ancient and Modern: Strauss Contra Straussianism on the Art of Political-Philosophical Writing," *Political Theory*, 34 (2006): 33–61.

Gourevitch, Victor, "Philosophy and Politics, I and II," *Review of Metaphysics*, 22 (1968): 58–84, 281–328.

Green, S. J. D., "The Tawney-Strauss Connection: On Historicism and Values in the History of Political Ideas," *Journal of Modern History*, 67 (1995): 255–277.

Gunnell, John, "The Myth of the Tradition," *American Political Science Review*, 72 (1978): 122–134.

Gunnell, John, "Strauss Before Straussianism: Reason, Revelation, and Nature," *Review of Politics*, 53 (1991): 53–74.

Jaffa, Harry V., "Crisis of the Strauss Divided: The Legacy Reconsidered," *Social Research*, 54 (1987): 579–603.

Jannsens, David, "Questions and Caves: Philosophy, Politics, and History in Leo Strauss's Early Work," *Journal of Jewish Thought and Philosophy*, 10 (2000): 111–144.

Jannsens, David, "The Problem of the Enlightenment: Strauss, Jacobi, and the Pantheism Controversy," *Review of Metaphysics*, 56 (2003): 605–632.

Kennington, Richard, "Strauss's *Natural Right and History*," *Review of Metaphysics*, 35 (1981): 57–86.

Kochin, Michael, "Morality, Nature, and Esotericism in Strauss's *Persecution and the Art of Writing*," *Review of Politics*, 64 (2002): 261–283.

Lenzner, Steven J. "Strauss's Three Burkes: The Problem of Edmund Burke in *Natural Right and History*," *Political Theory*, 19 (1991): 364–390.

Lenzner, Steven J. "A Literary Exercise in Self-Knowledge: Leo Strauss's Twofold Interpretation of Maimonides," *Perspectives on Political Science* (Fall, 2002): 225–234.

Levene, Nancy, "Athens and Jerusalem: Myths and Mirrors in Strauss's Vision of the West," *Hebraic Political Thought*, 3 (2008): 113–154.

Luz, Ehud, "How to Read the Bible According to Leo Strauss," *Modern Judaism*, 25 (2005): 264–284.

McWilliams, Carey Wilson, "Leo Strauss and the Dignity of American Political Thought," *Review of Politics*, 60 (1998): 231–246.

Meier, Heinrich, "How Strauss Became Strauss," *Enlightening Revolutions: Essays in Honor of Ralph Lerner*, ed. Svetozar Minkov (Boulder, CO: Rowman & Littlefield, 2006), 363–382.

Melzer, Arthur, "Esotericism and the Critique of Historicism," *American Political Science Review*, 100 (2006): 279–295.

Mewes, Horst, "Leo Strauss and Martin Heidegger: Greek Antiquity and the Meaning of Modernity," *Hannah Arendt and Leo Strauss: German Emigrés and American Political Thought After World War II*, ed. Peter Graf Kielmansegg, Horst Mewes, and Elisabeth Glaser-Schmidt (Cambridge, UK: Cambridge University Press, 1995), 105–120.

Miller, Eugene F., "Leo Strauss: Philosophy and American Social Science," *Leo Strauss, the Straussians, and the American Regime*, ed. Kenneth L. Deutsch and John A. Murley (Lanham, MD: Rowman & Littlefield, 1999), 91–102.

Momigliano, Arnaldo, "Hermeneutics and Classical Political Thought in Leo Strauss," *Essays on Ancient and Modern Judaism*, trans. Marua Masella-Gayley, ed. Silvia Berti (Chicago: University of Chicago Press, 1994), 178–189.

Novak, David, "Philosophy and the Possibility of Revelation: A Theological Response to the Challenge of Leo Strauss," *Leo Strauss and Judaism: Jerusalem and Athens Revisited* (Lanham, MD: Rowman & Littlefield, 1996), 173–192.

Patch, Andrew, "Leo Strauss on Maimonides' Prophetology," *Review of Politics*, 66 (2004): 83–104.

Pelluchon, Corine, "Strauss and Cohen: The Question of Enlightened Judaism," *Interpretation*, 32 (2005): 219–230.

Pines, Shlomo, "On Leo Strauss," *Independent Journal of Philosophy*, 5/6 (1988): 169–171.

Pippin, Robert, "The Modern World of Leo Strauss," *Political Theory*, 20 (1992): 448–472.

Pippin, Robert, "Being, Time, and Politics: The Strauss-Kojève Debate," *History and Theory*, 22 (1993): 138–161.

Pippin, Robert, "The Unavailability of the Ordinary: Strauss on the Philosophic Fate of Modernity," *Political Theory*, 31 (2003): 335–358.

Rosen, Stanley, "Leo Strauss and the Possibility of Philosophy," *Review of Metaphysics*, 53 (2000): 541–564.

Sadri, Mahmoud and Ahmad, "Intercultural Understanding: Max Weber and Leo Strauss," *International Journal of Politics, Culture, and Society*, 1 (1998): 392–411.

Schweid, Eliezer, "Religion and Philosophy: The Scholarly-Theological Debate Between Julius Guttman and Leo Strauss," *Maimonidean Studies*, 1 (1990): 163–195.

Sfez, Gérald "Leo Strauss: Un Criticisme de la Preuve," *Revue Philosophique* 130 (2005): 3–19.

Shell, Susan, "Taking Evil Seriously: Schmitt's 'Concept of the Political' and Strauss's 'True Politics,'" *Leo Strauss: Political Philosopher and Jewish Thinker*, ed. Kenneth L. Deutsch and Walte Nicgorski (Lanham, MD: Rowman & Littlefield, 1994), 175–193.

Smith, Steven B., "Leo Strauss as a Modern Jewish Thinker," *The Cambridge Companion to Modern Jewish Thought*, ed. Michael Morgan and Peter Gordon (Cambridge, UK: Cambridge University Press, 2007), 147–169.

Smith, Steven B., "How to Commemorate the 350th Anniversary of Spinoza's Expulsion or Leo Strauss's Critique of Hermann Cohen," *Hebraic Political Studies*, 3 (2008): 155–176.

Smith, Steven B., "Philosophy as a Way of Life: The Case of Leo Strauss," *Review of Politics* 71 (2009): 1–17.

Söllner, Alfons, "Leo Strauss: German Origin and American Impact," *Hannah Arendt and Leo Strauss: German Emigrés and American Political Thought After World War II*, ed. Peter Graf Kielmansegg, Horst Mewes, and Elisabeth Glaser-Schmidt (Cambridge, UK: Cambridge University Press, 1995), 121–137.

Stauffer, Devin, "Reopening the Quarrel between the Ancients and the Moderns: Leo Strauss's Critique of Hobbes's 'New Political Science,'" *American Political Science Review*, 101 (2007): 223–233.

Susser, Bernard, "Leo Strauss: The Ancient as Modern," *Political Studies*, 36 (1988): 497–514.

Tarcov, Nathan, "Philosophy and History: Tradition and Interpretation in the Work of Leo Strauss," *Polity*, 16 (1983): 5–29.

Tarcov, Nathan, "On a Certain Critique of 'Straussianism,'" *Review of Politics*, 53 (1991): 3–18.

Tarcov, Nathan, "Will the Real Leo Strauss Please Stand Up?" *The American Interest* (September/October, 2006), 120–128.

Velkley, Richard, "On the Roots of Rationalism: *Natural Right and History* as a Response to Heidegger," *Review of Politics*, 70 (2008): 245–259.

Ward, James F., "Political Philosophy and History: The Links Between Strauss and Heidegger," *Polity*, 20 (1987): 273–295.

INDEX

Note to index: An *n* following a page number denotes a note on that page.